How to Do Everything with

Adobe® Acrobat® 6.0

Doug Sahlin is an author, graphic designer, and web site designer living in Lakeland, Central Florida. He is the author of 11 books on graphic design and computer software, including *How To Do Everything with Adobe Acrobat 5* and *How To Do Everything with Macromedia Contribute.* Sahlin's articles and product reviews have appeared in national publications such as *Computer Graphics World*, *3D* Magazine, *Video Systems*, and *Corel* Magazine, and his tutorials have been featured at numerous web sites devoted to graphic design. Sahlin has also authored online multimedia tutorials, CD-ROM tutorials, and presented seminars for government agencies.

How to Do *Everything* with

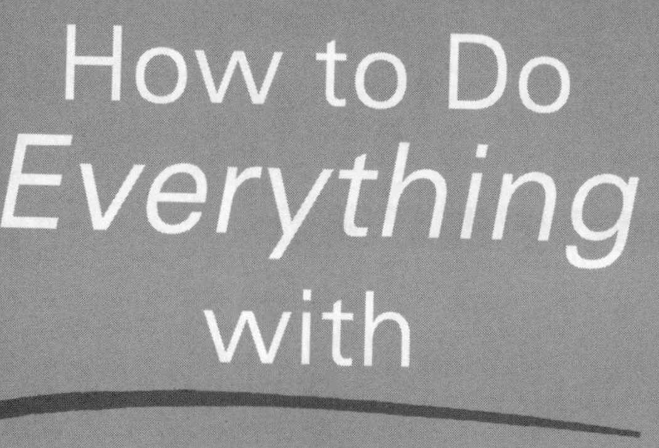

Adobe® Acrobat® 6.0

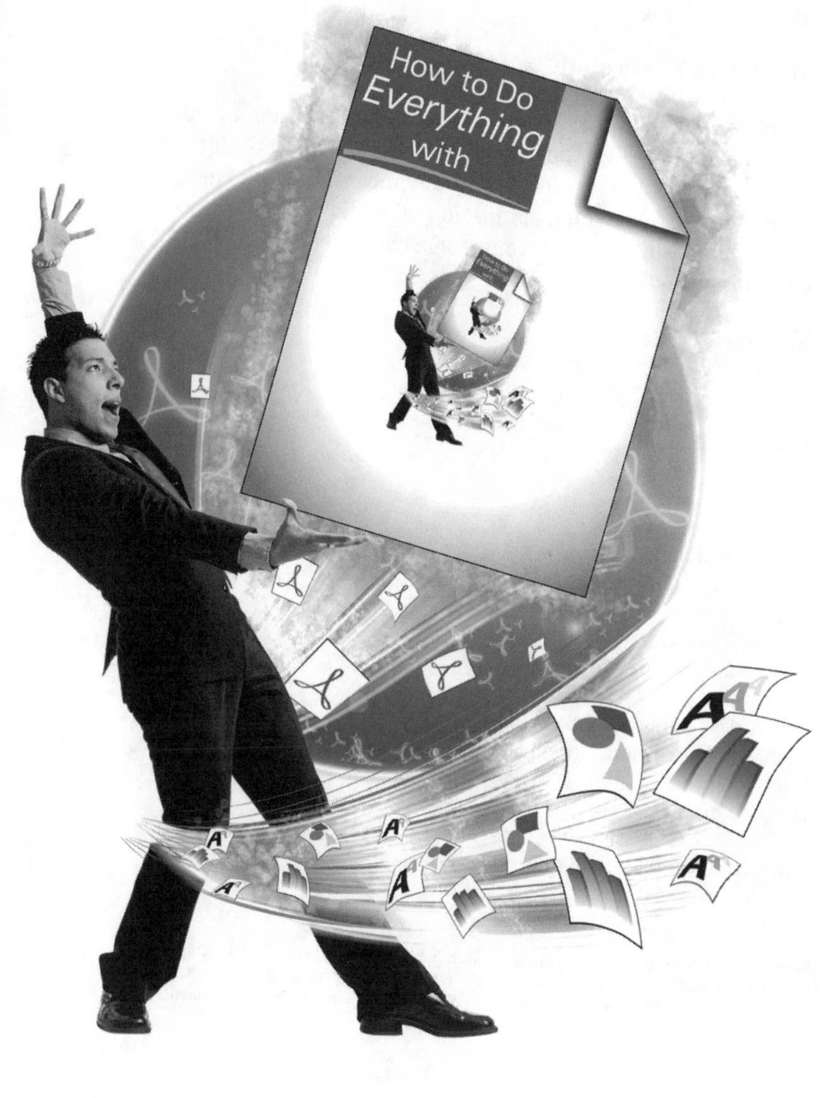

Doug Sahlin

McGraw-Hill/Osborne

New York Chicago San Francisco
Lisbon London Madrid Mexico City
Milan New Delhi San Juan
Seoul Singapore Sydney Toronto

The McGraw·Hill Companies

McGraw-Hill/Osborne
2100 Powell Street, 10th Floor
Emeryville, California 94608
U.S.A.

To arrange bulk purchase discounts for sales promotions, premiums, or fund-raisers, please contact **McGraw-Hill**/Osborne at the above address. For information on translations or book distributors outside the U.S.A., please see the International Contact Information page immediately following the index of this book.

How to Do Everything with Adobe® Acrobat® 6.0

34567890 FGR FGR 019876543

ISBN 0-07-222946-2

Publisher	Brandon A. Nordin
Vice President & Associate Publisher	Scott Rogers
Acquisitions Editor	Marjorie McAneny
Project Editor	Jennifer Malnick
Acquisitions Coordinator	Tana Allen
Technical Editor	Dave Wraight
Copy Editor	Andrea Boucher
Proofreaders	Emily Rader, Linda Medoff
Indexer	Claire Splan
Computer Designers	Tara A. Davis, Lucie Ericksen
Illustrators	Kathleen Fay Edwards, Melinda Moore Lytle, Lyssa Wald
Series Design	Mickey Galicia
Cover Series Design	Dodie Shoemaker

This book was composed with Corel VENTURA™ Publisher.

This book is dedicated to my mother, Inez, my mentor, my confidant, and my best friend. Your memory lives on forever.

Contents at a Glance

PART VI Appendixes

Contents

PART IV **Add Security and Distribute PDF Documents**

Acknowledgments

Writing is a solitary endeavor. When a book project is finished, the author's name appears on the cover, which in many ways seems unfair. A book project of this magnitude is not possible without the support of many. This book is no different.

I'd like to begin by thanking the publishing team at Osborne. Thanks to the ambitious and blonde Margie McAneny, for making this opportunity possible. And thanks to Megg Morin, for pinch hitting in the final stages of this project while Margie gave birth to her daughter. Thanks to Tana Allen, for making sure my manuscripts and screenshots got to the proper parties at the proper time. I would be remiss if I did not thank Project Editor Jenny Malnick, for filling my inbox when I thought it was once again safe to check my e-mail. Kudos to the talented copyeditor from Indy, Andrea Boucher. Special thanks to the Tech-Editor-Wonder-From-Down-Under, Dave Wraight. As always, thanks to my literary agent, Margot Maley Hutichson, for being the perfect liaison between author and publisher.

Many thanks to my friend and fellow author Bonnie Blake, for her upbeat attitude and support. Best wishes for success with all your endeavors.

As always, copious amounts of thanks to my friends, family, and mentors—life would indeed be difficult without them. Special thanks to my loving sister, Karen, and my cousin Ted (a.k.a. Theodoric of Annandale).

Introduction

Welcome to *How To Do Everything with Adobe Acrobat 6.0*. If you've used previous versions of Acrobat, you know that it's the premier solution for electronic publishing. You can use the Acrobat Distiller and Acrobat PDFMaker to publish documents as PDF (Portable Document Format) files that can be viewed by anyone with a copy of Acrobat, or the free Adobe 6.0 Reader installed on their computer. When you publish a PDF document, it retains the look and feel of the original document, which makes it possible for you to share information with others who have the Adobe Reader 6.0, without needing to invest in the software used to author the original document.

Adobe is distributing two versions of Acrobat 6.0: Standard and Professional. Owners of Acrobat Standard can use the software to create PDF documents from within authoring applications, and then enhance documents by including interactive objects such as navigation devices. Acrobat Standard has commenting tools that you use to annotate a document. Acrobat Professional has all of these features and more. With Acrobat Professional, you can create PDF documents from within Microsoft Visio and Project. Acrobat Professional users will also be able to create sophisticated PDF forms and add multimedia elements such as sound files, video files, and Flash SWF movies to their documents. Acrobat Professional owners will also be able to use Acrobat Catalog to create searchable indexes of PDF documents.

About this Book

You will find coverage of both Acrobat Standard and Acrobat Professional in this book. You can use this book as a standalone reference to understand and utilize the powerful features of both Acrobat versions.

This book is divided into five parts. The chapters in the first part of the book familiarize you with Acrobat and what you can do with it. The middle chapters show you how to create PDF documents and add interactivity to them. The final chapters show users of Acrobat Professional how to use the enhanced features of the software to create PDF forms, add multimedia elements to PDF files, as well as how to automate frequently performed tasks with batch processing. There are two appendixes as well that list the keyboard shortcuts to popular Acrobat commands and Acrobat Internet resources.

Part I: Welcome to Adobe Acrobat 6.0

In Part I, you'll get a general overview of Acrobat. You'll be introduced to the various tasks you can accomplish with Acrobat and gain a working knowledge of the Acrobat workspace. You'll learn how to use Acrobat to read and navigate PDF documents. You'll also find sections devoted to the new features in Acrobat.

Part II: Create PDF Documents

The chapters in Part II contain the information you need to create PDF documents. You'll learn how to create PDF documents from within authoring applications using the Adobe PDF printer, from within Microsoft office applications using the Acrobat PDFMaker, as well as how to create PDF documents by capturing them from web pages and scanned documents. The final chapters show you how to add enhanced interactivity to PDF documents in the form of navigation devices.

Part III: Edit PDF Documents

In Part III you'll learn how to edit PDF documents. You'll discover how to add pages, crop pages, and replace pages in the PDF documents you edit, as well as how to use Acrobat's powerful commenting tools to add notes and annotations to a document. You'll also learn how to initiate an e-mail review with other colleagues and keep track of the review with the new Review Tracker.

Part IV: Add Security and Distribute PDF Documents

In this part of the book you'll learn how to password protect the PDF documents you distribute with Acrobat Password Security. You'll also learn how to work with Digital IDs and create a list of Trusted Identities by exchanging Digital IDs with other colleagues and associates. When you work with trusted certificates, you can apply enhanced Certificate Security to documents, which enables you to set different user permissions for each member of your Trusted Identities list. Other topics of discussion show you how to optimize and distribute PDF documents.

Part V: Create Enhanced PDFs with Acrobat Professional

Part V is for Acrobat Professional users; here you'll find detailed instructions on how to create PDF forms. You'll also find a chapter devoted to using Acrobat Professional to add multimedia elements to PDF documents. In the final chapter of the book, Chapter 16, you'll learn how to use Acrobat Professional's batch processing feature to automate tasks you perform on a regular basis as well as how to master Acrobat Professional Catalog to create searchable indexes of PDF documents.

Conventions Used in this Book

Acrobat Standard and Professional are available for the Windows and Macintosh platforms. This book was written using the Windows version of Acrobat. Therefore, if you are a Macintosh user, you may notice some minor differences in certain dialog boxes. Whenever a menu command differs between platforms, it will be noted with the Windows command listed first, followed by the Macintosh equivalent. For example: right-click (Windows) or CTRL-click (Macintosh).

Italic type is used to designate a new phrase or term.

SMALL CAPITAL LETTERS are used to designate keyboard entries such as CTRL, SHIFT, or ESC.

`Courier type` is used to designate any JavaScript code.

When you are instructed to use a menu command, it will be referred to like this: choose Document | Pages | Insert. This is the path to the command you'll use to perform the task being discussed. The previous example shows how to open the Insert Pages dialog box by choosing the Insert command, which is one of the Pages commands, which is found on the list of Document menu commands.

You'll also find useful information about Acrobat and related topics in the How To..? and Did You Know sections of this book as well as informative sidebars. Tips on how to streamline your workflow and notes pertaining to specific topics are sprinkled throughout the book.

In Closing

My goal is to provide you with a book that you can use as a standalone reference for creating, editing, and adding interactivity to PDF documents. In addition, I have provided information that you will not find in the program manual, such as how to optimize images for PDF documents, tips to help you streamline your workflow, and other useful tidbits, such as how to use JavaScript to display the current date in a PDF document. After you read this book, keep it within arm's reach for an instant refresher course on a particular topic. You can also use Appendix A as a handy reference for the most popular Acrobat keyboard shortcuts. In Appendix B, you'll find the URLs to web sites featuring useful information about Acrobat as well as sources for third-party plug-ins.

Part I

Welcome to Adobe Acrobat 6.0

Chapter 1

Get to Know Adobe Acrobat 6.0

How to...

- Utilize the power of Acrobat
- Create PDF documents
- Create PDF documents for the Web
- Capture web sites as PDF documents
- Optimize PDF documents

Most computer users are familiar with Acrobat in some form or another. Many think that Acrobat is the application that pops up when they double-click a file with the *PDF* (Portable Document Format) extension. That little gem is Adobe Reader 6.0. But there's much more to Acrobat than the Reader. Major corporations, software manufacturers, and businesses use the full version of Acrobat to create and publish documents for electronic distribution. The fact that you are reading this book probably means that you either own the full version of Acrobat 6.0 or will soon purchase the program to create interactive electronic documents that retain the appearance of the original.

If you have used Acrobat before, you know that it is chock-full of features—so many features that it takes a while to learn them all. If you're brand-new to Acrobat, the prospect of publishing sophisticated electronic documents might seem a bit daunting. But don't worry—as you read this book, whether you own Acrobat Standard or Acrobat Professional, you'll learn to harness the power of Acrobat to create and publish electronic documents you never thought possible. Whether you need to create a simple electronic memo, an employee manual, or an indexed electronic catalog, Acrobat is the tool for you.

In this chapter, you'll also learn about the different components that come with Acrobat and the many uses for the software. If you've just upgraded from Acrobat 5.0, you've likely already noticed that there are many changes to the software. If you are an experienced Acrobat user, you may be tempted to skip this chapter. However, even if you're an Acrobat publishing veteran, I suggest that you browse through this chapter, especially when you consider the plethora of new features, new tools, menu commands, and so on. As you read this chapter, you may discover an application for the program you never knew existed. As you learn about the new features and enhanced functionality of Acrobat 6.0, you may develop ideas of how to best utilize the software for your publishing needs.

About Adobe Acrobat

Adobe Acrobat isn't quite as old as dirt, but it has been around for some time. Adobe created the product for individuals and corporations that needed to publish documents for distribution in electronic format (also known as *ePaper*). The premise of the product was to create a format for electronic documents that could be viewed by anyone, on any computer, with the only required software being the free Adobe Reader 6.0. Adobe accomplished this goal and then some. Initially, the product found great favor with software manufacturers who used Acrobat to create online manuals for their products. The manuals could easily be bundled on program installation disks with a free copy of Adobe Reader 6.0. Many software manufacturers opted to publish program manuals only in PDF format. Software companies, selling programs with manuals published in this manner, saved on packaging and shipping costs, enabling them to price their software more competitively. Help manuals published in PDF format are easy to navigate and read. Figure 1-1 shows the Adobe Acrobat Help manual as viewed in Acrobat Standard with the How To..? pane hidden.

As Acrobat grew in popularity, Adobe added more features to the product. Newer versions of the software featured enhanced usability, the addition of document security, and the ability to create a searchable index of multiple PDF documents. Users of the software found new applications for PDF documents; the documents soon appeared as corporate memos, portable product catalogs, and multimedia presentations for salespeople. Most popular browsers support the Adobe Reader 6.0 plug-in, so many companies post PDF documents at their web sites. The PDF acronym aptly describes the published file, as it is truly a portable document, viewable by any users with Adobe Reader 6.0, or earlier versions of the Acrobat Reader, installed on their computer.

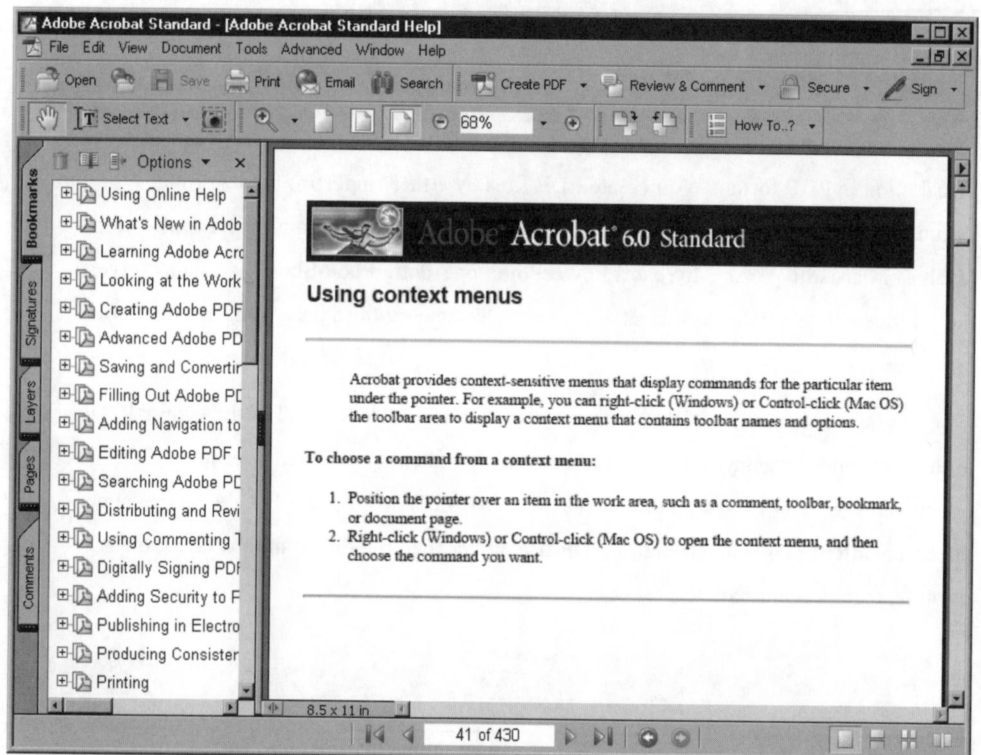

FIGURE 1-1 Many software manufacturers publish their Help manuals in PDF format.

You use Acrobat software to create and publish documents for electronic distribution in PDF format. You create PDF files by either importing into Acrobat documents authored in other applications or documents created in authoring applications (such as Microsoft Word, Microsoft PowerPoint, or Adobe Photoshop) and then converted the original file to a PDF document. There have been several third-party plug-ins available for working with PDF files in previous versions of Acrobat, a trend that is bound to continue with Acrobat 6.0. Many scanning utilities such as Omni-Page 12.0 and AverScan feature PDF output as an option.

When you create a PDF document, it retains the look and feel of the original. All the fonts and images you used in the original document are carried over to the PDF document. Figure 1-2 shows a document in Microsoft Word; Figure 1-3 shows the same document after being converted to a PDF file. Other than the different interfaces, the documents look identical.

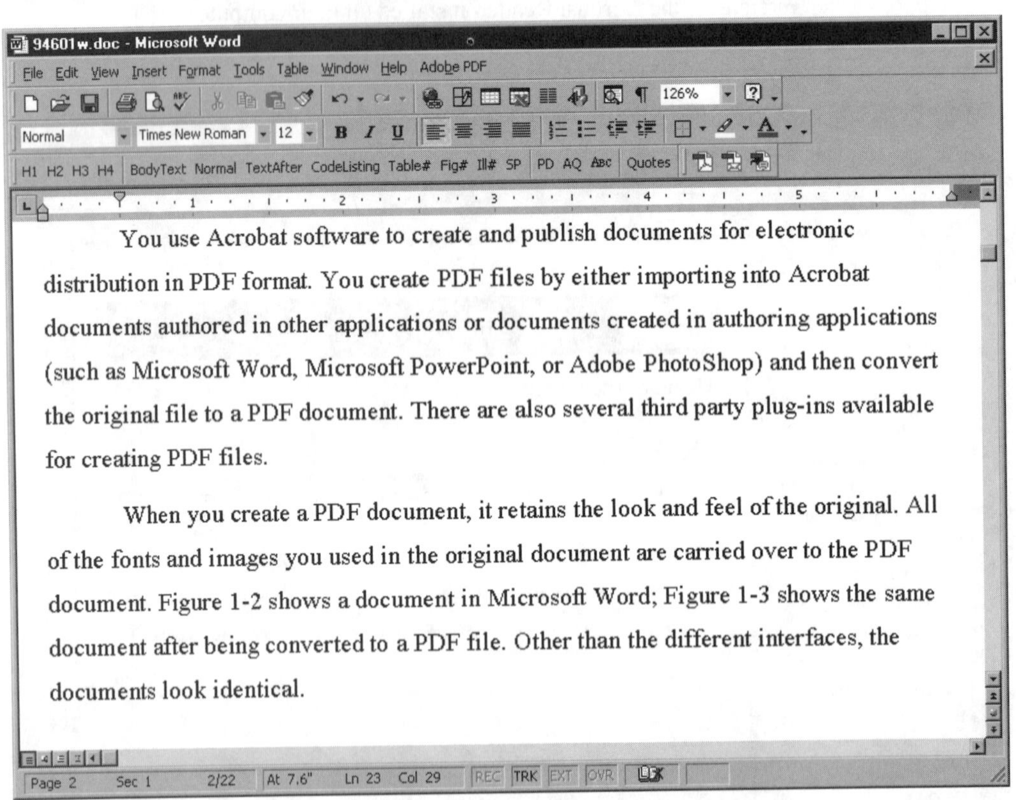
94601w.doc - Microsoft Word
File Edit View Insert Format Tools Table Window Help Adobe PDF
126%
Normal
Times New Roman
12
H1 H2 H3 H4 BodyText Normal TextAfter CodeListing Table# Fig# Ill# SP PD AQ ABC Quotes
You use Acrobat software to create and publish documents for electronic distribution in PDF format. You create PDF files by either importing into Acrobat documents authored in other applications or documents created in authoring applications (such as Microsoft Word, Microsoft PowerPoint, or Adobe PhotoShop) and then convert the original file to a PDF document. There are also several third party plug-ins available for creating PDF files.
When you create a PDF document, it retains the look and feel of the original. All of the fonts and images you used in the original document are carried over to the PDF document. Figure 1-2 shows a document in Microsoft Word; Figure 1-3 shows the same document after being converted to a PDF file. Other than the different interfaces, the documents look identical.
Page 2 Sec 1 2/22 At 7.6" Ln 23 Col 29 REC TRK EXT OVR

FIGURE 1-2 You can create PDF documents in an authoring program such as Microsoft Word.

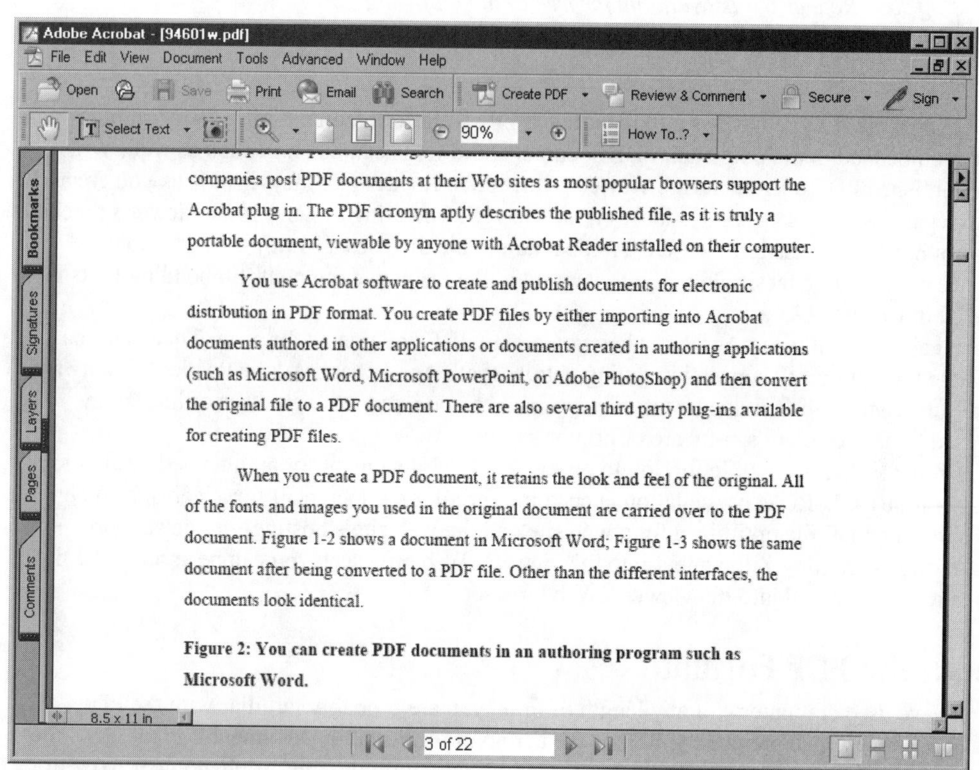
Adobe Acrobat - [94601w.pdf]
File Edit View Document Tools Advanced Window Help
Open
Save
Print
Email
Search
Create PDF
Review & Comment
Secure
Sign
Select Text
90%
How To..?
Bookmarks
Signatures
Layers
Pages
Comments
companies post PDF documents at their Web sites as most popular browsers support the Acrobat plug in. The PDF acronym aptly describes the published file, as it is truly a portable document, viewable by anyone with Acrobat Reader installed on their computer.
You use Acrobat software to create and publish documents for electronic distribution in PDF format. You create PDF files by either importing into Acrobat documents authored in other applications or documents created in authoring applications (such as Microsoft Word, Microsoft PowerPoint, or Adobe PhotoShop) and then convert the original file to a PDF document. There are also several third party plug-ins available for creating PDF files.
When you create a PDF document, it retains the look and feel of the original. All of the fonts and images you used in the original document are carried over to the PDF document. Figure 1-2 shows a document in Microsoft Word; Figure 1-3 shows the same document after being converted to a PDF file. Other than the different interfaces, the documents look identical.
Figure 2: You can create PDF documents in an authoring program such as Microsoft Word.
8.5 x 11 in
3 of 22

FIGURE 1-3 When you convert the document to PDF format, it maintains the look and feel of the original.

When you use different applications to publish documents for electronic distribution, the documents can be read only if the recipients have a copy of the authoring software installed on their computer. If you work for a large corporation and need to electronically distribute documents to a large number of coworkers, your employer ends up spending a fortune in software licensing fees. However, if you publish the document in PDF format, any coworker can read it as long as a copy of Adobe Reader 6.0 is installed on their computer. Adobe does not charge licensing fees when you distribute copies of Adobe Reader 6.0. As you can see, sending documents in PDF format is a cost-effective way to distribute documents within large organizations.

If your published PDF documents are included on a web site, most popular Web browsers are equipped with the proper plug-in to display PDF files within the browser. In the event that your viewer doesn't have Adobe Reader 6.0 or an earlier version installed, you can add a direct link from your web site to the Adobe web site where your viewer can download the Reader for free.

Adobe Reader 6.0 is available for free at the following URL: http://www.adobe.com/products/acrobat/readstep.html.

Another benefit you have as a PDF author is cross-platform compatibility. Any graphics you use are embedded in the published PDF document, and fonts can be embedded as well. When your published PDF documents are viewed with Adobe Reader 6.0, they display as you created them, regardless of resources available on the viewer's operating system. If the viewer's machine does not have a font used in the PDF, Acrobat automatically uses a Multiple Master font to produce a reasonable facsimile of the fonts used in the original document. Embedding fonts is covered in Chapter 12.

You also benefit using Acrobat when you create PDF documents for print. Thanks to the available formatting and conversion setting options, both Acrobat and Adobe Reader 6.0 software make sure your published documents always print as you intended regardless of limitations imposed by the recipient's software or printer.

Acrobat makes it possible for you to optimize a PDF document for an intended destination whether it be a CD-ROM presentation, a customer proof, or a document for a web site. When you publish a PDF file optimized for a web site and the web site's hosting service supports *byteserving* (streaming a document into the viewer's Web browser), you can be assured the file will quickly download into the viewer's Web browser.

About the PDF Format

If you have used computers for any length of time, you are probably familiar with the PDF format. As mentioned previously, PDF is the acronym for Portable Document Format. PDF files are indeed portable. You can view them on any computer with the free Adobe Reader 6.0. For example, if someone sends you a PDF file created on a Macintosh computer using Adobe PageMaker, you can view it on a PC (Personal Computer) that has Adobe Reader 6.0. PDF files can also be viewed on portable devices such as the Palm Pilot. The file you view with Adobe

How Streaming Works

Many file formats that are viewed over the Internet are streamed into the user's browser. When a file is streamed into a browser, it does not have to download completely before viewers can see the file. The first part of the file (or frame, if the file is a Flash movie or a streaming movie) is displayed as soon as enough data has been downloaded. Byteserving a PDF document works in the same manner; as soon as enough data has downloaded, the first page of the document appears in the user's browser.

Reader 6.0 on a PC looks identical to the Macintosh-created PDF file. All the elements used to create the file on the Macintosh are saved when the author converts the file to PDF format, which is the reason it appears identical when viewed with Adobe Reader 6.0 on a PC. PDF files can also be viewed in supported Web browsers where Adobe Reader 6.0 functions as a plug-in or helper application. Whenever a PDF file posted at a web site is selected, Acrobat or Adobe Reader 6.0 launches in the viewer's Web browser.

Many people confuse Acrobat with Adobe Reader 6.0, the little program you download from the Adobe web site. If you are new to Acrobat, you will quickly learn that Acrobat is a full-fledged application for publishing electronic documents in PDF format. If you have used previous versions of Acrobat, you are already familiar with the program's basic premise. In the sections to follow, you'll learn about the new features and uses for Acrobat 6.0.

About Adobe Acrobat 6.0

With Acrobat 6.0, Adobe created two versions: Acrobat Standard for the small business or individual needing to convert existing files to the PDF format, and Acrobat Professional for task-oriented users needing to create PDF files with objects like forms and multimedia elements. Acrobat Professional has several features for the "power user." The general capabilities of each version are listed in the following sections.

Acrobat Standard

With Acrobat Standard, you can easily create a PDF document from any number of sources. You can create PDFs from within authoring applications such as Microsoft Word, as discussed in Chapter 5, or you can create PDFs from within Acrobat Standard from a single file, multiple files, a web page, or from a document in your scanner as outlined in Chapter 6. Acrobat Standard enables you to send documents for review and track the review process. You can also mark up a PDF document with notes, text, or graphic elements. Reviewing and marking up PDF documents is covered in detail in Chapter 10.

Did you know?

About Acrobat Elements

Adobe has yet another tool to create PDF documents: Acrobat Elements. Large organizations can use Acrobat Elements to convert Microsoft Office documents to PDF formats. Acrobat Elements is a product you can license through Adobe. For more information, visit the Acrobat Elements web page at http://www.adobe.com/products/acrobatel/main.html.

Acrobat Professional

Acrobat Professional has the same feature set as Acrobat Standard with some powerful additions. With Acrobat Professional, you can create PDF documents from within AutoCad, Microsoft Project, and Microsoft Visio. Acrobat Professional also features additional commenting tools, enhanced multimedia support, and much more. Part V of this book covers the features unique to Acrobat Professional. However, there are some features that don't fall within the context of these chapters.

Within this book, whenever an Acrobat Professional tool or feature is discussed, it will be designated by the parenthetical reference, (Professional Only), in the section heading.

About the Acrobat CD-ROM Installation Disc

As mentioned previously, Acrobat 6.0 comes in two flavors: Standard and Professional. The Acrobat CD-ROM ships with the following components.

Adobe Acrobat

This is the core application. You use Acrobat to publish and edit PDF documents. In future chapters, you'll learn how to use the program features to create and publish PDF files for a variety of mediums. You'll also use Acrobat to capture web pages and save them as PDF files, as well as scan printed documents into Acrobat and save them as PDF files.

Adobe Reader 6.0

This application is used to read published PDF documents. You don't need to install the reader; PDF documents can be read within the Acrobat application. Adobe includes Adobe Reader 6.0 with the application CD-ROM so you can bundle it with applications you create for distribution on CD-ROM or zip disk. You can distribute Adobe Reader 6.0 without paying a licensing fee as long as you comply with the Adobe distribution policy that requires you distribute the *EULA* (End User License Agreement) and information that is included with the installation utility.

Acrobat Catalog (Professional Only)

This application is used to create indexes of PDF documents. When you create a PDF index, you create a searchable index of several—or several hundred—PDF documents. After you create a PDF index, you can use the Acrobat Search command to search the index documents for specific information.

Acrobat Distiller

Acrobat Distiller is used to create a PDF document from PostScript files in *EPS* (Encapsulated PostScript) or *PS* (PostScript) format. The Distiller *Conversion Settings* help you optimize the document for its intended destination. Acrobat Distiller is a separate application that can also be accessed from the core application.

What's New in Adobe Acrobat 6.0

Acrobat 6.0 has many new features that enhance usability when creating files within a network environment. You can easily share your PDF documents within a team. Individual team members can review PDF documents using Acrobat 6.0's enhanced commenting tools to create annotations, add audio and written comments, and much more. For example, if you use Acrobat Professional to create PDF documents, you can easily create interactive forms to gather information from within a corporate environment. These forms can be filled in and printed out, or they can be filled in and submitted on a corporate intranet. Recipients of your form can use either Adobe Reader 6.0 or Acrobat to fill out a form. In the sections that follow, you'll learn the exciting new features at your disposal in Acrobat 6.0.

New Features

Whether you've purchased Acrobat Standard or Acrobat Professional, the first and most striking difference is the interface. Acrobat 6.0 consists of two separate entities named Acrobat and Acrobat Distiller. If you are an Acrobat Professional user, Adobe Catalog is now a plug-in within the core application. You use the Catalog to create a searchable index of PDF files. Even though Acrobat Distiller is a separate program used to create PDF files from EPS and PS files, you can launch it from within Acrobat.

Veteran users of Acrobat will notice the PDFWriter is missing. In previous versions of Acrobat, the PDFWriter was added as a system printer. You could use the PDFWriter to print a file in PDF format from within another application. When you install Acrobat 6.0, Adobe PDF is added as a system printer. Adobe PDF is actually Acrobat Distiller with a new moniker. You can choose Adobe PDF from an authoring application Print command to create a PDF file, or you can use the new Create PDF command to convert text files and image files to PDF documents. Another Acrobat 6.0 benefit is that the Create PDF command can create a PDF document from a single file or multiple files of different formats supported by Acrobat, from an Internet web page, from your scanner, or from content previously pasted to the system clipboard.

If you work on a PDF project with multiple authors, you and your team members can review and add comments to a PDF file from within a Web browser via the Internet or a corporate intranet. When you open a PDF file within your Web browser, every Acrobat commenting tool is at your disposal. You can freely annotate the PDF file and then save it, or share your comments with other authors through protocols such as *WebDAV* (Web-based Distributed Authoring and Versioning). If your team is working on a corporate intranet, you can set up a shared data repository by setting up a shared network folder, using *ODBC* (Open Database Connectivity) for connecting to such databases as *MDB* (Microsoft Access) or *SQL Server* databases, or *Microsoft Office Server extensions*.

If you create PDF files that are shared in a workplace, you will be pleased to know that the software can publish a document that is accessible by workers with visual disabilities. Acrobat supports high contrast monitor settings used by the visually impaired and a wide variety of screen readers.

With Acrobat 6.0, you can apply enhanced security features to the documents you create. Acrobat 6.0 features 128-bit encryption, which makes it possible for you to distribute confidential documents with complete peace of mind. If you author a confidential PDF document, you can limit access to the document by assigning a *password* to the file. You can also certify a document. When you certify a document, you attest to its contents by adding your *digital signature* to the document. When you certify a document, you can prevent tampering by specifying what changes can and cannot be made. A digital signature is like an electronic fingerprint; it identifies which member of the team worked with the document and when.

New User Interface

Acrobat 6.0 features an enhanced interface that you can easily customize to suit your working preferences. Acrobat 5.0 had a myriad of toolbars arranged below the menu bar. Tool choice could often be confusing as some of the tools had similar icons. With Acrobat 6.0, the most commonly used toolbars are neatly arranged below the menu bar. When you need to access additional tools, you open the toolbar using a menu command. The selected toolbar floats in the workspace and can be moved as desired. You can modify the appearance of toolbars and lock their positions in the workspace. When you arrive at an optimum setup to suit your working preference, Acrobat defaults to your new setup until you change it. You'll learn about the Acrobat interfaces in Chapter 2.

The window on the left side of the interface in Figure 1-4 is the Navigation pane. You click the various tabs in the Navigation pane to access features that you use to advance to various elements within a PDF document, such as document bookmarks or page thumbnails. You'll learn how to navigate within a PDF document in Chapter 3. The window in the center of the interface is the Document pane. This is where you view the Acrobat document you're working on. On the right side of the interface, you'll find a new addition: the How To..? pane. You use the How To..? pane to get task-oriented information. The How To..? pane does double duty by displaying different choices and windows when a large number of command options are available, for example when you use the Search command.

Enhanced Acrobat Tabs

In Acrobat you use tabs, previously known as palettes in Acrobat 5.0, to perform various tasks such as to navigate within the PDF document or to display a list of elements used in the PDF file. In Acrobat 6.0, you have the following new tabs at your disposal:

- **Content** The Content tab is opened from the View menu. This tab shows the elements in a document and is used to reflow the structure of the document without changing the author's content.
- **Comments** The Comments tab is located near the bottom of the Navigation pane. You use the Comments tab to display a list of all comments within a PDF document and to navigate to their respective locations within the document. When you display comments, the tab expands horizontally to fill the lower part of the interface.

- **Info** The Info tab is opened from the View menu. This tab is a window that displays the *X*, *Y* coordinates of the mouse. You may find this tab useful for aligning objects such as form fields. You'll learn how to create forms in Chapter 14.
- **Fields (Professional Only)** The Fields tab is accessed from the View menu. The Fields tab is used to display all form fields contained in a PDF document.
- **Layers** The Layers tab is opened from the View menu. The Layers tab is used to display layers present in the document.
- **Tags** Tags are the *metadata*—the description of the structure of the elements contained within the document. This metadata can be exported to XML.

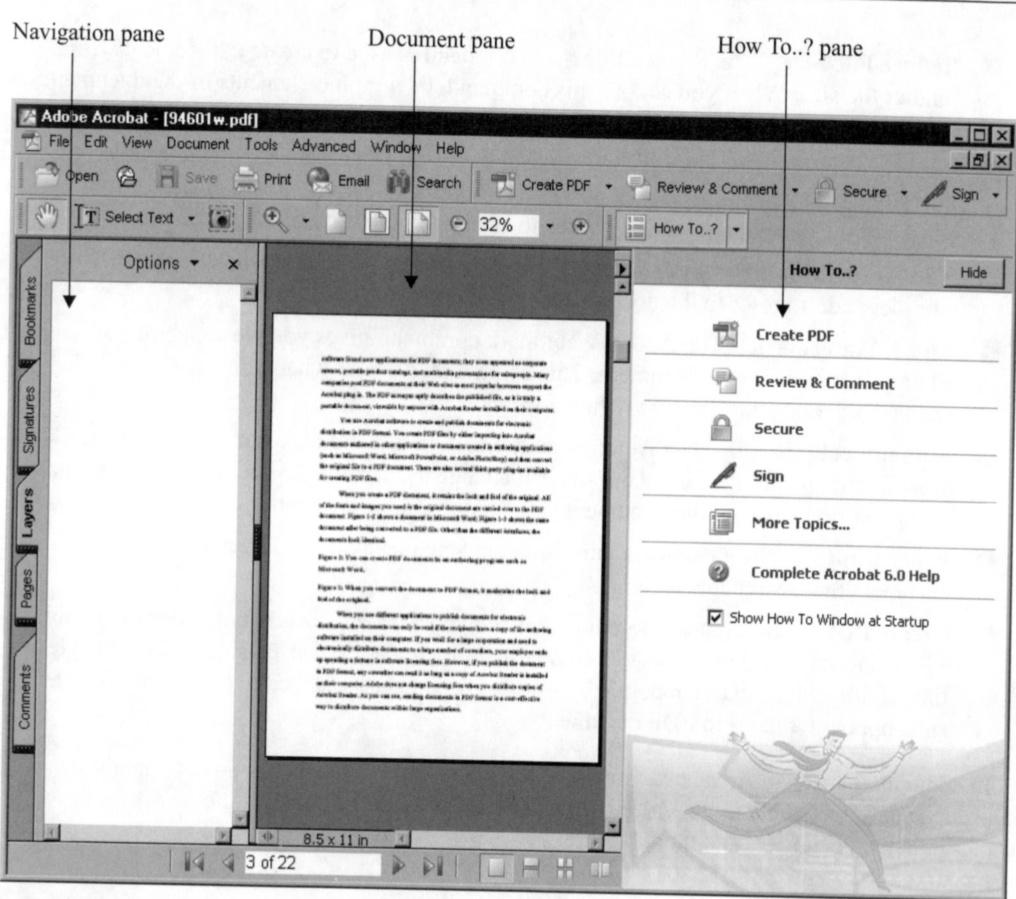

FIGURE 1-4 You can easily customize the Acrobat workspace to suit your preference.

Enhanced Export and Import Features

Acrobat 6.0 makes it possible to repurpose PDF content for other formats. You can use the Export All Images command to extract images from PDF files in either JPEG, JPEG 2000, PNG, or TIFF image formats. You can use the Save As menu command to export PDF content in EPS or PS format. You can also save the current PDF document as an HTML, JPEG, JPEG 2000, Microsoft Word, PNG, Text, TIFF, or XML file as well as an *RTF* (Rich Text Format) file.

New Menu Commands

In Acrobat 6.0, you have new menu commands available to streamline workflow and increase productivity. In upcoming chapters, you will find in-depth information about the following new commands:

- **Reduce File Size** The Reduce File Size command is used to create a document with a smaller file size. When you choose this command, the graphic elements of the document are compressed, resulting in a poorer quality document with a smaller file size.
- **Save As Certified Document** The Save as Certified Document command enables you to verify the contents of a document with your digital signature. You can also restrict editing of the document by other parties to ensure the integrity of the document.
- **Add Headers And Footers** The Add Headers and Footers command allows you to add a header and/or footer to the document.
- **Add A Watermark** The Add A Watermark command gives you the capability of adding a watermark to a document. This command is useful when you want to include visible corporate identification with a document.
- **Automatically Scroll** The Automatically Scroll command makes it easy for you to browse through a long document. You can change the scrolling speed and stop scrolling when you find a part of the document you want to examine in detail.
- **Paper Capture** The Paper Capture command enables you to convert a scanned document into searchable text.
- **Create PDF** The Create PDF command encompasses the different methods of creating a PDF document within Acrobat. You can use the command to convert single files, multiple files of different formats supported by Acrobat, web pages, scanned images or documents, and clipboard images to PDF documents.

In addition, there is an Advanced section of the menu bar where you'll find commands to make documents accessible to the visually impaired, launch the Acrobat Distiller, work with JavaScript in the document, and more.

Create a PDF Document

The flexible tools in Acrobat give you several different options for producing a PDF document. You can create PDF documents from within an authoring application, capture them from documents you scan, or capture them from web sites.

After you create or open a PDF document created by another author, you can add interactive elements such as text hyperlinks, image hyperlinks, and with Acrobat Professional, multimedia elements such as QuickTime movies, Flash SWF movies, and sound files. You can append an existing PDF file by inserting other documents. You can also do other housekeeping chores such as extract graphic elements from a PDF file, crop the file to delete unwanted elements, or remove unnecessary pages from the document. Acrobat has a set of *Touch Up* tools that let you make minor modifications to graphic and text elements in the document. If you need to extensively modify text in a PDF document, it is better to save it as an RTF or Word file and edit the exported file in a text editor or Microsoft Word. After you edit the file, you can then use the Print command to access the Adobe PDF printer and convert the edited file back to PDF format.

Create PDF Documents from Authoring Applications

The easiest way to create a PDF document is to create a file in an authoring application and then convert it to a PDF file. You can create PDF files from any of these popular Microsoft programs (Microsoft Office 97 or newer):

- **Microsoft Word** Microsoft Word is a word processing application. Within limits, you can add graphic elements to the content.
- **Microsoft Excel** Microsoft Excel is a spreadsheet program. Excel also has limited support for graphic elements.
- **Microsoft PowerPoint** Microsoft PowerPoint is software used to create presentations. A PowerPoint presentation is similar to a slide show. You can add graphic elements to your presentation and then convert it to a PDF file. The slide show transitions and other effects are preserved in the resulting PDF document.
- **AutoCad (Professional Only)** AutoCad is a 2-D and 3-D drafting software used to design products. The software can be used to create, view, and share design drawings.
- **Microsoft Project (Professional Only)** Microsoft Project is project management software. With the software, you can track schedules and project resources, as well as communicate and report the project status to others.
- **Microsoft Visio (Professional Only)** Microsoft Visio is used to create floor plans, flowcharts, software diagrams, and more. The software dovetails seamlessly with Microsoft Project to create project schedules.

When you install Acrobat, it detects the Microsoft products previously listed and installs the Adobe PDF shortcut shown on the following toolbar. The icon on the left converts the current document to a PDF file. The icon in the middle converts it to a PDF file and launches your default e-mail program, enabling you to send the PDF file as an e-mail attachment. The icon on the right converts the document to a PDF file and sends the file for review. Acrobat also adds an Adobe PDF menu to the Microsoft Office application. This menu gives you one additional command, the ability to change conversion settings. You'll learn how to convert Microsoft Office documents to PDF documents in Chapter 5.

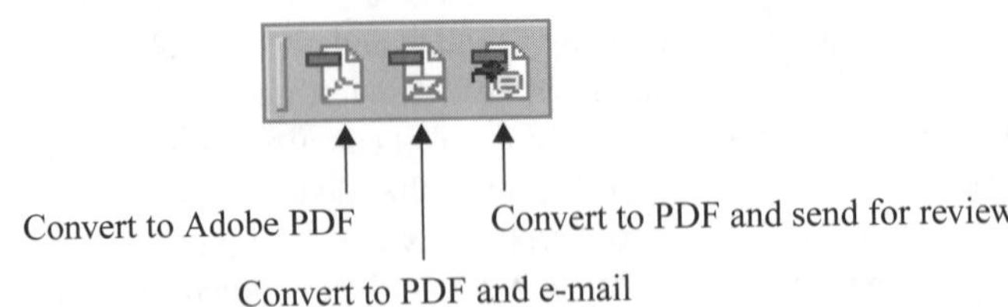

If you own certain Adobe products such as PageMaker and Photoshop, you can use a plug-in to export a document in PDF format. Other illustration programs such as CorelDraw, Quark, and Freehand also have the capability to export files in PDF format.

You can publish PDF files from any other application you use to generate images, illustrations, or text files. When you install Acrobat, Adobe PDF is added as a system printer. To publish a PDF file directly from an authoring application, choose the Print command and then choose Adobe PDF from the list of available printers. You can then open the PDF file in Acrobat to add enhancements such as links and form fields.

Create PDF Documents from EPS Files

If you create illustrations and documents in illustration or page layout programs and publish files in EPS or PS format, you can convert these files to PDF format with Acrobat Distiller. After you launch Distiller and select an EPS or PS file, select one of the preset Distiller Conversion Settings or create your own conversion setting. You use *Conversion Settings* to optimize a PDF file for an intended destination, such as print, screen, or the Web. You can use Distiller to create complete PDF documents or to convert an illustration to PDF format. For example, if you are a graphic designer, you can use Distiller to create a PDF proof of an illustration you are creating for a client. After you save the file in PDF format, you can then e-mail it to a client for approval.

You can quickly create a PDF document by dragging and dropping a supported file icon from your desktop onto the Acrobat shortcut icon. After you release the mouse button, the file opens in Acrobat. If the file is not supported, Acrobat displays a circle with a diagonal slash. If you have the Distiller shortcut on your desktop, you can create a PDF document by dragging and dropping an EPS or PS file onto the Distiller icon.

Create PDF Documents for the Internet

If you design web sites, you can use PDF documents in a variety of effective ways. For example, you can create a product catalog, interactive PDF tutorials, or publish a manual all in PDF format. The web site visitor can choose to view the document in the Web browser or download the complete file for future viewing. Most popular Web browsers support Adobe Reader 6.0 as a plug-in or helper application. Figure 1-5 shows a published document as displayed in Internet Explorer. Note that the figure shows a document displayed in the plug-in version of Acrobat Standard, not Adobe Reader 6.0.

Capture Web Sites as PDF Documents

If you do a lot of research on the Internet, you can capture web pages for future reference. When you capture a web page, Acrobat downloads the text and graphic elements from the web page, complete with hyperlinks. If you want to add additional pages from the same site to the PDF file, simply click the desired hyperlink in the captured page and Acrobat will append the document by downloading the linked page. You can use the Acrobat *Web Capture* feature to download complex

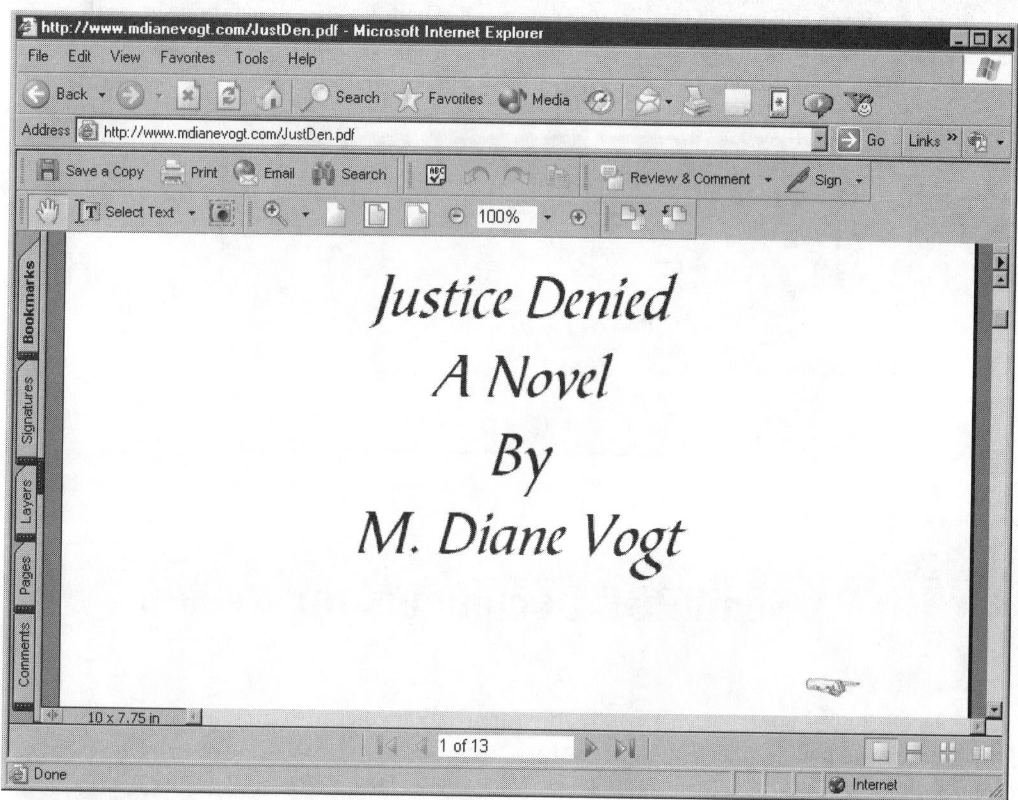

FIGURE 1-5 Acrobat is available as a plug-in or a helper application for most popular web browsers.

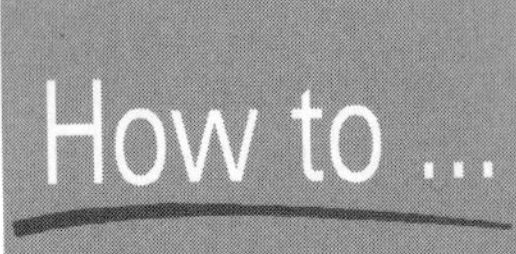

Send PDF Documents via E-Mail

You send a PDF document via e-mail when you need to share information with a coworker or client who may or may not have the program you used to create the original document. If you create the document in a Microsoft Office application supported by PDFMaker, you can e-mail it directly from the authoring application; otherwise, you can open the file in Acrobat and e-mail it from there. Sending PDF documents via e-mail will be discussed in detail in Chapters 5 and 13.

tutorials from the Internet and save them as PDF files for easy reference. If you download numerous web pages for reference and own Acrobat Professional, you can create a searchable index of your reference files with the *Catalog* command. The following illustration shows the dialog box that appears when you use Web Capture to download a web page. You'll learn how to capture web pages in Chapter 6.

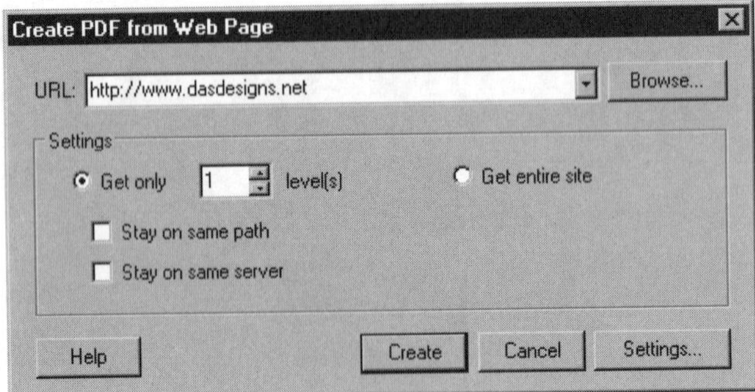

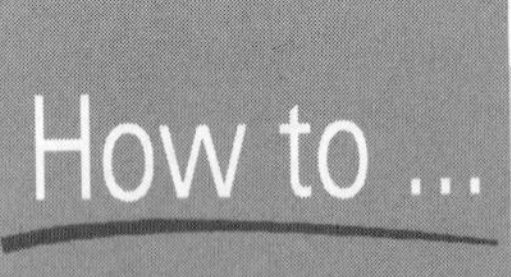

Send PDF Documents for Review

With the click of a button in a Microsoft Office application you can convert a document to PDF format and then initiate an e-mail or browser-based review. You can also initiate reviews from within Acrobat using menu commands. After you begin a review, you can use the Review Tracker to keep tabs on the reviewing process.

Convert Scanned Documents to PDF Format

If you have hard copies of documents, such as contracts or product brochures, that you need to share with coworkers or clients, Acrobat is very user-friendly. You could send the documents by fax, but in most cases what your recipient receives isn't anything near a reasonable facsimile of the original. To overcome the difference in resolution and quality of fax machines, create a PDF file for the document you want to share. If you have a scanner hooked up to your system, the Acrobat install utility adds the TWAIN information of the scanner as a device in the Create PDF from Web Page dialog box. Then it's simply a matter of choosing From Scanner from the Create PDF task button or menu. After you scan the document into Acrobat, save it as a PDF file and then e-mail it. When your document is received and viewed in Adobe Reader 6.0, it looks identical to what you scanned into Acrobat. As an example, you can also use the Scan command to archive dog-eared magazine articles for future reference in PDF format. A new Acrobat feature enables you to convert the scanned document into searchable text, a powerful feature if you scan multipage magazine articles or documents for conversion to PDF files. You learn how to convert scanned documents to PDF files in Chapter 6.

Create PDF Documents for Print

In previous versions of Acrobat, you had few options to print a hard copy of a PDF file. After you optimize a file for print, Acrobat 6.0 gives you more options for sending the file to the output device. The Print dialog box in Acrobat 6.0 has an *Advanced* button. When you click the Advanced button, a separate dialog box opens, allowing you to specify print options previously unavailable to Acrobat. If you own Acrobat Professional, you can specify options such as trim marks, transparency levels, and the capability of omitting images when printing a proof of the PDF file. If you use Acrobat Professional, you can view and print separations.

Create Interactive PDF Documents

When some Acrobat users create PDF documents for the first time, they tend to think that the document will be read in linear fashion. However, the Acrobat *Link* tool lets you create documents

Paperless Publishing

The planet on which we live has limited resources, resources that we have been taking for granted for hundreds of years. Paper is one of those resources. Whenever paper is used to publish a document, trees will inevitably have to be chopped down and processed into paper to replenish the supply. Trees should be sacrificed sparingly as they give oxygen to our planet. As you explore the possibilities of Acrobat, think of ways you can use the software to cut down on your paper usage. For example, if you work in the Human Resources department of a large organization, consider using Acrobat Professional to convert documents such as W-2 forms and employee evaluation forms into PDF documents that can be filled out and submitted via your corporate intranet.

that can be navigated like web pages. You can use the Link tool to change static text or images into hyperlinks. When you create a link in a PDF document, it serves many purposes. You can use the link to open up another PDF document, to navigate to a specific page in the current PDF document, to link to a URL on the Web, and much more. A link in a PDF document functions identically to a link in an HTML page. When you drag your mouse over the link, the cursor changes to a pointing hand. Interactive navigation for PDF documents is covered in Chapters 7 and 8.

Create PDF Documents for Multimedia Presentations (Professional Only)

The age of electronic education is very much upon us. Fluctuating demands in the workplace make lifelong learning a necessity. People in all stages of life need to increase their knowledge base. Most lifelong learners don't have time for formal classroom education and instead use online education to learn at their own pace. Online learners can log on and take a lesson according to their schedule. Other lifelong learners purchase interactive CD-ROMs and play the discs in their spare time to educate themselves.

If, on the other hand, you're authoring a PDF document for an online or CD-ROM presentation, you can accomplish the task with Acrobat. When you create a PDF document for an online or CD-ROM presentation, Acrobat Professional gives you the necessary tools to elevate your presentation to the next level. *Multimedia* is the current buzzword for online education, educational CD-ROMs, and business presentations. With Acrobat Professional, you can create PDF documents with multimedia elements such as movie clips, music, and the spoken word. You can use the *Sound* tool in Acrobat Professional, or the Sound Attachment tool in Acrobat Professional and Acrobat Standard to add a prerecorded sound clip to a document. After you add interaction, you can create links within the document to play multimedia clips or have them play when a document page is opened. In Chapter 15, you'll learn to create PDF files with multimedia elements.

Create PDF Documents for Internal Distribution

Many modern companies realize the futility of using paper to distribute information. Paper is bulky, it takes up room, and it is an expensive way to distribute written information with a short life span. If the company is a multilocation operation, there is also the cost of transporting published documents between locations. A much better solution for disseminating information is the PDF document. It can be efficiently distributed over the corporate intranet, sent via e-mail, or distributed on disk. An employee manual in print form might take up hundreds of pages plus a hefty portion of the employee's workspace. The same document can be created in PDF format and distributed to employees on a floppy disk or CD-ROM. A PDF employee manual uses fewer resources, is easier to distribute, and is easier to use. An employee looking for specific information can use the powerful Acrobat *Search* command (as shown in Figure 1-6) to navigate to specific information.

You can also use PDF documents to distribute memos. If you author a confidential memo, you can password-protect the document and add Acrobat security measures to prevent editing by

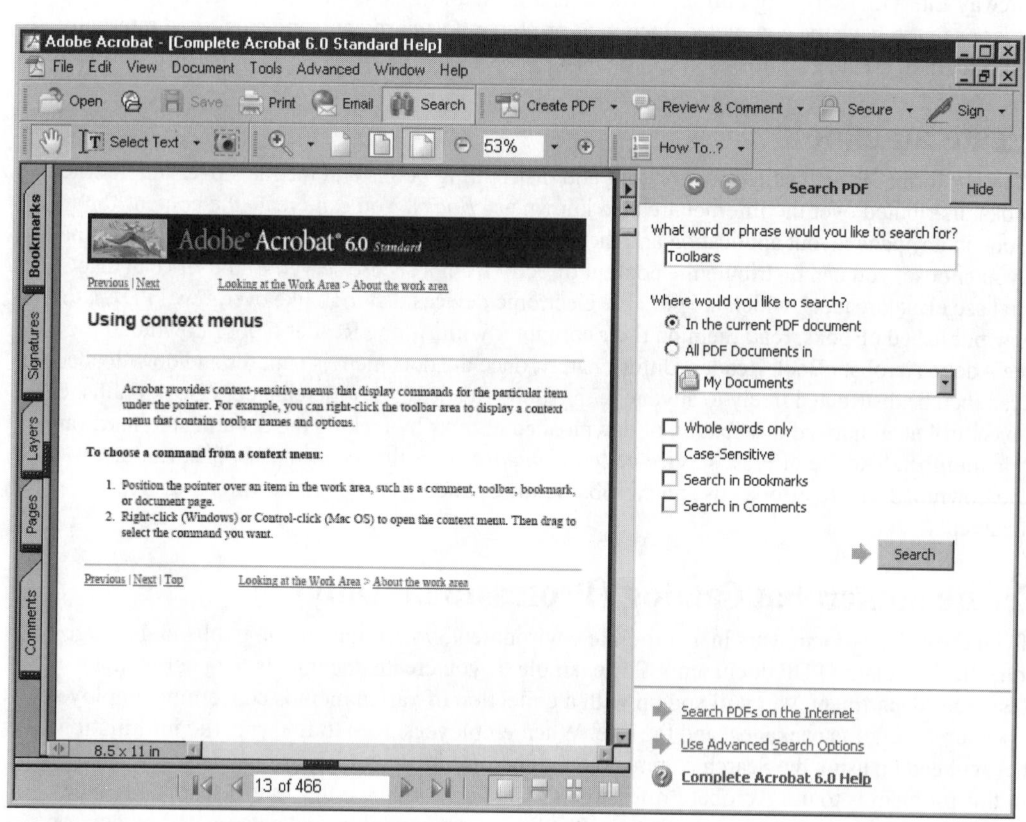

FIGURE 1-6 The Search command makes it easy to locate specific information in a multipage document.

unauthorized personnel. If you need to edit a confidential document, you can always change the security settings to allow editing and then disable editing after you have made the changes.

When you create a document for internal distribution, recipients can sign off on the document using the *Digital Signature* feature. Digital Signatures and document security are discussed in Chapter 11.

Create a PDF Form (Professional Only)

Acrobat Professional 6.0 has advanced tools that you can use to create forms to accumulate data. You can create forms complete with text boxes for collecting data, radio buttons and check boxes for selecting form options, and buttons for navigating the form or submitting the form data to a Web server. You can even create a drop-down list of form choices. You can use *CGI* (Common

Gateway Interface) scripting options to route data from a form submitted over the Web to a server or opt to have the completed document printed out as hard copy and submitted internally. You'll learn to create PDF forms in Chapter 14.

Create an eBook

The PDF format is well suited for creating and distributing books and manuals over the Internet. Books distributed over the Internet are also known as *eBooks*. You can create the content for an eBook in any page layout application and then use Adobe PDF to convert the file into PDF format. If you choose, you can distribute the content directly from a secure server. End users can also purchase eBook readers, which are portable electronic devices that look like overgrown PDAs, to view published eBooks, read them on their computer with Adobe Reader 6.0, or download the free Adobe Acrobat eBook Reader. Unfortunately, once the document is paid for and downloaded, it can then be distributed freely to anyone with Adobe Reader 6.0. A merchant or eBook publisher can control unauthorized distribution of downloaded eBooks by locking the document to hardware serial numbers. Adobe offers a service called *Content Server* that encrypts eBooks. End users who download secure eBooks use an Acrobat feature called *Web Buy* to download encrypted documents.

Create an Acrobat Catalog (Professional Only)

If you create PDF documents in a corporate environment, you might end up publishing a large collection of related PDF documents. For example, if you create documents for your Human Resources department, you will end up with a collection of varied memos concerning employee procedures, benefits packages, and the like. When employees need to find specific information, they will end up using the Search command on numerous documents to find the data. The solution for this problem is to use Acrobat Professional's Catalog command to create a searchable index of PDF files. After you create an index, use the Search command to find data related to a query. You'll learn to create a searchable index in Chapter 16.

Optimize Documents for Distribution

If you have created images and documents for different destinations, you know that a file needs to be formatted correctly for the intended destination. The file you create for print has different requirements than the file you create for a web site, both of which are different than the file you create for a multimedia CD-ROM presentation. When you create files for print, you need to optimize them for the output device, matching the file as closely as possible to the printer resolution. On the other hand, when you create a PDF file for a multimedia CD-ROM application, you need to worry only about screen resolution. When you create a document for the Web, you need to create a happy medium between image quality and bandwidth. (*Bandwidth* is the amount of information that can be downloaded per second at a given connection speed—for example, 56Kbps.)

Acrobat Distiller comes with preset Conversion Settings to optimize a document for an intended destination. If you create a PDF file from a Microsoft Office application, the PDFMaker plug-in has several presets that you can choose from the Change Conversion Settings command. If none of the presets suit the document you are publishing, you can modify a preset to create and save the parameters as a custom Adobe PDF Settings File with the .joboptions extension. Chapter 12 is devoted to optimizing PDF documents.

Use Acrobat as a Publishing Solution

If you have read this chapter from the start, you are beginning to realize the power and diversity of Acrobat. You can use Acrobat as a publishing solution within a large corporation, use it to distribute documents over the Internet, and use it to share documents with clients who do not own the software you used to create the original document. Acrobat can be used to create a simple electronic interoffice memo, a form for collecting data, or a complex presentation with interactive navigation and multimedia elements. Acrobat makes it possible for you to create a single document in an authoring program such as Microsoft Excel and publish the file as different PDF documents optimized for different destinations.

Summary

In this chapter, you learned about the powerful new features in Acrobat 6.0 and how you can utilize the software as a "paperless" publishing solution. You were introduced to the new features in Acrobat 6.0 and learned the difference between Acrobat Standard and Acrobat Professional. In Chapter 2, you get a look at the nuts and bolts that make it possible for you to create a wide variety of PDF documents. You'll learn how to navigate the Acrobat interface and how to customize the tools and tabs to suit your working preferences.

Chapter 2

Navigate the Acrobat Workspace

How to…

- Navigate the Acrobat workspace
- Customize the Acrobat interface
- Select Acrobat tools
- Set Acrobat preferences

When you launch Acrobat 6.0 for the first time, you are presented with a completely new interface. The tools you have grown accustomed to are no longer in their familiar places. It's like walking into your house after someone has completely rearranged it; you can't find a thing. However, the change in the Acrobat interface marks a huge step forward in usability. Whether you're just beginning with Acrobat or a seasoned electronic publishing veteran, after reading this chapter, you will be familiar with the new interface layout.

In this chapter, you will discover what you can accomplish with the wide variety of tools on the Acrobat toolbar. As an author of PDF documents, you'll spend a good deal of time working in Acrobat. In this regard, you'll find it imperative to know the layout of the Acrobat workspace as well as you know the back of your hand. When you begin working with Acrobat, you'll find that panes and tool groups are logically arranged for productive workflow. However, no two people work alike. For example, after you familiarize yourself with Acrobat, you may find the How To..? pane intrusive. If so, you'll be happy to know that you can hide the How To..? pane, which expands the document pane and gives you a better view of the document you're working on. You can also rearrange the layout of the toolbars to suit your working preference.

About the Adobe Reader 6.0 Interface

As of this writing, the members of the Adobe Acrobat team are still developing the newest version of the Reader, version 6.0. As an author of PDF documents, you may not feel it is imperative to learn how to use Adobe Reader 6.0. After all, you'll be doing most of your work in the full version of Acrobat Standard or Acrobat Professional. However, the people who receive and view your PDF documents may not have the full version of Acrobat. You will also be sending PDF documents to people with varying levels of computer savvy. From time to time, the recipients of your documents may require assistance with the Reader. Therefore, you should take some time to familiarize yourself with the Adobe Reader 6.0 menu commands and tool groups. If this latest version follows suit with previous versions, the tools and layout will be similar to what you'll use in the full version of Acrobat.

Navigate the Acrobat Interface

Acrobat Standard and Acrobat Professional share a similar interface. When you open a document in either application, the workspace consists of three panes, several toolbars, and a menu bar, as shown in Figure 2-1. The additional features in Acrobat Professional are not readily apparent until you start opening the various tool groups or menu commands. The majority of the features and tools that are unique to Acrobat Professional will be covered in the last part of this book. In the sections that follow, you'll find a brief overview of each tool group and the various menu commands for both versions of Acrobat. You will find concise information on how to use each tool in the remaining chapters of this book. The tools that are unique to Acrobat Professional will be parenthetically referred to as follows: (Professional Only).

Use the Navigation Pane

The Acrobat Navigation pane has five titles that look like tabs on a file folder. You click a title to open its associated tab (tabs were known as *palettes* in Acrobat 5.0) in order to navigate to

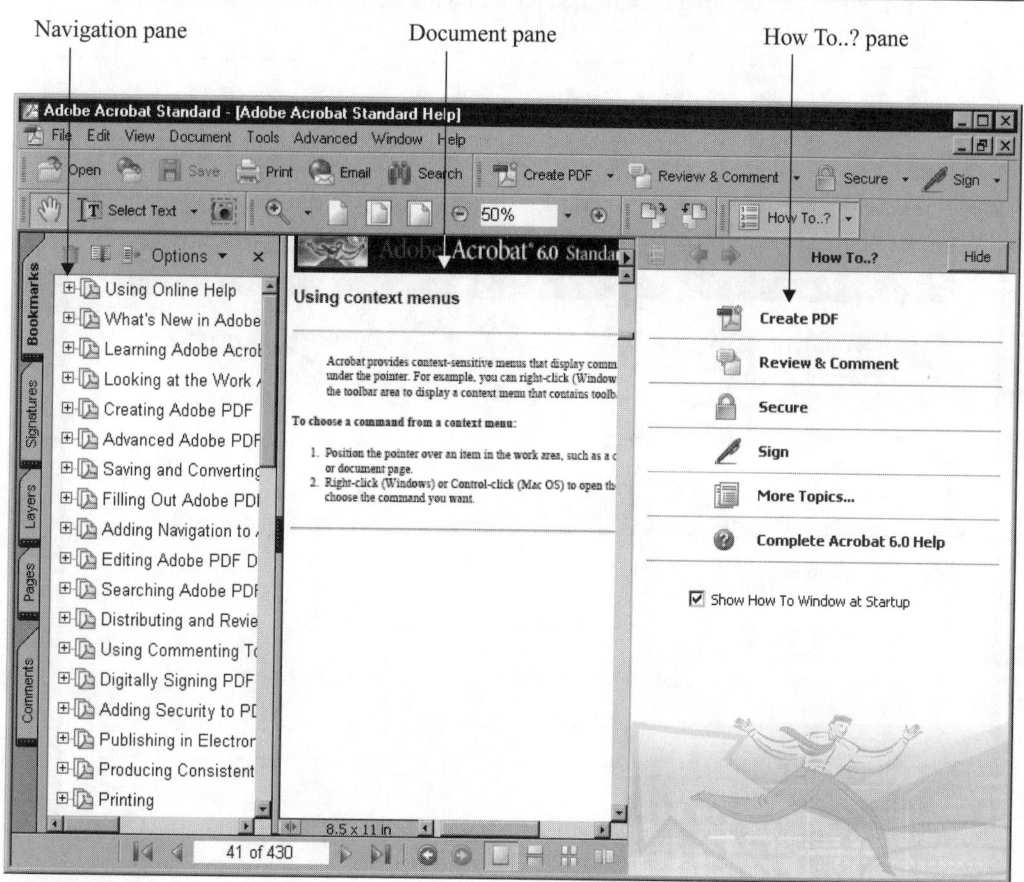

FIGURE 2-1 The Acrobat interface consists of three panes, a menu command bar, and several toolbars.

specific items in a document. You use the *Bookmarks* tab to display a list of the bookmarks in the document. Within the *Pages* tab, you find thumbnail images of each page in the document. You open the *Signatures* tab to review the list of digital signatures that have been applied to the document. Within the *Layers* tab, you'll find a list of layers in the document. This tab allows you to toggle the visibility properties of layers, as well as flatten, or merge, layers. When you open the *Comments* tab, you'll see a list of all comments added to the document and the names of people who authored them. Whenever you open a tab, you click an icon or text area to navigate to a specific point in the document. Figure 2-2 shows the five tabs in the Navigation pane. Notice in this figure the tabs are floating as opposed to their default docked position previously shown in Figure 2-1. You'll learn to float interface objects in the upcoming "Float Toolbars" section of this chapter.

In addition to using these tabs for document navigation, you also use them to perform specific functions such as adding or deleting bookmarks, changing the size of thumbnails, adding or

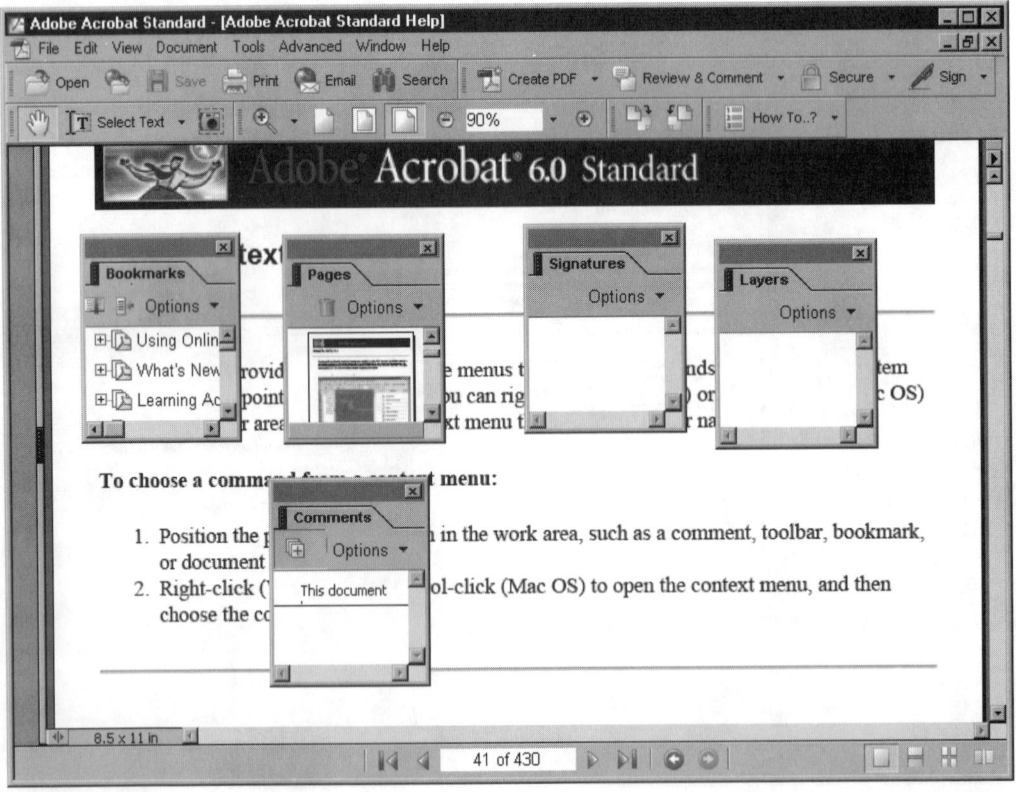

FIGURE 2-2 You use the tabs from the Navigation pane to advance to specific elements in a PDF document.

deleting pages, and so on. To the right of each tab name, you find an icon labeled *Options*. Click the icon to open a tab menu, as shown in the following illustration. The operations you can perform differ depending on the selected tab. You find many of the tab commands duplicated in menu command groups. You'll learn the different ways you can achieve the same result when specific topics such as bookmarks and digital signatures are covered in upcoming chapters.

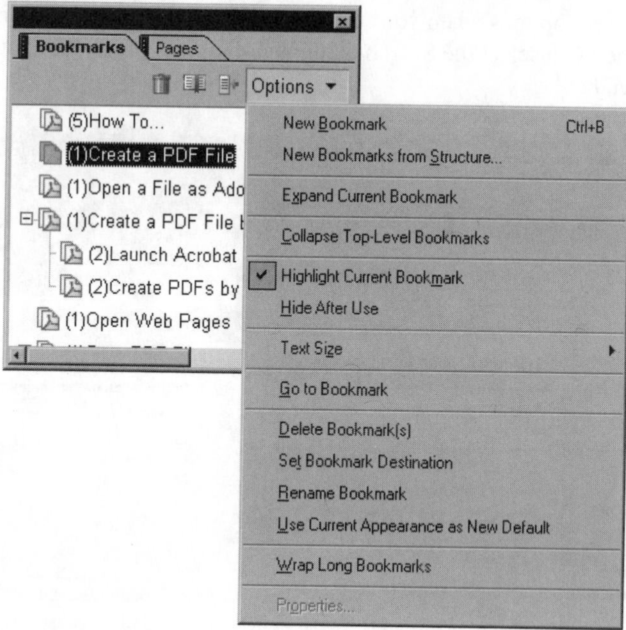

In addition to the Options menu, you'll see other icons that vary in accordance with the tab you have selected. The universally recognized garbage can icon is used to delete selected items from the tab. In the upper-right corner of each tab's window, you'll find an X. Click the X to close the Navigation pane. Click a tab name to open the Navigation pane to that particular tab.

About the Document Pane

You use the Document pane (the large window to the right of the Navigation pane, previously shown in Figure 2-1) to edit a PDF document as well as read it. At the bottom-left of the Document pane is a toolbar that contains various information about the displayed PDF file, as well as tools you can use to navigate to a specific page or change the number of pages Acrobat displays in the Document pane. In Chapter 3, you'll learn how to use these tools.

bout the How To..? Pane

To the right of the Document pane, you find another of Acrobat's new features, the How To..? pane (also shown in Figure 2-1). The How To..? pane contains task-oriented information for specific topics. To reveal information for a topic, click the topic's name. For example, when you click the Review & Comment title, you'll find a list of topics pertaining to reviewing a document and adding comments to it. This book provides the same information (and more) that you find displayed in the How To..? pane, but this pane will come in handy if you're working in a remote location and don't have this book available.

When you initially launch Acrobat, the How To..? pane is displayed by default. The pane changes to reveal different options when you select a command that needs an extensive dialog area. For example, when you select the Search command, the right pane of the interface is reconfigured, as shown here:

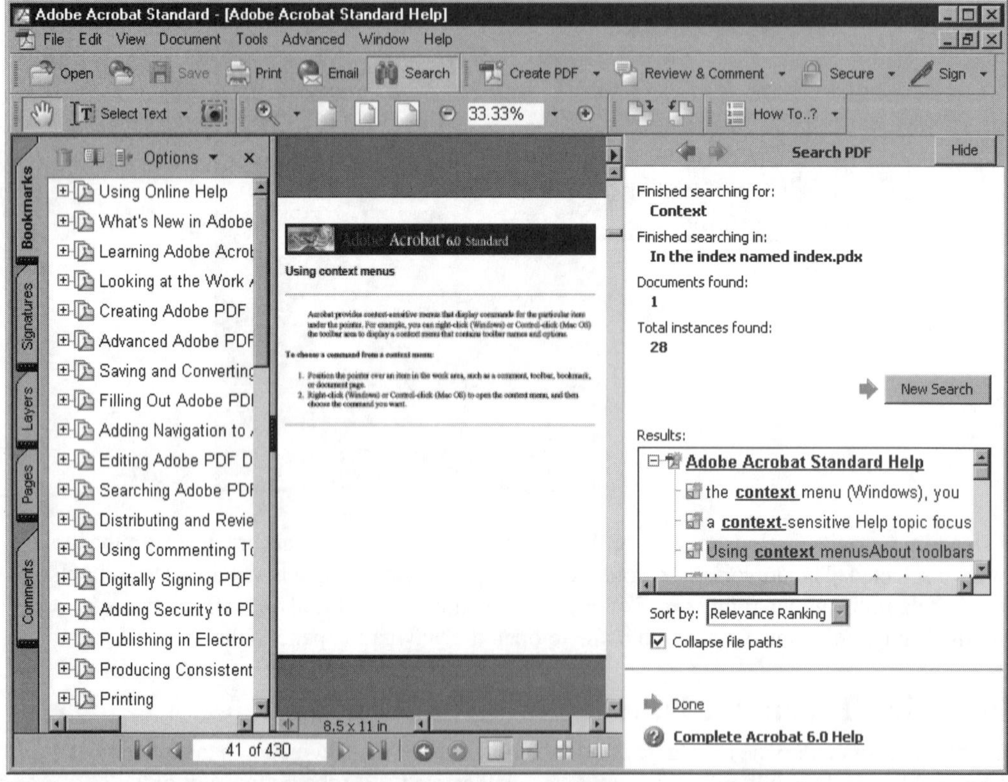

You can recover the space used by the How To..? pane, or any other dialog area that appears in the right pane, by clicking Hide (shown in the preceding illustration). To display the hidden How To..? pane, click the How To..? button on the toolbar.

If you prefer, you can prevent the How To..? pane from displaying at startup by clicking the Show How To Window at Startup to deselect the default option (refer to Figure 2-1). Alternatively, you can click the How To..? button and deselect the Show How To..? Window at Startup option.

TIP *Right-click (Windows) or* CTRL*-click (Macintosh) to reveal the How To..? pane context menu. Here you'll find commands to dock the pane on the right side (the default option) or left side of the interface as well as a command to hide the pane. Alternatively, you can press* F4 *to open or close the How To..? pane.*

Use the Acrobat Menu Commands

You find the Acrobat menu commands at the top of the interface, grouped by command type. Acrobat has eight command groups named File, Edit, View, Document, Tools, Advanced, Window, and Help. In upcoming chapters, you'll learn to use the commands from these menus to unlock the powerful features of Acrobat, such as capturing web pages. Individual menu commands will be presented in detail when they pertain to the topic of discussion. From left to right on the menu bar, you find the following command groups:

- **File** The commands in this list are used to create PDF files, and open, close, and save documents. You also have additional commands to e-mail PDF files, reduce the file size of a PDF document, and view document information, as well as initiate an e-mail or browser-based document review.
- **Edit** As the name implies, the commands in this group are used to perform edits to the current PDF document. You also have edit commands to search for items in the current document, search for items in PDF documents stored in folders on your computer, and set Acrobat preferences. You'll learn how to set Acrobat preferences in the upcoming "Set Preferences" section of this chapter.
- **View** The commands in this group are used to alter your view of the document. You will also find commands in this group to access Navigation tabs, enable the grid, initialize the Review Tracker, and much more.
- **Document** The commands in this group are used to add, delete, and crop pages, as well as add headers, footers, watermarks, or backgrounds to the document you are editing.
- **Tools** The commands in this group are used to access Acrobat tools. The tools are divided into five groups in Acrobat Standard: Commenting, Advanced Commenting, Basic, Zoom, and Advanced Editing. Acrobat Professional has one additional tool group: Measuring. Within each tool group, you'll find related commands and the option to show or hide the group's toolbar.
- **Advanced** The commands in this group are used to access the enhanced features of Acrobat. You can launch the Acrobat Distiller from within this menu group, as well as make a document accessible to the visually impaired, export images from a document, manage Digital IDs, and perform advanced Web capture commands.
- **Window** The commands in this group are used to select documents you currently have open, as well as arrange the view of multiple documents.

- **Help** In this command group, you find access to the How To..? pane, complete program help, and the Adobe JavaScript guide. You'll also find links to online help and program updates, plus a new Acrobat feature you can use to detect missing or corrupt program files and repair them.

Use Acrobat Toolbars

The tools you most often use to unleash the full power of Acrobat are conveniently grouped and laid out on a toolbar. You can access the rest of the Acrobat tools by choosing View | Toolbar and then selecting the desired toolbar. Prior versions of Acrobat had every tool displayed on the toolbar, which made selecting the proper tool difficult as the interface was cluttered with toolbars and many of the icons looked similar. In the default display of toolbars, you find tools that perform operations related to an Acrobat feature such as Reviewing and Commenting, Creating a PDF file, and so on. In the other toolbars, you find related tools to edit, view, navigate documents, and so on. Many of the toolbars are collapsed to save working space. A *collapsed toolbar* is signified by a downward pointing triangle. Click the triangle to view other tools in the toolbar, as shown in the following illustration. You can click the Show command at the bottom of each toolbar to display it as a floating toolbar as outlined in the upcoming "Float Toolbars" section. Certain toolbars such as the Advanced Editing toolbar can be displayed by clicking its icon on the main toolbar. You can dock a toolbar to the workspace, or leave it floating in the workspace. When no longer needed, you can close a toolbar by clicking its Close button.

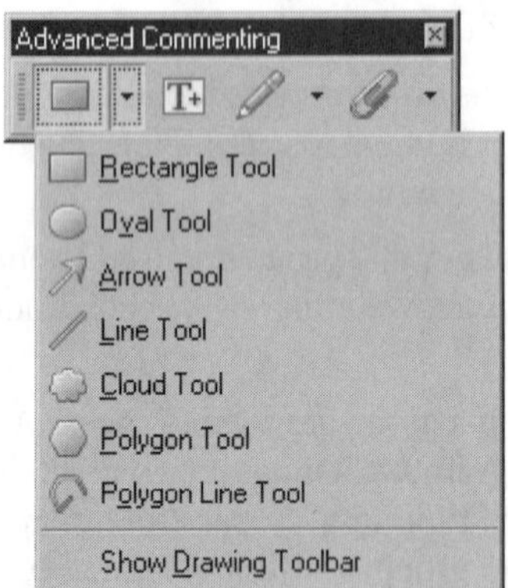

You can do most of your work in Acrobat using the toolbars. If you prefer working with menus, most of the tools have equivalent menu commands. Most Acrobat users find it convenient to work with a combination of menu commands, tools, context menus, and shortcuts. For a list of popular Acrobat shortcuts, refer to Appendix A. Figure 2-3 shows the default display of Acrobat toolbars.

The following sections list the default display of toolbars as they appear below the menu bar. In each toolbar section, individual tools are listed with a brief description of the task for which they are used. In future chapters, you'll find detailed information about using a specific tool in conjunction with a related task.

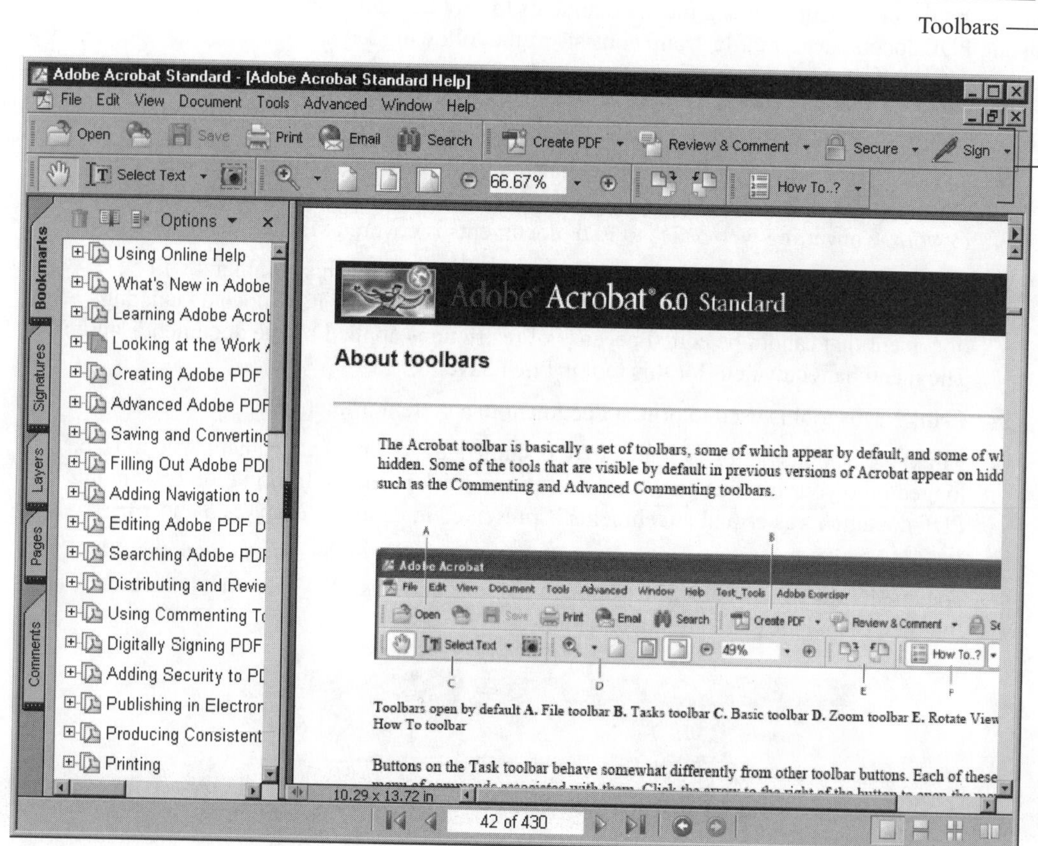

FIGURE 2-3 You use Acrobat tools to edit, navigate, and view PDF documents.

Acrobat Professional has additional toolbars you use to access the program's enhanced features. These toolbars are designated by the parenthetical reference (Professional Only).

About the File Toolbar

The File toolbar, as shown in the next illustration, consists of six tools that you use for file maintenance, printing, and search tasks. Within this toolbar, you'll also find tools to capture web pages as PDF documents and e-mail PDF documents. You'll augment the functionality of these tools with menu commands. For example, after you capture a web page as a PDF document, you can append the document by using menu commands to capture additional web pages or insert existing PDF documents. The file group consists of the following tools:

- **Open** Click this button to navigate to and open an existing PDF file stored on your computer or network.
- **Create PDF From Web Page** Click this button to download a web page into the Document pane. You must be connected to an Internet Service Provider for this tool to work. Converting web pages to PDF documents is covered in detail in Chapter 6.
- **Save** This tool is used to save the current PDF document. This command will be dimmed out if you open an existing document and do not edit it, or open an existing document that cannot be edited because of restrictions applied by the document's author. The menu bar equivalent for this tool is File | Save.
- **Print** This tool is used to print a document to a system printer.
- **Email** Click this button to send a PDF document as an e-mail attachment. You must be logged onto your Internet server for this tool to work properly. Information on sending PDF documents as e-mail attachments is presented in detail in Chapters 5 and 13.
- **Search** Click this button to search for a word or phrase in the current document, PDF documents stored in a folder on your computer or network, PDF documents on the Internet, or an index of PDF documents.

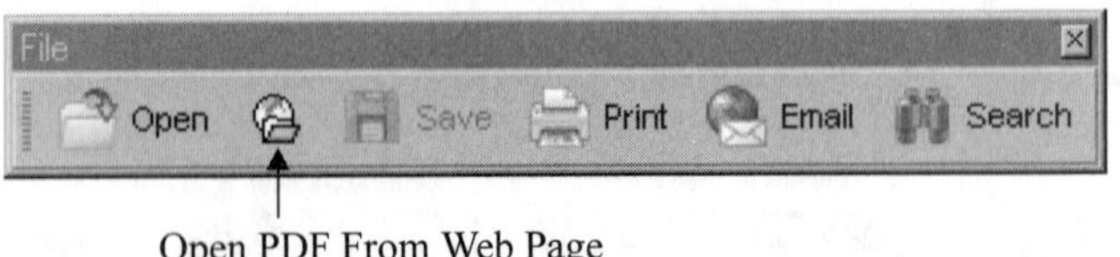

About the Tasks Toolbar

The default display of the Tasks toolbar comprises five task buttons (six when you open a document with graphic elements) you use to create PDF documents, review and comment PDF documents, secure PDF documents, and sign PDF documents. The upcoming sections give you a brief overview of what you can accomplish with the commands you access when you click a task button. There is an additional task button for eBooks that will be covered in the "About the eBooks Task Button" section of this chapter and one for Picture Tasks that will be covered in the "About the Picture Tasks Button" section of this chapter.

About the Create PDF Task Button

You click this task button to access commands used to create a PDF document. When you click this button, a drop-down menu appears where you'll find all of the commands you need to create PDF documents from files stored on your computer, from web pages, and from documents you scan into the Document pane, as well as images you've copied to the system clipboard. The

Create PDF task button shown in the following illustration opens a menu with the following commands:

- **From File** Click this button to navigate to a file on your computer and convert it to a PDF document. Creating PDF documents from supported files is covered in detail in Chapter 4.
- **From Multiple Files** Click this button to select several files and convert them to a PDF document. The files that you select can be different formats. For example, you can select a combination of Microsoft Word documents, PostScript files, or image files and convert them to a multipage PDF document. After you select the files, you can arrange the order in which they appear in the PDF document, add additional files, and remove files. Creating PDF documents from multiple files is covered in Chapter 4.
- **From Web Page** Click this button, and a dialog box appears where you enter the URL of the web page you want to convert to a PDF document. After converting the Web page, you can modify it by choosing Advanced | Web Capture and then choosing the desired command. Capturing web pages is covered in Chapter 6.
- **From Scanner** Click this button to create a PDF document from a scanner or digital camera that is attached to your computer. Capturing PDF documents from scanners and digital cameras is covered in detail in Chapter 6.
- **From Clipboard Image** Click this button to create a PDF document from material you copied to the clipboard from another application. You can also use this command after using the Snapshot tool to copy a selection to the clipboard from another PDF document. The Snapshot tool is covered in detail in Chapter 3.

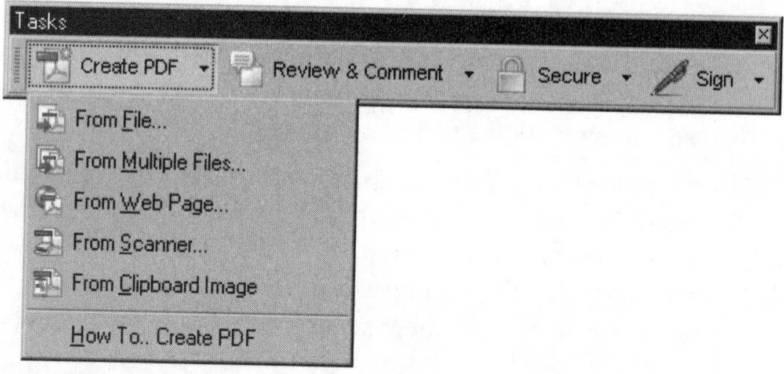

About the Review & Comment Tool Task Button

You use this task button to open a menu with commands you use to add comments (or as they were referred to in early versions of Acrobat, *annotations*) to a PDF document. Your comments can be in the form of notes, free-form text, file attachments, and sound files. Within the task button, you'll also find two toolbars:

- **Commenting** Use this toolbar to annotate a PDF document and put your stamp of approval on a document.
- **Advanced Commenting** Use this to add shapes to PDF documents, mark up text, and spell check form fields and comments.

The tasks you perform with the commenting tools in this group are discussed in detail in Chapter 10.

The Review & Comment task button has two toolbars and six menu commands. The expanded task button is shown in Figure 2-4.

The first toolbar available from the Review & Comment task button is used to annotate a document. With the tools in the Commenting toolbar shown in the following illustration, you'll find five buttons that you can use to add notes, text editing comments, and stamps to a PDF document to highlight text, and to display or hide comments in a document.

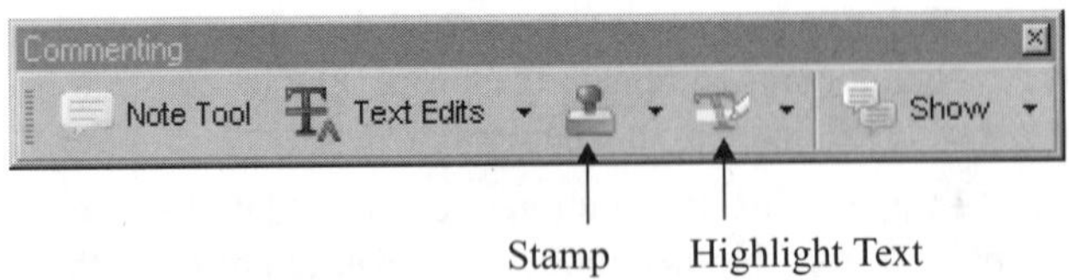

- **Note Tool** Click this button when you want to add a note or comment to a PDF file. After you create the note, an icon that looks like a sticky note appears in the document. Readers click the icon to read the note.
- **Text Edits** Click this button to display a list of commands you can use to indicate text in a document that needs to be edited. You can select text and mark it as text to be deleted and then add a note with the text you want displayed instead.
- **Stamp** This tool is used to add your stamp of approval (or other annotations) to a document. Click Stamp to choose a stamp from three major categories. Each category is subdivided into a wide array of presets, such as *Confidential, Approved,* and *Draft*. You can specify the color and size of the stamp as well as create custom stamps. The Stamp tool is the electronic equivalent of a rubber stamp, without the messy inkpads.

To the right the Stamp tool, you'll find three tools for marking up text. The icon for the tool last used is displayed (in this case, the Highlight Text tool). Click the triangle to the right of the tool to select a different markup tool. You have three highlighting tools from which to choose:

- **Highlight Text** This tool, the electronic counterpart of a felt-tipped highlighter, is used to highlight text. You can change the color of a highlight from the Acrobat default yellow to any color available in your system color picker by changing a highlight tool

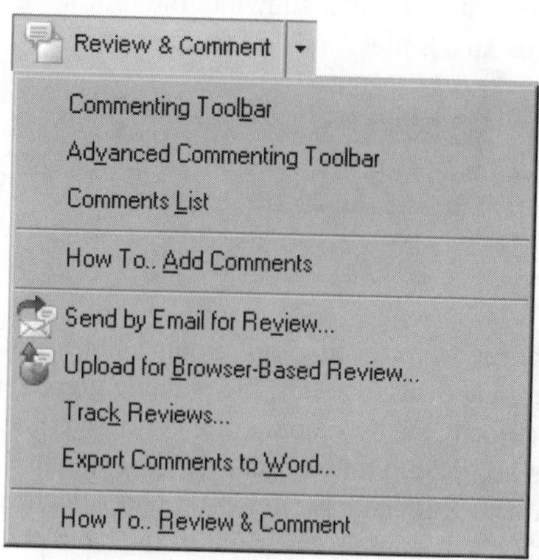

FIGURE 2-4 You use the Review & Comment task button to annotate a PDF document and much more.

annotation's properties after you highlight text with the tool. You can also use the Highlight Text tool to create a note that pops up when a viewer clicks the highlighted text.

- **Cross-Out Text** This tool is used to strikethrough selected text. You can change the color of the strikethrough and you can create a pop-up note with the Strikethrough Text tool as well.
- **Underline Text** This tool is used to highlight text by underlining it. You can specify the color of the underline and use this tool to create a clickable pop-up note as well.

TIP *If you frequently annotate PDF documents with the tools from the previous list, click the triangle to the right of the currently active highlighting tool and choose Show Highlighting Toolbar to display the Highlighting toolbar shown next:*

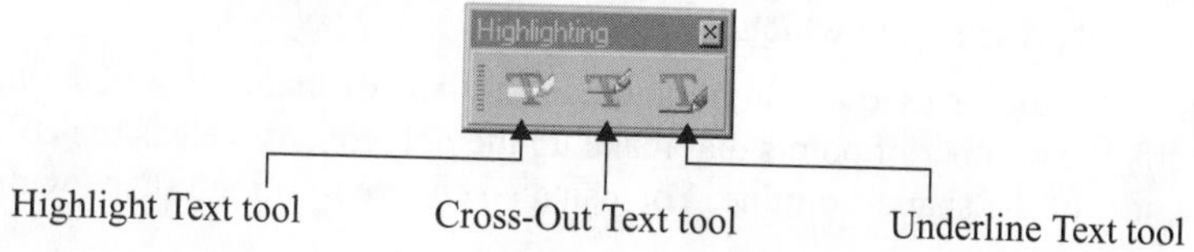

The last tool on the Commenting toolbar is used to display or hide comments:

- **Show** Click this button, and you can choose from a list of commands relating to commenting. From within this menu, you can open the Comments tab and determine which comments are displayed or hidden.

You use the Advanced Commenting toolbar shown in the following illustration to annotate a document with graphic elements, attach files, and add text notes:

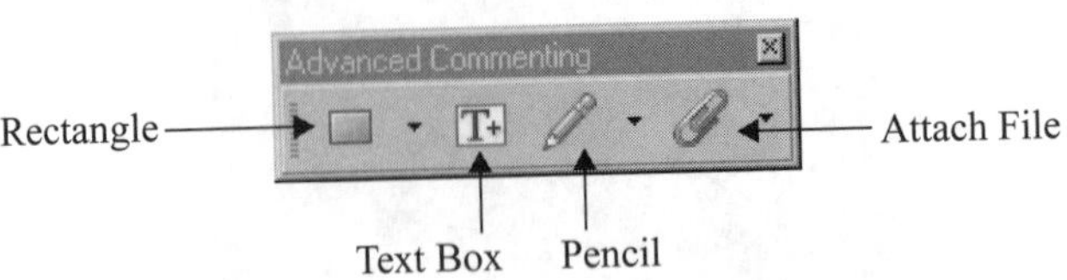

The first button in the Advanced Commenting tool group enables you to add graphic elements such as straight lines, rectangles, and ovals to a PDF file. Adding graphic elements draws attention to specific objects within a document, such as a paragraph or image that needs to be revised or deleted before the document is acceptable for publication. As explained in Chapter 10, each graphic element you add to a document can have a pop-up note attached. The icon for the tool you last used is displayed. Click the triangle to the right of the icon to select a different shape tool. You can annotate PDF documents with any of the following shapes:

- **Rectangle** This tool is used to add a square or rectangle to a PDF file. You can specify the thickness and color of the border and whether or not the shape is filled with color.
- **Oval** This tool is used to create circles and ovals. You can specify the thickness and color of the border and whether or not the shape is filled with color.
- **Arrow (Professional Only)** This tool is used to add lines with arrowheads to a PDF document. You specify the color, opacity, and thickness of the line, as well as the shape of the arrowhead, and whether one end of the line has an arrowhead or both.
- **Line** This tool is used to add straight lines to a PDF document. You specify the color and width of the line. You can even modify the appearance of the line by adding a shape such as a diamond to either end of the line.
- **Cloud (Professional only)** This tool is used to annotate a PDF document with shapes that look like clouds. You specify the color, opacity, shape, and thickness of the cloud's outline, and whether or not the cloud is filled with a solid color. Acrobat gives you different cloud presets from which to choose.
- **Polygon** This tool is used to add polygonal (multisided) shapes to a PDF document. You specify the number of points that make up the polygon, as well as the color, opacity, and thickness of the shape's outline. You can also choose to fill the shape with solid color or not.
- **Polygon Line** This tool is used to add freeform lines to a PDF document. You specify the number of points that make up the line, and the line color, opacity, and thickness.

TIP *If you frequently use the shape tools to annotate your document, click the triangle to the right of the last used tool and choose Show Drawing Toolbar from the menu to display the Drawing toolbar, as shown next.*

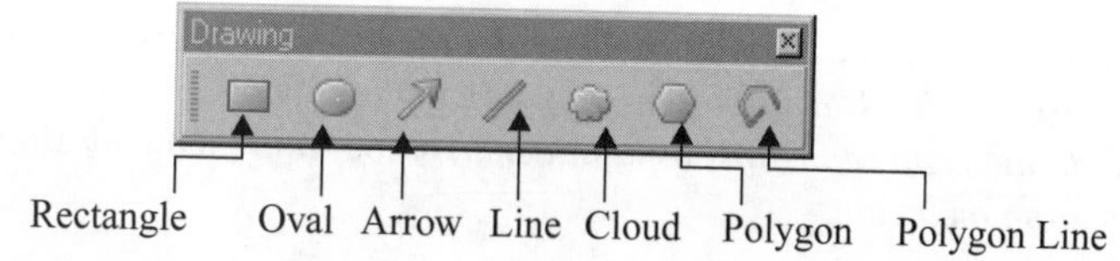

The next tool on the Advanced Commenting is the Text Box tool. This takes the place of the Free Text tool found in Acrobat 5.0.

- **Text Box** Use this tool to add free-form text notes to a PDF document. When you annotate a document with this tool, you can specify the color, opacity, and thickness of the text box border, as well as the text box fill color. If desired, you can create a text box with no fill.

The next button on the Advanced Commenting toolbar activates the Pencil tool. If you frequently use the Pencil tool to mark up PDF documents, you'll be happy to know Acrobat 6.0 provides a Pencil Eraser tool.

- **Pencil** This tool is used to add a free-form line to a PDF file. You can modify the color and thickness of lines you draw. Acrobat smoothes the line after you create it; however, your drawing skill with a mouse determines the final appearance of the line.
- **Pencil Eraser** This tool is used to erase lines created with the Pencil tool. You can use this tool to erase all or part of a line.

TIP *You can display the Pencil tool and Pencil Eraser on the Advanced Commenting toolbar by clicking the triangle to the right of the currently selected pencil tool and then clicking Expand This Button.*

You use the last button on the Advanced Commenting toolbar to attach the contents of the clipboard, files, or sounds to a document. The button for the last tool you used is displayed. Click the triangle to the right of the button to display all of the attachment tools.

- **Attach File** This tool is used to attach a file to a PDF document. After you use this tool, an icon appears in the document. When the icon is double-clicked, the file opens up in the appropriate program (for example, Microsoft Word for a file with the .doc extension).
- **Sound Attachment** This tool is used to insert audio files in a document or to record an audio note. After you use this tool, a speaker icon appears in the document. When a viewer double-clicks the icon, the recorded note or sound plays.
- **Paste Clipboard Image** This tool is used to paste an image from the clipboard into a PDF document. The image can be one you pasted to the clipboard from another application, or one that you captured from another PDF document using the Snapshot tool.

TIP

If you frequently annotate documents with attached files, sounds, or clipboard images, you can display the Attach toolbar shown in the following illustration by clicking the triangle to the right of the last used attachment tool and then choosing Show Attach Toolbar from the menu.

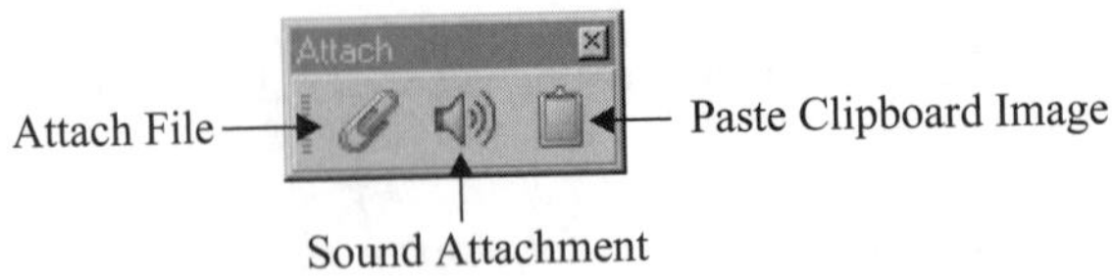

About the Secure Task Button

With the commands in this task button, you can restrict access to a document, create an encrypted document, or display the security and restrictions applied to the currently selected document. When you click the Secure task button, you can choose from the following commands:

- **Restrict Opening and Editing** With this command, you can password protect a document. Furthermore, you can restrict editing so that a password must be used in order to edit the document. When you choose this command, you can specify the level of encryption.
- **Encrypt for Certain Identities Using Certificates** You use this command to restrict access to the document by choosing the digital IDs of the parties you want to have access to the document. When you choose individual IDs, you can restrict the level of access permitted to the bearer of the digital ID.
- **Display Restrictions and Security** You use this command to display the restrictions applied to the document you are viewing. If the document is password protected and you have the proper password, you can modify the restrictions and security applied to the document.

About the Sign Task Button

You use the commands in this task button to digitally sign a document and verify any signatures that have been applied to the document. When you click this button, you have access to the following commands:

- **Sign This Document** You use this command to apply your digital signature to a document.
- **Validate All Signatures in This Document** You use this command to validate all digital signatures that have been applied to the document. A signature is validated if it is part of your trusted indentities list.

About the Picture Tasks Button

When you open a document with images, the Picture Tasks button becomes available, which you can use to work with images in the file. When you click this button, you have access to the following commands:

- **Export Pictures** You use this command to export pictures from a document into a folder on your computer.
- **Export and Edit Pictures** You use this command to export pictures from a document and edit them in Photoshop or Photoshop Elements.
- **Print Pictures** You use this command to print pictures in a document on your local printer.
- **Order Prints Online** You use this command to order prints of pictures in a document from an online printing service. Your prints are delivered by mail.
- **Order Project Online** You use this command to order prints from a PDF document that was created with specific Photoshop Elements 2.0 templates or Photoshop Album 1.0. After selecting this command the project is uploaded to a printing service whereupon you can choose which items from the project you want printed.

About the Basic Toolbar

The tools in this toolbar (as shown in the following illustration) are used to manually navigate to different parts of a document and activate links in the document. The enhanced features of these tools will be discussed in Chapter 3. This group also has tools used for selecting text and graphic elements in a document. Selecting text and graphics for use in other applications will also be discussed in detail in Chapter 3.

- **Hand** This aptly named tool is used to manually navigate through the pages of a PDF document. First, click the tool to select it; then when you click inside the document pane to navigate with this tool, your cursor becomes a closed fist. To navigate from the top to bottom of a page and vice versa, select the Hand tool, move the tool over the document, and then click and drag. Release the left mouse button to stop scrolling the page. The Hand tool is also used to find and activate links within the document. When you pass your cursor over a document link or a bookmark in the Bookmark tab, the cursor becomes a pointing finger. Click the link or bookmark to navigate to the specified destination within the document.

The button to the right of the Hand tool expands to display three tools used to select elements within the document. The tool last used is displayed. Click the triangle to the right of the current to access a different tool. You have three selection tools at your disposal.

- **Select Text** This tool is used to select a block of text within a PDF document. You can copy the selected text to the clipboard and save it for use in another application.
- **Select Table** This tool is used to select a table within a PDF document. After selecting the table, you can copy it to the clipboard or use it within a spreadsheet application such as Microsoft Excel.

- **Select Image** This tool is used to select an image in the document. After selecting the image, you can copy it to the clipboard for use in another application.

If you frequently select items from PDF documents, you can display the Selection toolbar shown in the following illustration by clicking the current selection tool and then choosing Show Selection toolbar:

- **Snapshot** The last tool on the Basic toolbar is used to select an area of the document and then paste it to the clipboard. You can then use that selection to create another PDF document. You can also paste the selection into another application.

About the Zoom Toolbar

The tools in this toolbar (shown in the following illustration) are used to change the magnification of the document and change the way the document is displayed in the Document pane. The toolbar consists of six buttons and a magnification window.

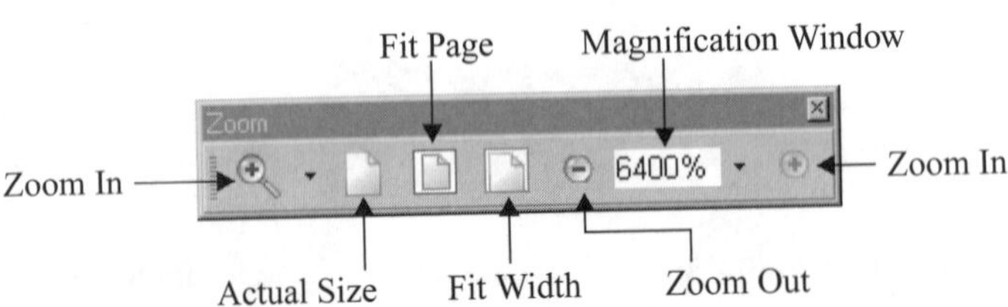

The first button on the toolbar displays the zoom tool you last used. You have three zoom tools at your disposal:

- **Zoom Out** This tool is used to zoom to the next lowest level of magnification. The menu bar equivalent for this tool is View | Zoom Out.
- **Zoom In** This tool is used to zoom to the next highest level of magnification. The menu bar equivalent for this tool is View | Zoom In.
- **Dynamic Zoom** This tool is used to dynamically zoom in and out on the document. After selecting the tool, you click and drag within the Document pane to change magnification levels.

If you use the zoom tools frequently, you can float the Zoom toolbar (the Acrobat Professional Zoom toolbar is shown above) by clicking the triangle to the right of the currently selected zoom tool and then choosing Show Zoom Toolbar.

If you own Acrobat Professional, you have two additional zoom tools at your disposal. They are

- **Loupe (Professional Only)** This tool enables you to select a portion of the document you want to examine in greater detail. The selection is displayed in another window with a magnification level slider you use to set the magnification level for the selection. You can drag the tool to different parts of the document, and the window refreshes with a magnified view of the area over which your cursor is hovering.
- **Pan & Zoom Window (Professional Only)** This tool displays the document in another window that you can use to interactively pan to different areas of the document as well as change the magnification level.

The next tools on the Zoom toolbar are used to change the way the document is displayed in the document pane. The buttons for these tools look like pages of a document and are as follows:

- **Actual Size** This tool is used to return the document page to its originally published size. The menu bar equivalent for this tool is View | Actual Size.
- **Fit Page** This tool is used to resize a document so that a single page is displayed within the Document pane. The menu bar equivalent for this tool is View | Fit Page.
- **Fit Width** This tool is used to conform the document width to the current width of the Document pane. The menu bar equivalent for this tool is View | Fit Width.

The final elements of the Zoom toolbar are two buttons separated by a window. These tools are used to change the document level of magnification.

- **Zoom Out** This tool is used to zoom out to the next lowest level of magnification.
- **Magnification Window** Acrobat displays the current percentage level of magnification in this window. You can click the triangle to the right of the window and select a magnification percentage from the drop-down menu, or you can enter the desired level of magnification directly into the window and then press ENTER or RETURN to apply. You can also specify a magnification level by choosing View | Zoom To and then enter a value between 8.33% and 6400% in the Zoom To dialog box (the available range of magnification in Acrobat).
- **Zoom In** This tool is used to magnify all or part of a document.

About the How To..? Toolbar

The How To..? toolbar is used to display the How To..? pane when it is hidden. The toolbar has five commands (Acrobat Standard) or seven commands (Acrobat Professional) that you use to open task-specific information within the How to..? pane. For example, when you click the Create PDF button, information on creating PDF documents is displayed in the How To..? pane. There is also an option to open the complete Acrobat 6.0 Help document in a separate window. If you find the How To..? pane is using too much of the workspace, you can hide it at startup by clicking the triangle to the right of the How To..? button and then deselecting Show How To.. Window at Startup.

TIP *If you prefer working with button icons and no text, choose View | Toolbars and then deselect the default Show Tool Button Labels.*

Use the Other Acrobat Task Buttons and Toolbars

In previous sections, you learned about the task buttons and toolbars that are displayed by default. The designers of Acrobat have uncluttered the interface by hiding infrequently used task buttons and toolbars. You can, however, display these toolbars as needed by choosing the proper command from the View menu. The sections that follow describe one additional task button and the other toolbars.

About the eBooks Task Button

If you use Acrobat to collect and read eBooks, you can use the eBooks task button to add to your eBook collection or read an eBook. To access the eBooks task button, choose View | Task Buttons | eBooks. After choosing this command, the eBooks task button is added to the Task Buttons toolbar with the following commands:

- **Get Books Online** This command enables you to download books from the Internet after activating Acrobat as an eBook Reader.
- **My Bookshelf** The command enables you to manage and read eBooks you have downloaded.

About the Acrobat Standard Advanced Editing Toolbar

The Advanced Editing toolbar provides the tools you need to add interactivity to your PDF documents. On this toolbar, you'll find tools to add links, crop pages, touch up text, and more. To access the Advanced Editing toolbar shown in the following illustration, choose View | Toolbars | Advanced Editing. After choosing the toolbar, you can modify a PDF document using the following tools:

- **Select Object** This tool is used to select objects in a PDF document.
- **Article** This tool is used to select a portion of a PDF document and give it a name, known in Acrobat as an *article*. An article can be a single block of text or several blocks of related text dispersed throughout the document. When readers view your document, they can follow the thread of the article.
- **Crop** This tool is used to reduce the size of the page or remove elements, such as unwanted graphics and extraneous text, from a PDF document page. If you have used cropping tools in image editing programs, you'll find this tool performs in a similar manner.
- **Link** This tool is used to add interactivity to your documents. You can create visible or invisible links. You can use document links for navigation or to trigger an event, such as opening a file or opening a web page. Acrobat calls these events *actions,* and you have a wide variety of actions from which you can choose. Detailed uses for this tool are discussed in Chapter 7.

- **TouchUp Text** This tool is used to make minor corrections to text objects in a PDF document. After selecting this tool, you can replace text, add text, and change text color, font, size, or style.

About the Acrobat Professional Advanced Editing Toolbar

If you own Acrobat Professional, you have additional tools on the Advanced Editing toolbar. In addition to the tools listed in the previous section, you can enhance a PDF document with the tools shown in the following illustration. The final two groups of buttons on this toolbar are expanded. When you initially display the Advanced Editing toolbar, only two tools are visible at the end of the toolbar, the Movie tool and the TouchUp Text tool. In the following illustration, these buttons have been expanded:

The first additional tool on the Acrobat Professional Advanced Editing toolbar houses seven tools. These tools are used to add form fields and digital signature fields to a document. PDF forms will be covered in detail in Chapter 14. Click the triangle to the right of the currently selected tool to display the following tools:

- **Button** This tool is used to add interactive buttons to a PDF document. The buttons work like buttons in an HTML document.
- **Check Box** This tool is used to add check boxes to a PDF document. Check boxes can be used as items in a PDF form that you use to gather information. You can create a series of check boxes when you want viewers to be able to select more than one item from a list of choices; for example, a viewer survey asking why a certain product is used.
- **Combo Box** This tool is used to add combo boxes to a PDF document. A combo box displays a single item from a pop-up menu. Viewers of the PDF document click a button to reveal the entire list.
- **List Box** This tool is used to add list boxes to a PDF document. A list box is used to display a list of items from which users can choose. With a list box, the entire list is displayed as opposed to a combo box that displays only one item from the list.

- **Radio Button** This tool is used to add radio buttons to a document. Radio buttons are used when you want viewers to choose only one item from a list—for example, the type of credit card they use.
- **Text Field** This tool is used when you want to add a text field to a PDF document. Text fields can be used to gather information from viewers of a PDF document or display read-only information.
- **Digital Signature Field** This tool is used to add a placeholder for a digital signature.

TIP *If you're creating a PDF document with several form fields, you may find it beneficial to display the Forms toolbar shown in the following illustration. To float the Forms toolbar in the workspace, display the Advanced Editing toolbar as described previously. Click the triangle to the right of the currently selected form tool and then choose Show Forms Toolbar.*

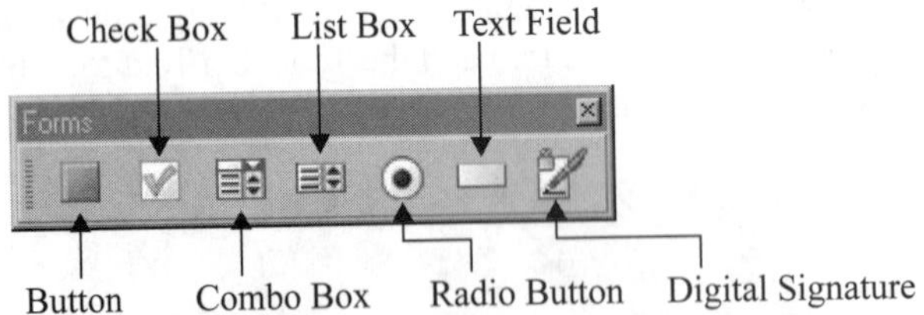

When you display the Advanced Editing toolbar, the next tool displayed is the Movie tool. To the right of this tool is a triangle that, when clicked, displays the Sound tool. Below the Sound tool is a command to expand the button, which displays both tools on the Advanced Editing toolbar, as shown previously.

- **Movie** This tool is used to add movies and Flash SWF movies to your PDF files. You specify the location where the movie will play in the document and the trigger used to begin the movie. You can choose to display the first frame of the movie, which, when clicked, will start play, or choose to leave the movie invisible until a button is clicked to begin play.
- **Sound** This tool is used to add sound clips to a PDF document. You specify the location where the sound will play in the document and the trigger used to begin playing the sound.

The next tool on the Acrobat Professional Advanced Editing toolbar is the TouchUp Text tool. It performs the same functions as the TouchUp Text tool discussed in the "About the Acrobat Standard Advanced Editing Toolbar" section. When you click the triangle to the right of the tool, you have access to the TouchUp Object tool. Below the TouchUp Object tool is the command "Expand This Button" as discussed previously.

- **TouchUp Object** This tool is used to make changes to objects in a document. You can use the tool to select an object such as an image, and then move it to a different location within the document.

About the Measuring Toolbar (Professional Only)

The Measuring toolbar gives you a set of tools with which you can accurately measure the distance between objects. This toolset is especially useful if you're working with PDF documents that were created from AutoCad documents. To access the Measuring toolbar shown in the following illustration, choose View | Toolbars | Measuring:

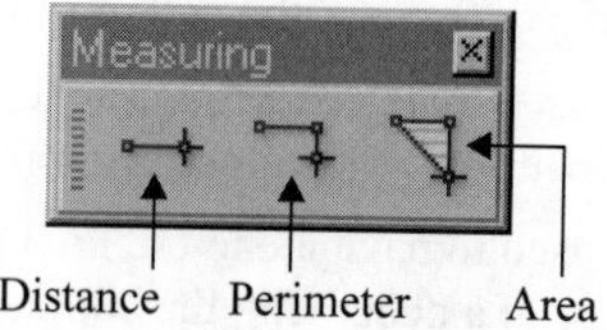

- **Distance** This tool is used to measure the distance between two points.
- **Perimeter** This tool is used to measure the distance between multiple points.
- **Area** This tool is used to measure the area within points that you create with the tool.

About the Edit Toolbar

If you prefer the convenience of toolbars when editing a document, the Edit toolbar is right up your alley. You can undo and redo commands with this toolbar, as well as copy selected items to the clipboard and spell check comments and form fields. To float the Edit toolbar in the workspace, choose View | Toolbars | Edit. The Edit toolbar, as shown next, contains the following tools:

- **Spell Check** This tool is used to spell check comments and form fields.
- **Undo** This tool undoes the last command you performed.
- **Redo** This tool redoes the last command you performed.
- **Copy** This tool copies selected objects to the clipboard.

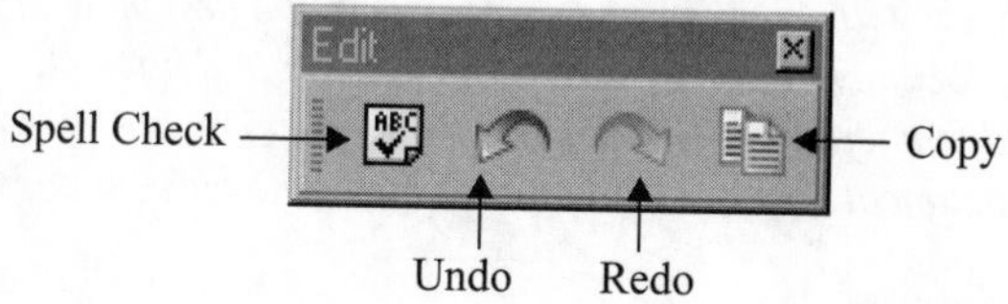

About the Navigation Toolbar

The tools from the appropriately named Navigation toolbar (as shown in the following illustration) are used to go from page to page within a document and back again. There are also tools within this group that you use to navigate to the start or end of the document. The Acrobat designers have included the tools from the Acrobat 5.0 Navigation tool group to this toolbar so that you can now perform all necessary document navigation from a single toolbar.

- **First Page** This button is used to navigate to the start of a PDF document. If you are at the start of the document, the button is dimmed out.
- **Previous Page** This button is used to go to the previous page in a document. If you are viewing the first page of a document, the button is dimmed out.
- **Next Page** This button is used to advance to the next page in a document. If you are viewing the last page of a document, the button is dimmed out.
- **Last Page** This button is used to navigate to the final page of a document. If you are already viewing the last page of a document, the button is dimmed out.
- **Previous View** This button is used to return to the previous view of the last page you visited. It is the button that looks like a Back button in a Web browser. If you are at the start of a document, or have navigated to your first view of the document, the button is dimmed out.
- **Next View** This button is used to advance to the next available view you selected in a document. It is the button that looks similar to the Forward button in a Web browser. If you are at the end of a document, the button is dimmed out.

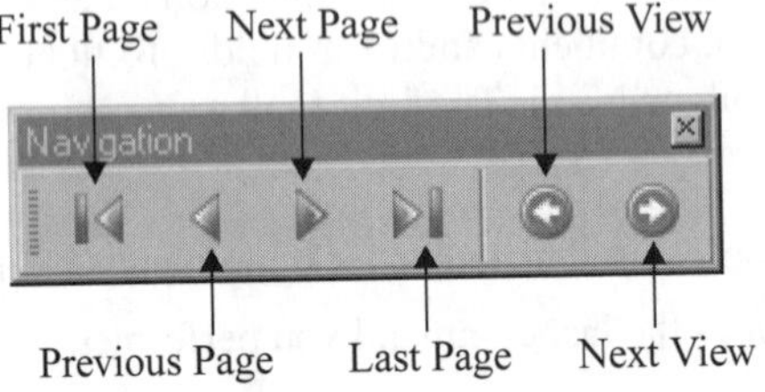

You can also use the Previous View and Next View tools to navigate between documents; you can navigate from the last view in one document to the first view in the next document. If you have closed a document during an Acrobat session and have navigated to the first view of the current document, you can use the Previous View button to open the previous view of the closed document that you had open prior to the current document.

About the Rotate View Toolbar

The tools from this toolbar give you the ability to rotate a page clockwise or counterclockwise in 90-degree increments. You can rotate the document more than 90 degrees with additional applications of the desired rotation tool. To float the Rotate View toolbar, shown in the following illustration, choose View | Toolbars | Rotate View.

- **Rotate Clockwise** This tool is used to rotate the page you are viewing 90 degrees in a clockwise direction. The menu bar equivalent for this tool is View | Rotate View | Rotate Clockwise.

- **Rotate Counterclockwise** This tool is used when you want to rotate the current document page 90 degrees in a counterclockwise direction. The menu bar equivalent for this tool is View | Rotate View | Rotate Counterclockwise.

About the Properties Bar

If you've used Acrobat previously, you know that objects such as comments, links, and form fields have properties that you can edit. In previous versions of Acrobat, you accessed an object's properties through a context menu, a paradigm that continues with Acrobat 6.0. However, if you are going to be editing properties of several objects, you can choose View | Toolbars | Properties Bar to display the Properties bar, shown in the following illustration. After displaying the Properties bar, select an object to reveal and edit the object's properties.

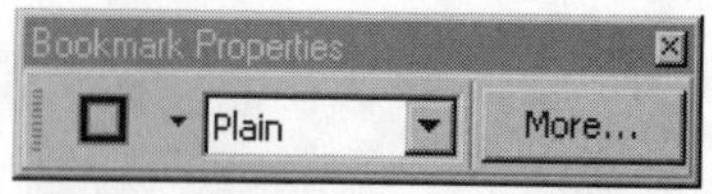

NOTE *When you open the context menu of a floating tab or toolbar, you must place your cursor below the tab or toolbar title bar before you right-click (Windows) or* CTRL*-click (Macintosh). If you open a context menu with your cursor on the tab title bar using Acrobat with the Windows operating system, the context menu displays system options for closing, moving, or resizing the tab. On a Macintosh system, no context menu is displayed when you* CTRL*-click with your cursor over the title bar.*

Customize the Workspace

As you become more comfortable with Acrobat, you'll find there are certain tools that you use more often than others. Adobe has engineered flexibility into the program, making it possible for you to customize the workspace to suit your working preference. You can customize the workspace by floating toolbars and tabs, as well as by expanding toolbars that you frequently use.

Float Toolbars

When you edit PDF documents and perform the same task numerous times, reaching up to select a tool from the command bar can be distracting. If this is the case, or if you prefer working with a certain toolbar in a different position, you can float any toolbar to a different position. To float a toolbar displayed on the command bar, click the vertical line at the left edge of the toolbar and drag it. Release the mouse button when the toolbar is where you want it. To float a toolbar that is not displayed, choose View | Toolbars and then select the toolbar that you want to float in the

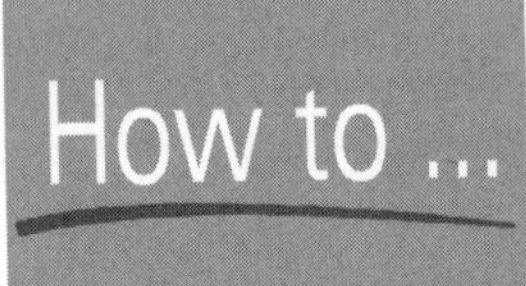

Save Time with Context Menus

Acrobat Standard and Acrobat Professional have context menus that can streamline your production and speed up your workflow. Context menu options will vary depending upon the tool you use and the pane in which you work. For example, if you access a context menu in Acrobat after selecting a block of text with the Select Text tool, you have a list of several options or commands you can perform on the selected block of text. Open the context menu in Acrobat while in the Signatures tab, and you have a different set of options that pertain to digital signatures within the document and their properties. Individual tab context menu commands and options are discussed in detail in future chapters of this book. The following is the context menu for the Acrobat Bookmarks tab. To open a context menu associated with a tab, position your cursor within the tab and then right-click (Windows) or CTRL-click (Macintosh). To open a context menu specific to an object, select the object and then right-click (Windows) or CTRL-click (Macintosh).

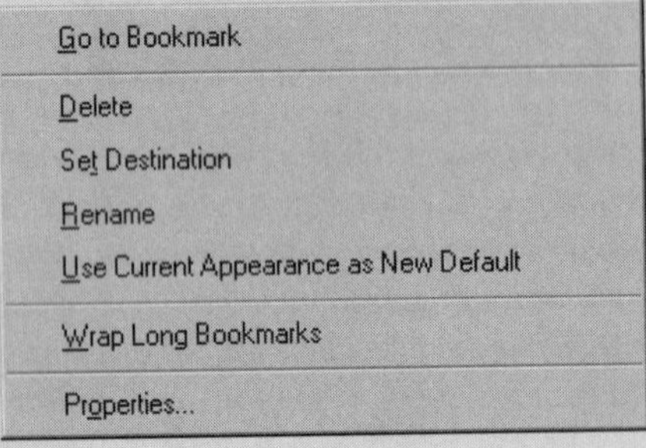

workspace. To move a floating toolbar, click its title bar, drag it to a new position, and release the mouse button. Figure 2-5 shows several floating toolbars in the Document pane.

To dock a floating toolbar to the command bar, click the toolbar title and than drag and drop it on the command bar. When you close a floating toolbar, it does not redock itself. When you open the toolbar again, it floats in the last position you left it.

Float Navigation Pane Tabs

You can float any tab in the Navigation pane by clicking its name and dragging it out of the Navigation pane. Release the mouse button when the tab is in the desired position. After you float a tab, you can change its height by clicking and dragging the horizontal bar at the base of the tab. You change the width of a floating tab by clicking and dragging the vertical bar on the

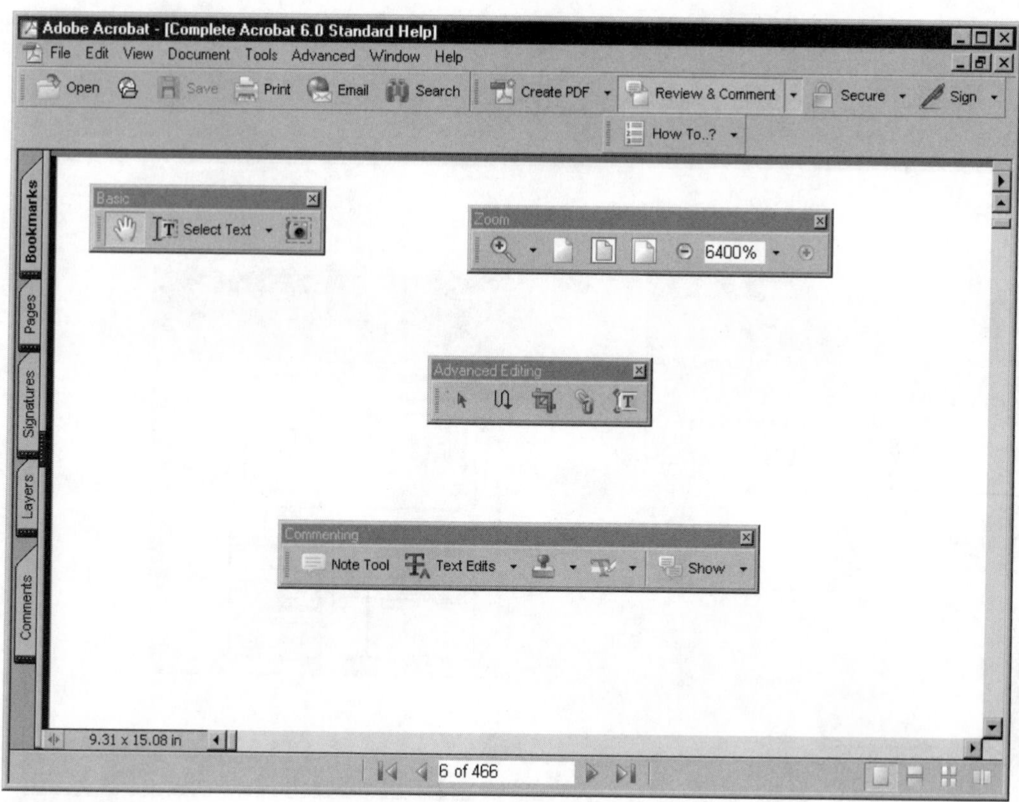

FIGURE 2-5 You can float a toolbar by clicking and dragging it to another position.

left or right side of the tab. Figure 2-6 shows two floating tabs in the Document pane. The tab on the right has been resized.

To redock a tab in the Navigation pane, click its name and then drag and drop it into the pane. Note that when you redock a tab, it appears at the bottom of the pane but above the Comments tab, regardless of its original position. If you float and then redock the Comments tab, it reassumes its default position at the bottom of the Navigation pane.

Group Tabs

When you have more than one tab floating in the Document pane, you can group them to conserve monitor space. To create a tab group, click the name of a floating tab and drag it into

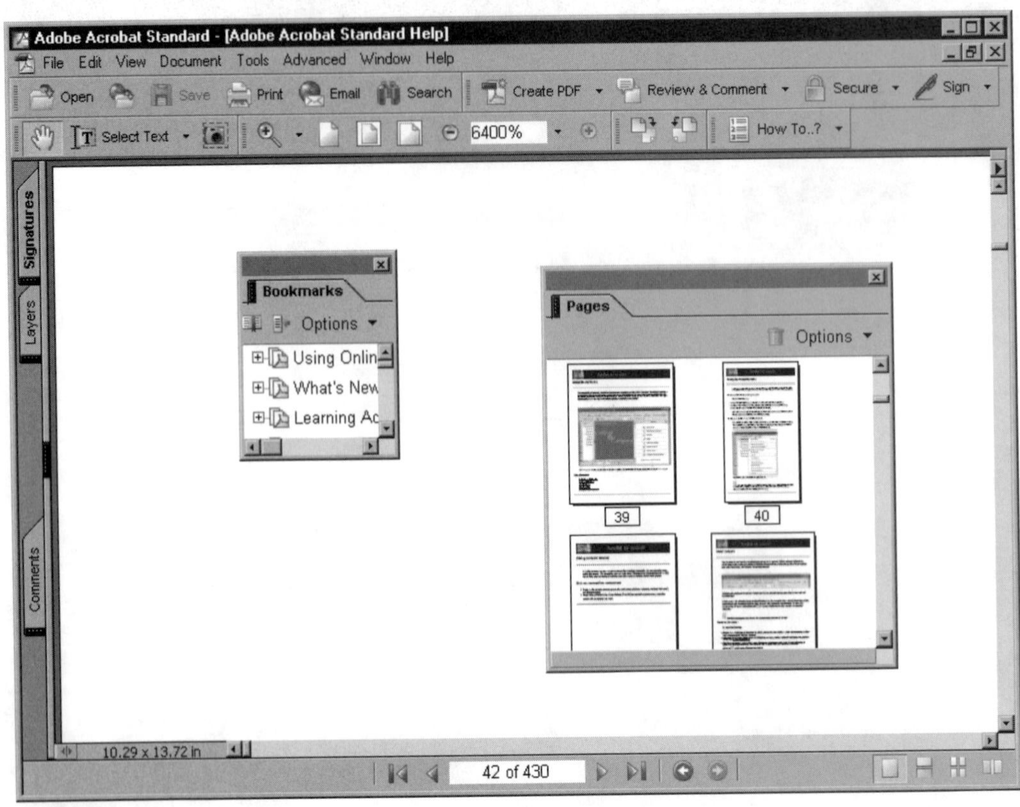

FIGURE 2-6 You can float and resize tabs to suit your working preference.

another floating tab. You can group as many tabs as needed. To access an individual tab in a group, click its name. Note that you can combine Navigation pane tabs with tabs opened from menu commands such as the Destinations and Articles tabs. In Figure 2-7, you see a custom tab group consisting of Navigation pane tabs and tabs accessed from the View menu.

TIP

If you frequently use tabs (like the Destinations and Articles tabs), you can dock them within the Navigation pane or leave them floating in the Document pane. To dock a tab to the Navigation pane, choose the desired tab from the View menu. After the tab appears in the Document pane, click its name and drag it into the Navigation pane. The next time you launch Acrobat, the tab will be in its new home.

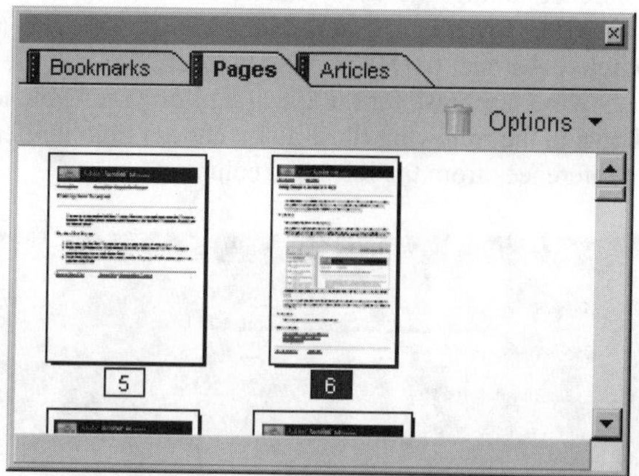

FIGURE 2-7 You can create a tab group by dragging and dropping one tab onto another.

Get Complete Acrobat 6.0 Help

This book covers every major aspect of Acrobat. However, if you need more information about a specific topic, you can search the Acrobat 6.0 Help document (which, of course, is a PDF document) or choose another topic from the Acrobat Help menu. To open the complete Acrobat 6.0 help document, choose Help | Complete Acrobat 6.0 Help.

About the Detect and Repair Command

If after using Acrobat for a while, it doesn't perform as you'd expect, you may have a corrupt or missing file from within the program. If you suspect this is the case, choose Help | Detect and Repair. After choosing this command, the Acrobat installer launches and examines the files associated with the software. If anything is amiss, Acrobat repairs the program by reinstalling corrupt files or replacing missing files.

Set Preferences

Many people find the Acrobat configuration easy to work with upon installation. However, you can change many Acrobat defaults by selecting the appropriate title in the General Preferences dialog box. There is a preference setting for virtually every Acrobat task you perform. Unfortunately, the sheer volume of parameters you can change is beyond the scope of this book. When preference setting options are important to an individual task, the options will be covered in that section of the book. Many of the preference settings are easily understood even by casual computer users and therefore will not be covered. However, if you need more information on an individual setting, choose Help | Complete Acrobat 6.0 Help. After the Acrobat Help file opens, click the Search tab and enter the key word or phrase for the specific information you need. To open the Preferences dialog box shown in the following illustration, choose Edit | Preferences and then select one of the specific preferences from the left-hand column:

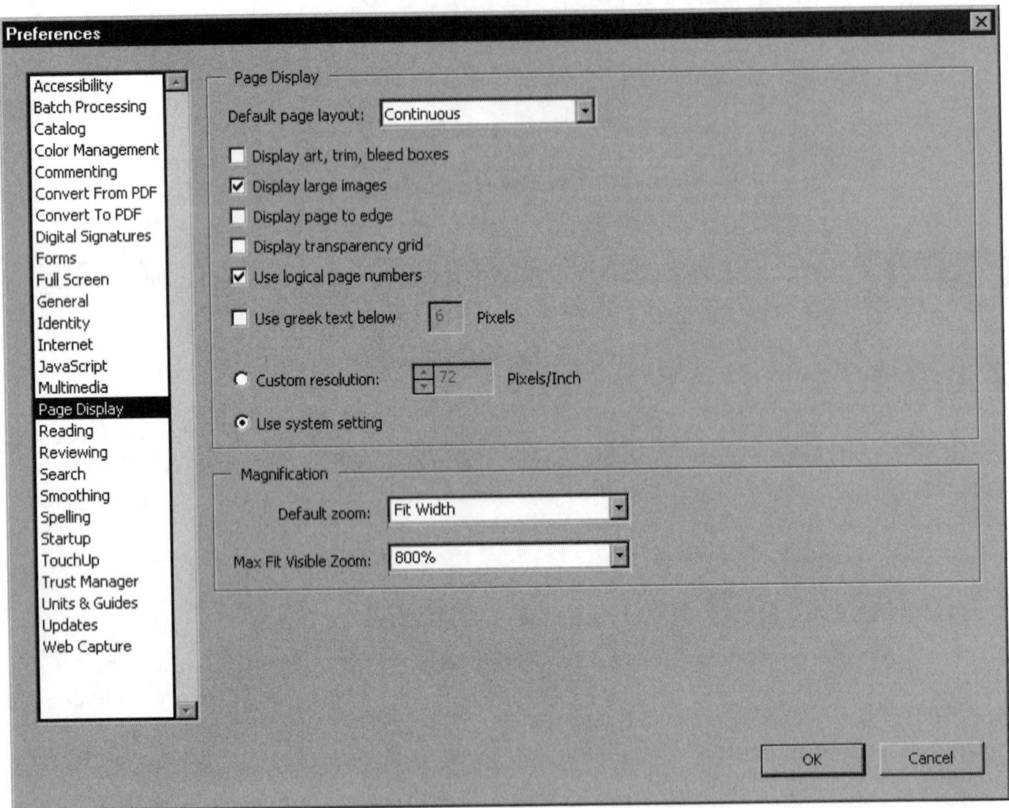

Summary

In this chapter, you learned to navigate the Acrobat workspace. You were also introduced to the toolbars and task buttons that you'll use to edit and add interactivity to PDF documents. You were shown the differences between the Acrobat Standard and Acrobat Professional toolset, and you learned how to customize the workspace to suit your working preferences. In the next chapter, you'll learn to read PDF documents with Acrobat as well as extract text and graphic elements from PDF files.

Chapter 3

Read PDF Documents with Adobe Acrobat 6.0

How to…

- Open and navigate documents
- Change document view
- View multiple documents
- Search PDF documents
- Search a PDF index

You purchased Acrobat—and for that matter, this book—to create and distribute electronic documents. Many people will read your PDF documents in linear fashion from start to finish, which is fine with a one- or two-page document but cumbersome when reading a large document. With Acrobat, when you publish documents with several hundred pages, your readers can choose which parts of the document they view. Acrobat and Adobe Reader 6.0 can be used to read PDF files. Both programs have the tools you need to navigate to specific parts of a document or to find and navigate to key words or phrases. You can also use the Acrobat and Adobe Reader 6.0 Search feature to search a single document, a folder of documents, or an index of several PDF documents. In this chapter, you'll learn how to use Acrobat and Adobe Reader 6.0 to view a document.

NOTE *In this chapter, Acrobat will be used generically to refer to both Acrobat and Adobe Reader 6.0.*

Open a PDF Document

Authors of PDF documents can specify what viewers will see when they open a PDF document. A PDF document can be set to open to a certain page, at a certain magnification, or at full screen view.

NOTE *If the document opens at Full Screen view, the toolbar, command bar, and other navigation aids are not visible. If you prefer, you can exit full-screen mode by pressing ESC or by pressing CTRL-L (Windows) or COMMAND-L (Macintosh). You can change how you view documents in full screen mode by choosing Edit | Preferences | Full Screen and selecting the desired options from the Preferences dialog box.*

To open a PDF file, choose File | Open and use the Open dialog box, shown in Figure 3-1, to navigate to the PDF file you want to view. Select the files you want to view and then click Open. To select multiple files from a folder, hold down the SHIFT key and click the files you want to select.

NOTE *You can quickly open a recently viewed document by choosing File and then clicking the document filename. The last five documents you viewed appear at the bottom of the menu. You can modify the number of documents shown on this menu by choosing Edit | Preferences, and in the General section, specifying a larger number of files to display in the Recently Opened Documents lists.*

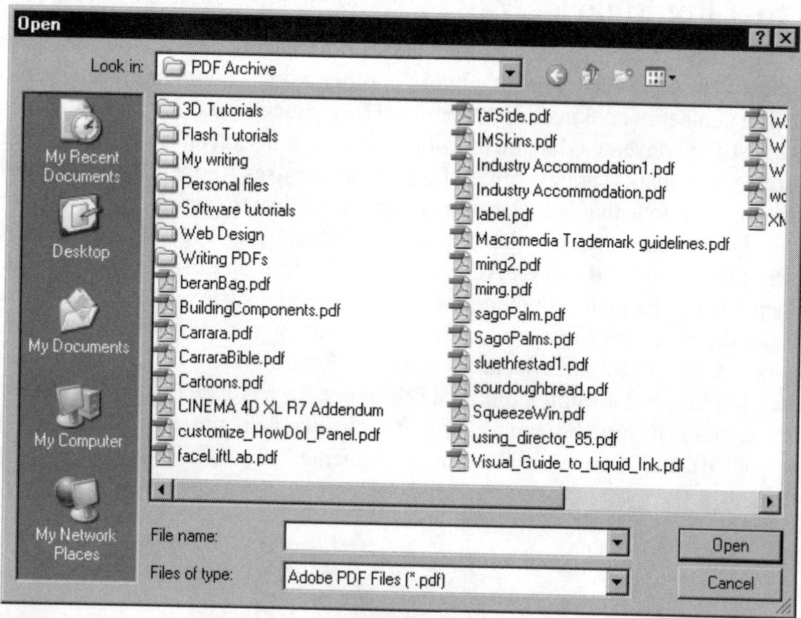

FIGURE 3-1 Use the Open dialog box to open PDF files you want to view or edit.

If you prefer, you can access the Open dialog box by clicking the Open tool, as shown here. Alternatively, you can launch Acrobat and open a file by double-clicking a PDF file icon on your desktop or within any file folder you navigate to using Explorer (Windows) or Finder (Macintosh).

Navigate the Document

After you open a PDF document, you can begin viewing the first page, or you can use the Acrobat viewing tools to navigate to specific parts of a document. If you are viewing an eBook or similar document, you may find the author has added a menu or index that you can use to navigate to specific pages. If this is not the case, you can use the Navigation pane tabs for navigation. Adobe Reader 6.0 has two tabs named Bookmarks and Pages, while Acrobat has three additional tabs named Comments, Layers, and Signatures. The Comments tab is covered in Chapter 10 while the Signatures tabs is covered in Chapter 11.

Navigate to a Bookmark

You use the Bookmarks tab to navigate to bookmarks within the document. *Bookmarks* are similar to chapters and section headings in a book; in other words, a bookmark is a specific place in a document. The number of bookmarks is determined by the method used to create the document. When Acrobat Distiller converts a document to PDF format, it uses features from the original document to create bookmarks. For example, if a PDF author uses Adobe PDF (the plug-in for Microsoft Office applications that launches the Acrobat Distiller) to convert a Word document to PDF format, a bookmark is created wherever a Word Heading style is used. If you use the application's Print command and choose Adobe PDF as the printing device, no bookmarks will be created. When you open a PDF document, the Bookmarks tab usually appears in the Navigation pane. If this is not the case, you can open the Bookmarks tab by choosing View | Navigation Tabs | Bookmarks. A typical Bookmarks tab is shown in Figure 3-2.

A bookmark is a link to a specific point in a document. To navigate to a bookmark, open the Bookmarks tab, click the desired bookmark icon (it looks like a document with the Acrobat logo and one corner folded), and Acrobat displays the bookmarked page or view.

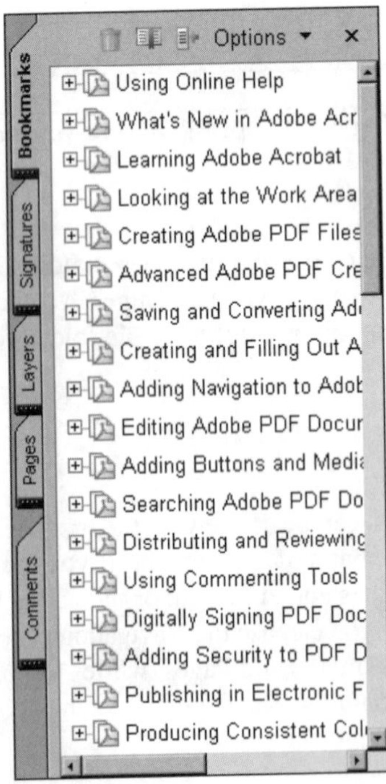

FIGURE 3-2 You use the bookmarks in this tab to navigate to a specific page in a PDF document.

Expand a Bookmark

Many PDF documents you view have bookmarks with a plus sign (+) beside them. This designates that the bookmark can be expanded to show more bookmarks that are nested within the parent bookmark. Bookmarks give a document structure and make it easier for you to find specific information. To expand a bookmark, click the plus sign, and Acrobat displays the bookmarks related to the subject heading. If you are viewing a complex document with several heading levels, the expanded bookmark may include bookmarks with additional subheadings that are also signified with a plus sign. To view the additional subheadings, click the section heading plus sign. The following illustration is a bookmark expanded to several levels:

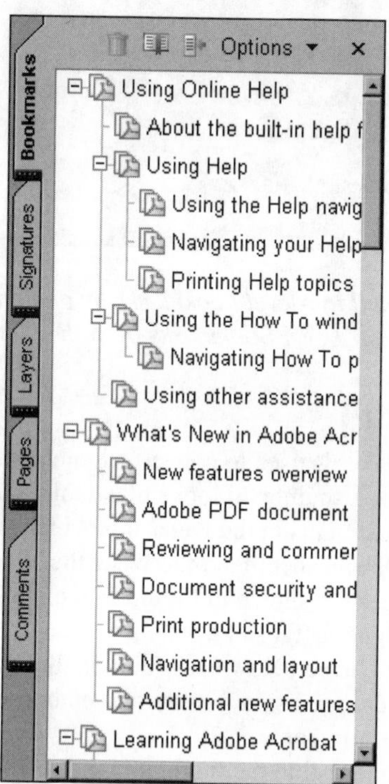

Collapse a Bookmark

When you view a complex document with several heading levels and expand the bookmarks, you end up with an indented treelike structure that displays all the document bookmarks. You know a bookmark can be collapsed when you see a minus sign (–) to the left of the bookmark. When you expand several bookmarks, the Bookmark tab becomes quite cluttered, making it difficult to find a specific bookmark. You can easily regain control by clicking the minus sign to the left of a bookmark to collapse it.

Use the Bookmarks Options Menu

You can also navigate to expand and collapse selected bookmarks by choosing commands from the Bookmarks Options menu. To open the Bookmarks Options menu shown here, click the Options icon at the top of the Bookmarks tab:

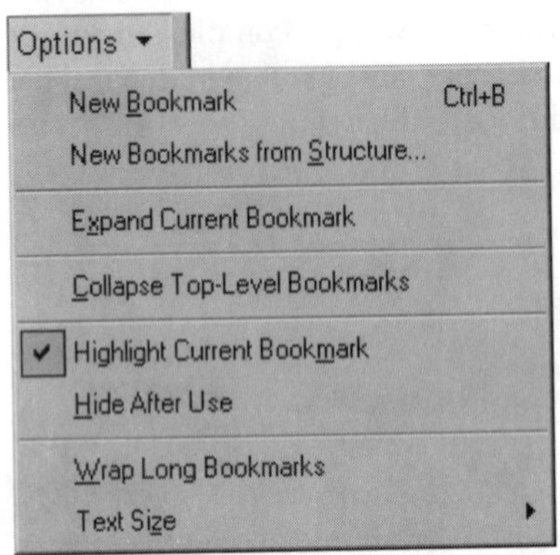

You can quickly collapse all top-level bookmarks by opening the Bookmarks tab and then choosing Collapse Top-Level Bookmarks from the Options menu.

Navigate to a Thumbnail

When Acrobat Distiller or PDFMaker is used to convert a document to PDF format, it creates a thumbnail of each document page. A thumbnail looks like a miniature snapshot of a full-size PDF page. You find document thumbnails in the Pages tab, which is located in the Navigation pane. Unless the author of the PDF file specified otherwise, the Navigation pane opens when the document does. To access the Pages tab shown in Figure 3-3, click Pages in the Navigation pane. Alternatively, choose View | Navigation Tabs | Pages.

Notice that the page number is listed below each thumbnail. You can navigate to a specific page by clicking its thumbnail. Acrobat displays a light green border around the current page's thumbnail and highlights the page number.

Acrobat displays a red rectangle within the thumbnail that shows you a miniature representation of the page as displayed in the Document pane. You can use the red rectangle to scroll the page by clicking either the top or the bottom border of the rectangle and dragging, as shown in the following illustration. Or you can resize the view by clicking and dragging the red square at the bottom-right corner of the rectangle.

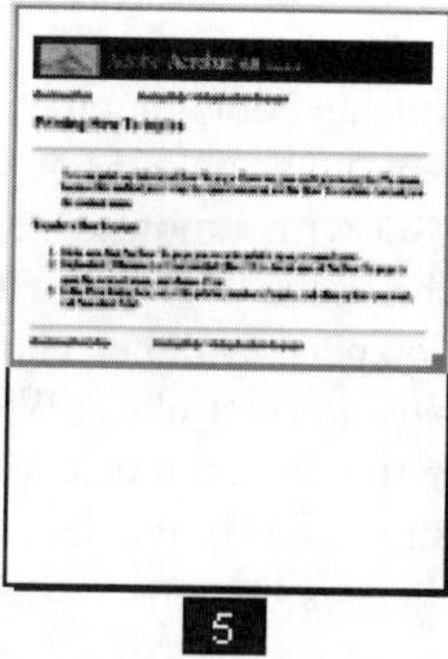

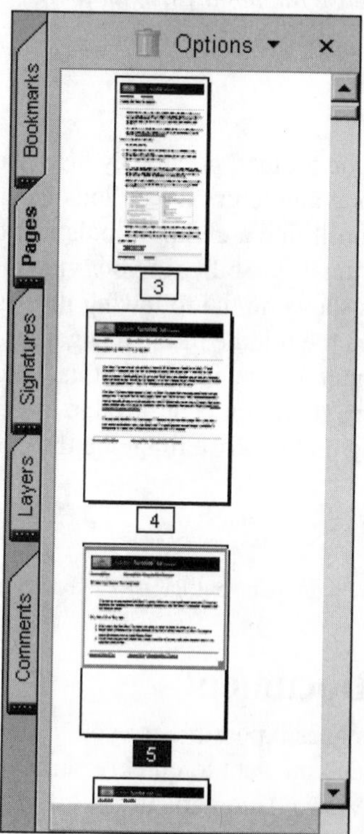

FIGURE 3-3 You can use thumbnails to navigate to a document page.

When you initially open the Pages tab, Acrobat displays the thumbnails in a neat column. You can display additional thumbnails by clicking and dragging the border between the Navigation pane and Document pane. However, this may not be feasible if you are working on a monitor with a desktop smaller than 1024×768. If you work with a monitor resolution of 800×600 or less, you can shrink the size of the thumbnails. To shrink the thumbnails to the desired size, click the Options icon at the top-right corner of the Navigation pane, and then choose Reduce Page Thumbnails from the Pages Options menu. Alternatively you can right-click (Windows) or CTRL-click (Macintosh) and choose Reduce Page Thumbnails from the context menu. You can apply this command several times to shrink page thumbnails to the desired size. To increase the size of page thumbnails, choose Enlarge Page Thumbnails from either the Pages Options menu or context menu.

If you reduce the size of the thumbnails to the point where you're displaying a dozen or more, Acrobat may become sluggish as it refreshes the thumbnails when you change pages. If this happens, increase thumbnail size until your system starts responding normally again.

Navigate to a Page

You can use the tools in the Navigation toolbar, previously discussed in Chapter 2, to navigate a PDF file in linear fashion or to jump to and return to previous views you specified. At the lower-left corner of the Document pane, you'll find a group of tools that duplicate the Navigation tools along with other tools that add additional flexibility to your viewing and navigation tasks. Use the navigation tools in this group, as shown in the following illustration, in the same manner as the tools in the Navigation toolbar. In the middle of the navigation tools is a window that displays the current page of the document. Enter a page number in this window and then press ENTER or RETURN to navigate directly to that page. If you enter a value larger than the last page of the document, Adobe displays a warning dialog box telling you the page is not in the document.

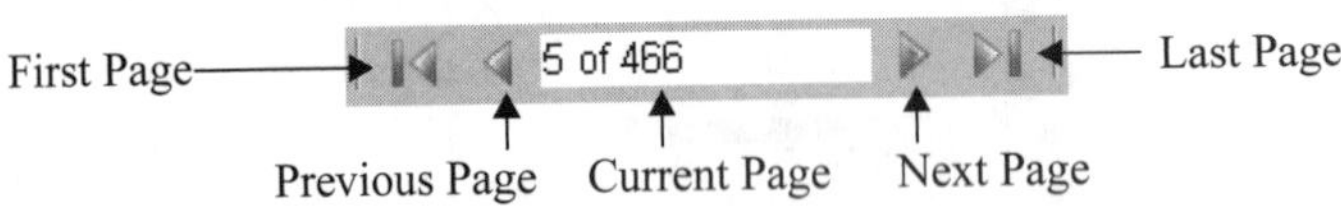

Automatically Scroll a Document

Acrobat 6.0 has a new feature that makes it possible for you to automatically scroll through a document. This option is handy when you want to quickly peruse a document. To automatically scroll through a document, choose View | Automatically Scroll. Press ESC to stop scrolling.

Change Document View

When you view a PDF document, you have a wide variety of viewing options available to you. Unlike a printed document, where you have to contend with the font size and page size chosen by the author, you can modify the magnification of the PDF document, change how much of the document is displayed in the Document pane, change the number of pages displayed in the Document pane, and rotate the document. You can use tools, menu commands, or context menus to change the way Acrobat displays a document.

Change View Options

In the lower-right corner of the Document pane, you'll find another group of tools, as shown in the next illustration. You use these tools to change the way you view the document. You have the following viewing options at your disposal:

- **Single Page** Click this button to view a single page of the document. You can use the Hand tool to scroll through the page but not to advance to another page. Alternatively, you can choose View | Page Layout | Single Page to enable this mode.
- **Continuous** Click this button to view a multipage document in Continuous mode. In this mode, you can use the Hand tool to scroll through the document a page at a time. Alternatively, you can choose View | Page Layout | Continuous to achieve the same result.
- **Continuous Facing** Click this button, and Acrobat reconfigures a multipage document so that the pages are displayed side by side. In Continuous Facing mode, you can use the Hand tool to scroll through the document. Alternatively, you can choose View | Page Layout | Continuous Facing to view a document in this format.
- **Facing** Click this button, and Acrobat reconfigures a multipage document so that the pages are displayed side by side. In Facing mode you can use the Hand tool to scroll through the currently displayed pages but not to scroll to the next pages in the document. Alternatively, you can choose View | Page Layout | Facing to view the document in this format.

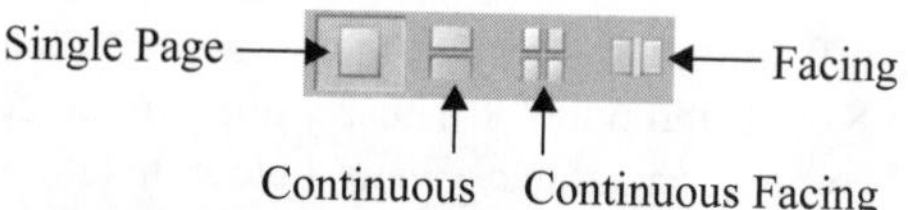

Magnify the Document

You can use Acrobat to view a wide variety of documents created by authors on machines with different desktop sizes. Even though Acrobat is cross-platform and the document you view is identical to what authors create on their computers, you may find it necessary to make modifications to comfortably view the document. When you view a PDF document with small font sizes or tiny graphics, you can magnify the document. You can choose from preset levels of magnification or choose to zoom in on a specific portion of a document. When you are finished viewing the magnified document, you can zoom out. You can use tools from the Zoom toolbar, as shown in the following illustration, or menu commands to change the magnification of a document you are viewing. Note that the following illustration shows the expanded version of the Acrobat Professional Zoom toolbar. The Acrobat Standard Zoom toolbar is identical with the exception of the Loupe Tool and Pan & Zoom Window options, which are not present in Acrobat Standard.

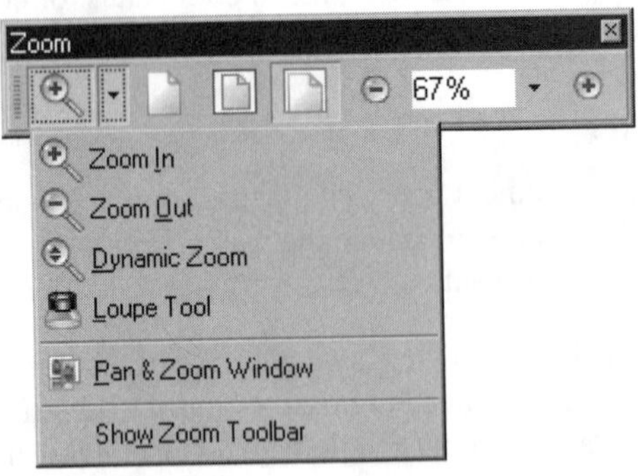

Zoom In or Out on a Document

You have many different ways to change the magnification of a document you view. Your first set of magnification tools is in the Viewing tool group. Change the magnification of a document with the following Viewing tools:

- Click the Zoom In tool, which looks like a plus sign (+), to zoom in to a higher level of magnification.
- Click the Zoom Out tool, which looks like a minus sign (–), to zoom out to a lower level of magnification.
- Click the triangle to the right of the Magnification window and choose a preset magnification value from the drop-down menu.
- Enter a value in the Magnification window and then press ENTER or RETURN. You can enter any value between 8.33% and 6400%. These values are percentages of the original size of the document. If you enter a value above or below this range, Acrobat selects the appropriate default value.

You also have a second set of magnification tools in your Acrobat tool pouch. You find these in the Zoom toolbar group. From this toolbar, you can use the Zoom In, Zoom Out, and Dynamic Zoom tools to define the area of the document you want to view. Adobe uses a magnifying glass icon for these tools so you don't confuse them with their identically named counterparts that reside further down the toolbar. The zoom tool you used last is displayed on the toolbar. To select a different tool, click the triangle to the right of the current zoom tool and choose the desired tool from the drop-down menu. Alternatively, you can choose Show Zoom toolbar from the drop-down menu to float the Zoom toolbar in the workspace. You change magnification of a document with the following tools:

- **To zoom in on a document** Select the Zoom In tool and click the document to zoom to a higher level of magnification. When you have zoomed to the maximum level of magnification, the plus sign (+) disappears from the icon.

- **To zoom in on a specific portion of the document** Select the Zoom In tool, click a point on the document, and then drag right or left and up or down to define the boundaries of the area. As you drag the tool, a rectangular bounding box appears, giving you a preview of the area you are defining. When the bounding box encompasses the area you want to view, release the mouse button and Acrobat zooms to the defined area.
- **To zoom out** Select the Zoom Out tool and click anywhere inside the Document pane to zoom to the next lowest level of magnification. When you have zoomed out as far as you can go, the minus sign (–) disappears from the icon.
- **To zoom out to a specific portion of the document** Select the Zoom Out tool and then drag to define the boundary of the area you want to view. As you drag, a rectangular bounding box appears. This bounding box defines an area of the document; however, the tool is zooming out so the bounding box does not designate the area you will actually be viewing when you release the mouse button.
- **To zoom dynamically** Select the Dynamic Zoom tool, click anywhere inside the document, and then drag up or right to zoom in on the document, left or down to zoom out. You can also drag diagonally to zoom in and out.

Use the Acrobat Professional Zoom Tools

In addition to the zoom tools mentioned in the previous section, Acrobat Professional has two additional tools: the Loupe tool and the Pan & Zoom window.

To change magnification using the Loupe tool, follow these steps:

1. Choose Tools | Zoom | Loupe Tool. Alternatively, you can click the Loupe tool from the Zoom toolbar.
2. Click inside the document to define the area you want to examine more closely. The selected area appears in another window.
3. Drag the slider, shown in the following illustration, to set the magnification level:

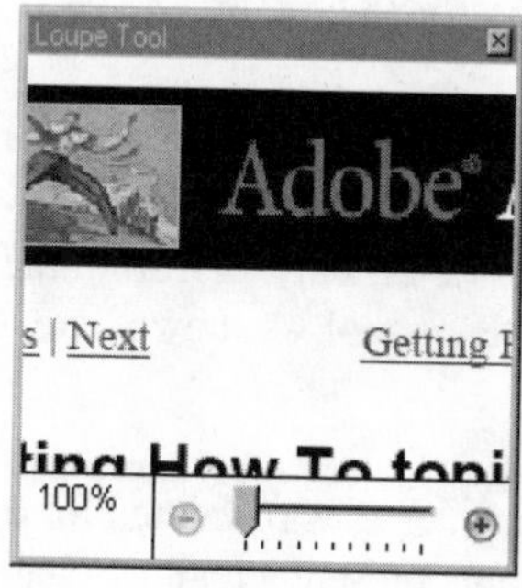

4. To examine a different area of the document, click and drag the tool to a different position in the Document pane. Release the mouse button when the bounding box is over the desired area.

To change document magnification using the Pan & Zoom window, follow these steps:

1. Choose Tools | Zoom | Pan & Zoom to open the Pan & Zoom window shown in the following illustration. Alternatively, you can click the Pan & Zoom tool from the Zoom toolbar. Within the Pan & Zoom window, you'll find a smaller view of the current page surrounded by a red bounding box that designates the section of the document being viewed.

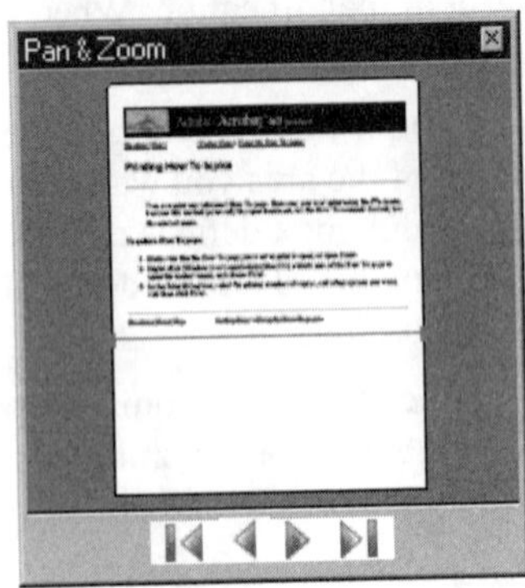

2. Drag one of the corner handles diagonally to zoom in or out on the document.
3. Place your cursor inside the red rectangle and then click and drag to pan to a different view.
4. Click a button at the bottom of the Pan & Zoom window to advance to another page while preserving the same view.
5. Click Close to exit the Pan & Zoom window.

View Document at Actual Size

After viewing a document at a different magnification, you often need to shrink the document back to its original size. You can accomplish this easily by clicking the Actual Size tool, as shown here, or by choosing View | Actual Size.

Fit Document in Window

You can change your view of a document so an entire page of the document is sized to the window. You accomplish this by using the Fit Page tool from the Zoom toolbar. To fit a document in the window, click the Fit Page tool, as shown here, or choose View | Fit Page.

Fit Document to Width

Many of the PDF files you open are narrow, thus formatted for destinations like Internet web sites. Narrow documents with small fonts present a reading challenge even to people with perfect vision. Fortunately, Adobe has a tool to expand the width of documents and make them easier to read. You can expand the document to fit the current width of the Document pane by clicking the Fit Width tool, as shown here. Alternatively, you can choose View | Fit Width.

Fit Text and Graphics to Document Pane Width

Another useful option is to resize the document so that the width of the text and graphics expands to fit the current size of the Document pane. You can accomplish this task by choosing View | Fit Visible.

View Document at Full Screen

If you prefer to read a document without Acrobat toolbars, choose Window | Full Screen. When you view a document at Full Screen, it is easier to read. However, it is difficult to navigate if the author has not provided navigation devices such as buttons or text links. To return to normal viewing mode, press ESC.

If you choose Continuous or Continuous Facing mode and then switch to Full Screen, Acrobat will set the viewing mode to the default Single mode and you will not be able to scroll pages with the Hand tool.

Rotate a Document

Adobe has also provided you with the necessary tools to rotate pages in a document. Choose View | Toolbars | Rotate View to float the Rotate View toolbar in the workspace. You can then rotate the view of a document 90 degrees clockwise or 90 degrees counterclockwise by clicking the appropriate tool. To rotate a page an additional 90 degrees, click the button again. The Rotate View toolbar is shown here:

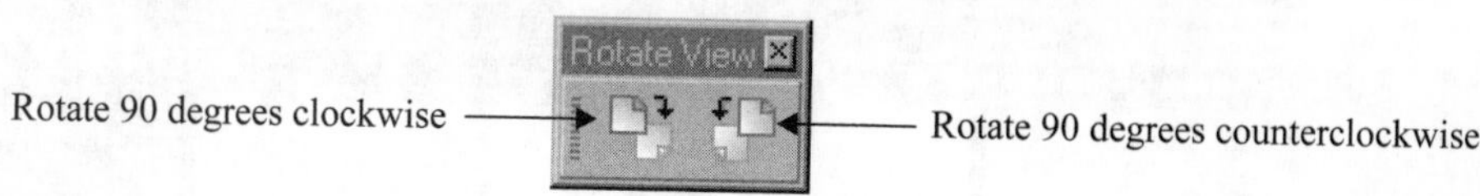

You can also choose View | Rotate View and then choose Rotate Clockwise or Rotate Counterclockwise.

View a Document in Two Windows

If you're viewing a complex document and you need to zoom in on certain parts of the document while still seeing the big picture, you can view the document in split window mode. When you view a document in split window mode, you can change magnification or navigate to a different page in one window without affecting the document view in the other window. To view a document in two windows, choose Window | Split. Click a window to make it the active window. When you're finished viewing the document in two windows, invoke the command again to return to single window mode, whereupon Acrobat uses the magnification settings of the previously active window.

ew Multiple Documents

When you do research or create a PDF file that will include several existing PDF documents, it is convenient to work with all of the documents open—or as many as your system resources allow—at the same time. When you have multiple documents open, you can switch from one document to another by choosing Window and then selecting another document from the list at the bottom of the menu, or you can choose to have Acrobat arrange the documents in a cascading or tiling fashion.

Cascade Documents

When you work with multiple documents, you can speed up your workflow considerably if you have easy access to each document. You can have Acrobat arrange multiple documents in cascading fashion by choosing Window | Cascade. When you choose this viewing option, Acrobat overlaps each PDF file. You can see each document title as well as its Navigation pane, which is collapsed to conserve working space. To switch to a document while in cascading mode, click its title bar. After you select a document, you can expand it by clicking Maximize. Click Minimize, and Acrobat returns the document to its position in the cascade. In Figure 3-4, you see several documents arranged in cascading format.

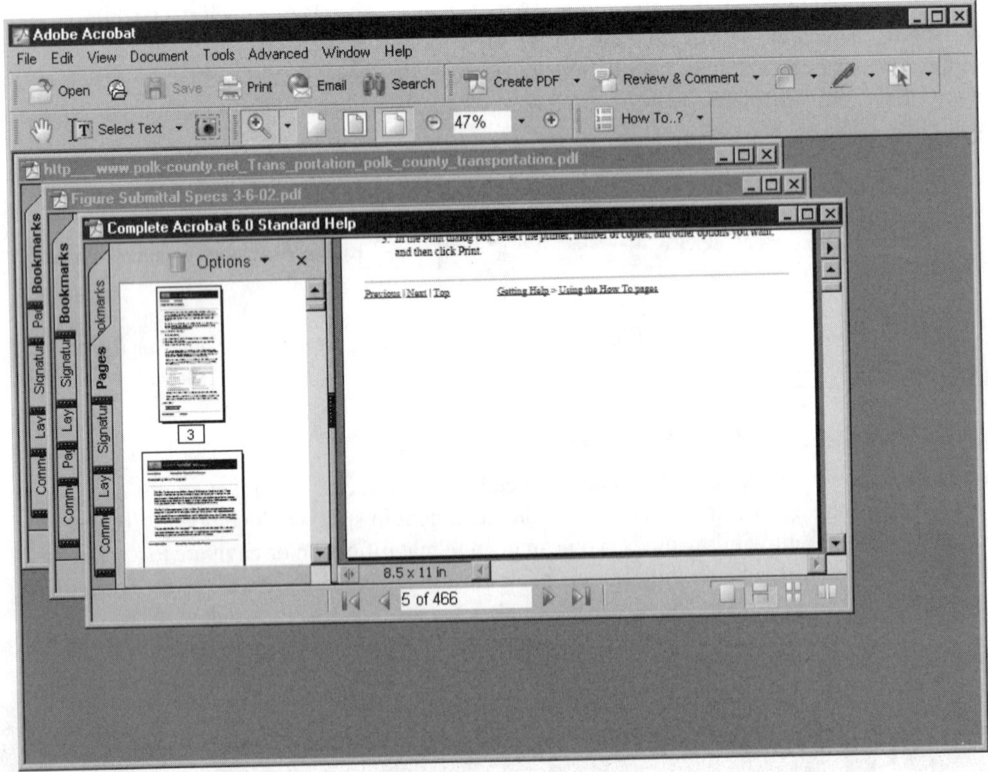

FIGURE 3-4 You have ready access to multiple documents when you choose the Cascade command.

Tile Documents

If you prefer to view multiple documents neatly arranged in checkerboard fashion, choose Window | Tile. Choose this command, and you have the following two tiling options available: vertical and horizontal. When you view tiled documents, you can see the document title bar and part of its contents. To select a document, click its title bar. Click Maximize to expand the document; click Minimize to return it to its tiled position. After you've selected a document from the tile, you can use Acrobat tools to navigate within the document. Experiment with both options to find out which option best suits your working preference. Figure 3-5 shows two documents tiled horizontally.

Search for a Word or Phrase

When you are viewing a multipage PDF document, you can use bookmarks to navigate to parts of the document that appear to have the information you seek, or you can cut right to the chase and find instances of a specific key word or phrase within the document by using the Search

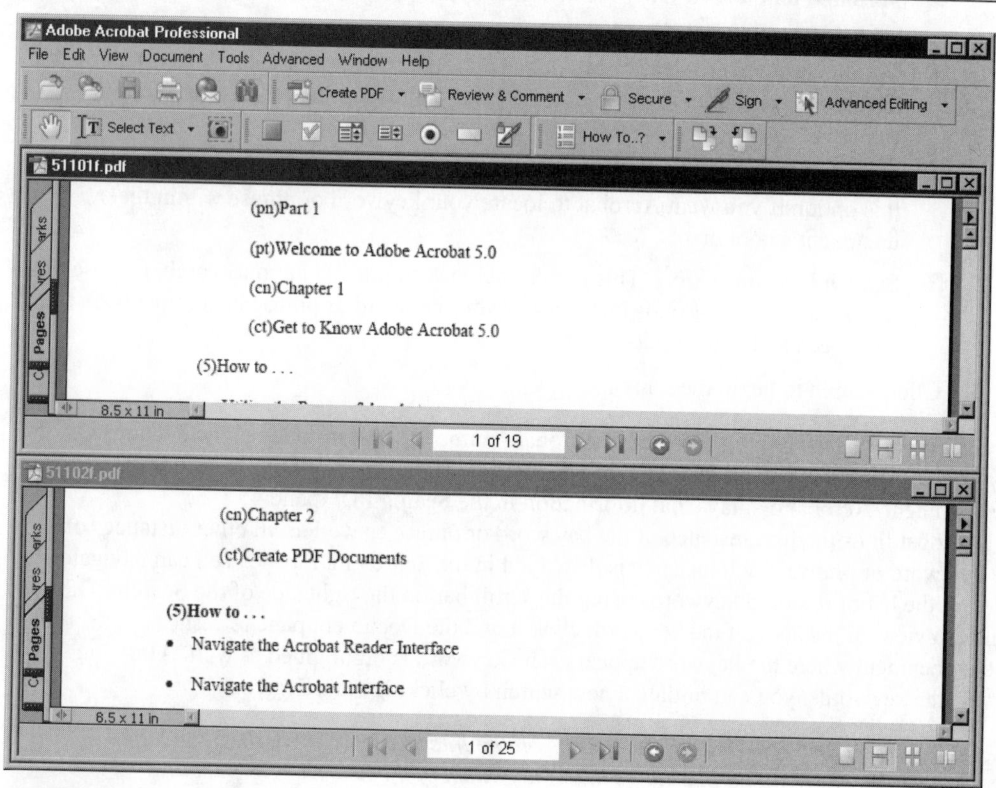

FIGURE 3-5 You can view documents tiled horizontally.

command. This powerful Acrobat feature can help streamline your work. What could be easier than typing a key word or phrase and letting Acrobat take care of the grunt work? You can search the current document, search PDF files in a folder on your computer or network, and search for files on the Internet. To search for information:

1. Click the Search tool that looks like a pair of binoculars as shown here. Alternatively, choose Edit | Search to open the Search PDF pane in the right pane of the workspace.

2. Enter the key word or phrase you want to find.
3. Choose from the following options:
   - **In The Current PDF Document** Choose this option, and Acrobat searches for the key word or phrase in the current document.
   - **All PDF Documents In** Choose this option and then navigate to a folder in your computer or network that contains the PDF document you want to search.
4. Choose from the following options:
   - **Match Whole Word Only** Choose this option, and Acrobat finds only matches for the exact word or phrase you enter.
   - **Match Case** Choose this option, and Acrobat returns words or phrases that match the case you enter. For example, enter **Query** and Acrobat returns instances of *Query*, not *query*.
   - **Search In Bookmarks** This option includes bookmarks in your search. Choose this option if you want Acrobat to locate your keyword or phrase within the document's bookmarks.
   - **Search In Comments** This option includes comments in your search. Choose this option, and Acrobat finds instances of your keyword or phrase in comments that have been added to the document.
5. Click Search to begin the search.

When you use the Search command, Acrobat returns the first instance in the document of the key word or phrase you enter in the Search dialog box. If the key word or phrase does not exist in the document, Acrobat displays that information in the Search PDF pane.

Acrobat finds the first instance of the key word or phrase as well as all other instances of the key word or phrase. Each instance is displayed in the Search PDF pane. You can navigate through the list of returned keywords using the scroll bar on the right side of the Search PDF pane. To view an instance of the keyword, click it and the Document pane refreshes to the point in the document where the keyword appears. The keyword is highlighted as well. After you review the keywords, you can initiate a new search by clicking New Search.

TIP *You can also search PDF documents on the Internet by clicking the Search PDF Documents On The Internet icon at the bottom of the Search PDF pane.*

Search an Index of Documents

Many authors of PDF documents use the Acrobat Professional Catalog command to launch Acrobat Catalog and create an index of PDF documents. (Creating indexes with the Catalog command is covered in Chapter 16.) Acrobat has a sophisticated search function that lets you search for a specific word or phrase in one or more indexed catalogs. To take advantage of this powerful feature, you use the Search command, use Advanced Search options, and then specify which indexes you want included in the search.

In order to search an index of documents, you must first specify the list of indexes to search as outlined in the following section, "Add an Index." If you own Acrobat Professional and create your own indexes, you can add the indexes that may contain the information you seek. When you install Acrobat, the Acrobat 6.0 Online Guides index is installed by default.

Add an Index

In order to search other indexes, you add the files to the Available Indexes list. To display the indexes currently available for searching, follow these steps:

1. Click Search. The Search PDF pane appears on the right side of the interface.
2. Click the Use Advanced Search Options icon at the bottom of the Search PDF pane. The Search PDF pane is reconfigured as follows:

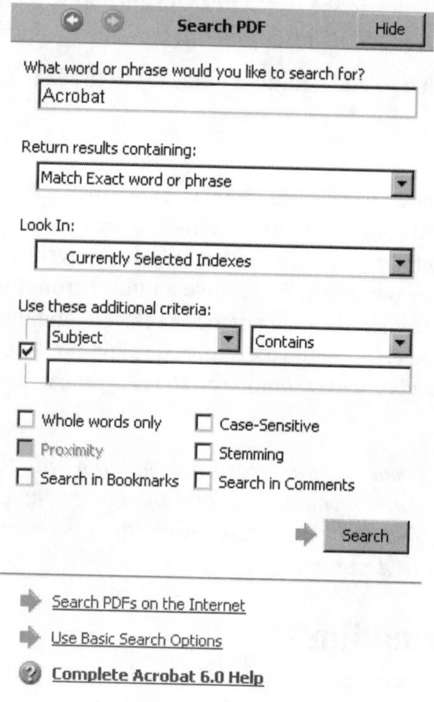

3. Click the triangle to the right of the Look In field and then choose Select Index from the drop-down menu. The Index Selection dialog box appears, as shown here:

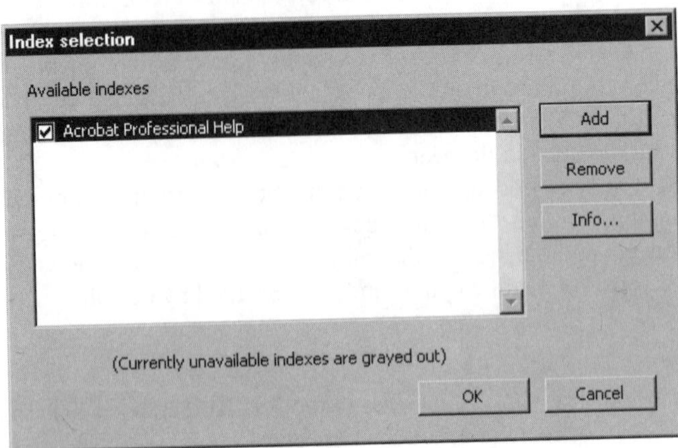

4. Click Add to display the Open Index File dialog box.
5. Navigate to the Index you want to add to the list. Acrobat indexes have the PDX file extension.
6. Click Open to add the index to the list. After you click Open, the Open Index dialog box closes, and the newly selected index appears in the Index Selection dialog box.
7. Repeat Steps 4 through 6 to add additional indexes to the list.

Remove an Index

You can enable or disable an index from a search by clicking the check box to the left of the index name. Using the check box is the preferred method of enabling or disabling an index in a search. However, if you are no longer using an index, or have moved it to a different location on your hard drive, you can remove the index. To remove an index from the list, open the Index Selection dialog box just shown, click the index name to select it, and then click Remove to delete the index from the list. When you click Remove, Acrobat displays no warning, and the index is removed from the list. If you inadvertently remove an index, you can use the Add button to restore it to the list.

The best way to limit a search of indexes is by enabling only the indexes you want Acrobat to use for the search you are performing. For example, if you have ten PDF indexes, but feel only five of them contain information pertinent to your search, disable the ones you don't want Acrobat to search.

Display Index Information

When an indexed PDF catalog is created, certain information is recorded with the file. If you have several indexes to choose from, or you are sharing indexes with coworkers on a network, this information can be valuable when deciding whether or not the PDF files included in the index contain the information you require. If the author of the index accepted the Acrobat default name of Index, using the Info option is the only way to know what is contained in the index. To access information about an index, open the Index Selection dialog box shown previously, select an index, and then click the Info button to display the Index Information dialog box, as shown here:

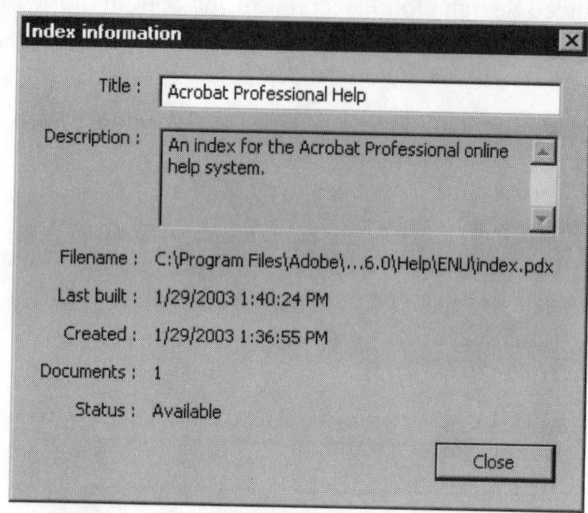

After you open the Index Information dialog box, you have the following information available:

- **Title** This is the title entered by the creator of the index. When you build your own indexes, it is advisable to specify a title that describes the contents of the PDF files being indexed. Refer to Chapter 16 for information on naming an index.
- **Description** This information describes the contents of the PDF index as entered by the author of the index.
- **Filename** This line displays the path to the index and the full filename of the index.
- **Last Built** This information shows you when the index was last updated. If the index has not been updated, the date is the same as when the index was created.
- **Created** This line shows you the time and date the index was originally created.
- **Documents** This line displays the number of PDF files in the index.
- **Status** If Acrobat successfully identified the file when you added it, it is Available. Unavailable indexes are listed as such and are shown dimmed out in the list.

Create a Query

When you search an index of PDF files or multiple files, you create a *query*. Your query tells Acrobat exactly what information to retrieve. You can specify which indexes to search and which key word or phrase you want Acrobat to find. You can fine-tune the search by specifying whether you want Acrobat to return exact matches or similar matches. To create a query, do the following:

1. Choose Edit | Search to open the Search PDF pane. Alternatively, click the Search tool that looks like a pair of binoculars.
2. Click the Use Advanced Search Options icon near the bottom of the Search PDF pane. The Search PDF pane is reconfigured to show the advanced search options, as shown here:

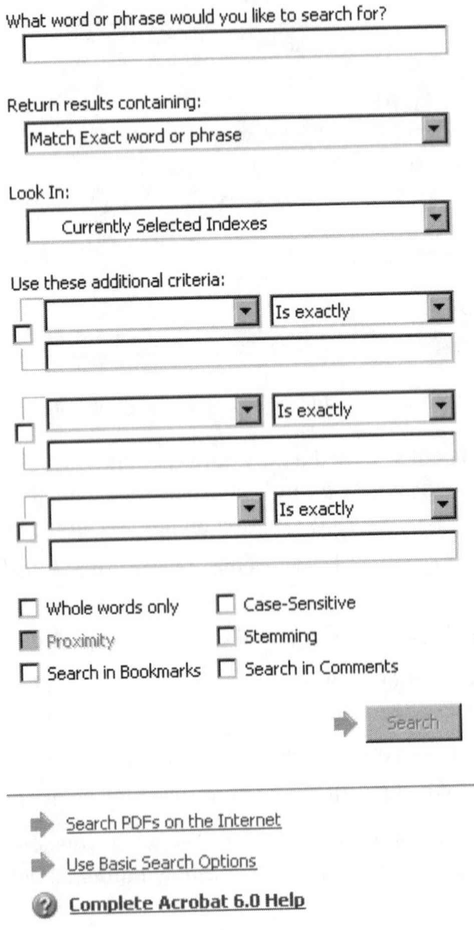

3. Click the triangle to the right of the Look In field and choose Currently Selected Indexes. To add an index to the list, follow the steps in the earlier section, "Add an Index." You can also select a folder on your hard drive or network that contains PDF documents you want to search.

4. Enter the word or phrase for which you want to search in the What Word Or Phrase Would You Like To Search For? field.

5. Click the triangle to the right of the Return Results Containing field and choose one of the following options:

   - **Match Exact Word Or Phrase** This option returns results from PDF documents where the exact word or phrase appears as entered in your query.
   - **Match All Of The Words** This option returns results from PDF documents where all the words in your query appear. The words do not have to be in the order as entered in your query. This option is available only in multiple document searches.
   - **Match Any Of The Words** This option returns results from PDF documents that contain any of the words in your query. This option returns the most documents; however, not all the documents may be relevant.
   - **Boolean** This option enables you to fine-tune a search by telling Acrobat exactly the information for which you are searching. You can combine words and phrases and omit certain words from your query. This option is available only in multiple document searches.

6. In the Use These Additional Criteria section, choose from the following options:

   - **Whole Words Only** When you select this option, Acrobat returns only whole words that match your query and not words that contain your query. For example, if your query is the word **text**, Acrobat will return all instances of the word *text* in the documents you are searching, but not the word *context*.
   - **Case-Sensitive** When you select this option, Acrobat finds only the words that match the case of your query. For example, if you enter **Adobe**, the search returns instances of the word *Adobe*, but not *adobe*.
   - **Stemming** When you select this option, Acrobat finds words that stem from the word you enter. For example, if you enter the word **index**, Acrobat returns instances of the words *indexed*, *indexes*, and *indexing* (if these words appear in the files you are searching, of course).
   - **Proximity** When you choose this option when searching for results that match any of the words in your query, using the AND Boolean operator, Acrobat returns one pair of matches per file for the words you entered. The match Acrobat returns will be within the first three pages of the document. If there are several matches for the pair of words you are searching for, Acrobat ranks the relevancy of the match on the proximity of the words. For example, if you enter the query, **Adobe AND Portable**, Acrobat looks for the words *Adobe* and *Portable* in a document and highlights the first instance of each word, provided they appear within the first three pages of the document. If further instances of either word occur in the document, they are not selected or highlighted as Acrobat is returning instances of the key words with the closest proximity to each other.

- **Search in Bookmarks** When you select this option, Acrobat returns instances of your query when it appears in the bookmarks of documents you are searching.
- **Search in Comments** When you select this option, Acrobat returns instances of your query when it appears in the comments of documents you are searching.

7. Click Search.

Your search results are displayed in the Search PDF pane that displays a list of documents that contain instances of your query. A New Search button also becomes available. After perusing the search results, you can click New Search to create a search with different parameters or click Done. When you click Done, the Search PDF pane reverts to the How To..? pane.

You can also use the Advanced Search Options on a single document if you want to include proximity and stemming in your search criteria.

About Search Results

After you click Search, Acrobat searches for occurrences of your query in the selected documents or indexes. The results Acrobat returns depend on the key word or phrase you entered and the parameters you selected. Results are displayed in the Search PDF pane, as shown here:

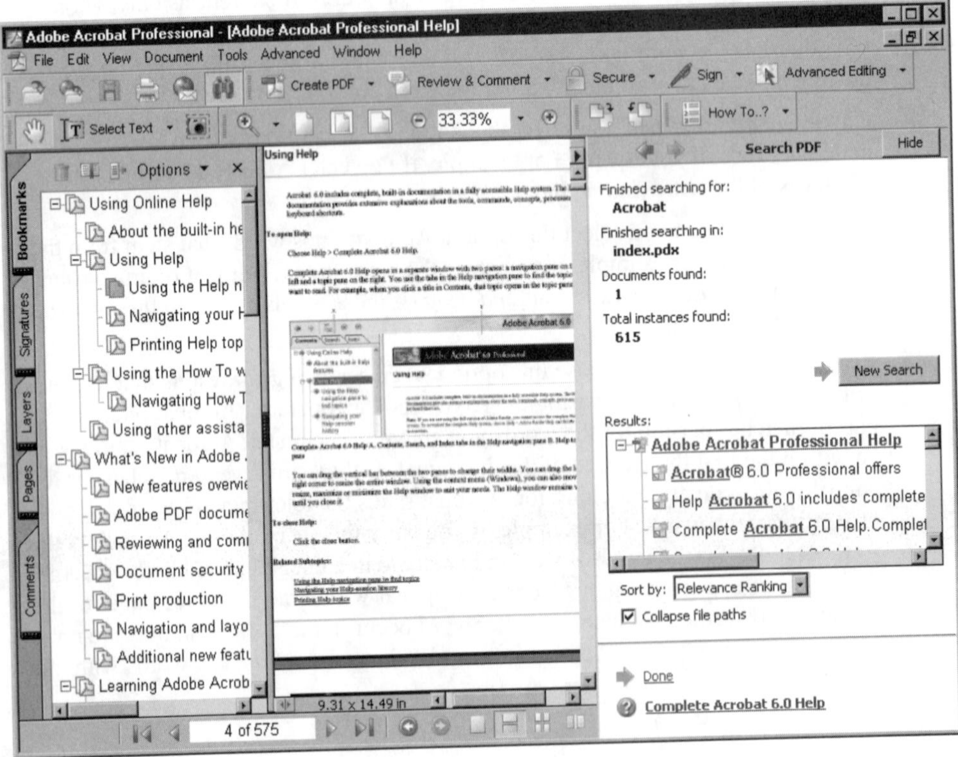

Did you know?

Boolean Logic

When you perform a Boolean search in Acrobat, or perform a Boolean search on the Internet, Boolean logic is at work in the background. Boolean logic was developed in the mid-1800s by an Englishman named George Boole. In 1854 Boole published a treatise, *An investigation into the Laws of Thought, on Which are founded the Mathematical Theories of Logic and Probabilities.* The information in this treatise became the logic behind Boolean algebra, which today finds applications in computer construction, switching circuits, and the like.

Your search results are displayed in descending order according to relevancy or score. The documents at the top of the list are more relevant to the parameters of your query; in other words, these documents contain a higher percentage of instances of the key words or phrases in your query.

View Query Results

After Acrobat finishes the search, you can select a result from the list by clicking its name. After viewing the result, you can view additional results by clicking a name in the Search PDF pane.

If you decide to hide the Search PDF pane in order to get a better view of the document, you can advance to the next occurrence of your query by choosing View | Search | Next Result. After viewing a few results, you may want to jump back to a previous result, a task you accomplish by choosing View | Search | Previous Result. If the Previous Result command is dimmed out, you are at the first occurrence of your query in the document. When you reach the last occurrence in a document of the key word or phrase you searched for, choosing the Next Result command opens the next document Acrobat returned for your search. You can also view the first result of a query in the next document by choosing View | Search | Next Document. To view the first result in a previous document, choose View | Search | Previous Document.

onduct an Advanced Search

When you conduct an advanced search by clicking the Use Advanced Search Options icon, you can refine a search by searching for documents by key words or phrases. In addition, you can choose an option from the Use These Additional Criteria section of the Search PDF pane Advanced Search Options to search for documents by Title, Subject, Author, Keywords, or by Date info. You can add up to three search parameters, as shown in Figure 3-6. Note that in this figure, only one field is available because of screenshot size constraints.

To conduct an advanced search, follow these steps:

1. Click Search to open the Search PDF pane and then click the Use Advance Search Options icon. The Search PDF pane is reconfigured as shown in Figure 3-6.

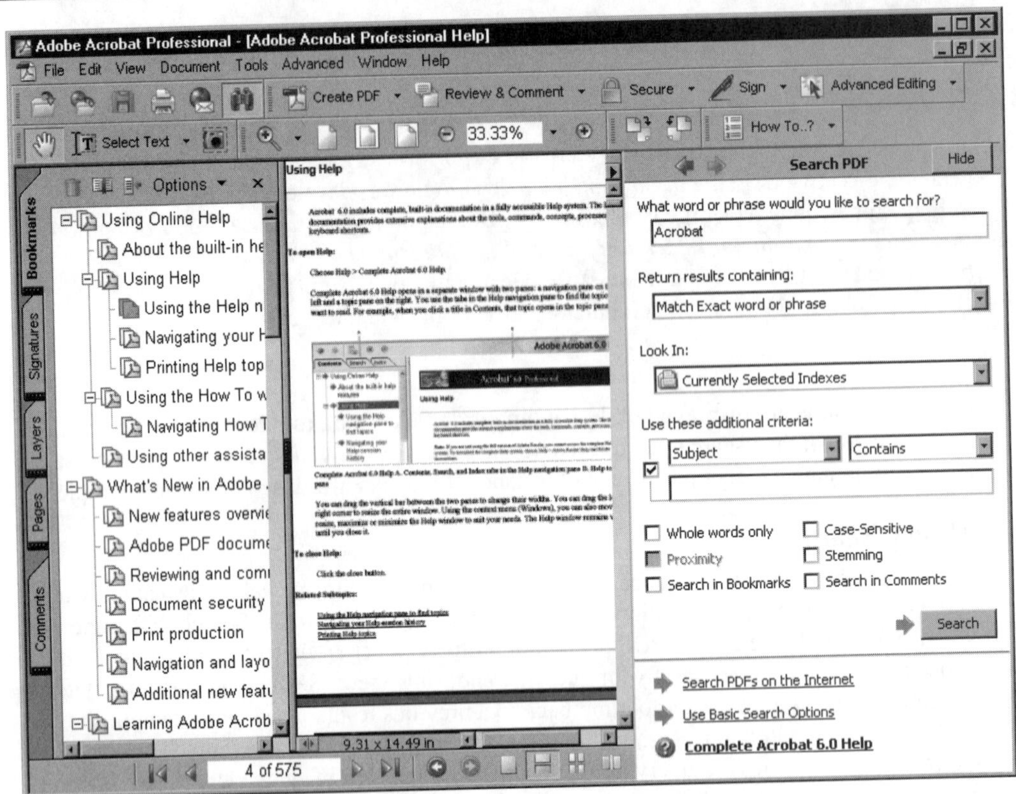

FIGURE 3-6 You can refine a search by using all available fields in the Search PDF pane.

2. Enter the word or phrase you for which you want to search and enter your other search parameters as outlined in the "Create a Query" section earlier in the chapter.
3. Click the first check box in the Use These Additional Criteria section.
4. Click the triangle to the right of the first blank field and choose one of the following criteria options:
   - **Date Created** Choose this option when you want to search for documents using the date created as a search criterion.
   - **Date Modified** Choose this option when you want to search for documents using the date modified as a search criterion.
   - **Author** Choose this option when you want to search for documents created by a particular author.

- **Subject** Choose this option when you want to search for documents pertaining to a specific subject.
- **Filename** Choose this option when you want to use a document filename as a search criterion.
- **Keywords** Choose this option when you want to search for documents containing specific keywords.
- **Bookmarks** Choose this option when you want to use the contents of a document's bookmarks as a search criterion.
- **Comments** Choose this option when you want to use the contents of a document's comments as a search criterion.
- **JPEG Images** Choose this option to search any text that is added to artifacts that are added to JPEG images.
- **XMP Metadata** Choose this option to search any text present in the document's XMP metadata. This metadata is present when you add tags to a document, and is also present with the various tags you find in the Contents tab.

5. Click the triangle to the right of the next field to reveal a drop-down menu with factors that apply to the criterion you selected from the previous field. For example, the applicable factors for the date criteria are Is Exactly, Is Before, Is After, and Is Not.
6. Enter the keyword or phrase you want to match the criterion you selected. For example, if you want to find all documents created by Adobe, you'd choose Author in Step 4, Contains in Step 5, and then enter **Adobe** in the text field.
7. If desired, add additional criteria to the search by clicking one or both of the remaining criteria check boxes and then following Steps 4 through 6.
8. Click Search. Acrobat performs the search and returns the results of your query in the Search PDF pane.

After performing your search, you can select from the results. If desired, you can sort the results of your search as outlined in the next section.

Sort Your Search

After you perform a search using the advanced options, Acrobat uses the default method of sorting and returns the results according to relevance ranking. However, you can sort the search results according to different criteria by clicking the triangle to the right of the Sort By field and then choosing one of the following options:

- **Relevance Ranking** This default option sorts search results in descending order starting with the most relevant.
- **Date Modified** This option sorts search results according to the date the document was modified starting with the most recent date.

- **Filename** This option sorts search results in alphabetical order according to the document's filename.
- **Location** This option sorts search results according to the folder where the document is stored. If you search for documents across a network or multiple hard drives, the path to the folder is also factored into the sort.

By default, Acrobat collapses the path of a search result to the directory and document filename. If desired, you can display the full path by deselecting the Collapse Paths option at the bottom of the Search PDF pane.

Refine Your Search with Boolean Operators

When you search for information in an index that contains a large number of documents, Acrobat finds every document that matches your query. If the sheer volume of documents is overwhelming, you can fine-tune your search by conducting a Boolean query. When you conduct a Boolean query, you can limit your search by using Boolean operators. To conduct a search using a Boolean query to filter your search results, follow these steps:

1. Click Search to open the Search PDF pane. Alternatively, you can choose Edit | Search.
2. Click Use Advanced Search Options.
3. Click the triangle to the right of the Look In field and then choose the location where you want to search.
4. Click the triangle to the right of the Return Results Containing field and then choose Boolean Query.
5. In the What Word Or Phrase Would You Like To Search For? field, enter your query using one of the following Boolean operators:
   - **AND** Use this Boolean operator between two words to find all instances of both words in the PDF documents you are searching. For example, entering **Adobe AND Acrobat** would return documents that contain the words *Adobe* and *Acrobat*.
   - **NOT** Use this operator between two words to find all documents that contain the first word but not the second. For example, enter **cat NOT dog** to find all PDF documents that contain the word *cat* but not *dog*.
   - **OR** Use this Boolean operator between two words to locate PDF documents that contain either word. For example, entering **Adobe OR Acrobat** and your search yields documents that contain either word.
   - **Quotation marks** Use quotation marks to search for documents with words that appear in the exact order you enter them between quotation marks. For example, enter **Boolean query** to find all documents that contain the phrase *Boolean query*.
   - **Quotation marks** Use quotation marks to search for documents that contain phrases with Boolean operators. For example, enter **John or Jane** to find PDF

documents that contain the phrase *John or Jane*, as opposed to a Boolean search phrased *John OR Jane*, which would return PDF documents that contained the names *John* or *Jane*.

Get Document Properties

When you search for PDF documents from an index, the document's title in the list of search results generally gives you a good idea of what is contained in the document. You can find more information about documents Acrobat finds in a search by clicking the document title and then choosing File | Document Properties. When you open a PDF file received via e-mail, or one that is part a multimedia presentation, you can find out more about the document by choosing File | Document Properties and then choosing an option from the Document Properties dialog box shown here:

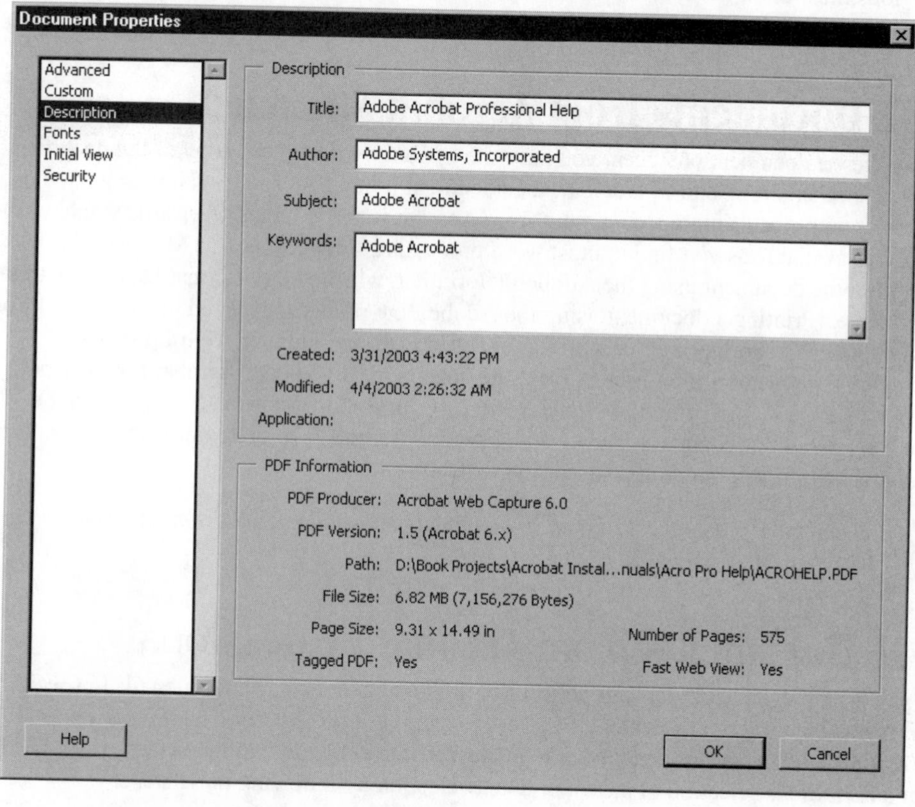

Many of the options from this dialog box are applicable to creating a PDF document and are covered in Chapter 4. If you choose this command while using Adobe Reader 6.0, you only have two options, Summary and Fonts. When you choose one of these options in Adobe Reader 6.0,

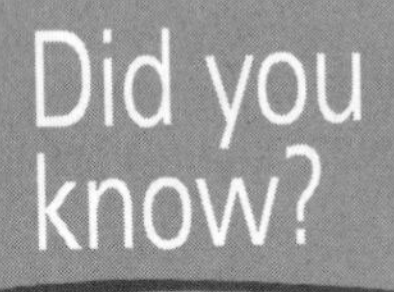

Using Boolean Operators

If you've used Boolean operators such as =, ~, +, <, and so on to perform Internet searches, you can use these operators in an Advanced Options search. Use quotes on your query words and use the desired Boolean operator to refine your search. Acrobat supports all Boolean operators except the * or ? wildcards.

all the fields are dimmed out, which means you cannot modify the information. However, in Acrobat, all the fields are available; you can modify the properties and save them with the document. The previous illustration is a typical Acrobat Document Properties dialog box. Notice that some of the fields are the same ones you specify when conducting a search.

Print PDF Documents from Acrobat Standard

After you view a document onscreen, you have the option to print a hard copy of the document. Herein lies another strong suit of Acrobat; the document prints out exactly as it was created on the author's computer. Printing a document from Acrobat is pretty straightforward. You have the same options available as you find in most word processing software such as Microsoft Word. You can print the document using the Adobe PDF printer, which is the Acrobat Distiller with a different name. (Printing a document using the Adobe PDF printer is covered in Chapter 4.) You can also choose a network printer or a printer attached to your computer. Your options vary depending on the type of printer used to print the document. If you own Acrobat Professional, you have a wide variety of printing options, which are covered in the next section. To print a document from Acrobat Standard, choose File | Print. After the Print dialog box appears, select a printer and then follow the prompts to print the document.

TIP *You can print a document as well as comments attached to the document by choosing File | Print With Comments.*

Print PDF Documents from Acrobat Professional

When you print a document, you can print the entire document or select thumbnails to specify the pages you want to print. You can also print a selection of text by using the Select Text tool to drag a marquee around the text you want to print. You can set printing options and print a hard copy of a PDF file, a selection of pages, or a text selection by following these steps:

1. To open the Print Setup box shown next, choose File | Print Setup. You can use this dialog box to set general parameters for the print job such as page orientation, size,

printer, and so on. After choosing Print Setup parameters, click OK to close the dialog box. This step is needed only if you want to change the default printer and page size.

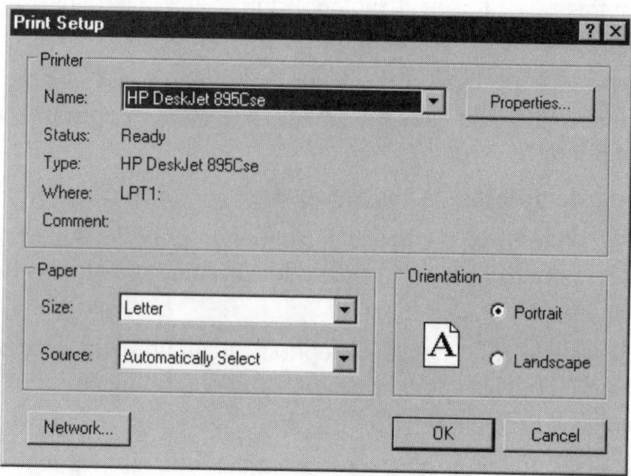

2. After selecting a printer, choose File | Print or click Print to open the Print dialog box shown here:

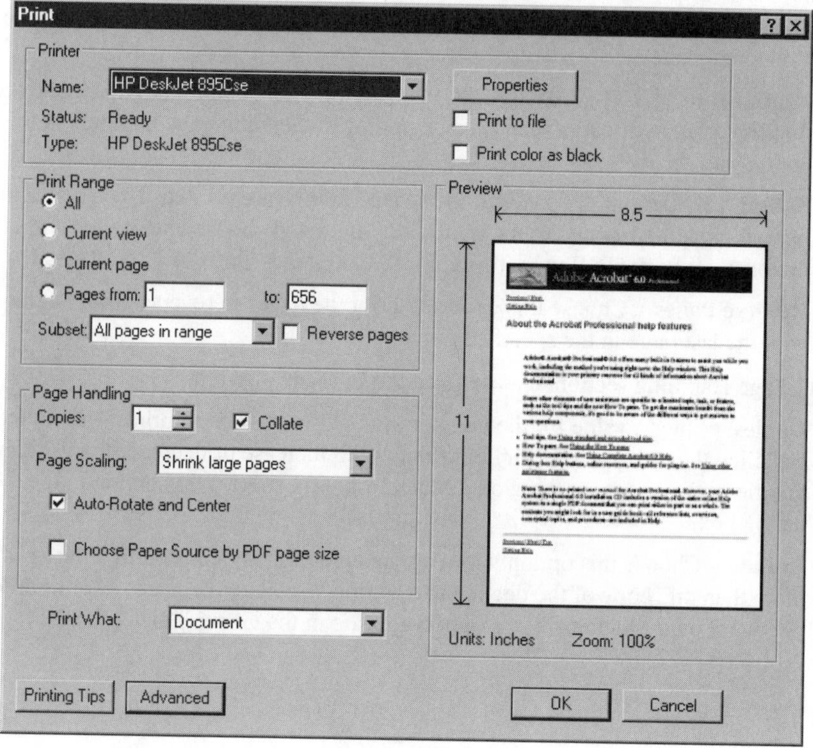

3. In the Printer section you can choose from the following options:
   - **Name (Windows) or Printer (Macintosh)** Your system default printer is displayed in this field. To select another printer, click the triangle to the right of the text field and choose a printer from the drop-down menu.
   - **Properties (Windows)** Click this button to set parameters for the currently selected printer. After you click this button, a dialog box appears that is specific for the selected printer.
   - **Destination (Macintosh)** Your choices are either Printer or File.
   - **Print To File (Windows)** Choose this option to print the document to file in PRN (Printer Files) format. This is redundant, however, as you already have the file in PDF format.
   - **Print Color As Black** Choose this option and all non-white areas of the document are printed as black. This option is useful if you're printing an AutoCad file converted to PDF that has thin-colored lines.
4. In the Print Range section, you can choose from the following options:
   - **All** Choose this option to print all pages in the document.
   - **Current View** Choose this option to print the page as it is currently visible in the Document pane. This option prints any visible comments as well.
   - **Current Page** Choose this option to print the page currently visible in the Document pane.
   - **Pages From [ ] To [ ]** By default, the beginning and ending pages are entered. To print a range of pages, enter the beginning and ending page numbers in the appropriate field.
   - **Subset** By default, all pages in the selected range are printed. To choose a different option, click the triangle to the right of the field and choose one of the following options: All Pages In Range (the default), Odd Pages Only, or Even Pages Only.
   - **Reverse Pages** Choose this option to print the pages in reverse order beginning with the last page in the specified range.
5. In the Page Handling section, choose from the following options:
   - **Copies** Enter a value for the number of copies you want to print. Alternatively, you can click the arrows to the right of the field to increase or decrease the value in the text field. If you are working on a Macintosh, you specify this option in the General dialog box.
   - **Collate** Choose this option if you are using double-sided printing or are printing more than one copy of the document to properly collate the pages in print order. If you work on a Macintosh, this option appears in the General dialog box.

6. In the Page Scaling section, choose one of the following options:
   - **None** Prints the document at its current size beginning at the upper left-hand corner or center (if the Auto Rotate and Center option is selected). If the document dimensions exceed the paper size, the document is cropped.
   - **Fit To Paper** Scales the document to fit the currently selected paper size. If you select a section of the document to print, the printed output is scaled to fit the printable area of the currently selected paper.
   - **Shrink Large Page** Choose this option, and Acrobat shrinks oversized pages to fit the selected paper size. This option comes in handy if the PDF file you are printing has different page sizes within the document. If you choose this option and the document has pages smaller than the currently selected paper sizes, the small pages are not enlarged.
   - **Tile Large Pages** Choose this option, and Acrobat divides pages or selections larger than the currently selected paper size into tiles. Small pages are not upsized when you use this option.
   - **Tile All Pages** Choose this option, and Acrobat divides all pages or selected areas into tiles.
   - **Auto-Rotate And Center** Choose this option if the PDF file you are printing contains pages in both landscape and portrait format. While printing is in progress, Acrobat changes page orientation as needed.
   - **Choose Paper Source By PDF Page Size (Windows)** Choose this option, and Acrobat uses the PDF page size to choose the paper tray on the output device. Choose this option if your printer has multiple paper trays when you're printing a document with varied page sizes.
7. Click the triangle to the right of the Print What field and choose one of the following options:
   - **Document** Choose this option, and Acrobat prints the selected pages from the document as well as form fields.
   - **Document And Comments** Choose this option, and Acrobat prints the selected pages from the document, comments, and form fields.
   - **Form Fields Only** Choose this option, and Acrobat prints only the form fields from the specified pages or selected area.

NOTE *Form fields will not print if the document author selected the Visible But Doesn't Print option when creating the field.*

   - **Advanced** Click this button to open the Advanced Print Setup dialog box. Use this option if your printer, or the printer on which the document will be printed, supports marks and bleeds, transparency, and so on. Refer to your printer manual to select the proper settings for your device.
8. Click OK to print the document.

3

Use Text and Graphics from PDFs in Other Applications

You can capture text and graphic elements from a PDF document that you want to use in another application. You can select text, tables, or graphic elements from a document and then copy them to the system clipboard for use in another PDF document or a document in a different application that supports the elements you've captured from the PDF document.

NOTE *You may not be able to capture text or graphic elements if Acrobat Security has been applied to the document.*

Capture Text from a PDF Document

You can easily select any text elements in a PDF document with the Acrobat Select Text tool. With the Select Text tool, you can select a single letter, a word, a sentence, an entire paragraph, or more. If there are graphic elements dispersed in the text you are selecting, Acrobat ignores them and selects only text. To capture text from a PDF document:

1. Launch Acrobat and open a PDF file.
2. Select the Select Text tool from the Basic toolbar, as shown here: Select Text
3. After you select the tool, drag it into the Document pane. Note that your cursor is now in the shape of an I-beam.
4. To select the text, click the point where you want to begin selecting text, drag your cursor to the right, and release it when you have selected the desired text. To select text from more than one line, click to define the beginning point and then drag diagonally to select contiguous sentences. Acrobat highlights the selected text.
5. Choose Edit | Copy, and Acrobat copies the selected text to your system clipboard. Alternatively, you can right-click (Windows) or CTRL-click (Macintosh) and choose Copy To Clipboard from the Context menu.
6. Open your favorite word processing program and choose the Paste command. You can now edit the pasted text and save it for future reference.

Capture Tables from PDF Documents

You can use the Table Select tool to select a table within a PDF document. After you select the table, you can then copy it to the clipboard for use in a spreadsheet application. You can select a table using the Select Table tool as follows:

1. Open the PDF document that contains the table you want to select.
2. Select the Select Table tool shown here: Select Table
3. Click inside the table to select the entire table. Alternatively, you can click and drag to select contiguous rows and columns.

4. To use the selection in another application, do one of the following:
   - Right-click (Windows) or CTRL-click (Macintosh) and choose Copy Selected Table.
   - Right-click (Windows) or CTRL-click (Macintosh) and choose Save Table As. This enables you to save the selection for use in another application.
   - Right-click (Windows) or CTRL-click (Macintosh) and choose Open Table in Spreadsheet. Choosing this option opens the selection in a *CSV* (Comma Separated Values)–compliant spreadsheet application such as Microsoft Excel.
5. If you copied the table to the clipboard, launch your spreadsheet software and then paste the selection into a document.

TIP *If you have Acrobat and a CSV-compliant spreadsheet program open at the same time, resize and arrange both applications so that they are visible at the same time. You can then use the Select Table tool to select a table and drag it into your spreadsheet application as CSV text.*

Capture Graphic Elements from PDF Documents

When you open a PDF document with embedded graphics, the PDF retains the look and feel of the graphics as they were originally created. If the PDF document has a relatively low level of compression applied, the graphic elements will be crisp and clear. You can use the Acrobat Select Image tool to select a graphic element, such as a photograph or logo, from a PDF document as follows:

1. Launch Acrobat and open the PDF file that contains the graphic element(s) you want to select.
2. Select the Select Image tool as shown here: Select Image
3. Within the PDF document, navigate to the page that contains the graphic you want to select. Note that your cursor becomes a crosshair when you move it over an image.
4. Click to the above-left (or above-right) of the graphic you want to select and then drag diagonally. As you drag, a dotted rectangular bounding box appears, giving you a preview of the area you are selecting.
5. When the bounding box surrounds the graphic, release the mouse button.
6. To use the graphic in another application, do one of the following:
   - Choose Edit | Copy, and Acrobat copies the graphic to the system clipboard.
   - Right-click (Windows) or CTRL-click (Macintosh) and choose Copy Image To Clipboard.
   - Right-click (Windows) or CTRL-click (Macintosh) and choose Save Image As to open the Save Image As dialog box and save the selection to a folder on your system or network.

- Drag the selection into an open document in an application that supports graphic elements such as Microsoft Word or Adobe Photoshop.

If you copied the graphic to the system clipboard, you can paste it into another application.

TIP *You can select a portion of a graphic (known in photo editing circles as* cropping*) by releasing the mouse button when the rectangle surrounds the desired portion of the graphic.*

Using the Snapshot Tool

You can use the Snapshot tool to copy a combination of text and graphics to the clipboard. You can select an entire page, a portion of a page, or a portion of a graphic. After copying the selection to the clipboard, you can paste it into another application. To select text and graphics with the Snapshot tool, follow these steps:

1. Select the Snapshot tool shown here: 
2. Copy a selection to the clipboard by doing one of the following:
   - Click anywhere inside the document pane to select the current view of the page.
   - Click to define the edge of a selection and then drag diagonally. As you drag, Acrobat displays a dashed bounding box that indicates the area of the current selection. Release the mouse button when the bounding box encompasses the area you want to copy to the clipboard.
   - Click and drag to select a portion of a graphic element within the page.

After doing any of the above, Acrobat displays a dialog box informing you the selection has been copied to the clipboard. You can paste the selection into another application.

NOTE *Although you can use the Snapshot tool to capture text, the text is captured as an image, and as such, is not editable. If you need to capture text that you'll edit in another application, use the Select Text tool.*

Summary

In this chapter, you learned to use the Acrobat tools to navigate a document and Acrobat tabs to navigate to specific elements in a document. You also learned to use Acrobat's powerful Search command to search through a single document, a folder of documents, or an index of PDF documents. In the latter part of the chapter, you learned to use Acrobat tools to select elements from documents for use in other applications. In the next chapter, you'll learn to create PDF documents.

Part II

Create PDF Documents

Chapter 4

Create a PDF Document

How to...

- Create a PDF file
- Use Acrobat Distiller
- Set conversion settings
- Set document properties
- Save PDF files
- Save PDF files in other formats

Acrobat gives you the capability of creating PDF documents from many sources. You can create a PDF file from within many authoring applications (which are covered in Chapter 5), or you can create documents directly in Acrobat. When you create a document within Acrobat, you have many options available to you. You can save a document using Acrobat defaults, or you can modify the document properties and add security to confidential documents. You can even use Acrobat to save documents in other formats. In this chapter, you'll learn the nuts and bolts of creating a bare-bones PDF file.

Create a PDF File

You can use Acrobat to quickly create PDFs from existing files. Choose between two methods: the Create PDF command or the drag-and-drop method. When you create a PDF file using one of these methods, Acrobat converts the original file into PDF format. After Acrobat converts the file, you can save it in PDF format or export it using another supported format for use in another application. You can also create a PDF document from within an authoring application by exporting the file in PDF format (if supported) or by using the application Print command and choosing Adobe PDF as the printing device. Creating a PDF file from within an authoring application is covered in Chapter 5.

Use the Create PDF Command

You use the Create PDF command or task button to open supported files formats as PDFs. When you choose this command and select a file(s) to open, Acrobat converts the file from its current format into PDF format. You can open the following formats as PDF files:

- **AutoCad Files** You can create technical drawings using the popular AutoCad software. You can create PDF documents from AutoCad documents with DWG or DWT file extensions.
- **BMP Files** You can export *BMP* files from most popular photo-editing programs such as Adobe PhotoShop, CorelDraw Graphics Suite 11, and Macromedia Fireworks. Image files saved in this format can have color depth as high as 24 bit.

- **CompuServe GIF Files** *GIF* (Graphic Interchange Format) files have 8-bit (256 color) color depth. You can open GIF files saved in the GIF 87 format or GIF 89a format as PDF files. You can also open an animated GIF; however, only the first frame of the animation is converted to PDF format.
- **HTML Files** *HTML* (Hypertext Markup Language) files are created for use on the Internet. You can open HTML files as PDF documents. When you open an HTML file as a PDF file, Acrobat reads any image tags (<img src= "yourimage.jpg">) and converts the associated files to PDF in the exact position they appear when the HTML document is opened in a Web browser. If the image is not available, Acrobat creates a bounding box with the dimensions of the Alt (Alternate Text) tag and displays the Alt text. Converting a web page to PDF format is a great way to create a client proof of a web site under construction. You can also use the Capture web Page command to open a web page from your hard drive or download a web page from the Internet. Web capture is discussed in Chapter 6.
- **JPEG Files** *JPEG* (Joint Photographic Experts Group) files are used for Web graphics and multimedia presentations. JPEG files are compressed for quick download from the Web or to save file space in a multimedia presentation.
- **JPEG 2000 Files** JPEG2000 can be thought of as JPEG's big brother. It is an advanced image compression format that features progressive download and will be used by next-generation digital imaging devices. JPEG2000 files are designated with the .JPF, .JPX, .JP2, J2K, J2C, or .JPC file extension.
- **Microsoft Office** You use Microsoft Office applications to create Word documents, Excel spreadsheets, and PowerPoint presentations. In addition to being able to create a PDF document from within a Microsoft application, you can now create a PDF document from within Acrobat by choosing File | Create PDF | From File and then opening a Microsoft Office document, a feature that was not available in previous versions of Acrobat.
- **Microsoft Project** You use Microsoft Project to manage projects. You can use the software to communicate the status of a project, as well as manage project resources with colleagues in your organization.
- **Microsoft Visio** You use Microsoft Visio to create diagrams and flowcharts that enable you to document and share information and ideas with colleagues.
- **PCX Files** Image files in the Windows-only *PCX* (**Pi**Cture E**X**change) format can be exported from most popular image-editing programs. The PCX format is native to the Windows Paintbrush program; however, many applications such as CorelDraw Graphics Suite 11 offer full support of the PCX format. Consult your image-editing software user manual to see if the format is supported. The PCX format supports 24-bit color depth and can be opened directly in Acrobat as PDF files.
- **PICT Files (Macintosh only)** Image files saved in the Macintosh *PICT* (PICTure) format support 32-bit color depth. While PICT files can be created in Windows-based image-editing programs, only the Macintosh version of Acrobat can open PICT images as PDF files.

- **PNG Files** *PNG* (Portable Network Graphics) files are not compressed and support 24-bit color.
- **PostScript/EPS Files** *EPS* files are used in illustration programs such as Adobe Illustrator, CorelDraw, and Macromedia FreeHand MX. EPS files can be comprised of vector and bitmap graphics.
- **Text Files** You can open text documents saved in *TXT* format as PDF documents. Text files can be created in programs as sophisticated as Microsoft Word or as humble as the Notepad utility included with versions of the Microsoft Windows operating system.
- **TIFF Files** *TIFF* (Tagged Image File Format) files can be compressed or uncompressed and support 32-bit color. People who create images in both platforms for print favor this format because of the high image resolution and clarity.

Create PDF from File

In Acrobat 5.0, you used the Open As PDF command to open a single file or multiple files. Acrobat 6.0 refines this process considerably. When you need to open a single document, you use the Create PDF From File command. You can still use this command to open multiple files; but another command, the Create PDF From Multiple Files command, gives you more options that provide better control over the PDF creation process.

To convert an existing file to a PDF file, do the following:

1. Choose File | Create PDF | From File to access the Open dialog box, as shown in the following illustration. Alternatively, you can click the Create PDF task button and choose From File.

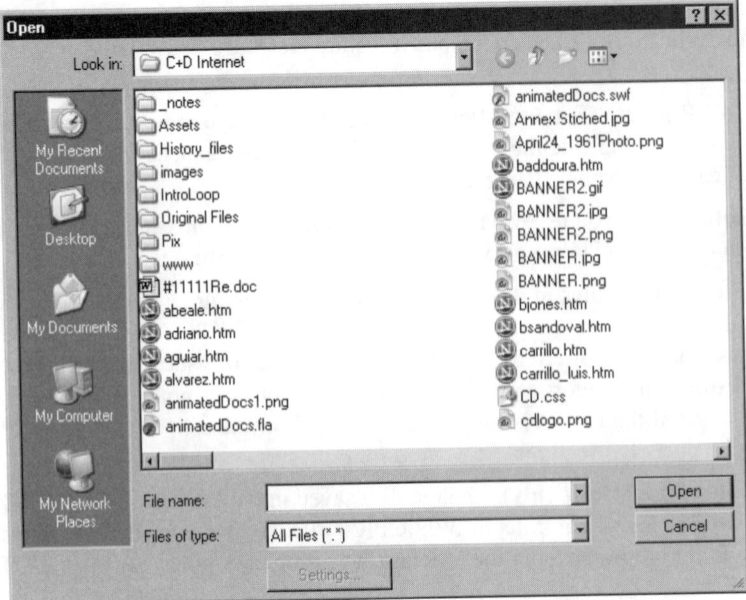

2. Click the triangle to the right of the Files Of Type field and choose an option from the drop-down menu or accept the default All Files option. If you select a specific file type, only files of that type will be visible for selection.
3. Select the file you want to open.
4. If you specify a file type, after you select a file, the Settings button may become available. The available settings options vary depending on the selected file type. Compression and color management settings are covered in the next section.
5. Click Open, and Acrobat converts the file in PDF format. Figure 4-1 shows a JPEG image converted to PDF format.

After you open a file in PDF format, you can work with the file directly in Acrobat. You can then save the file in PDF format or other formats supported by Acrobat. Saving files is covered in the "Save PDF Files" section of this chapter.

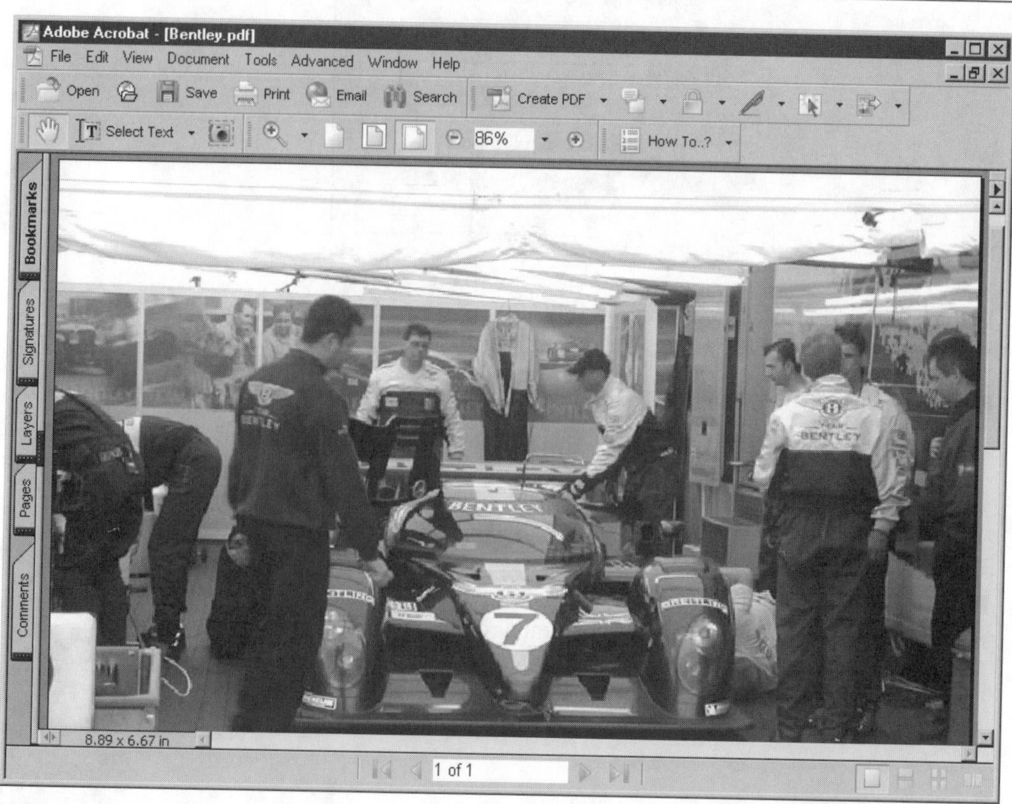

FIGURE 4-1 Use the Create PDF command to convert other file formats to PDF files.

Choose Compression and Color Management Settings for Image Files

When you convert an image file into a PDF document, you can control how much compression is applied to the image, as well as color management. Compression settings are dimmed out when you convert JPEG or JPEG2000 files to PDF documents. When you choose the Create PDF From File command and choose an image format, the Settings button becomes available. Click the Settings button to display the Adobe PDF Settings dialog box, shown here:

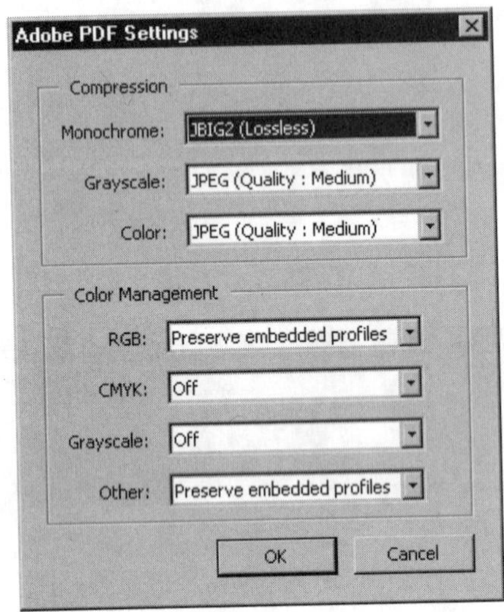

With all image formats except JPEG and JPEG 2000, you can specify the following compression settings from the Adobe PDF Settings dialog box:

- **Monochrome** For 1-bit monochrome images, choose CCITT G4 to achieve good image quality, JBIG2 (Lossy) for better image quality, and JBIG2 (Lossless) for the best image quality. When an image is compressed, data is lost, hence the term "lossy." The amount of data lost depends on the amount of compression applied. When little or no compression is applied to an image, the image is sharp and crisp, and little or no quality is lost, hence the term "lossless."
- **Grayscale** For 8-bit grayscale images, choose ZIP to convert images or documents with images that have large areas of similar color or repeating patterns; choose JPEG quality for photos; or choose JPEG 2000 to take advantage of the format's superior

compression and progressive download. When you choose JPEG 2000, choose from six options that range from Minimum (high compression, small file size, and low image quality) to Maximum (low compression, largest file size, and best image quality).

- **Color** For images with thousands (16 bit) to millions of colors (32 and 48 bit), you can specify ZIP, JPEG, or JPEG2000 with the same compression settings as discussed in the previous bullet.

With all image formats, you can specify color management settings. From within the Color Management section of the Adobe PDF Settings dialog box just shown, you can specify color management for RGB (colors mixed with shades of **R**ed, **G**reen, and **B**lue), CMYK (colors mixed with shades of **C**yan, **M**agenta, **Y**ellow, and blac**K**), Grayscale, and Other by choosing one of the following options for each format:

- **Preserve Embedded Profiles** Choose this option to use an ICC color profile that has been embedded with the image.
- **Off** Choose this option, and Acrobat color profiles will be used in lieu of color profiles embedded with the image.
- **Ask When Opening** Choose this option, and Acrobat displays color profiles embedded with the option, giving you the option to use them or not.

NOTE *When you create a PDF document from a nonimage format, the Settings button may also be available. The settings differ for each format and will be discussed in future chapters when applicable.*

Create PDF from Multiple Files

You can create a PDF document from multiple files in formats supported by Acrobat. When you create a PDF document from multiple files, you can specify the order in which the files appear in the converted PDF document. You can also use this command to append all currently open PDF documents.

To convert multiple files into a PDF document:

1. Choose File | Create PDF | From Multiple Files to open the Create PDF From Multiple Documents dialog box. Alternatively, you can click the Create PDF task button and choose From Multiple Files from the drop-down menu. When you choose this command,

any currently open PDF documents are displayed in the Files To Combine window, as shown in the following illustration. Note that several files have already been added.

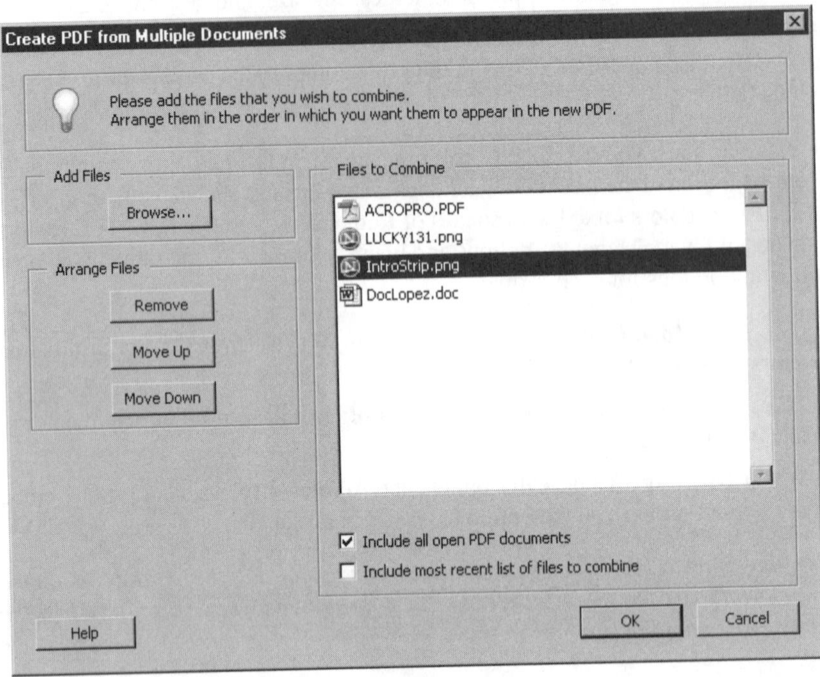

2. Click Browse to display the Open dialog box. Choose the files you want to convert to a PDF document. You can choose multiple files by clicking them while holding down the CTRL key.
3. Click Add to add the files to the list in the Files To Combine window. To add additional files to the list, repeat Steps 2 and 3. You can select a file and click any of the following buttons to modify the list. These buttons are dimmed out if you have not selected a file.
   - **Remove** Removes the selected file from the list.
   - **Move Up** Moves the file to the next highest position in the list. The order that the files appear in the list is the order in which they appear in the converted PDF document. You can click this button as needed to move the file further up the list. This button is dimmed out when you select the first file or reach the top of the list.
   - **Move Down** Moves the file to the next lowest position in the list. You can click this button as needed to move the file further down the list. This button is dimmed out when you move a file to the bottom of the list or select the last file.
4. Click the Include All Open PDF Documents check box (selected by default) to append all currently open PDF documents with the selected files. Deselect this option to remove all currently open PDF documents from the list.

NOTE *If you have several PDF documents open, you can select the ones you don't want included in the conversion process and then click Remove.*

5. Click the Include Most Recent List Of Files To Combine check box to add to the list the files you combined the last time you used this command.
6. Click OK. Acrobat converts the selected files into a single PDF document.

NOTE *When you combine files of different formats using this command, Acrobat uses the current settings for each file type. For example, if you add Microsoft Word files to the list, Acrobat uses the conversion settings currently in effect for Microsoft Office files.*

Create a PDF File by Dragging and Dropping

You can quickly open one or several files as PDFs by dragging the file icon from your desktop or an open file folder and dropping it on the Acrobat icon. You can also drag-and-drop a file from a file folder directly into the Acrobat application.

When you create PDF files by dragging and dropping, you have the same options and limitations imposed by the Create PDF From File command. If you select several files to open as PDF documents using the drag-and-drop method, Acrobat creates a separate PDF file for each file you select.

TIP *If you have a project folder with several files you are converting to PDF documents, resize Acrobat and the open file folder so that both are visible on your desktop. Then it's a simple matter of dragging files from the folder and then dropping them into Acrobat.*

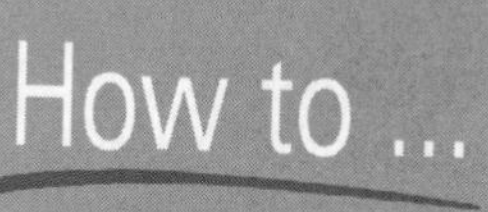

Launch Acrobat and Create a PDF File

You can launch Acrobat and create a PDF file on the fly by dragging a supported file format onto the Acrobat shortcut on your desktop. This method comes in handy when you work in other applications and decide you need an accompanying PDF file to the one you are currently editing. To open a file in this manner, do the following:

1. Select the file you want to open as a PDF document. You can select one or several files to open.
2. Drag the selected files to the Acrobat desktop shortcut and release the mouse button. After you release the mouse button, Acrobat launches and converts the selected files to PDF format. If you attempt to open a file that is not supported, Acrobat displays a warning dialog box.

Did you know?

ePublishing

The popularity of the Internet makes it possible to get a message out to millions of people. Anyone with a computer and a modem can point their browser to a web site and access all manner of information. With the advent of cable and DSL modems, people can retrieve complex information from a web site faster than ever. But the sheer magnitude of media available often means a message will be lost if the viewer doesn't have the proper plug-in. This is where Acrobat shines. Most Internet users have a version of Acrobat Reader installed on their computer, and this also functions as a browser plug-in. When you create a multipage PDF document with text and images, you can optimize it for the Internet. When viewers click a web site link to a PDF document, the first page quickly loads in the user's browser, and all the interactivity of the document is readily available. When you create PDF documents for distribution over the Internet, it's important to create a link to the latest version of the Acrobat Reader and advise web site visitors to update in order to properly read the document.

Open Web Pages

If you are a web site designer, you can use the Create PDF From Web Page command to create a PDF proof for client approval. This technique shows a customer your design before a Web host has been selected. Use this command to convert a single HTML document from your hard drive into a PDF document, or use it to convert the entire site into a PDF document, complete with links. To create a PDF document from HTML files, do the following:

1. Choose File | Create PDF | From Web Page to access the Create PDF From Web Page dialog box, as shown in the following illustration. Alternatively, you can click the Create PDF From Web Page button that looks like a file folder with a globe in front of it. If the command has been used before, the last site opened is listed in the URL field.

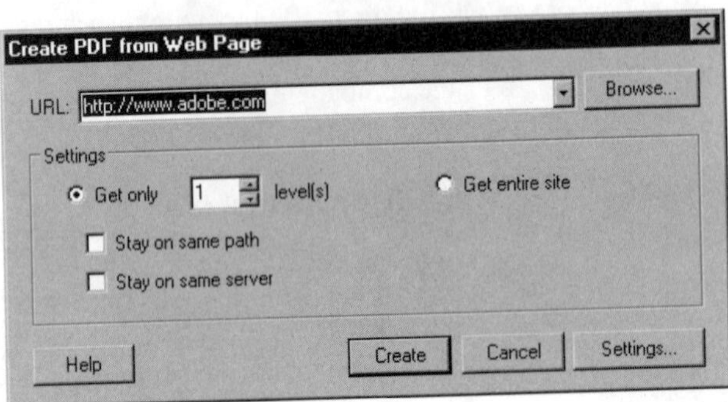

How to ... Add Headers and Footers to a PDF Document

Acrobat 6.0 has an exciting new feature that gives you the capability of adding headers and footers to a document. To add headers and footers to a document, choose Document | Add Headers and Footers to open the Add Headers and Footers dialog box, which looks similar to the Headers and Footers dialog box in most popular word processing programs. The dialog box is divided into two tabs: Header and Footer. Within each tab, you have three windows to which you can add the date, page number, or custom text for the header or footer you are creating. You can also specify how many pages the header or footer appears and how the margins are configured.

2. If you want to open a single HTML page, accept the default. If you want to open the entire site in PDF format, choose the Get Entire Site option.
3. Click Browse and Acrobat opens the Select File To Open dialog box.
4. Navigate to the HTML file you want to convert to PDF format and then click Open. If you choose the Get Entire Site option, select the Home page of the site.
5. Click Download. If you choose the Get Entire Site option, Acrobat displays a dialog box warning you of a potentially large download. Click Yes to begin the download; click No to abort. When you use this command to convert HTML documents stored in a folder on your hard drive, the download is relatively quick. However, when you download sites from the Internet, the download time depends upon the quality of your connection, your modem speed, your processor, and the size and complexity of the web site. Capturing web pages from the Internet is covered in detail in Chapter 6.

After you click Download, Acrobat begins converting the HTML pages into PDF format. Acrobat downloads the entire site, including images and accompanying files. Figure 4-2 shows a web site that has been converted to PDF format.

ve PDF Files

After you convert a file to PDF format, you can save it for future reference. When you save a PDF file, you can accept the Acrobat defaults, name the file, and save it, or you can modify the document properties, name the file, and save it. The properties you modify determine how the document appears when opened and what information is available for the Search

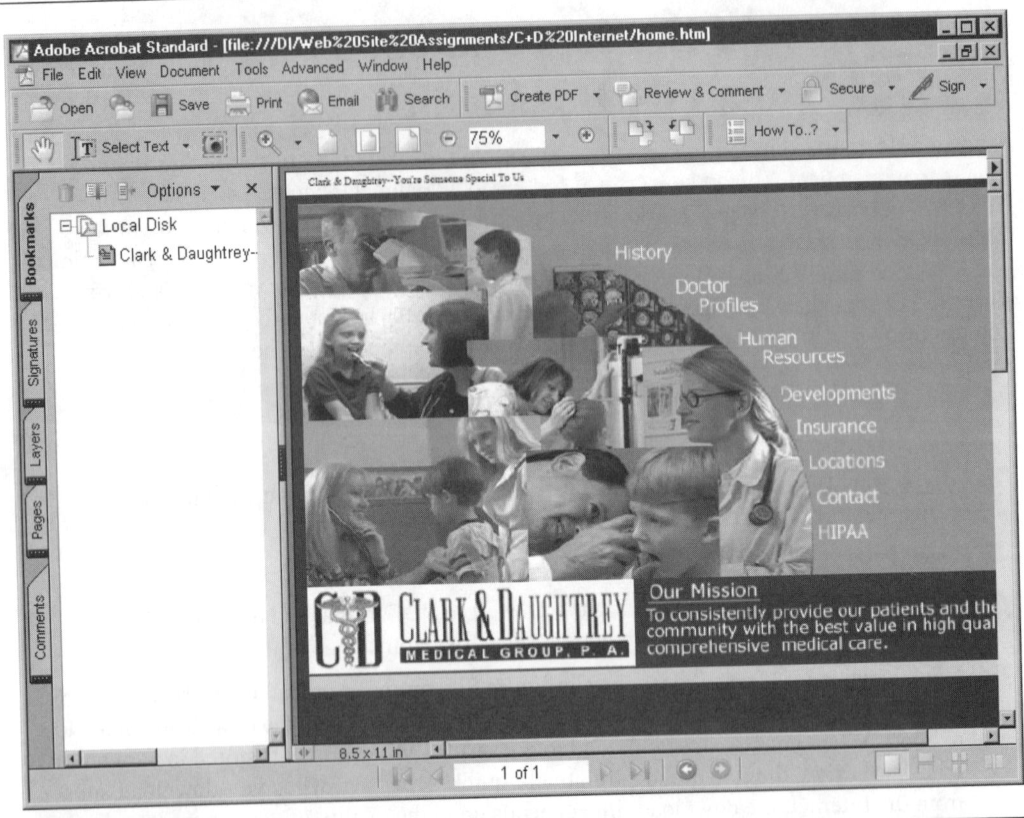

FIGURE 4-2 Use the Create PDF From Web Page command to create a customer proof of a Web design.

command (if the document is included as part of a PDF index). To save a PDF file using the Acrobat defaults, do the following:

1. Choose File | Save and Acrobat opens the Save As dialog box opens, as shown next.

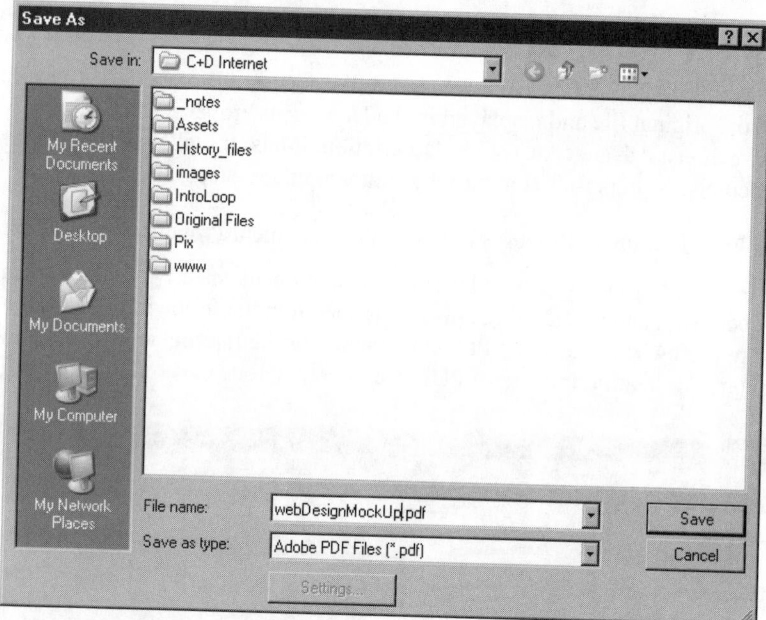

2. Navigate to the folder you want the file saved in and enter a name for the file. Accept the Save As Type default [Adobe PDF Files (*.pdf)] and click Save.

After you click Save, Acrobat saves the file in PDF format using the default Document Summary. If you are using the document for your own reference, the Acrobat defaults may be acceptable. However, if you distribute the document to colleagues or customers, it is to your advantage to modify the document properties, as discussed in the next section.

Set Document Properties

When you convert a file to PDF format or open a PDF document and modify it, you can change the document properties before saving the document. You can edit the document properties to include information you deem pertinent to your viewing audience. For example, you can set the document Initial View to change or specify what the viewer sees when the document is opened, and you can set the document security to limit access to the document while adding custom information.

Edit Document Properties

When you convert a file to PDF format, Acrobat records the document's properties. This information is gleaned from the original file and displayed in the Document Properties dialog box, which is divided into six sections: Advanced, Custom, Description, Fonts, Initial View, and Security. You can modify a document's properties summary by following these steps:

1. Choose File | Document Properties to open the Document Properties dialog box.
2. Click Advanced to specify a base URL for the document, specify an index to attach to the document, and set trapping options, as shown in the following illustration. Base URLs are used when you create PDF documents for the Internet and will be covered in Chapter 13. Creating indexes of PDF documents will be covered in Chapter 16.

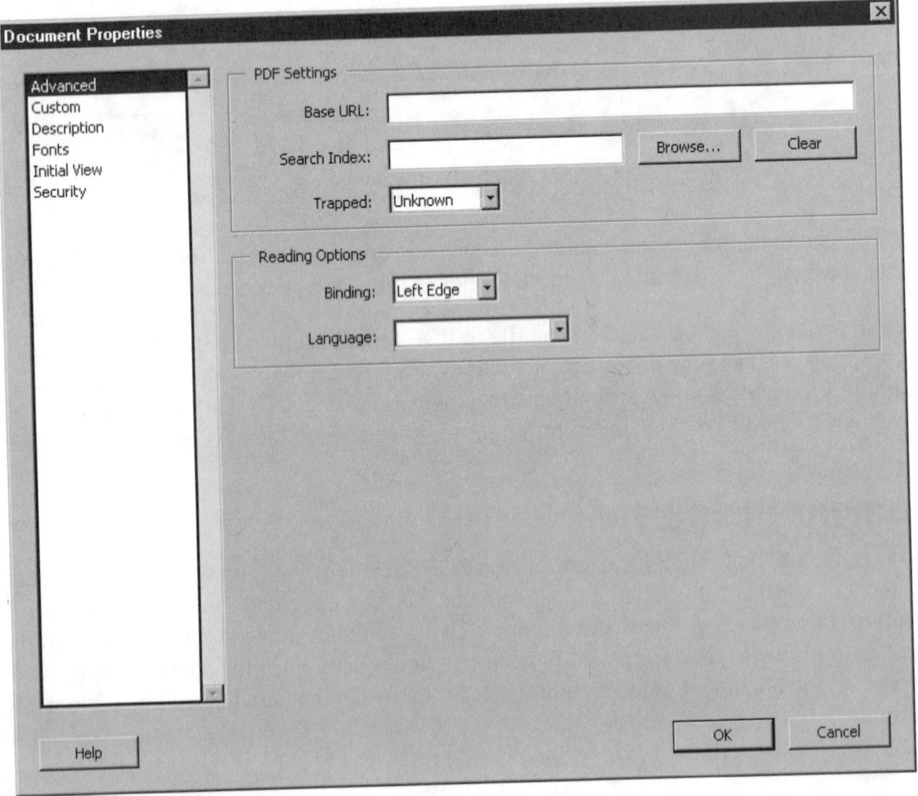

3. In the Reading Options area, click the triangle to the right of the Binding field and choose Left Edge or Right Edge from the drop-down menu. Binding is used when thumbnails are displayed or when a multipage document is displayed using the Continuous Facing mode.

4. Click Custom to define Custom Names and Values for the document. Custom names and values can be specified as search options in PDF Indexes. Creating indexes of PDF documents is covered in Chapter 16.
5. Click Description to open the Description section of the dialog box shown in the following illustration and modify the information in any or all of the following text fields: Title, Author, Subject, and Keywords. Remember that this information is often the first information your viewers see concerning your document, especially if they use the Search command to locate the information. Keep this information as relevant as possible.

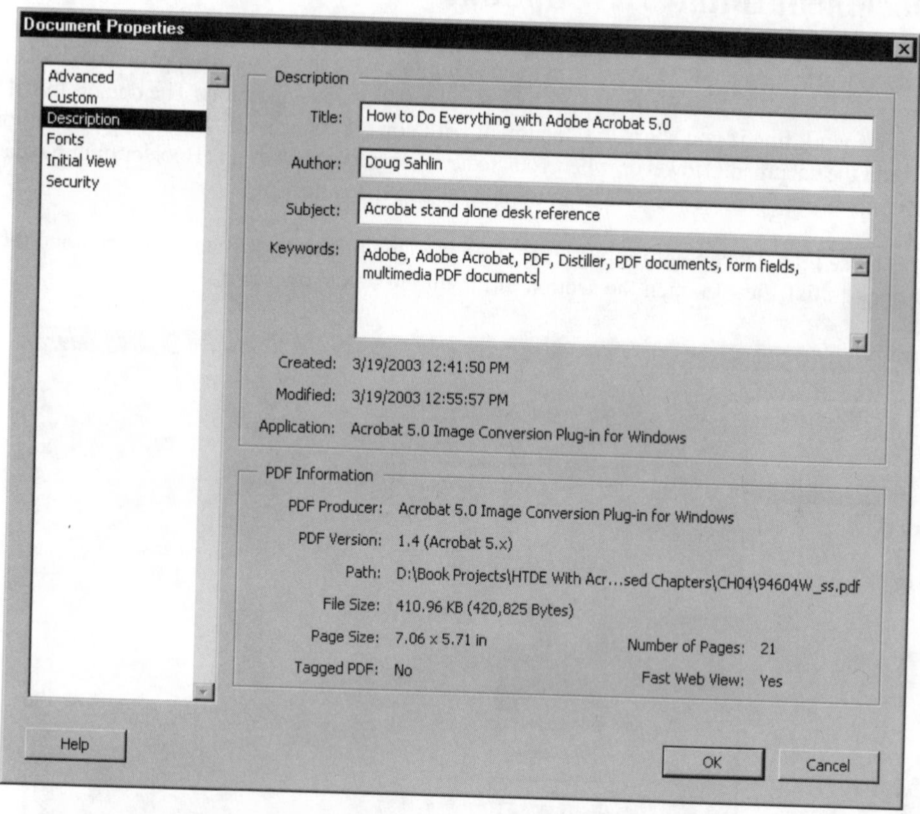

6. Click Fonts to display information about the fonts embedded in the document.
7. Click Initial View to set viewing options when the document is opened, as discussed in the upcoming "Set Document Initial View Options" section of this chapter.
8. Click Security to set document security options, as outlined in the upcoming "Set Document Security" section of this chapter.
9. Save the document as a PDF file, and Acrobat updates the information you entered along with other document summary information, such as the date modified.

Saving a document with pertinent information in the document summary makes it easier for other people who view the document to understand the information contained within. Time is valuable. In today's hustle-bustle world, people do not have the time to sift through a document to see if the information meets their needs. In addition to changing the Document Properties Description information, you can also specify what your viewers see when they open a PDF document. The information you include in the Document Properties can also be used in a search if the document is included in a PDF index. Creating a PDF index is covered in Chapter 16.

Set Document Initial View Options

If you save a PDF document with Acrobat defaults, when your viewers open the document, they see the first document page in the Document pane, complete with the Navigation pane bookmarks and thumbnails, and all of the Acrobat (or Adobe Reader 6.0) menus and tools. The default Initial View options work fine if you share the document with coworkers or work with a team of authors who will edit the document. However, when you create a document such as an eBook or multimedia presentation, you can change the default options by doing the following:

1. Choose File | Document Properties to open the Document Properties dialog box and then click Initial View to open the section of the dialog box shown here:

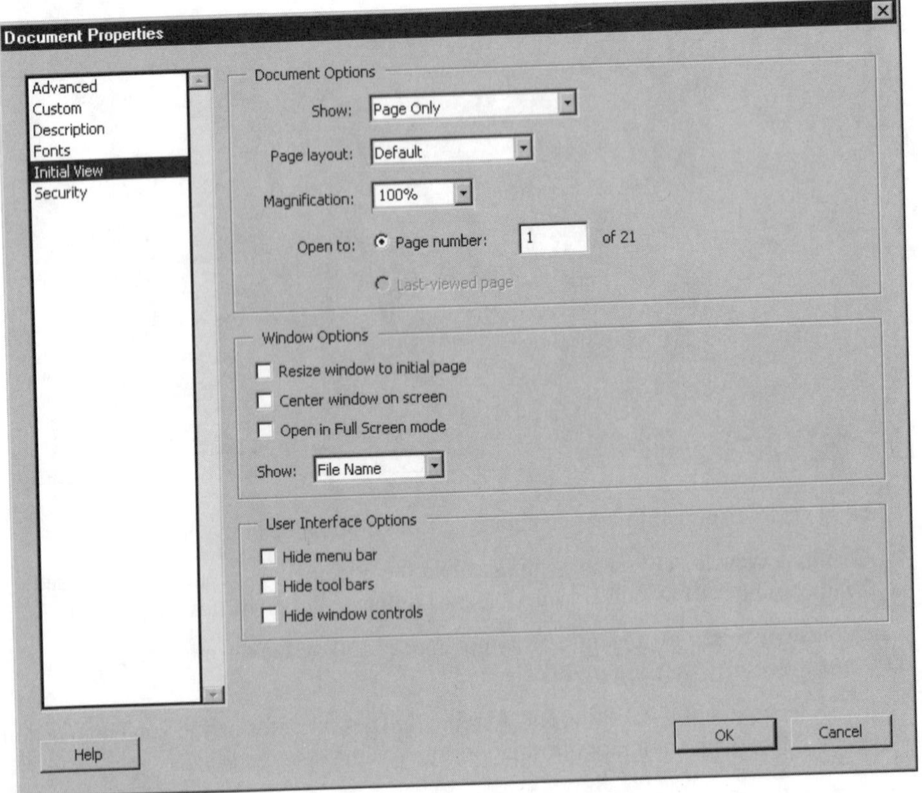

2. In the Document Options section, click the triangle to the right of the Show field and choose from the following options:
   - **Page Only** Choose this option so that when the document opens, the viewer sees the full page with only the tab titles visible in the Navigation pane.
   - **Bookmarks Panel And Page** Choose this option so that when the document opens, the viewer sees the full page with only the Bookmarks tab of the Navigation pane visible.
   - **Pages Panel And Page** Choose this option so that when the document opens, the viewer sees the full page with only the Pages tab of the Navigation pane visible.
   - **Layers Panel And Page** Choose this option so that when the document opens, the viewer sees the full page with only the Layers tab of the Navigation pane visible.
3. Click the triangle to the right of the Page Layout field and choose one of the following options:
   - **Default** Choose this option, and Acrobat configures the document according to the user's viewing preference.
   - **Single Page** Choose this option, and the document opens in single-page mode. Viewers will be able to use the Hand tool to navigate through a single page, but not to the next page.
   - **Continuous** Choose this option, and the document opens in continuous mode. Viewers will be able to use the Hand tool to scroll from page to page in the document.
   - **Facing** Choose this option, and the document opens with multiple pages arranged in the document pane.
   - **Continuous Facing** Choose this option, and the document opens with multiple pages displayed in the Document pane. Viewers will be able to use the Hand tool to scroll to different pages in the document.
4. Click the triangle to the right of the Magnification field and choose one of the following options:
   - **Magnification Levels** Choose one of the preset magnification values, and the document opens at that magnification. These are the numbers followed by the percent symbol. These values represent a percentage of the document size as it was originally published. You can also enter a value between 8.33% and 6400% in the Magnification Levels field to have the document open at a level other than one of the defaults.
   - **Fit Page** Choose this option, and Acrobat sizes the document to fill the entire Document pane when the file opens.
   - **Fit Width** Choose this option, and Acrobat fits the document to the current width of the Document pane when the file opens.
   - **Fit Visible** Choose this option, and Acrobat sizes the document so that only visible elements fit the width of the Document pane. If you choose this option, no margins will be visible.

- **Default** Choose this option, and Acrobat sizes the document according to the general preferences of the user.

5. In the Open To section, choose one of the following options:
   - **Page Number** Choose this option and in the text field, enter the number of the page you want visible when the document opens. If you enter an invalid page number, Acrobat displays a warning to that effect.
   - **Last Viewed Page** Choose this option, and the document opens to the last page viewed. This option is useful when you are creating an eBook because the document will open to the last page read by the user.
6. In the Window Options section, choose from the following options:
   - **Resize Window To Initial Page** Choose this option, and Acrobat resizes the Document pane to fit around the document.
   - **Center Window On Screen** Choose this option, and Acrobat opens the Document pane in the middle of the workspace.
   - **Open In Full Screen Mode** Choose this option, and the viewers see the initial page in Full Screen mode, without any toolbars, menu bars, or navigation tabs. Viewers will not be able to scroll a multipage document viewed in Full Screen mode; however, they can use the Page Down, Page Up, and arrow keys to navigate the document. If you choose Full Screen Mode and your document will be distributed to parties with limited Acrobat knowledge, it is a good idea to create an index or buttons that your viewers can use for navigation.
7. Click the triangle to the right of the Show field and choose one of the following options:
   - **File Name** Choose this option, and Acrobat displays the document filename in the application title bar.
   - **Document Title** Choose this option, and Acrobat displays the document title in the application title bar. If you did not specify a document title in the Description section of the Document Properties dialog box, the document filename and extension are displayed.

NOTE *You can select every option in the Window Options section. However, when options conflict, Acrobat applies the overriding option. For example, if you choose both Open In Full Screen Mode and Document Title, the document title is not visible because the application title bar is hidden in Full Screen viewing mode.*

8. In the User Interface Options section, choose any or all of the following options:
   - **Hide Menu Bar** When you choose this option, Acrobat opens the document with the menu bar hidden. Press F9 to unhide the menu bar.
   - **Hide Tool Bars** When you choose this option, Acrobat hides the toolbar when the document opens. If you do not choose the Hide Menu Bar option in conjunction with this option, the user can choose Window | Hide Tool Bars to unhide the toolbars or press F8.

- **Hide Window Controls** When you choose this option, Acrobat opens the document with the Navigation pane hidden.

NOTE *Even though it is possible for your viewers to reveal the menu bar and toolbars using keyboard shortcuts, many of your viewers may not know this. Therefore, you may want to consider including some navigation aids for your viewers if you hide either the menu or toolbars.*

9. Click OK to apply the options and close the dialog box.
10. Choose File | Save.

When you save the document, the new Initial View options are saved with it and will be applied the next time the document opens. Of course, a viewer with the full version of Acrobat can modify any of the changes you make to the document. To prevent viewers from tampering with your handiwork, change the security level of the document, as I describe in the following section.

Set Document Security

You add security to limit access to the document or prevent viewers from editing your document in the full version of Acrobat. You can use Acrobat Standard Security to password-protect confidential documents. When you password-protect a document, you set permissions for document accessibility; for example, you can prevent the document from being printed. Alternatively, you can choose to use Acrobat Certificate Security, which requires a user to log in. When you use Acrobat Certificate Security, you specify which users can access the document. Both forms of Acrobat security are covered in detail in Chapter 11.

se the Save As Command

You use the Acrobat Save As command to save the same document with different settings under another filename. Use this technique when you need to create different versions of the same document for different destinations—for example, to save a document optimized for print or to save a document optimized for a web page. To save the current PDF with a different filename, choose File | Save As to open the Save As Settings dialog box. Enter the new name for the document and click Save.

You can also use the Save As command to save the document in another format. This is known as *repurposing* content. After you save the file in another format, you can edit the resulting file in a program that supports that format.

ave PDF Files in Other Formats

When you open a document in Acrobat, you can save the file in PDF format, or you can repurpose the document into another format. After you repurpose a document, you can edit the contents in another program. For example, if you repurpose all of the text in a document by saving in *RTF*

(Rich Text Format), you can edit the text in any word processing program that supports the RTF format. Consult your word processing software documentation to see if RTF format is supported.

Save Text from a PDF File

Acrobat is a powerful program, but unless you have third-party plug-ins, you will not be able to edit wholesale portions of a document text. However, you can repurpose the document by saving all of the text in RTF format, as a Text file, or as a Microsoft Word file and then editing it in your favorite word processing program. If you use Microsoft Word for your word processing tasks, you can click one of the Adobe PDF buttons to export the edited text in PDF format. You can repurpose a PDF document as editable text by following these steps:

1. To save the text from a PDF file, choose File | Save As. Acrobat opens the Save As dialog box.
2. Name the document, click the triangle to the right of the Save As Type field, and choose Microsoft Word Document (*doc), Rich Text Format (*.rtf), Text (Accessible) (*.txt), or Text (Plain) (*.txt).
3. Click the Settings button to define parameters for the text option you choose. The settings vary depending on the file type you choose. The default options for each file type work well in most cases; however, you can modify the settings to suit the application in which you will be using the file. For example, you can have Acrobat generate images when the PDF document is repurposed or not.
4. Click Save to save the document to file.

Save PDF Files as Images

You can also repurpose PDF documents by saving them in image formats. You can save PDF documents in the following image formats: EPS, JPEG, JPEG2000, PNG, PS (PostScript), and TIFF. When you save a document in one of these image formats, you can modify the settings, which differ depending on the image format you use to save the file. The settings you choose determine parameters such as image compression, colorspace, and the resolution of the saved image.

Save as EPS

You can save a PDF file as an EPS for use in an illustration program such as Adobe Illustrator or Macromedia Freehand. When you save a file as EPS, you can modify the output settings to suit your needs. To save a PDF file in EPS format, follow these steps:

1. Choose File | Save As to open the Save As dialog box.
2. Choose Encapsulated PostScript from the Save As Type drop-down menu.

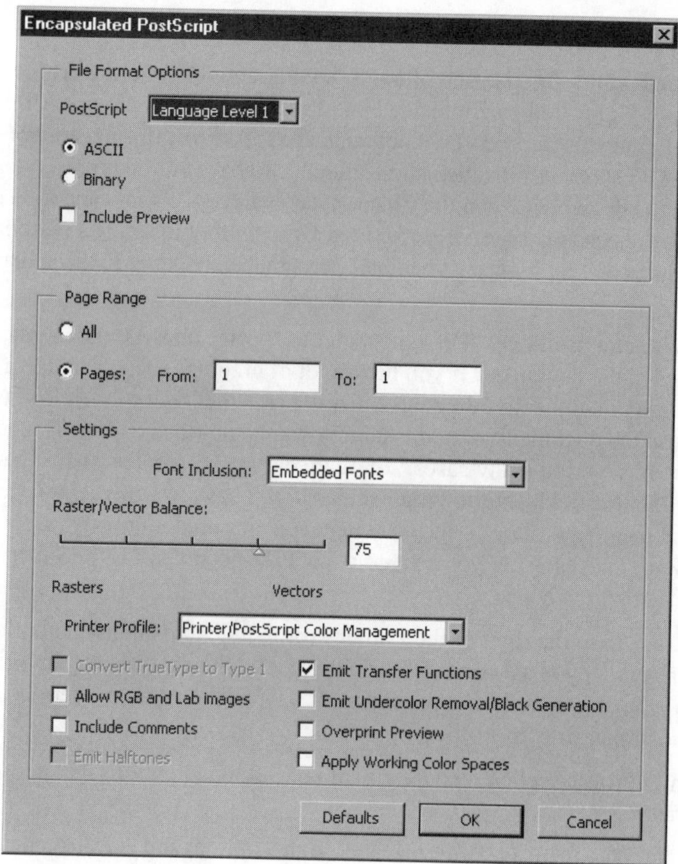

3. In the File Format Options section, choose from the following:
   - **PostScript** Choose one of the following from the drop-down menu: Language Level 1, Language Level 2, or Language Level 3.
   - **ASCII** Choose ASCII if you specified Language Level 1 PostScript.
   - **Binary** Choose this option if you specified Language Level 2 or Language Level 3 PostScript.
   - **Include Preview** Choose this option, and Acrobat exports a screen preview with the EPS file. If you do not choose this option, the preview will be displayed as a gray box when you open the file in another program. If you use the Windows version of Acrobat, you have one choice available: TIFF; with the Macintosh version, you can choose to generate a PICT or TIFF preview.
4. In the Page Range section, choose All to save all pages in the PDF file, or choose Pages and specify the range by entering values in the From and To fields.

5. In the Settings section, specify the following settings:
   - **Font Inclusion** Choose one of the following options from the drop-down menu: None, All Embedded, or Embedded and Reference. If you choose All Embedded, all fonts embedded in the PDF document are preserved. If fonts are not embedded in the PDF, choose Embedded and Reference to have Acrobat preserve the fonts used in the document when the file is saved as EPS. If a font cannot be distributed because of licensing issues, Acrobat uses a system font to create a reasonable facsimile of the document font you try to embed. Note that embedding fonts increases the size of the file.
   - **Raster/Vector Balance** Drag the slider to specify how Acrobat will compress the graphics in the document. If you have a lot of graphics such as logos or graphics with areas of solid color, drag the slider towards the Vector label; if you have lots of photos in the document; drag the slider towards the Raster label. The default setting of 80 works well in many cases. Alternatively, you can enter a value between 0 and 100 in the text field, entering high values if you have lots of vector type graphics in the document, low values if the document contains predominantly *raster* (also known as *bitmap*) images. After you convert a few PDF documents to EPS files, you'll know which setting to choose.
6. Click the triangle to the right of the Printer Profile field and choose an option from the drop-down menu. If you are unsure of which profile to choose, consult your printer manual; or if you are having the EPS file printed professionally, contact the service center support staff for the proper printer profile.
7. In the Printer Profile section, choose any of the following options that pertain to the file you are creating:
   - **Convert TrueType To Type 1** Choose this option, and Acrobat converts any True Type fonts in the document to Type 1 fonts. If there are no TrueType fonts in the PDF document, this option is dimmed out.
   - **Allow RGB And LAB Images** When you choose this option, Acrobat exports images in these color profiles as well as images with the CMYK color profile. If you neglect to include this option and there are images with these RGB or LAB color profiles, they are not included when the file is saved. This is especially important if your PDF documents will be printed by a service center. For more information on optimizing PDF documents for print, refer to Chapter 12.
   - **Include Comments** Choose this option, and any comments in the document are included when the document is saved as an EPS file. To open exported comments, the application you open the EPS file in must be capable of handling comments.
   - **Emit Halftones** If halftone screens are present in the PDF file, choosing this option keeps them intact when you save the file in EPS format. Halftones break an images into dots of solid colors that vary in size to give the illusion of blending colors. This option dims out if halftone screens are not present in the PDF file.
   - **Emit Transfer Functions** Choose this option, and if Transfer Functions are preserved in the PDF document, they will be exported with the EPS file.

- **Emit Undercolor Removal/Black Generation** If Undercolor Removal or Black Generation settings are included in the document's images, the settings are preserved when the document is converted to EPS format.
- **Overprint Preview** Choose this option, and if Overprint Previews are included in the PDF file, then they are included with the EPS file.
- **Apply Working Color Spaces** Choose this option, and ICC colors embedded in the PDF file are printed as Device colors. Device colors are derived from the printer's color profiles for grayscale colors, RGB (Red, Green, and Blue) colors, and CMYK (Cyan, Magenta, Yellow, and BlacK) colors.

8. Click OK to close the Encapsulated PostScript dialog box.
9. Navigate to the folder where you want the file saved, name the file, and click OK.

TIP *You can choose File | Save As and then choose one of the HTML or XML formats to save a PDF document as an HTML or XML file for use at your web site. For additional information, refer to Chapter 13.*

Save as JPEG

When you save a PDF file as a JPEG, you can specify the amount of compression applied to the image. JPEG is a "lossy" format; when the image is compressed, certain color information is *lost* to create a smaller file size. Image degradation occurs at high levels of compression. To save a PDF file as a JPEG, follow these steps:

1. Choose File | Save As to open the Save As dialog box.
2. Choose the JPEG Files option from the Save As Type drop-down menu.
3. Click Settings to open the Save As JPEG Settings dialog box, as shown here:

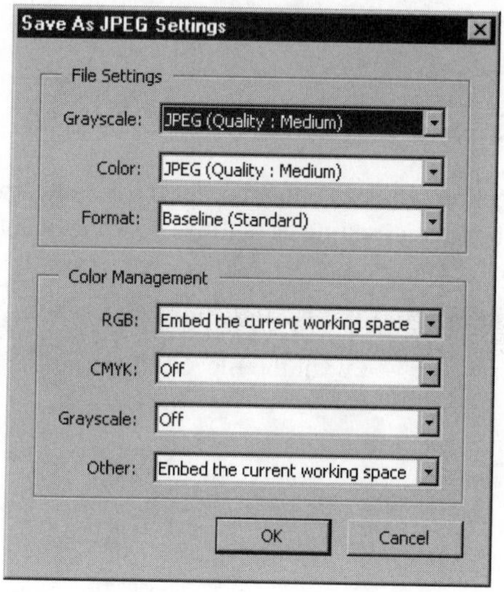

4. In the File Settings section, you can either accept the defaults (which work well in most instances) or choose a different setting, as outlined previously in the "Choose Compression and Color Management Settings for Image Files" section of this chapter.
5. Click OK to close the Save As JPEG Settings dialog box.
6. Navigate to the folder where you want the file saved, name the file, and click OK.

Save as JPEG2000

You can save PDF documents in the new JPEG2000 format and take advantage of the format's progressive loading feature and superior compression. To save a PDF document as a JPEG2000 image, follow these steps:

1. Choose File | Save As to open the Save As dialog box.
2. Choose the JPEG2000 option from the Save As Type drop-down menu.
3. Click Settings to open the Save As JPEG2000 Settings dialog box, as shown here:

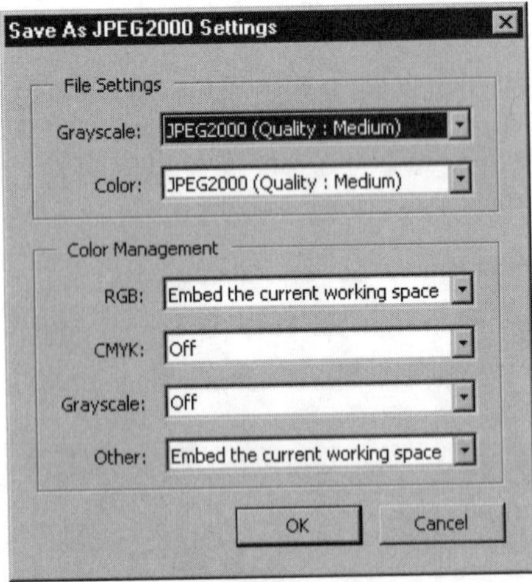

4. In the File Settings section, you can either accept the defaults (which work well in most instances), or choose a different setting as outlined previously in the "Choose Compression and Color Management Settings for Image Files" section of this chapter.
5. Click OK to close the Save As JPEG2000 Settings dialog box.
6. Navigate to the folder where you want the file saved, name the file, and click Save.

Save as Microsoft Word Document

You can save PDF documents in the Microsoft Word .DOC format. You can embed images with the document as well as comments. This option is handy when you have a PDF document that contains a lot of text you need to edit. After you edit the document in Microsoft Word, you can use the PDFMaker to convert the document back to a PDF file. To save a PDF document as a Microsoft Word file, follow these steps:

1. Choose File | Save As to open the Save As dialog box.
2. Choose the Microsoft Word Document option from the Save As Type drop-down menu.
3. Click Settings to open the Save As DOC Settings dialog box, as shown here:

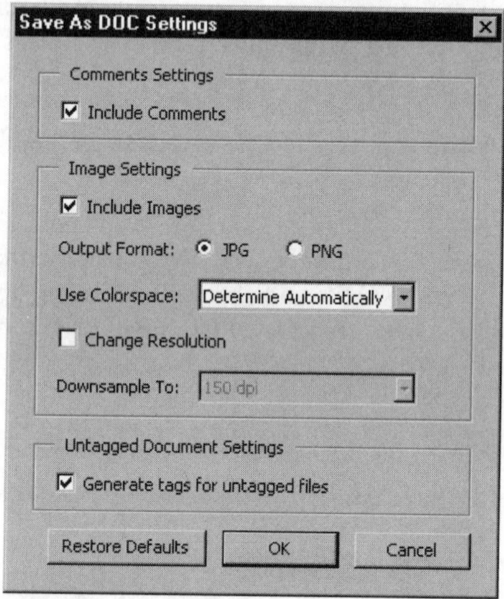

4. In the Comments Settings section, choose Include Comments (selected by default) to include any comments in the PDF document with the converted Word file.
5. In the Image Settings section, choose from the following options:
   - **Include Images** This option is selected by default. If you deselect the option, the resulting Word file will be text only.
   - **Output Format** If you select the default Include Images option, you can specify whether to save the images in the JPG or PNG format.

- **Use Colorspace** Click the triangle to the right of this field and choose one of the following options:
  - **Determine Automatically** Acrobat chooses the proper colorspace.
  - **Grayscale** Images are saved as 8-bit grayscale images in the specified output format.
  - **Color** Images are saved as 24-bit color images in the specified output format.

6. In the Image Settings section, click the Change Resolution check box if you want to resample images from the Acrobat default. After choosing this option, the Downsample To field becomes active and you can choose one of the following resolutions from the drop down menu: 72 DPI, 96 DPI, 150 DPI, or 300 DPI.
7. In the Untagged Document Settings section, select Generate Tags For Untagged Files (selected by default), and Acrobat creates tags if the PDF file has none.
8. Click OK to close the Save As DOC Settings dialog box.
9. Navigate to the folder where you want the file saved, name the file, and click Save.

Save as PNG

You can save PDF documents in the PNG (pronounced *ping*) image format. When you choose this file format, you can interlace the PNG file and choose the filtering option that supports the device where the PNG file will be viewed. To save a PDF file in PNG format, follow these steps:

1. Choose File | Save As to open the Save As dialog box.
2. Choose the PNG Files option from the Save As Type drop-down menu.
3. Click Settings to open the Save As PNG Settings dialog box, as shown here:

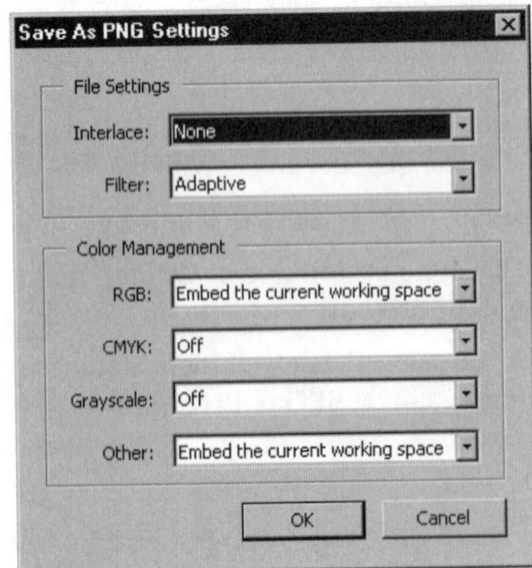

4. Click the triangle to the right of the Interlace field and choose either None (the default) or Adam7. When you choose Adam7 interlacing, the result is similar to an Interlaced GIF image that loads into a viewer's Web browser in stages.
5. Click the triangle to the right of the Filter field and choose a filtering option from the drop-down menu. You generally get good results with Adaptive (the default). However, you may achieve better results with one of the other filtering options. The old trial-and-error method works best here. Save the file using a different filename for each filtering option and compare the results onscreen to determine which works best for the PDF file you want to save.
6. Click the triangle to the right of one of the Color Management fields and choose an option. You have the same Colorspace choices as in the conversion settings previously discussed.
7. Click OK to close the Save As PNG Settings dialog box and apply the settings.
8. Navigate to the folder where you want the filed saved, name the file, and click Save.

Save as PostScript

Converting a PDF file to *PostScript* (PS) format is like printing a PS file to disk from an illustration program. After you save a file as PS, you can use Acrobat Distiller to save the file with optimized settings for a specific destination, such as a web site or multimedia production. To save a PDF file as PS:

1. Choose File | Save As to open the Save As dialog box.
2. Choose PostScript from the Save As Type drop-down menu.
3. Click Settings to open the PostScript dialog box. The file format settings for PS are identical to those for EPS with the exception of Include Preview, which is not a PS option. Refer to the "Save as EPS" section earlier in this chapter for detailed information on available options and their settings.

Save as TIFF

When you save a PDF document in *TIFF* (Tagged Image File Format) format, Acrobat creates a file that is recognized by most image-editing programs. When you save a PDF as a TIFF image, you can specify monochrome and color compression, as well as resolution. To save a PDF document as a TIFF image, follow these steps:

1. Choose File | Save As to open the Save As dialog box.
2. Choose the TIFF Files option from the Save As Type drop-down menu.

3. Click Settings to open the Save As TIFF Settings dialog box, as shown here:

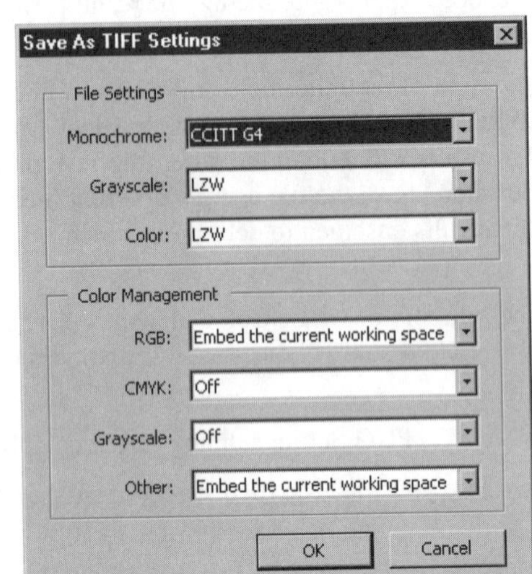

4. Click the triangle to the right of the Monochrome Compression field and choose a compression method from the drop-down menu. The default (CCITT G4) performs well in most instances.
5. Click the triangle to the right of the Grayscale and Color fields and from the drop-down menus choose a compression option. The default (LZW) compression method is widely used by printers and achieves excellent results.

You can tweak TIFF compression settings by saving the file with a different filename for each compression method. Compare the results onscreen to see which method yields the best results for the PDF document you are working with.

6. In the Color Management section, choose the settings that apply to the document you are converting to a TIFF file. These are the same settings discussed previously in the "Choose Compression and Color Management Settings for Image Files" section of this chapter.

Create PDF Files with Acrobat Distiller

In previous sections of this chapter, you learned to create PDF documents by converting supported file formats into PDF documents and then saving the files from within Acrobat. You can also use Acrobat Distiller to create PDF files. Acrobat Distiller is a separate program, but you can launch Acrobat Distiller from within Acrobat. When you install Acrobat, Acrobat Distiller is also added as a system printer under the moniker of Adobe PDF, which gives you the capability of printing a PDF file directly from within any application that supports printing. Printing from an authoring application is covered in Chapter 5.

Use Acrobat Distiller

Acrobat Distiller is a separate program that you use to convert EPS and PS files into PDF documents. With Acrobat Distiller, you have preset options available to optimize the file for an intended destination. Optimize a PDF document for a destination by choosing a specific setting. The Acrobat Distiller interface is shown in Figure 4-3.

As you can see, there is really not much of an interface at all—just a few menu options, an information section, and a progress section. To create a PDF file using Acrobat Distiller, follow these steps:

1. Launch the program by choosing Acrobat Distiller from your operating system program menu. Alternatively, you can launch Acrobat Distiller from within Acrobat by choosing Advanced | Acrobat Distiller, or by double-clicking the Acrobat Distiller desktop shortcut if available.
2. Click the triangle to the right of the Default Settings field and from the drop-down menu, choose the option that best suites the intended destination of the document. Choose from the following:
   - **High Quality** Choose this option when creating files that require higher image quality and will be printed.

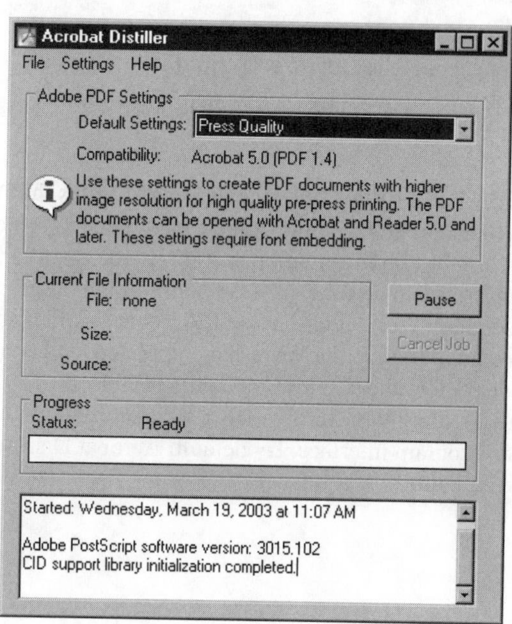

FIGURE 4-3 Create PDF documents from EPS and PS files using Acrobat Distiller.

- **Press Quality** Choose this option when you need the highest quality images in your files. This option is the way to go if you print your files on a high-end printer with PS capabilities. When you choose this format, minimum compression is applied to images.
- **Smallest File Size** Choose this option to create the smallest possible file size at the expense of image quality when the resulting PDF document will be distributed via e-mail or viewed on the Internet.
- **Standard** Choose this option when you create a PDF file for distribution across your corporate intranet or via CD-ROM for colleagues.
- **PDFX/1a (Professional only)** Choose this option to create a PDF document that supports only the CMYK color model and spot processing. This option is applicable if the PDF file will be printed on a specific device, such as a Web offset printer.
- **PDFX/3 (Professional only)** Choose this option to create a PDF document that enables a printing device that supports color management. This controls the document colors while printing, as well as CMYK and spot processing.

NOTE *You can modify a PDF setting to suit the intended destination for the document you distill. Modifying settings are discussed in detail in Chapter 12.*

3. To apply security to the distilled PDF file, choose Settings | Security. For more information about Acrobat security settings, refer to the "Set Document Security" section, presented earlier in this chapter.
4. Choose File | Open to access the Open PostScript File dialog box.
5. Navigate to the PS file you want to convert to PDF format, create a name for the file, and click Open.

After you click Open, Acrobat Distiller takes the reins and creates the PDF file. The Acrobat Distiller icon, which looks like a propeller, spins as the file is created. You can view information about the document in the Current File Information section. If you distill a large multipage PS file, the distilling process may take some time. You can monitor the progress by viewing the Status bar in the Progress section. As the file is created, Acrobat Distiller shows you which page is being printed, the percentage of the job that has been completed, and a visual reference in the form of a blue bar that moves across the window as the file is created.

After completion of the distilling job, Acrobat Distiller creates a report that appears in the window at the bottom of the program interface. By default, Acrobat Distiller also creates a job log that you can view in a text editor.

Set Distiller Preferences

When you use Acrobat Distiller, it seems like a straightforward process, and it is: choose a setting, load a file, and Acrobat Distiller does the rest for you. The real power of Distiller is in the number of settings parameters you can modify, and you learn how to do this in Chapter 12. You can also modify Acrobat Distiller to suit your working preference by doing the following:

1. Launch Acrobat Distiller.
2. Choose File | Preferences to open the Preferences dialog box, as shown here:

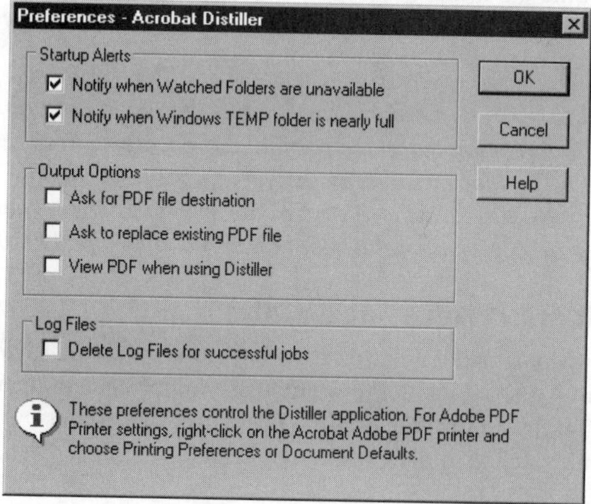

3. In the Startup Alerts section, you can modify the following options:
   - **Notify When Watched Folders Are Unavailable** When you choose this option (the default), Distiller as shipped with Acrobat Professional has the capability of monitoring a folder or directory on your computer. Distiller automatically distills PS files placed in watched folders. You learn how to create watched folders in the following section, "Create Watched Folders."
   - **Notify When Windows TEMP folder Is Nearly Full** Distiller needs to write temporary files to disk when creating a PDF file. Choose this option, and Distiller warns you when the startup volume is less than 1 MB.
4. In the Output Options section, you can modify the following:
   - **Ask For PDF File Destination (Windows only)** When you enable this option, Distiller prompts you for a folder to save the converted PDF file in. When this option is disabled (the default), the converted PDF file is stored in the same location as the PS file.

- **Ask To Replace Existing PDF File (Windows only)** This option is enabled by default and will prompt you when you try to overwrite an existing file. If you enable the Ask For PDF File Destination, this option is unavailable.
- **View PDF When Using Distiller (Windows only)** When you enable this option, upon completion of the distilling job, the default Acrobat viewer launches and the converted PDF file displays.

5. In the Log Files section you have one option available:
   - **Delete Log Files For Successful Jobs** Choose this option, and Distiller deletes the log file of the job if the file is successfully distilled. A *distiller log file* is a text file that is created during the distilling process. A log file is created and records any distilling errors, even if a PDF file is not created.

NOTE *Macintosh Acrobat users do not have the same Preferences options as their Windows counterparts. As noted in the section above, several Preferences options are Windows only. The Macintosh menu, however, does have an option not available to Windows users: Restart Distiller After PostScript Fatal Error. When this option is enabled, Distiller automatically relaunches after encountering a fatal PostScript error.*

Create Watched Folders (Professional Only)

If you own Acrobat Professional and regularly create PostScript files and save them to certain folders, you can configure Acrobat Distiller to watch these folders and automatically convert PostScript files to PDF files, plus move the original PostScript files to the Out folder or delete them. If you create several watched folders, each folder can have unique Distiller settings.

NOTE *If you work in a corporate environment where several authors create PostScript files, you cannot save them to watched folders on a network server. Set up a watched folder on your workstation for converting your own files. Other authors who need to convert PostScript files to PDFs must set up a watched folder at their workstations using a licensed version of Acrobat.*

To create a watched folder, follow these steps:

1. Launch Acrobat Distiller and choose Settings | Watched Folders to open the Watched Folders dialog box, as shown in the following illustration. Note that a file has already been added to the folder.

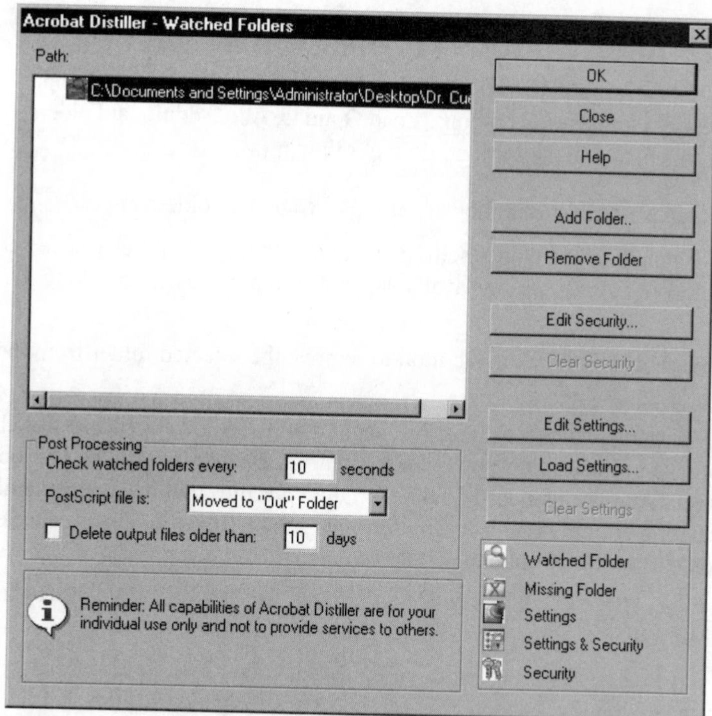

2. Click Add Folder to open the Browse For Folder dialog box.
3. Navigate to the folder you want Distiller to watch, select the folder, click OK, and the selected folder is added to the watched folders list. After you add the folder, Distiller automatically creates an In and an Out folder within the watched folder.
4. In the Checked Watch Folders Every ___ Seconds field, enter a value between 1 and 1,000 seconds. This value specifies how often Distiller checks a watched folder.
5. Click the triangle to the right of the PostScript File Is field and choose an option to determine whether the converted PostScript file is moved to the Out folder or deleted.
6. Click the Delete Output Files Older Than ___ days check box and enter a value between 1 and 999 in the text field. Distiller uses this value to determine when to delete PostScript files in the Out folder.
7. After you add a folder to the watched folders list, you can click OK to close the dialog box or click Add Folder to add additional folders to the list.

Set Watched Folder Options (Professional Only)

After you add one or several folders to the watched folders list, you can specify options for each folder, namely: Security Options, Job Options, Load Options, Add Additional Folders, or Remove Folders. To set options for a watched folder, do the following:

1. Launch Acrobat Distiller and choose Settings | Watched Folders.
2. Select the watched folder whose settings you want to modify. After you select a watched folder, additional buttons become available, as shown previously, for setting the following options:
   - **Remove Folder** Click this button to remove the selected folder from the watched folders list.
   - **Edit Security** Click this button to set and edit security for files distilled from the watched folder. After you click this button, the Security dialog box opens. You can apply Acrobat Standard Security to the PDF files that have been distilled. For information on individual security settings, refer to the "Set Document Security" section earlier in this chapter.
   - **Clear Security** Click this button to remove security for files distilled from the watched folder.
   - **Edit Settings** Click this button to open the Adobe PDF Settings dialog box. After the dialog box is open, you can specify settings for all files distilled within the selected folder. You can find information for the options in this dialog box in Chapter 12.
   - **Load Settings** Click this button to open the Load Adobe PDF Settings dialog box. Navigate to the folder that contains the settings file you want to load and click Open. Adobe PDF settings files have the. joboptions extension. For more information on creating custom settings, refer to Chapter 12.

TIP *If you create PS files for distillation into PDF files with different destinations, you can copy PS files to different watched folders and apply different job options to each watched folder. For example, you might create one folder for PDF files for the Internet and another for PDF files that will be printed. Apply the appropriate Adobe PDF settings to each folder, and Distiller takes care of the rest.*

   - **Clear Settings** This button becomes available after you specify job options for files distilled from this folder. Click the button to clear Adobe PDF settings applied to the PostScript files being distilled from this folder.
3. Click OK to apply the new settings and close the Watched Folders dialog box.

Summary

In this chapter, you learned to create PDF files from within Acrobat. You learned how to create PDF documents from single files and multiple files. You also learned how to save PDF documents in other file formats. In the latter part of the chapter, you learned to use the Acrobat Distiller to create PDF documents from PostScript files. In the next chapter, you'll learn to create PDF documents from within authoring applications such as Microsoft Word.

Chapter 5

Create PDF Documents in Authoring Applications

How to…

- Convert Microsoft Office documents to PDFs
- Set document conversion properties
- Convert using the Print command
- Convert document to PDF and then e-mail

As discussed in Chapter 4, you can use Acrobat to convert supported file types into PDF documents from within Acrobat. You can also create PDF files from within authoring applications. When you create a file in any application that supports printing devices, you can create a PDF file using the application Print command. Other software, such as FreeHand and CorelDraw, supports PDF exporting. You can also create PDF files from within Adobe graphics applications. Adobe offers extensive PDF support with many of their image-editing, illustration, and page-layout applications. Adobe has also teamed with Microsoft to create a plug-in that you use to create PDF files from within Microsoft Office applications.

When you create a PDF file from within an authoring application, you gain many benefits. Primarily, you can save the original version of the file in its native format, which makes it available for future editing when needed. Secondly, you can export the file in PDF format without leaving the host application. If you have several documents to create and convert to PDF format, this is a tremendous time saver. You can also export several PDF files from the original document, each optimized for a different destination.

Create PDF Files from Microsoft Office Software

When you install Acrobat, the install utility searches your machine for Microsoft Office applications. When a supported Microsoft Office application is found, Acrobat installs PDFMaker as a helper utility. With PDFMaker, you can create a PDF file that looks identical to the Microsoft Office file by clicking a Convert to Adobe PDF icon that is added to your Microsoft Office program when Acrobat is installed. If you prefer more control of the process, you can also modify the conversion settings to optimize a PDF file for its intended destination.

You can use PDFMaker to create PDF files from within the following Microsoft Office Applications:

- **Word 97, 2000, and XP** Use PDFMaker to convert documents you create with Word to PDF files. The resulting PDF file retains font information, embedded graphics, and header and footer attributes.
- **Excel 97, 2000, and XP** Use PDFMaker to convert an Excel spreadsheet to PDF format. The converted PDF file retains column formatting as well as column and row headers and embedded graphics.
- **PowerPoint 97, 2000, and XP** Convert PowerPoint presentations to PDF files and add additional functionality to the presentation with many features of Acrobat.

- **Project (Professional Only)** Convert Microsoft Project documents to PDF files. The converted file can be sent to other colleagues who don't have Microsoft Project but need to be privy to the information within the original document.
- **Visio (Professional Only)** Convert Microsoft Visio documents to PDF files. You can share the converted file with other colleagues who do not have Microsoft Visio installed on their computers.

The PDFMaker in all supported Microsoft Office applications is for all intents and purposes identical with the exception of the options available when modifying conversion settings. The next section covers all the major features of PDFMaker and shows you how to use it to convert documents to PDF format (with examples from Microsoft Word 2000).

Create PDF Files from Microsoft Word Files

When the installer finds a supported application, as previously mentioned, three icons and a menu group are added to the application toolbar. You use the icons shown in Figure 5-1 to convert a document to PDF format, to convert a document to PDF format and e-mail it, or to convert a document to PDF format and initialize a review. The Adobe PDF menu group contains commands that duplicate the button tasks and change PDF conversion settings.

Convert Word Files to PDF Files

When you create a document in Word, you can apply styles to the document. When you convert the Word document to PDF format, Acrobat uses these Word styles to create corresponding bookmarks in the PDF document. The Acrobat default setting uses Heading styles to create bookmarks; however, if desired, you can change the conversion settings to include other styles that exist in the Word document. When you convert the Word file to a PDF file, the resulting file retains the formatting and font information, as well as any graphics you may have embedded in the Word file.

The easiest way to convert a Word file to a PDF file is by using the Convert to Adobe PDF button. You can also use a menu command to achieve the same result. To convert a Word file to PDF file, do the following:

1. Click the Convert to Adobe PDF button, as shown in Figure 5-1. Alternatively, choose AdobePDF | Convert to Adobe PDF.

   If you have not saved the Word document, PDFMaker displays the Acrobat PDFMaker dialog box, as shown in the following illustration. Click Yes, and the Save PDF File As dialog box opens. Click No, and PDFMaker stops the conversion process.

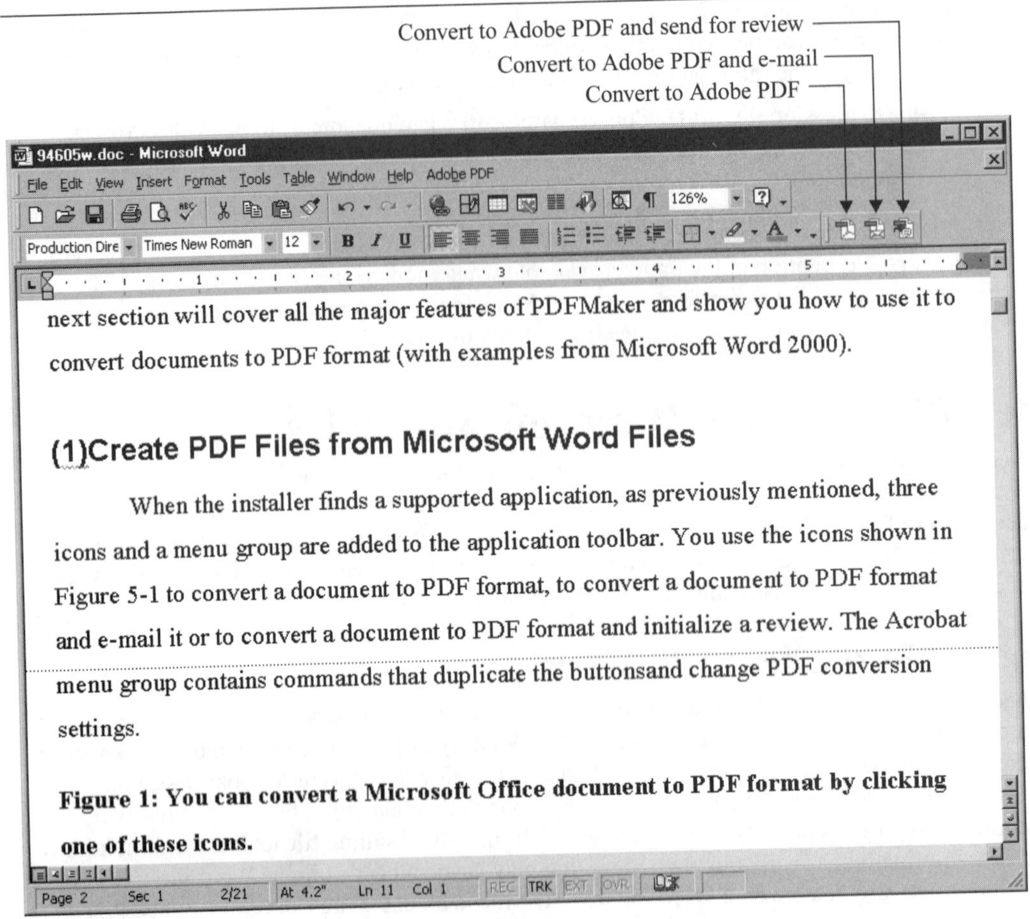
Convert to Adobe PDF and send for review
Convert to Adobe PDF and e-mail
Convert to Adobe PDF
94605w.doc - Microsoft Word
File Edit View Insert Format Tools Table Window Help Adobe PDF
126%
Production Dire
Times New Roman
12
next section will cover all the major features of PDFMaker and show you how to use it to convert documents to PDF format (with examples from Microsoft Word 2000).
(1)Create PDF Files from Microsoft Word Files
When the installer finds a supported application, as previously mentioned, three icons and a menu group are added to the application toolbar. You use the icons shown in Figure 5-1 to convert a document to PDF format, to convert a document to PDF format and e-mail it or to convert a document to PDF format and initialize a review. The Acrobat menu group contains commands that duplicate the buttonsand change PDF conversion settings.
Figure 1: You can convert a Microsoft Office document to PDF format by clicking one of these icons.
Page 2
Sec 1
2/21
At 4.2"
Ln 11
Col 1
REC
TRK
EXT
OVR

FIGURE 5-1 You can convert a Microsoft Office document to PDF format by clicking one of these icons.

2. In the Save PDF File As dialog box, accept the default name (the Word filename) and location (the directory the Word file is saved in), or specify a document name and directory.
3. Click Save to complete the conversion.

After you convert the document to PDF format, you can modify it in Acrobat. You can add interactive elements, such as links to external web sites, or add comments, annotations, or multimedia elements to the document. Figure 5-2 shows a PDF file in Acrobat that was converted from a Word document. Notice the bookmarks. PDFMaker created them using Word Heading styles. You learn how to change conversion settings later, in the "Change Conversion Settings" section of this chapter.

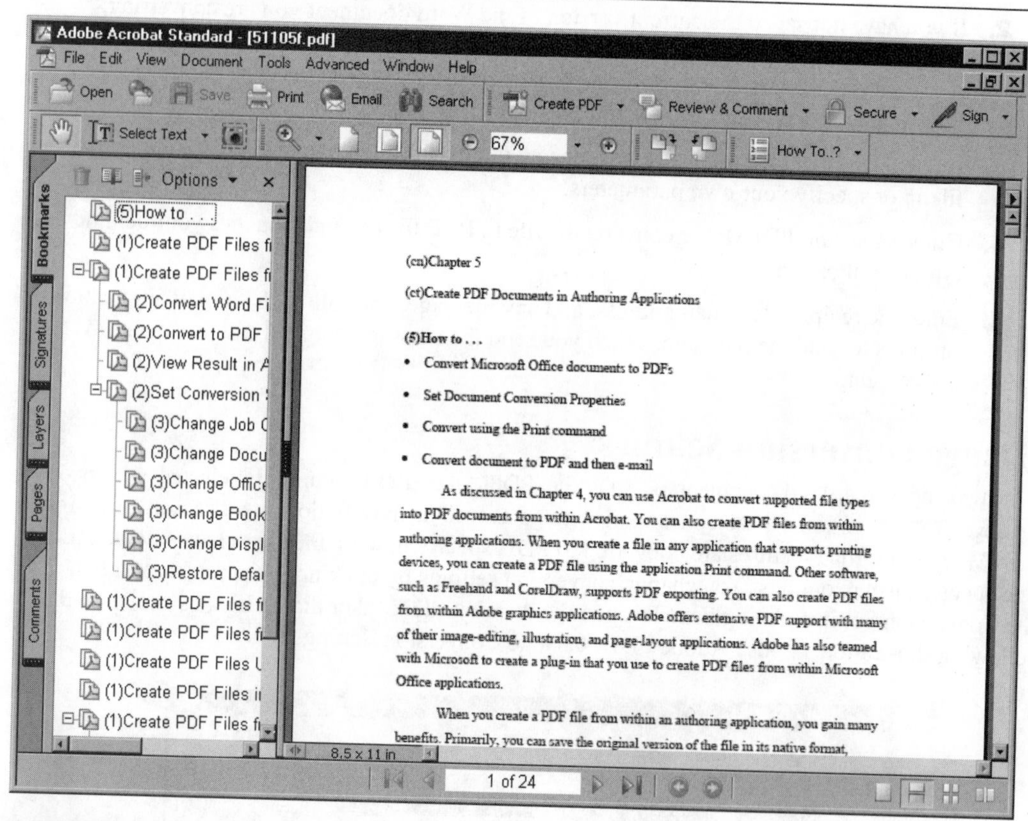

FIGURE 5-2 Use the PDFMaker to convert files from supported Microsoft Office applications to PDFs.

OTE *There is also a command and button that convert a document to PDF format and send it for review. Reviewing PDF documents will be covered in Chapter 10.*

Convert to PDF and Then E-Mail

Thanks to the Internet and e-mail, it is now possible to efficiently conduct business with faraway clients. Whether you are a one-person entrepreneurship or work in a large organization, you can convert a Word document to a PDF file and then e-mail it to a client or coworker. To convert a Word document to a PDF file and e-mail it, follow these steps:

1. Click the Convert to Adobe PDF and Email button, as shown previously in Figure 5-1. Alternatively, choose Adobe PDF | Convert to Adobe PDF and EMail.

2. If you have not saved the current version of the Word document you are converting, PDFMaker displays the Acrobat PDFMaker dialog box, as shown in the preceding section. Click Yes to save the current version of the Word file and open the Save PDF File As dialog box. Click No to stop the conversion process.
3. In the Save PDF File As dialog box, accept the default filename and location to save the file in or specify your own parameters.
4. Click Save, and PDFMaker converts the file to PDF format and launches your default e-mail application.
5. Enter the recipient's e-mail address, add any message, and follow the e-mail application prompts to send the message. When you send the message, the PDF file is sent as an attachment.

Change Conversion Settings

When you convert a Word document to a PDF file, PDFMaker uses the currently selected conversion settings. You can modify these conversion settings as well as modify document security, specify how Microsoft Office features are converted to PDF, specify how PDFMaker creates bookmarks, and specify display options. You change conversion settings by clicking the appropriate tab in the Conversion Settings dialog box. To open the Acrobat PDFMaker dialog box, as shown in the following illustration, choose Adobe PDF | Change Conversion Settings:

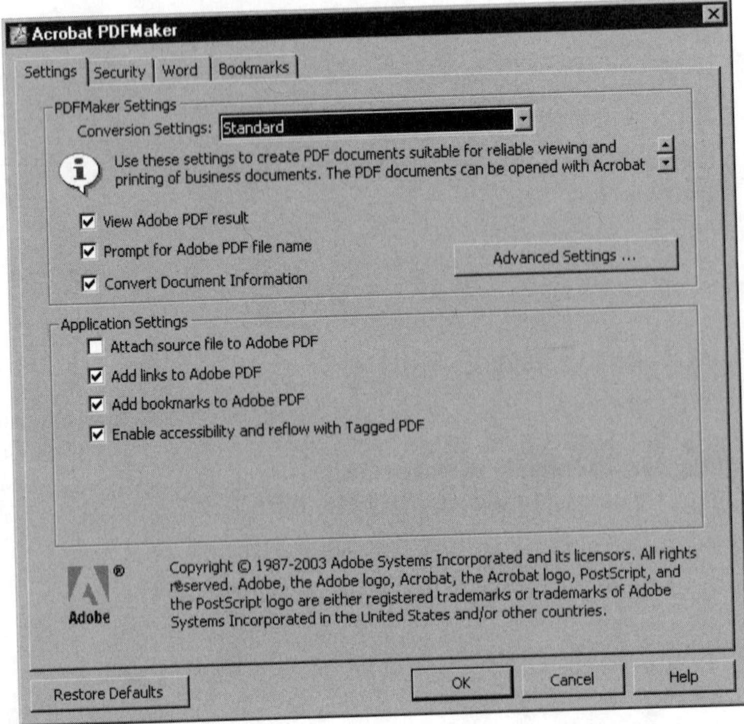

When you first open the Conversion Settings dialog box, the Settings tab is active, as just shown. In this section, you'll choose the setting that is the closest match for the intended destination of the PDF file, which you can then modify by following these steps:

1. Click the triangle to the right of the Settings field and choose one of the preset options (High Quality, Press Quality, Smallest File Size, Standard, XPDF1a [Professional Only] or XPDF3 [Professional Only]) or any custom conversion settings you created. These options are the same as the Distiller Job Options discussed in Chapter 4. To apply the new settings, click OK. To modify additional conversion settings, click the appropriate tab and modify the parameters to suit the intended destination of your document.
2. In the Conversion Settings section, the following options are selected by default:
   - **View PDF Result** This default option opens the document in Acrobat after the conversion process is completed.
   - **Prompt For Adobe PDF Filename** This default option prompts you for a filename before the document is converted to a PDF file. If you deselect this option, the resulting PDF file adopts the filename of the Microsoft Office document you are converting.
   - **Convert Document Information** This default option converts information from the Microsoft Office Properties dialog box into PDF Document Properties.
3. In the Applications Settings section, you can choose the following options:
   - **Attach Source File To PDF** This option attaches the source file to the converted PDF document; the file is signified by a file attachment icon in the upper-left corner of the PDF document. Viewers can open the source file by double-clicking the icon.
   - **Add Links To Adobe PDF** This default option preserves any links present in the Microsoft Office file. The links in the converted PDF file maintain a similar appearance to those found in the original file.
   - **Add Bookmarks To Adobe PDF** This default option uses headings or styles from the Microsoft Office document to create bookmarks in the PDF document. You can specify which styles are converted to bookmarks in the Bookmarks tab of the Adobe PDFMaker dialog box.
   - **Enable Accessibility And Reflow With Tagged PDF** This default option creates tags (objects that reference document structure objects such as images and text objects) in the PDF document based on the structure of the source Microsoft Office file. This structure can be used to reflow a document when viewed on different devices.
4. Click OK to apply the settings. Alternatively, click a different tab to modify additional settings.

OTE

You can create custom conversion settings by clicking Advanced Settings. After you click this button, PDFMaker opens the Adobe PDF Settings dialog box. For more information on creating a custom settings file, refer to Chapter 12.

5

Change Document Security Settings

When you convert a Word file to PDF format, you can specify document security from within Microsoft Word. You can assign a password to the converted file and limit permissions. Do the following to set document security:

1. Open the Acrobat PDFMaker dialog box as outlined previously.
2. Click the Security tab to reveal the security settings, as shown here:

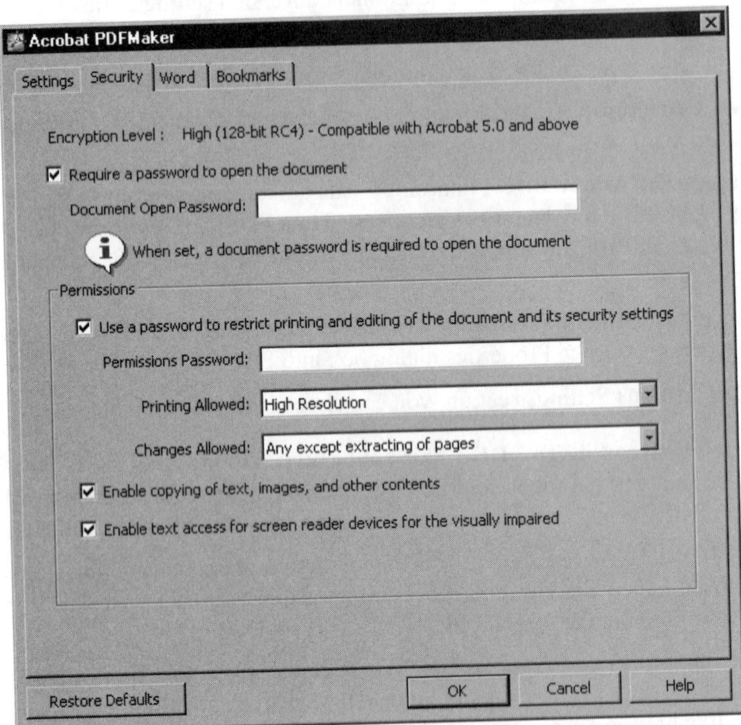

3. To assign a password to the PDF file, choose the Require A Password To Open The Document option. When you choose this option, the User Password field becomes active.
4. If you choose the Require A Password To Open The Document option, enter the password in the Document Open Password field.
5. To assign a master password to the PDF file, choose the Use A Password To Restrict Printing And Editing Of The Document And Its Security Settings option. When you choose this option, the Permissions Password field becomes available.
6. If you require a password to change permissions, enter the password in the Permissions Password field.
7. Click the triangle to the right of the Printing Allowed field and choose one of the following options:

- **Not Allowed** Choose this option, and users will not be able to print the document.
- **Low Resolution (150 DPI)** Choose this option, and users will be able to print a low-resolution copy of the PDF document.
- **High Resolution** Choose this option, and users will be able to print the document at high resolution.

8. Click the triangle to the right of the Changes Allowed field and choose one of the following options:
   - **None** Choose this option, and users with Acrobat 6.0 Standard or Professional will not be able to edit the document.
   - **Inserting, Deleting, And Rotating Of Pages** Choose this option, and viewers with Acrobat 6.0 Standard or Professional will be able to insert, delete, and rotate pages.
   - **Filling In Of Form Fields And Signing** Choose this option, and viewers with Acrobat 6.0 Standard or Professional will be able to fill in form fields and digitally sign the document. Adobe Reader 6.0 users will be able to fill in only the form fields.
   - **Commenting, Filling In Of Form Fields, And Signing** Choose this option, and viewers with Acrobat 6.0 Standard or Professional will be able to add comments to the document as well as fill in form fields and digitally sign the document.
   - **Any Except Extracting Of Pages** Choose this option, and viewers with Acrobat 6.0 Standard or Professional will be able to perform any editing with the exception of extracting pages from the PDF document.
9. The Copying Of Text, Images, And Other Contents option is selected by default. If you deselect the option, viewers will not be able to copy text, images, or other contents of the document.
10. The Enable Text Access For Screen Reader Devices For The Visually Impaired option is selected by default. If you deselect this option, visually impaired readers will not be able to access text with their screen readers.

NOTE *When you add security to a document, the document can be viewed only with Acrobat 5.0 (PDF 1.4) or newer. For more information on modifying document security settings, refer to Chapter 11.*

11. To apply the security settings, click OK. To modify additional settings, click the appropriate tab and modify the parameters as desired.

NOTE *Whether you assign a document password, a permissions password, or both, you will be prompted to verify the password(s) before the new settings are accepted.*

Change Word Settings

The settings you modify in this section determine how PDFMaker converts Office features and Word features. The actual wording of this tab varies depending on the program for which you are modifying conversion settings. For example, there is no tab for these settings in Microsoft Excel or Microsoft PowerPoint. To change Microsoft Word settings, do the following:

1. Open the Acrobat PDFMaker dialog box as outlined previously.
2. Click the Word tab to reveal the settings illustrated here:

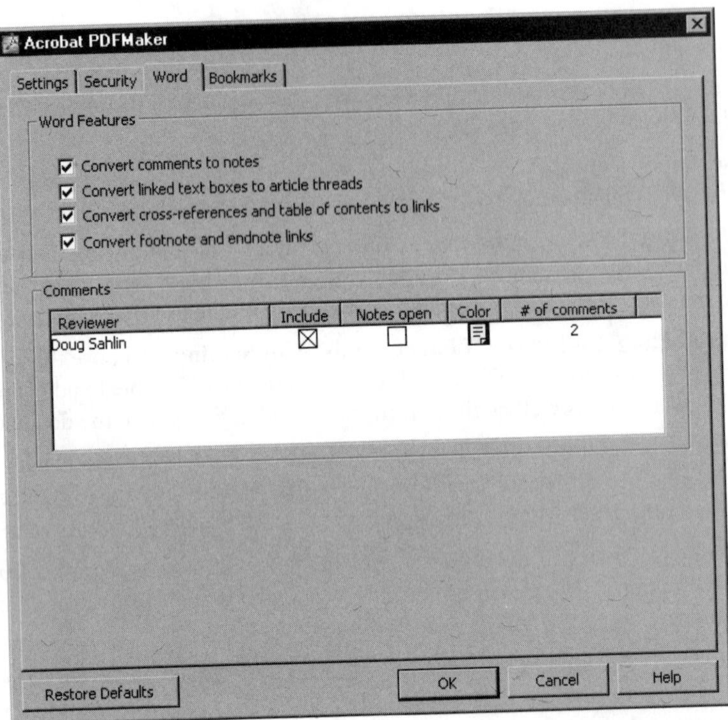

3. In the Word Features section, you can modify the following settings:
   - **Convert Comments To Notes** Choose this option (the default), and Word document comments are converted to notes in the resulting PDF document. If you choose this option, any comments in the document appear in the Comments window, as shown previously. Comments are segregated by reviewer, and the number of comments entered by the reviewer is noted in the # of Comments column.
   - **Convert Linked Text Boxes To Article Threads** Choose this option (the default), and linked text boxes are converted to article threads in the resulting PDF file.
   - **Convert Cross-References And Table Of Contents To Links** Choose this option (the default) to convert document cross-references and table of contents items into links to their destinations in the converted PDF document.
   - **Convert Footnote And Endnote Links** Choose this option to preserve endnote and footnote links in the converted PDF document.

4. If you choose to convert comments to notes, in the Comments window, you can perform the following tasks:
   - Click the check box in a reviewer's Include column to include the comment in the PDF file or not.
   - Click the check box in a reviewer's Notes Open column to have the note open when the page the note appears on opens, or not.
   - Click the icon in a reviewer's Color column to select a color for the note. Each time you click the icon, it changes to a different color. You can choose different colors for other reviewer's comments in the document.
5. To apply the Word settings, click OK. To modify additional settings, click the appropriate tab and modify the parameters as desired.

Change Bookmark Settings

The settings you modify in this section determine which Word text styles PDFMaker converts to bookmarks. To change bookmark settings for the document conversion, do the following:

1. Open the Adobe PDFMaker dialog box as outlined in previous sections.
2. Click the Bookmarks tab and modify the settings, as shown here:

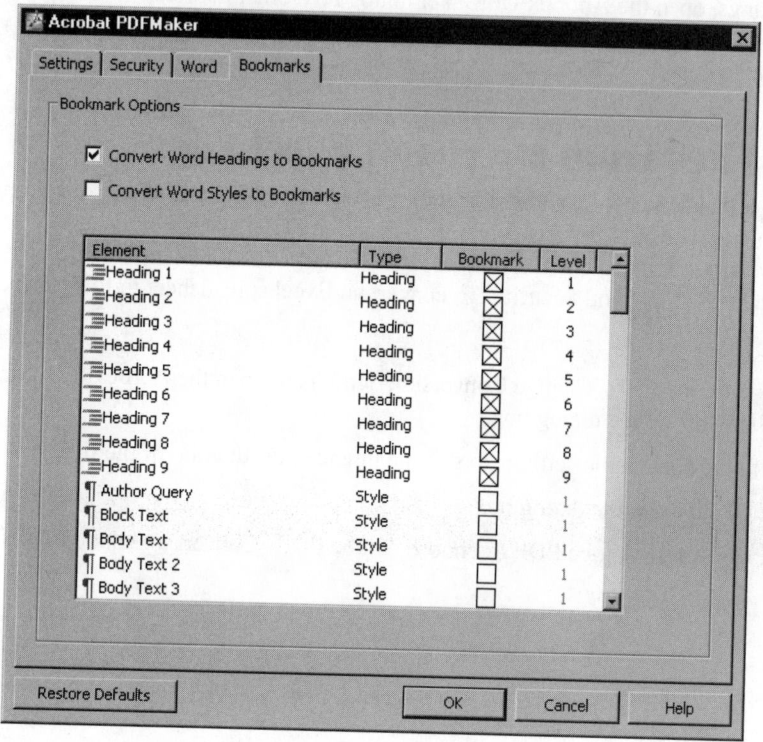

- **Convert Word Headings To Bookmarks** Choose this option (the default), and PDFMaker converts all Word headings in the document to PDF bookmarks. By default, Heading 1 through Heading 9 styles are converted to bookmarks. To modify which headings are converted to bookmarks, click a heading name in the Bookmark column to select or deselect it.
- **Convert Word Styles To Bookmarks** Choose this option, and all Word styles used in the document are converted to bookmarks when PDFMaker converts the document. By default, no Word styles are converted to bookmarks. Choose which styles PDFMaker converts to bookmarks by clicking the style name in the Bookmark column to select or deselect it.

NOTE *You can enable both options to determine how bookmarks are created from the source document. When you choose both styles and headings, you can select the desired styles and headings to suit the PDF document you are creating.*

3. Click OK to apply the new settings, or click another tab to make additional modifications to the document conversion settings.

Restore Default Conversion Settings

After you modify conversion settings, they remain active until you modify them again. To restore the default settings, open the Adobe PDFMaker dialog box, click the Restore Defaults button, and then click OK to complete the restoration. The next document you convert to PDF will be converted with the default PDFMaker conversion settings.

Create PDF Files from Microsoft Excel Files

You can also use PDFMaker from within Excel 97, Excel 2000, or Excel 2002 to convert spreadsheets to PDF documents. The only difference you find between PDFMaker in Excel and Word is the available conversion settings. The Excel Acrobat PDFMaker 6.0 for Microsoft Office dialog box has only two tabs: Settings and Security. To convert an Excel spreadsheet to PDF format, follow these steps:

1. Choose Adobe PDF | Change Conversion Settings to open the Acrobat PDFMaker for Microsoft Office dialog box.
2. Modify the conversion settings to suit the intended destination of the file.
3. Click OK to close the dialog box.
4. Click Convert to Adobe PDF or choose Adobe PDF | Convert to Adobe PDF.

NOTE *There are also buttons and menu commands to convert an Excel document to PDF and e-mail, as well as convert a document to PDF and send the PDF for review.*

Create PDF Files from Microsoft PowerPoint Files

If you use PowerPoint, you know it is a powerful program for creating presentations. It seems that PowerPoint presentations are everywhere these days, even on the Web. You may not think there is any advantage to converting a PowerPoint presentation to PDF format. However, if you want to share a presentation with someone who does not own PowerPoint or does not have a version of PowerPoint capable of opening your presentation, you can convert it to a PDF. All your recipient needs is Adobe Reader 6.0, and he or she can view your presentation.

You can also convert a PowerPoint presentation to a PDF and enhance it with Acrobat features. For example, you can use the File Attachment tool to open another file during your presentation.

The PowerPoint Adobe PDFMaker dialog box has two tabs, Settings and Security. You can convert a PowerPoint presentation to PDF format by doing the following:

1. Choose Adobe | Change Conversion Settings to access the Acrobat PDFMaker dialog box.
2. Modify the conversion settings to suit the intended destination of the converted PDF file.
3. Click OK to close the dialog box.
4. Click the Convert to Adobe PDF button, or choose Adobe PDF | Convert to Adobe PDF.

NOTE *You can also convert a PowerPoint presentation to PDF and e-mail, as well as convert a PowerPoint document to PDF and send it for review.*

Did you know?

Creative Collaborations

If you work for a large corporation, there's no doubt that computer-generated files are a fact of life. If these files need to be shared or reviewed with other colleagues, they will need the native application to open and edit these files. However, if the files need only to be reviewed, a corporation does not have to supply reviewers with the native software used to create these files. If the head of each department has Acrobat, the files can be converted to PDF documents and sent for review. Reviewers can use the powerful Acrobat annotation features to mark up a document and then send it back to the creator, who can then use the native software to modify the document per reviewers' comments. This is also a convenient way to share information between creative entrepreneurs such as graphic designers, web site designers, and their clients. The designer can convert the original artwork to PDF format and send it to the client for review.

Create PDF Files Using an Application Print Command

When you install Acrobat software, Adobe PDF (also known as the Acrobat Distiller) is automatically added as a system printer. You can use Adobe PDF to print the authoring application file to disk in PDF format in the same manner as you use a printer to print out a hard copy of a file. You can create a PDF file from any authoring application that supports printing by following these steps:

1. Choose the application Print command.
2. Choose Adobe PDF from the application Printer menu. The actual Print dialog box will vary depending upon your operating system and the software from which you are printing the file.
3. Click Properties to reveal the Adobe PDF Document Properties dialog box, as shown in the following illustration. As you can see, the dialog box has three sections separated by tabs:

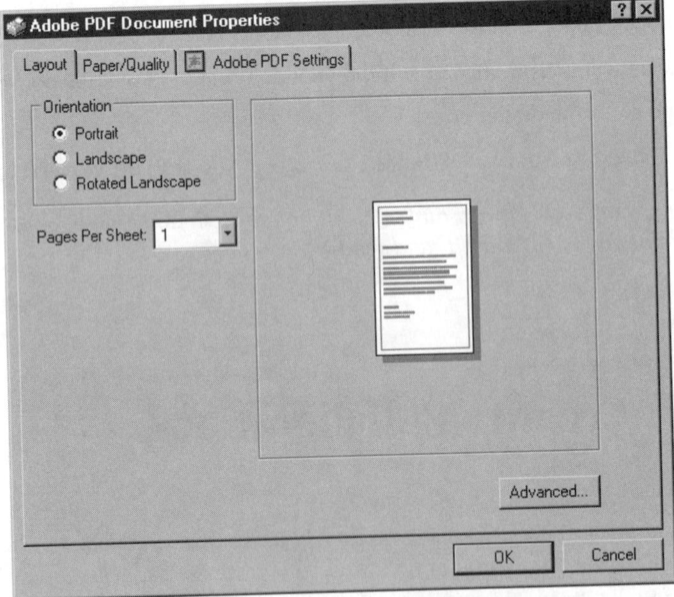

4. In the Layout section choose one of these orientation options: Portrait, Landscape, or Rotated Landscape.
5. Click the triangle to the right of the Pages Per Sheet field and from the drop-down menu, choose an option. The default option of 1 displays one document page on one PDF page. If you choose one of the other options, multiple pages of the original document will be displayed on a single PDF page.

6. In the Paper/Quality section, click the triangle to the right of the Paper Source field.
7. Click the desired icon to print the document in color or black and white.
8. Click Advanced to reveal the dialog box in the following illustration. Note that all options have been expanded, as they are discussed in the next steps:

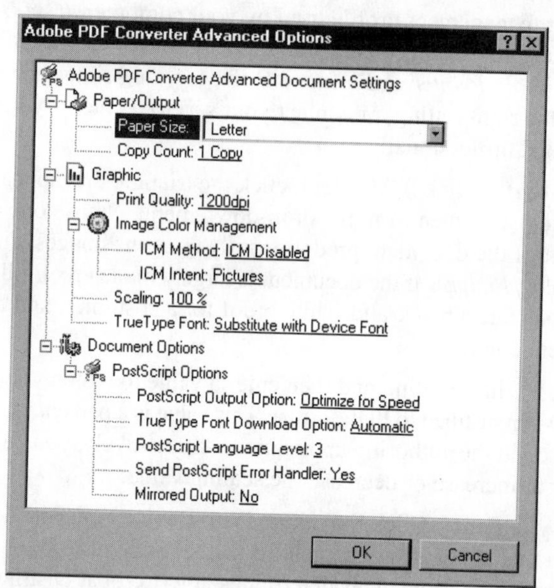

9. Click the triangle to the right of the Paper Size field and choose one of the presets from the drop-down menu.

   - **Copy Count** Click Copy Count and enter a value for the number of copies to print. When you choose this option, the Collate option is available. This option is enabled by default and causes Acrobat to collate the pages for each copy printed.

TIP *You can match the paper size to the file you are printing by choosing PostScript Custom Page Size from the Paper Size menu and then entering the desired dimensions in the PostScript Custom Page Size Definition dialog box.*

10. Click the plus sign (+) to the left of the Graphic title to set the following parameters:
    - **Print Quality** Click Print Quality, click the triangle that appears to the right of the field, and then choose an option from the drop-down menu. The default resolution, 1200 *dpi* (dots per inch), works well in most instances. If the document you are converting to PDF contains vector graphics and you will eventually print the file on a high-end printer, choose a resolution that closely matches the intended output device.

- **Image Color Management** Click the plus sign (+) to the left of the Image Color Management title to set the following parameters:
  - **ICM Method** Click ICM Method, click the triangle that appears, and then choose one of the following options: *ICM Disabled* to disable color management, *ICM Handled by Host System* to handle color management through the color management profile used by your computer, *ICM Handled by Printer* to handle color management through the output device, or *ICM Handled by Printer Using Printer Calibration.* Refer to your printer operation manual to choose the right setting, or contact your service center if you are having the file printed professionally.
  - **ICM Intent** Click ICM Intent, click the triangle that appears to the right of the field, and then from the drop-down menu, choose one of the following: *Graphics* if the document predominantly contains images with large areas of solid color; *Pictures* if the document is largely made up of full-color photographs; *Proof* to create a black-and-white proof for a customer; and *Match* to match the document colors.
  - **Scaling** Click Scaling and then enter a value to which you want the document scaled when distilled to PDF format. This value is a percentage of the document size as created in the authoring application. Alternatively, you can click the scroll buttons to increase or decrease the scaling value.
  - **True Type Font** Click Substitute With Device Font (the default); click the triangle that appears and then choose either Substitute With Device Font, or Download A Softfont. This determines how Acrobat Distiller handles True Type fonts used in the original document. The default option works well in most cases.

11. Click the plus sign (+) to the left of Document Options and then click the plus sign to the left of PostScript options to set the following parameters:
    - **PostScript Options** Click PostScript Options and then click the triangle that appears to choose one of the following options:
      - **Optimize For Speed** Choose this option to speed up the distilling process. However, if you choose this option, you may not be able to take advantage of print spooling if you work on a network.
      - **Optimize For Portability** Choose this option, and the distilled file conforms to *ADSC* (Adobe Document Structuring Conventions). When you choose this option, each PostScript page is independent of the other pages in the document. Choose this option if you are printing the file on a network spooler. When you use a network spooler, printing happens in the background, which frees up your workstation for other tasks. When you choose this option, the network spooler prints the PDF document one page at a time.
      - **Encapsulated PostScript (EPS)** Choose this option to create EPS files comprised of single pages in the authoring application that you intend to use in documents of other applications. Use this option if you want to create a high-quality image and use it in a document that will be printed from another application.

- **Archive Format** Choose this option to improve file portability. When you choose this option, printer settings that may prevent the distilled PDF file from printing on other output devices are suppressed.

- **TrueType Font Download Option** Click TrueType Font Download Option, click the triangle the appears to the right of the field, and then choose one of the following from the drop-down menu:
  - **Automatic** Choose this option to automatically embed any TrueType fonts from the source document to the resulting PDF file.
  - **Outline** Choose this option to embed any TrueType font in the source file as outlined in the resulting PDF file.
  - **Bitmap** Choose this option to convert TrueType fonts in the source file to bitmap images in the resulting PDF document. The resulting PDF document cannot be searched.
  - **Native TrueType** Choose this option, and TrueType fonts will not be embedded with the document. The resulting PDF file will download font information from the source computer from which the document is viewed.
- **PostScript Language Level** Click this option and then choose 1, 2, or 3.
- **Send PostScript Error Handler** Click this option and then choose Yes or No from the drop-down menu.
- **Mirrored Output** Click this option and then, from the drop-down menu, choose No to print the PDF document the same as the source file, or Yes to print the PDF document as a mirror image of the source document.

12. Click OK to close the Adobe PDF Converter Advanced Options dialog box.
13. Click the Adobe PDF Settings tab to set the parameters shown here:

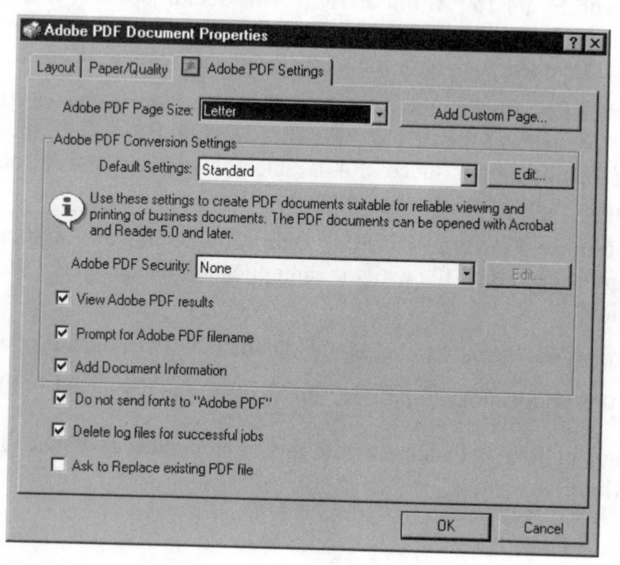

14. Click the triangle to the right of the Adobe PDF Page Size field, and choose the size for the resulting PDF document.
15. Click the triangle to the right of the Default Settings field and then choose one of the presets from the drop-down menu. These are identical to the settings previously discussed in Chapter 4.
16. Click the triangle to the right of the Adobe PDF Security field and choose one of the following options:
    - **Reconfirm Security For Each Job** You will be prompted for security settings each time you use the Adobe PDF printer.
    - **None** No security is applied to distilled documents.
    - **Use Last Known Security Settings** Acrobat will use the last security settings you specified on future printing jobs.
    - **Edit** The Edit button becomes available after you choose one of the above. Click the button to edit security settings. Acrobat security will be discussed in detail in Chapter 11.
17. In the Adobe PDF Conversion Settings section, choose one of more of the following options:
    - **View Adobe PDF Results** This default option opens the resulting PDF document in Acrobat. Deselect this option to print the document without previewing the end result.
    - **Prompt For Adobe PDF Filename** This default option prompts you for a filename whenever you use Adobe PDF to distill a source file. Deselect this option, and Acrobat uses the source document filename followed by the PDF extension as the PDF filename.
    - **Add Document Information** This default option adds information from the source document to the PDF file as Document Information.
    - **Do Not Send Fonts To "Adobe PDF"** This default option will not embed fonts from the source document in the resulting PDF file. Deselect this option, and Acrobat will embed document fonts as long as there are no licensing issues.
    - **Delete Log Files For Successful Jobs** Acrobat Distiller creates a log file whenever you use Adobe PDF to create a PDF file. By default, the file is deleted when the distilling job is successful. Deselect this option, and Acrobat will create a log file that can be viewed with a text editor.
    - **Ask To Replace Existing PDF File** Select this option, and Acrobat prompts you when overwriting a PDF file with the same filename as the one selected for the current printing job.
18. Click OK to apply the settings and close the Adobe PDF Document Properties dialog box.
19. Click OK in the Application Print dialog box to print the document in PDF format.

If you are printing a multipage document with lots of embedded graphics, the printing process may take a while.

Create PDF Files in Adobe Programs

Adobe has gone to great lengths to enhance interactivity between Acrobat and its graphics software. You can create a PDF file using the following Adobe software:

- **FrameMaker** FrameMaker is a page-layout program suitable for publishing long documents for viewing across multiple media. You can use the program to create content for the Web, CD-ROM, and print. FrameMaker offers extensive support for creating PDF documents. To create a PDF file in FrameMaker, you use the application's Print command.
- **Illustrator** Illustrator is a vector-based illustration program. Programs like Illustrator use mathematics to define a shape, which means the shape can be greatly enlarged without loss of fidelity. You can convert Illustrator documents to PDF format using the Save command. Illustrator 9.0 and newer versions support transparency, which is preserved when you save a PDF document with Acrobat 6.0 compatibility.
- **InDesign** InDesign is the latest page-layout software from Adobe. InDesign features extensive PDF support. Documents you create in InDesign are converted to PDF format using the Export command.
- **Photoshop** Photoshop is an award-winning image-editing software from Adobe. Use the Save As command and then choose the PDF format to save a Photoshop file in PDF format. When you use the Save As command to convert a Photoshop file to PDF, you can specify image compression and the color model. When you save a file from Photoshop in PDF format, layers are flattened; however, if you open the resulting PDF file in Photoshop, any layers and objects from the original file are preserved and available for editing.
- **PageMaker** PageMaker is a page-layout program. To create a PDF file from a PageMaker document, use the Export PDF 3.01 plug in, which can be downloaded from the Adobe web site at http://www.adobe.com.

Although the methods used to create PDF files differ between Adobe programs, many of the options are similar. Consult your software application manual for specific instructions on exporting the file as a PDF document. After you export the file, you can modify the file in Acrobat Standard or Acrobat Professional.

Create PDF Files from Vector-Drawing Software

If you create vector-based illustrations, you can convert them to PDF files using one of the following methods:

- Save the file in either EPS or PS format and then use Acrobat Distiller to print the file.
- Use the vector drawing program Print command and choose Adobe PDF for the printer.
- Export the file in PDF format if supported by the software.

The first two methods of creating PDF files have already been discussed. If you use Illustrator to create illustrations, you can create a PDF document by choosing PDF format from the Save command. Two other vector-based drawing programs offer enhanced support for PDF export. They are CorelDraw and FreeHand. If your vector-based program supports PDF export, consult the user manual for specific instructions.

Create Files from Adobe Illustrator

If you create illustrations with Adobe Illustrator, you can save documents in the PDF format. When you save an Illustrator document in PDF format, the Adobe PDF Format Options dialog box appears. There are two sections to the Adobe PDF Format Options dialog box: General and Compression. The settings in the General section allow you to specify whether to save the file with Adobe 4.0 (PDF 1.3) or 5.0 (PDF 1.4) compatibility. Future versions of Illustrator will most likely have Adobe 6.0 (PDF 1.5) compatibility. You also have the option of preserving Illustrator editing capabilities. When you choose this option, you can open the PDF file in Illustrator and edit layers, objects, text, and so on. You also have the option to embed fonts and subset fonts less than a certain percentage, as with the InDesign export options discussed previously. The Compression section of the Adobe PDF Format Options dialog box is identical to the compression setting of the InDesign Export PDF dialog box, with the exception of an additional option to compress text and line art.

Create PDF Files from CorelDraw Documents

If you use CorelDraw 10 or newer to create illustrations, you may not be aware that the program features extensive support of the PDF format. In fact, PDF documents you create in CorelDraw or Corel PhotoPaint are produced with the Corel PDF engine. When you want to publish a file from CorelDraw as a PDF document, you do not have to search for a command buried on an obscure menu or choose an option from a Save menu; CorelDraw puts the Publish to PDF file where you can easily find it—on the File menu. For more information on exporting a CorelDraw illustration as a PDF document, consult your software owner's manual.

Create PDF Files from Macromedia FreeHand Files

If you use FreeHand for creating illustrations, you can import PDF documents and edit them within FreeHand as well as export FreeHand documents as PDF files. FreeHand supports Acrobat Notes and URLs and assigns them to separate layers upon import. Note that if FreeHand is unable to determine the path of a note when importing a PDF, it imports notes as a rectangular block on the URL layer.

FreeHand 10 and FreeHand MX supports direct export of files as PDF documents. As this is written, FreeHand exports PDF files in Acrobat 4.0 or earlier formats only. By the time you read this, there may be a patch available at the Macromedia web site (www.macromedia.com) to support export in Acrobat 6.0 format. Currently, FreeHand cannot export the following effects in PDF format:

- Custom fills, PostScript fills, strokes, arrowheads, or textured fills.
- Alpha channel transparency.
- EPS images within the FreeHand document. (If the EPS image has a TIFF preview, only the preview image is exported with the file.)
- Text effects, such as drop shadows, highlights, and strikethroughs.

For specific information on exporting a FreeHand document as a PDF file, consult your software owner's manual.

Summary

In this chapter, you learned to create PDF documents from within Microsoft Office applications that support the PDFMaker. You also learned how to create PDF files from within applications that support printing and learned how to configure Adobe PDF as a PostScript printing device. In the next chapter, you'll learn to create PDF documents by capturing them from your scanner or from web pages.

Chapter 6

Capture PDF Documents

How to...

- Capture PDF documents from your scanner
- Capture images from digital cameras
- Use Paper Capture
- Capture web pages
- Append web pages

You create most of your PDF documents in authoring applications and then convert them to PDF files from within the authoring application (if supported) or by using Adobe PDF to print the document in PDF format. You can also create PDF files by printing a file to disk in either EPS or PS format and then using Acrobat Distiller to convert the PostScript file to PDF format. Both of these techniques are covered in Chapters 4 and 5. However, there are other ways to create PDF documents.

You can also create PDF documents with your scanner or by capturing pages from Internet web sites. Either method is a great way to build an information library. You can scan magazine articles of interest, convert them to PDF format, and discard the original to avoid paper clutter. You can also capture single web pages or an entire web site. With the wealth of information available on the Internet, capturing web pages is a wonderful way to build a PDF library on your hard drive. If you own Acrobat Professional, you can use the Adobe Catalog plug-in to create a searchable index of PDF documents captured from the Web. Creating PDF indexes is covered in Chapter 16.

Capture PDF Documents from a Scanner

If you have a scanner attached to your computer, you can capture PDF documents directly from your scanner using the Acrobat Scan plug-in. With the Acrobat Scan plug-in, it is possible to scan a document into Acrobat without leaving the program. After you scan the document, you can use Acrobat tools or menu commands to modify the document before saving it as a PDF file.

Your scanner probably has an interface or other software that makes the scanning process a relatively simple task. Most scanner applications let you crop the image, select a color model, and adjust the image resolution before scanning the document into an application. If your scanner is equipped with similar software, you can adjust the image to suit its intended destination before returning the scanned image to Acrobat.

NOTE

When you scan a document, it is temporarily written to disk before it is converted to PDF format. Make sure you have enough temporary disk space to avoid problems. You can increase disk space by deleting unnecessary temporary files. You can also increase disk space by copying infrequently used documents to a mass storage device such as a tape backup, zip disk or USB hard drive.

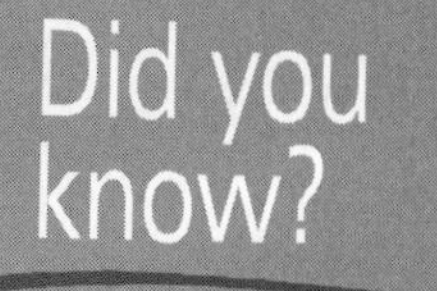

How TWAIN Got Its Name

When you install Acrobat, the install utility detects any TWAIN devices you have attached to your computer. As a note of interest, TWAIN originated from Rudyard Kipling's *The Ballad of East and West* ("and never the twain shall meet"), which, when the technology was in its infancy, reflected the difficulties of connecting a scanner to a personal computer. However, many people think TWAIN stands for *Technology Without An Interesting Name.* A TWAIN device contains drivers that convert the optical input from a scanner or digital camera into digital format that can be recognized by computer software. The TWAIN devices you have attached to your computer are listed on a drop-down menu in the Create PDF From Scanner dialog box.

Capture Images and Text

After you have a scanner up and running on your system with a TWAIN device that Acrobat recognizes, you can scan any document into Acrobat and save it as a PDF file. After you capture the document, you can use the Paper Capture command to convert the document into a PDF file with searchable text. To capture a document into Acrobat with your scanner:

1. Insert the document you want to capture in your scanner.

TIP *To create a better-looking PDF document, make sure the document is square with the edge of your scanner. If the page is clipped from a magazine, trim and square the edges for better results.*

2. Choose Create PDF | From Scanner to reveal the Create PDF From Scanner dialog box, as shown here:

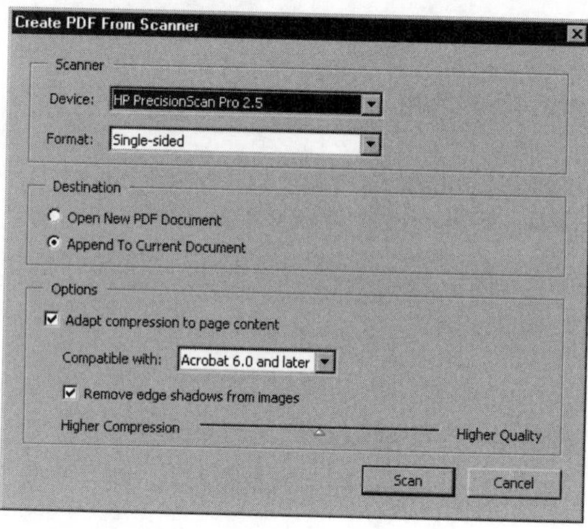

3. Click the triangle to the right of the Device field and choose the appropriate TWAIN device for your scanner from the drop-down menu.

NOTE *The menu for TWAIN devices may show two listings for each item. For best results, choose the manufacturer's software for your scanner if it is listed.*

4. In the Format field, there are two options, Single-Sided (the default) and Double-Sided. If your scanner supports double-sided scanning, choose Double-Sided; otherwise, accept Single-Sided.
5. If no document is currently open in Acrobat, Open New PDF Document is the only option available; otherwise, the Append To Current Document option is available and selected by default. Choose the option that applies and click Scan.
6. After you click the Scan button, the interface for the TWAIN device you selected opens. Follow the prompts to preview the scan and return it to Acrobat. Refer to your scanner user guide for specific instructions. The following illustration shows the HP PrecisionScan Pro 2.5 interface:

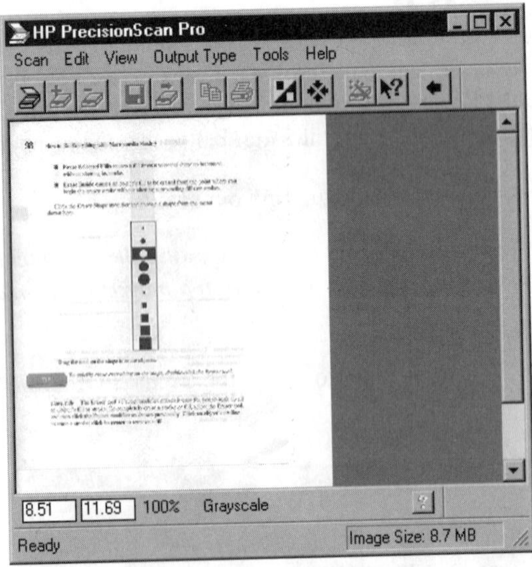

7. After the image is scanned into Acrobat, modify the document as needed and save the image. Figure 6-1 shows a page from a book as captured with the Acrobat Scan plug-in.

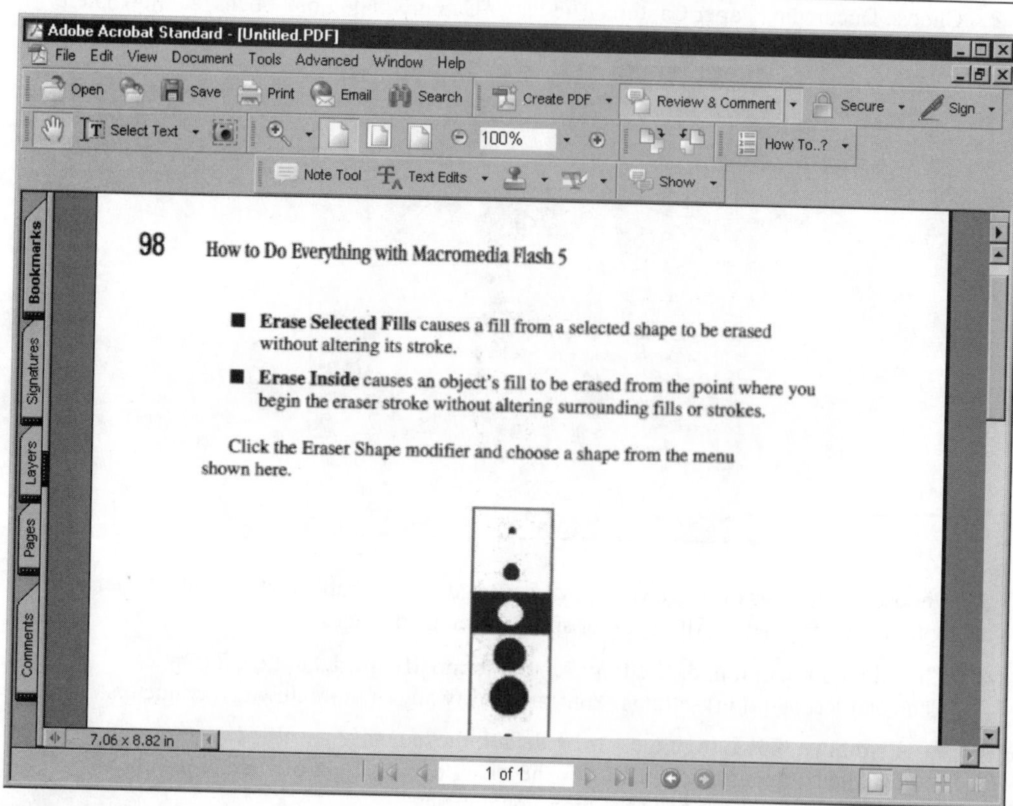

FIGURE 6-1 You can use your scanner to capture paper documents as PDF files.

8. Choose File | Save to save the scanned image as a PDF file.

Convert Scanned Captures to Searchable Text

When you convert a document to a PDF file by scanning it, the document is captured as an image and the text is not searchable. You can use the Paper Capture command to convert the captured document to searchable text by following these steps:

1. Open the PDF file you want to convert to searchable text. Alternatively, you can use the Paper Capture command immediately after scanning the document.

6

2. Choose Document | Paper Capture. The Paper Capture dialog box opens, as shown here:

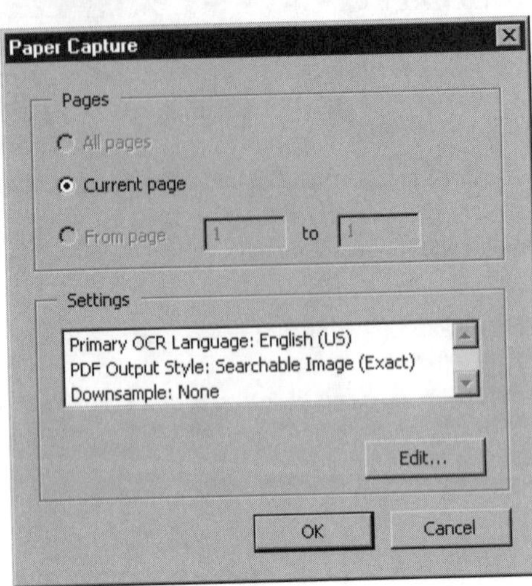

3. Choose the number of pages you want converted to searchable text. Accept the default option (Current Page), All Pages, or specify a range of pages.
4. Click the Edit button in the Settings section to modify the default *OCR* (Optical Character Recognition) settings. You can modify any of the following parameters:
   - **Primary OCR Language** Is by default the language specified when Acrobat was installed on your computer. Click the triangle to the right of this field to choose a different language from the drop-down menu.
   - **PDF Output Style** Determines the type of PDF document output by the Paper Capture command. Choose from Searchable Image (Exact), which places the searchable text behind the image as captured from your scanner; Searchable Image (Compact), which places the searchable text behind the image as captured from your scanner with image compression applied; or Formatted Text & Graphics, which converts the scanned image into searchable text with graphic objects. The latter option results in the largest file size.
   - **Downsample Images** Determines how much compression is applied to images in the converted document. Choose from None, Low (300 DPI), Medium (150 DPI), or High (72 DPI). When you choose higher compression settings, the document file size is smaller, but the image quality suffers.
5. Click OK to convert the document to searchable text.

TIP *When you use the Paper Capture command to convert a scanned document into searchable text, an OCR program reads bitmaps of words and recognizes them as text. During the conversion process, Acrobat creates a "suspect" when it is uncertain that the word has been converted correctly. You can correct suspect words by choosing Document | Paper Capture | First OCR Suspect, or Document | Paper Capture | Find All OCR Suspects. Suspect words are displayed in a dialog box, which enables you to accept the suspect word as correct or correct the suspect word with the TouchUpText tool. You can use the First OCR Suspect command to open the Find Element dialog box, which gives you a drop-down menu of elements you can search for such as unmarked content or unmarked links.*

Capture Images from Digital Cameras

6

If you have a digital camera connected to your computer, with a TWAIN driver that is recognized by Acrobat, you can use it to capture images directly into Acrobat. To capture an image from a digital camera, the device must be connected to the computer (the most common hookup being a USB cable) or you must have a device connected to your computer that supports your camera memory cards. To capture an image from your digital camera, choose File | Import | Scan; then choose the TWAIN device that supports your camera and follow the prompts to capture the image.

Pictures you take with a digital camera are generally in JPEG, or if you own a more advanced digital camera, TIFF format. In the majority of cases, there are better methods for capturing photographs from your digital camera, especially when you have to edit the image after photographing it. However, capturing an image with a digital camera, converting it to PDF, and then attaching it to an e-mail message is any easy way to send images of people or products to friends and coworkers who may not have computer software capable of opening images in their native formats.

Capture PDF Documents from Web Sites

The Internet is a treasure trove of information. You can find out almost anything about any subject by typing relevant keywords into one of the many online search engines. After you submit the search, the search engine usually returns several pages of web sites that contain information that pertains to your search. The first three or four pages contain the sites with information that closely matches your query, but searching through 10 or 15 web sites can be time consuming. If you have a slow Internet connection and the returned pages are filled with graphics, this only exacerbates the problem. The solution is to use the Acrobat Web Capture command to download the page into Acrobat. You can download a single page or the entire site. After the download is complete, you can save the page(s) in PDF format for review at your leisure. Figure 6-2 shows a web page that has been downloaded into Acrobat.

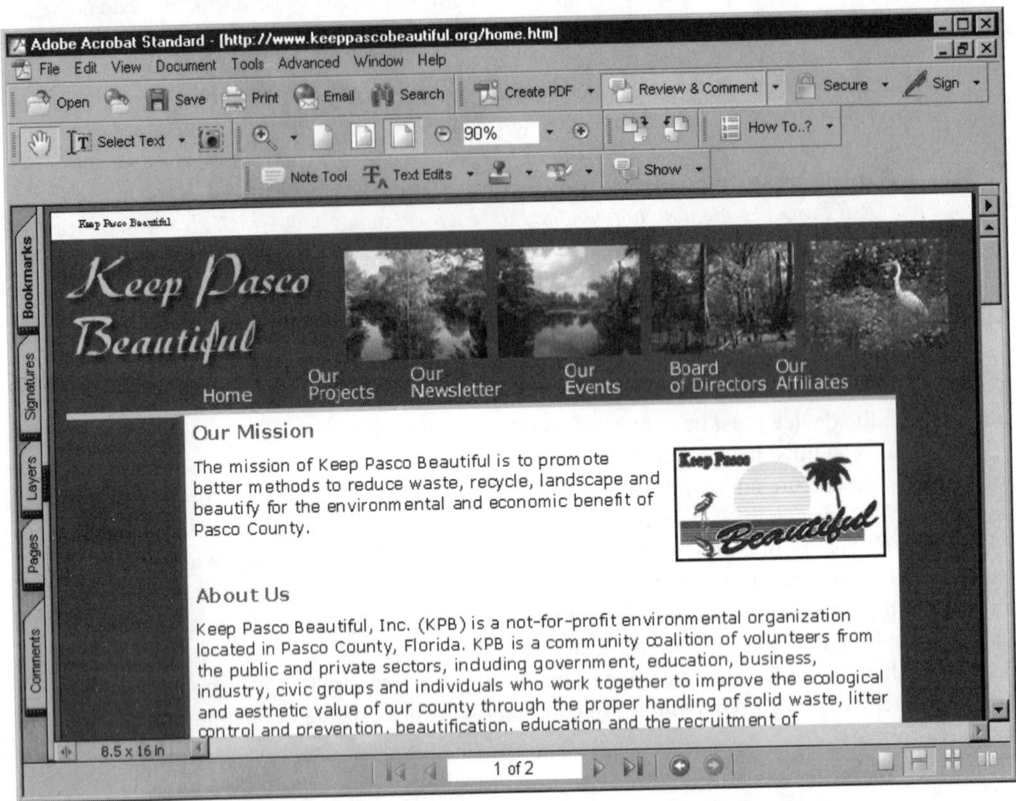

FIGURE 6-2 You can download a web page into Acrobat for future reference.

Set Web Capture Preferences

Create PDF From Web Page is a powerful command that can save you hours of time online. You can configure Web Capture to suit your working style by changing Web Capture Preferences as follows:

1. Choose Edit | Preferences | Web Capture to open the Web Capture section of the Preferences dialog box, as shown next.

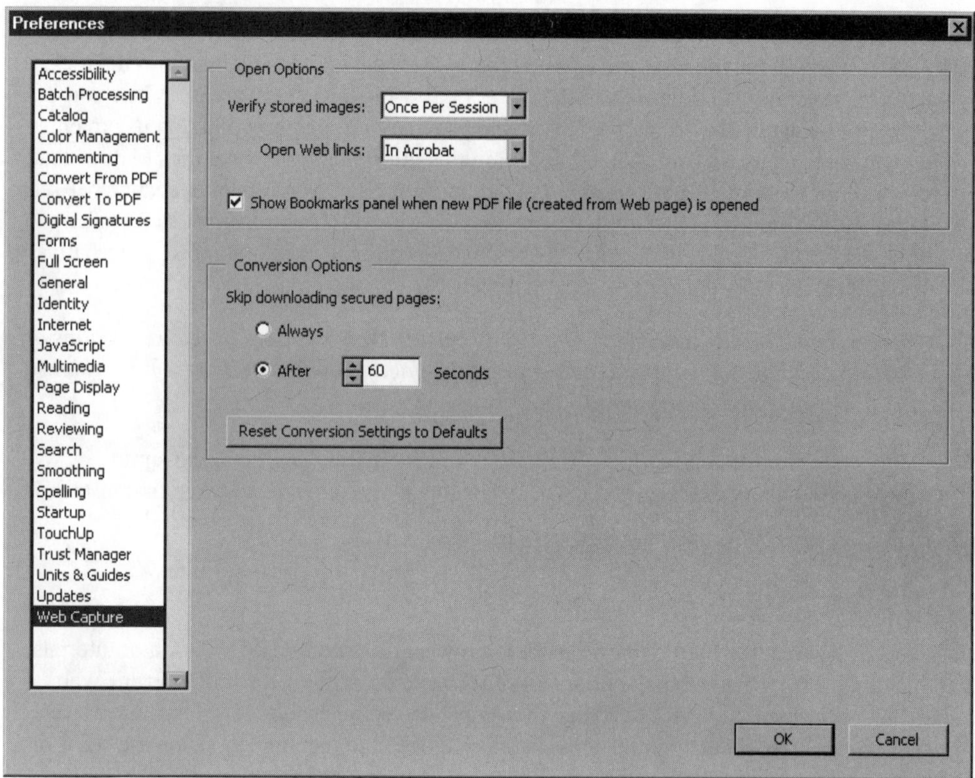

2. Click the triangle to the right of the Verify Stored Images field and from the drop-down menu, choose Once Per Session, Always, or Never. The default option, Once Per Session, checks the web site you captured pages from to see if the images stored with the captured pages have changed at the site. If the images have changed, new images are downloaded.
3. Click the triangle to the right of the Open Web Links field and from the drop-down menu, choose In Acrobat (the default) or In Web Browser. This option determines what device is used to open a page when a captured web page button or hyperlinked text is clicked.
4. When you enable Show Bookmarks Panel When New PDF File (Created From Web Page) Is Opened (the default), after the captured web page downloads completely, the Navigation pane opens and the document bookmarks are displayed. Disable this option and when the download is complete, the document opens with the Navigation pane closed; however, bookmarks have been created.

5. Choose a Skip Downloading Secured Pages option. The default option skips a secured page if it is not downloaded within 60 seconds. Acrobat can download secured pages, but you generally need permission to access password-protected areas. When you attempt to download a secure page, Acrobat provides a dialog box that you use to enter a login name and password. After you submit this information, Acrobat tries to download the page for the time interval specified in the Seconds field. You can enter a value between 1 and 9,999 seconds. If the allotted time has passed and Acrobat has not successfully downloaded the page, a warning dialog box appears and the page is skipped. Alternatively, you can choose Always, and Acrobat will never try to download a secure page.

NOTE *If the web site server is set up to allow only certain Web browsers in secure sections of the site, Acrobat may not be able to capture the page, even though the right username and password have been entered.*

6. Click Reset Conversion Settings To Default, and the settings in the Web Capture Preferences dialog box are restored to the default values Acrobat had when first installed.
7. Click OK to apply the settings and exit the dialog box.

Download Web Pages

Whether you are surfing the Internet for pleasure or browsing for product information or tutorials, you can quickly download a web page or an entire web site using the Create PDF From Web Page command. When you capture a web page in Acrobat, the entire page is downloaded, complete with images. When Acrobat encounters an unsupported object, a rectangular shape the color of the web page background is displayed in lieu of the unsupported object. If an animated GIF is part of the page being captured, only the first frame of the animated GIF appears after Acrobat downloads the page. When you are on the Internet and find a web page you want to download, do the following:

1. If it is not already open, launch Acrobat.
2. Choose Create PDF | From Web Page to access the Create PDF From Web Page dialog box shown next. Alternatively, you can click the Create PDF From Web Page button on the toolbar.

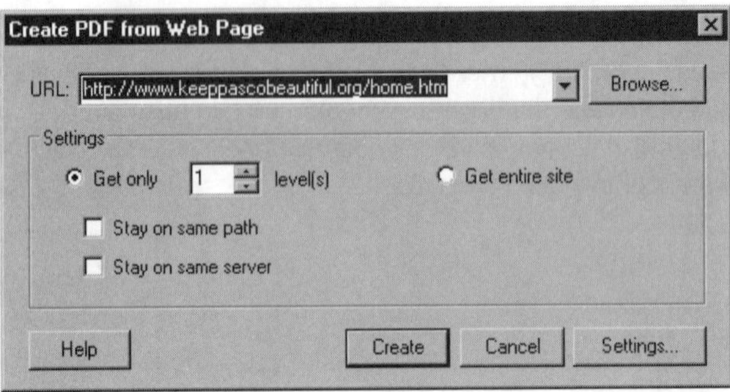

3. In the URL field, enter the URL for the page you want to capture.

TIP

Some URLs are very long. Instead of manually entering the entire Web address, you can select the Web address in your Web browser and then press CTRL-C *(Windows) or* COMMAND-C *(Macintosh) to copy the Web address to your operating system clipboard. Switch to Acrobat, click inside the URL field, and then press* CTRL-V *(Windows) or* COMMAND-C *(Macintosh) to paste the URL into the field.*

4. In the Get Only [ ] Level(s) field, enter the number of levels to download, or use the spinner buttons to increase or decrease this value. Alternatively, you can choose Get Entire Site to download every level (and subsequently every page) in the site.

AUTION

Some web sites are several levels deep; for example, a site home page (Level 1) could branch out to five sections (Level 2). Each section on Level 2 could branch out to other pages (Level 3), and so on. When you download a site that is several levels deep, you use a considerable amount of your system resources and run the risk of exceeding available system resources and perpetrating a system crash. If you are downloading a site with many levels, you are advised to download the first level, browse through the downloaded page in Acrobat, and then click a link to download an additional page.

6

5. If you specify the number of levels to download, you can specify the following options:
   - **Stay On Same Path** Choose this option, and Acrobat downloads all pages along the path of the specified URL.
   - **Stay On Same Server** Choose this option, and Acrobat downloads pages from the server of the specified URL only, disregarding links to URLs on another server.
6. Click the Settings button to modify Acrobat web capture conversion settings. This feature is explained fully in the "Specify Web Page Conversion Settings" section, later in the chapter.
7. Click the Create button to begin capturing the page. As the site is downloading, Acrobat keeps you informed of the download progress by opening the Download Status dialog box.
8. To save the captured page in PDF format for future reference, choose File | Save to open the Save As dialog box. Enter a name for the file, specify the folder to save the file in, and then click Save.

When the download is complete, Acrobat displays the captured page in the Document pane according to the specified web capture preferences. At the top of the document you'll find the title of the captured page. This same title is displayed in your Web browser when you view the page on the Internet. You can change the document by choosing File | Document Properties and then entering another name in the Title field of the Description section in the Document Properties dialog box; however, this changes the title only as it pertains to an index, to which you may add the PDF file. When you reopen the document after assigning the new title, the title you saved the PDF document with appears in the Document pane, not the title you specified in the Description section of the Document Properties dialog box.

NOTE

Certain web page features will not download, such as pop-up menus, multistate JavaScript buttons, and JavaScript image swaps. Pop-up menus and similar web page features are created using JavaScript. You should also be aware that Acrobat will not convert certain CGI files, Java applets, or RealMedia to PDF. Although JavaScript is supported in bookmarks, links, and form fields you create in Acrobat, JavaScript features are not downloaded with a web page.

Append Web Pages

After you successfully capture a web page, you may decide to add additional pages from the same site to the document, download the rest of the site, or append the document with web pages from another site. You can append the current web page by clicking links on the captured page or using menu commands.

Append with Web Links

As you view a captured page in Acrobat, you may decide that another page from the same site, or a page from another site that is linked to the captured page, contains information you would like to archive in PDF format. To append a page using a Web link, follow these steps:

1. From the captured page, move your cursor over the link to the page you want to capture. Your cursor becomes a document with a plus sign (+) in it. This signifies you can append the document by clicking the link.
2. Click the link and Acrobat downloads the page.
3. To add another page to the document, click the desired link and accept the default Open In Acrobat behavior. Acrobat downloads the page to the document, unless you've modified the Web Capture section of the Preferences dialog box to open Web links in the browser. Acrobat creates a bookmark and thumbnail for the added page, as shown in Figure 6-3.
4. When you have finished adding pages to the document, choose File | Save.

Use the View Web Links Command

To view all the Web links within a captured page, you use the View Web Links command. You can use this command to add additional web pages to the document as follows:

1. Choose Advanced | Web Capture | View Web Links, and Acrobat opens the Select Page Links To Download dialog box, as shown next.

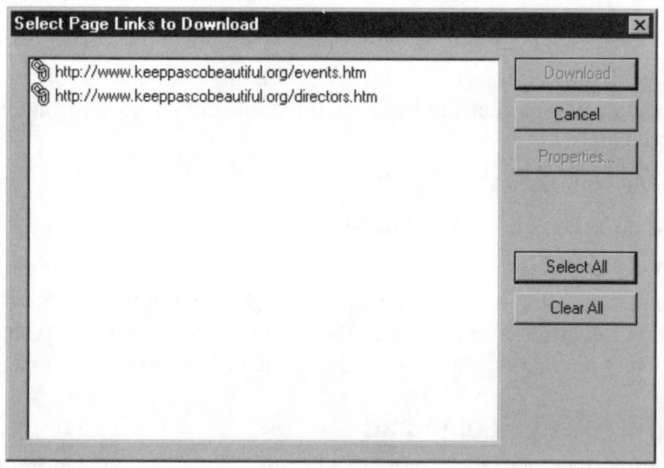

6

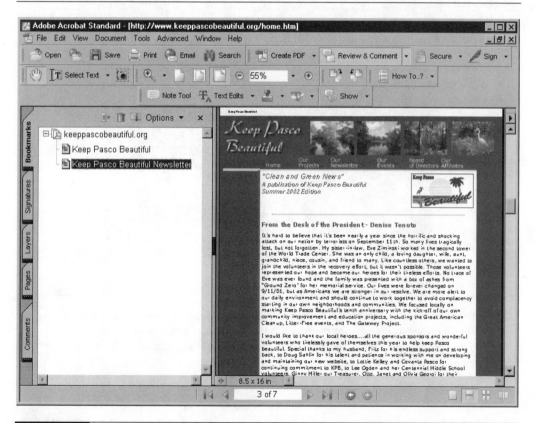

FIGURE 6-3 You can append a captured web page by clicking a link within the document.

2. To add additional web pages to the current document, do one of the following:
   - To add contiguous links to the selection, click the link while holding down the SHIFT key. To add noncontiguous links to the selection, click the link while holding down the CTRL key.
   - To select all links, click Select All.
   - To clear the selection, click Clear All.
3. Click the Download button to begin the download. After you do so, Acrobat opens the Download Status dialog box and displays the progress of the operation. When the download is complete, Acrobat appends the document with the downloaded pages and adds additional bookmarks and thumbnails for the new pages.

Use the Append Web Page Command

You can use the Append Web Page command to add additional pages to the current document. If you are appending the current document with links from within the same site, either click a link within the document or use the View Web Links command to view the links within the document and then select the links you want to add to the document. However, if the link you want to add to the captured web page does not appear on the page, do the following:

1. Choose Advanced | Web Capture | Append Web Page to open the Add To PDF From Web Page dialog box, as shown here:

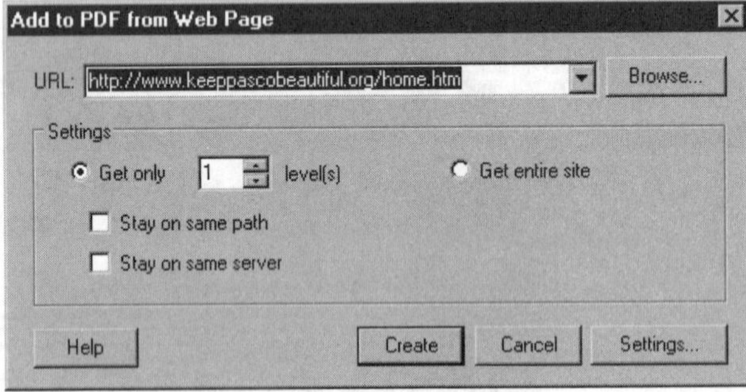

2. In the URL field, enter the address for the web page you want to add to the document.
3. In the Get Only [ ] Level(s) field, enter the number of levels to download or use the spinner buttons to increase or decrease the value in the Levels field. Alternatively, you can choose Get Entire Site to download every level (and subsequently every page) in the site.
4. Choose Stay On Same Path, and Acrobat downloads all pages along the path of the specified URL.
5. Choose Stay On Same Server, and Acrobat downloads only pages from the server of the specified URL, disregarding links to URLs on another server.

6. Click the Create button to begin capturing the page. Acrobat opens the Download Status dialog box, which you can use to monitor download progress.
7. After the page downloads, you can invoke the command again to add additional pages to the document, or choose File | Save.

NOTE *When you append a web page, you can modify the settings for the new pages by clicking the Settings button in the Add To PDF From Web Page dialog box. For more information on settings, refer to the upcoming "Specify Web Page Conversion Settings" section of this chapter.*

When you append a captured web page with pages from another web site, Acrobat creates a bookmark for the URL of the site. Captured pages from each site are listed under the site's URL bookmark.

Append All Links on a Page

After you download a web page, you can use any of the methods previously discussed to append the page, or you can download every page that is linked to the captured page by choosing Advanced | Web Capture | Append All Links. After you choose this command, Acrobat downloads the linked pages one at a time and displays the download progress in the Download Status dialog box. This operation may take a considerable amount of time if the page has several links. After the linked pages are downloaded, you can view the downloaded pages by clicking a link in the main page or by opening the Bookmarks tab or Thumbnails tab and clicking a bookmark or thumbnail. You can apply the Append All Links command on any of the newly downloaded pages to add additional pages to the document.

After you have added all the desired pages to the document, you can disable Web links by choosing Advanced | Links | Remove All Links From Document. This opens the Remove Web Links dialog box, with which you can specify how many pages of links to remove. After you apply this command, Web links will be visible in the document but will no longer function as links to URLs. However, links to other downloaded web pages will still be functional and open the proper document page when clicked. When you remove Web links, you reduce the size of the PDF file.

TIP *You can also create links from URLs in a document by choosing Advanced | Links | Create From URLs In The Document.*

Specify Web Page Conversion Settings

You can modify the conversion settings used to capture web pages and convert them to PDF format. When you modify these settings, it is a global action that applies to future web pages you capture until you modify the settings again. To modify web capture conversion settings, do the following:

1. Choose File | Create PDF | From Web Page to open the Create PDF From Web Page dialog box shown previously. Alternatively, you can click the Open Web Page button or click the Create PDF task button and then choose From Web Page.

2. In the Create PDF From Web Page dialog box, click the Settings button to open the Web Page Conversion Settings dialog box shown in Figure 6-4. You can modify parameters for General options and Page Layout options, as detailed in the following sections.

Modify General Conversion Settings

When you open the Web Page Conversion Settings dialog box, the General section is selected by default. As shown in the Figure 6-4, the supported file types Acrobat can convert to PDF are listed in the File Type Settings window. To modify the General web page conversion settings, follow these steps:

1. Open the Web Page Conversion Settings dialog box, as outlined previously. The General tab is selected by default.
2. You can modify the following options in the PDF Settings section:
   - **Create Bookmarks** Choose this option to have Acrobat generate a new bookmark for each additional page you capture. This option is selected by default.
   - **Create PDF Tags** Choose this option to have Acrobat create a document structure that conforms to the layout of the HTML document. If you choose this option, Acrobat adds bookmarks for HTML items such as paragraphs, lists, tables, and so on. The tagged document can be reflowed for easier reading on devices with smaller viewing areas. For more information on tagged documents, refer to the "About Tagged Documents" section of Chapter 12.
   - **Place Headers & Footers On New Pages (Windows) or Put Headers And Footers On New Content (Macintosh)** Choose this option to have Acrobat add a new header and footer to each captured web page. The header shows the web page title as it appears in the browser, and the footer displays the web page URL plus the date and time the file was downloaded. If the URL is exceptionally long, it may be truncated to allow room for the page number.
   - **Save Refresh Commands (Windows) or Save Update Commands (Macintosh)** Choose this option to have Acrobat save a list of all URLs associated with the captured page and remember the order in which they were downloaded. Choose this option, and you will be able to update the content of the converted PDF document to match the current version of the web page from which the document was created. Updating captured web pages is covered in the upcoming "Update Converted Web Pages" section of this chapter.

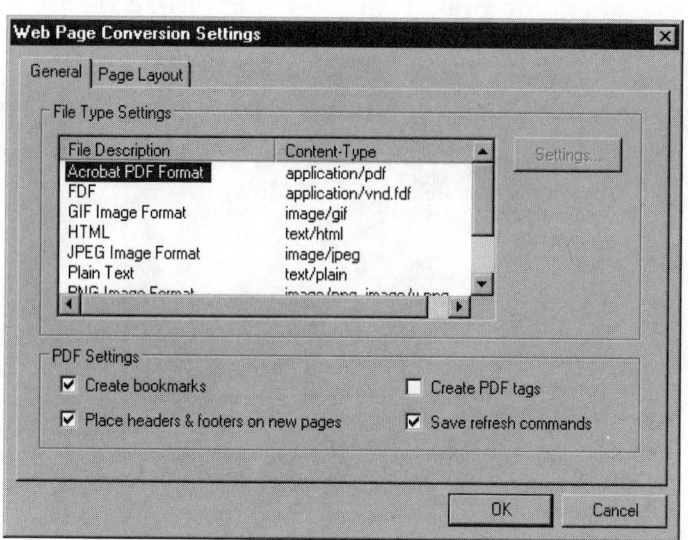

FIGURE 6-4 You can modify several parameters for capturing web pages as PDF documents.

3. In the File Type Settings window, you can modify settings for two file types: HTML and Plain Text. To modify the HTML settings and Plain Text settings, refer to the "Modify HTML Display Settings" section, which is next.
4. To save the settings, click OK to close the Web Page Conversion Settings dialog box and return to the Create PDF From Web Page dialog box.

Modify HTML Display Settings

When you capture a web page as a PDF, you can modify the look of the captured page by changing the HTML display settings. You can modify font style, font color, and other parameters of the converted page, such as background color and table cell colors. To modify the display characteristics of captured web pages, do the following:

1. Open the Web Page Conversion Settings dialog box as outlined previously.
2. In the File Type Settings window, click HTML to activate the Settings button.

6

3. Click the Settings button to open the HTML Conversion Settings dialog box, as shown here:

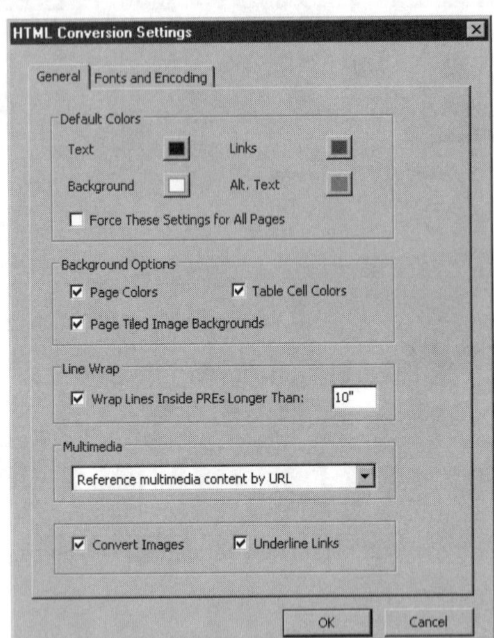

4. In the Default Colors section, you can modify the color of Text, Links, Background, and Alt Text by clicking the color button to the right of an item to open a color palette. Choose a color for the item and then click OK to close the palette and apply the change. Repeat as needed to change the color of other items.
5. Choose Force These Settings For All Pages, and the colors you specify in the previous step are applied to all pages you capture, regardless of the colors specified in the actual HTML document. If you do not choose this option, Acrobat applies the colors you specified in the previous step only to HTML documents that do not have colors specified in the document HTML code.
6. In the Background Options section, Page Colors, Table Cell Colors, and Page Tiled Image Backgrounds are enabled by default. If you disable these options, the captured PDF document may look different from the actual web page but may be more legible when printed.
7. In the Wrapped Lines Inside PREs Longer Than field of the Line Wrap section, enter a value. Acrobat will wrap preformatted lines of HTML longer than the value you specify (10 inches is the default) to fit onscreen.
8. Click the triangle to the right of the Multimedia field and choose one of the following options:

- **Disable Multimedia Capture** Captures HTML and images but does not capture multimedia content such as Flash movies.
- **Embed Multimedia Content When Possible (the default option)** Embeds multimedia formats supported by Acrobat 6.0.
- **Reference Multimedia Content By URL** Creates a placeholder for the media that is linked to the URL from which you downloaded the web page. When you open the file, Acrobat plays the multimedia file by accessing the URL from which the page was captured provided you are connected to the Internet; otherwise, you'll just see the placeholder for the rectangle the same size as the multimedia content. This option creates a smaller file size but is not recommended if you distribute the document to recipients that view the files on machines without Internet connections or have a slow Internet connection. Also, the file will not play if the parent web site removes the multimedia file or moves it to a different URL.

9. Choose Convert Images (the default option) to have Acrobat include images from the captured web page. If you disable this option, Acrobat replaces the image with a colored border and the image Alt text, if specified within the HTML document.
10. Choose Underline Links (the default option) to have Acrobat underline all text links when converting the document to PDF format, whether they are underlined or not in the HTML page.
11. Click the Fonts And Encoding tab to open the fonts section of the HTML Conversion Settings dialog box, as shown in the following illustration. In this section, you can modify the font style for body text, headings, or preformatted text, and change the base font size.

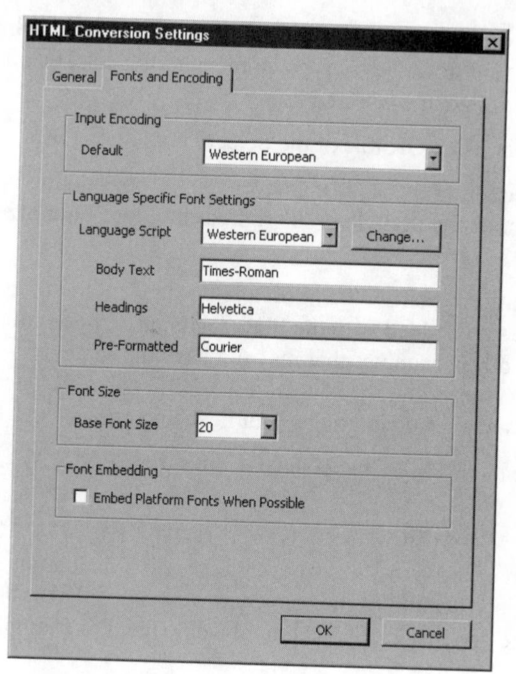

12. In the Input Encoding section, accept the default option or click the triangle to the right of the field and choose the appropriate encoding system from the drop-down menu.
13. In the Language Specific Font Settings section, accept the defaults or click Change to display the Select Fonts dialog box, shown here:

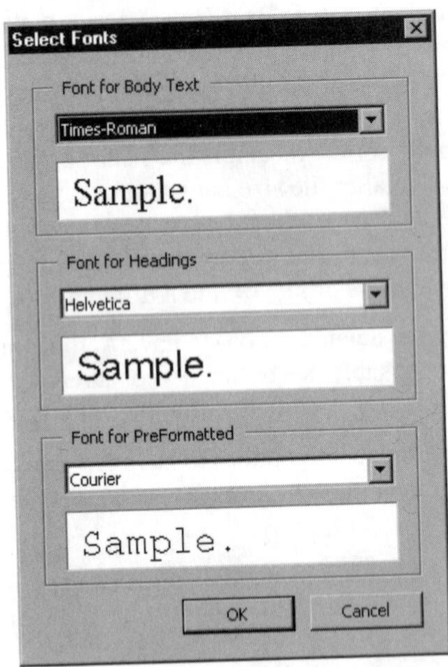

14. In the Select Fonts dialog box, click the triangle to the right of each font section and choose the desired font from the drop-down menu. After selecting a font, the sample window updates to reflect the selected font.
15. After selecting fonts, click OK to exit the Select Fonts dialog box.
16. In the Font Size section of the HTML Conversion Settings dialog box, accept the default base font sizes or click the triangle to the right of the Base Font Size field and select the desired font size.
17. Choose Embed Platform Fonts When Possible if you want the fonts you specify for the captured web pages embedded with the PDF document. Choose this option if the file will be viewed on other machines that may not have the same fonts you have on your machine. Note that embedding fonts increases the file size of the document. If you embed fonts, make sure you are not violating a font licensing agreement.
18. Click OK to close the HTML Conversion Settings dialog box.

Modify Page Layout Options

In the Page Layout section of the Web Page Conversion Setting dialog box, you can modify the size, margins, orientation, and scaling of the converted web pages. These options come in handy if you want to maintain the dimensions of a captured web page. For example, if you know each page in a web site is configured to a certain size, say 760 pixels × 420 pixels (a Web browser maximized at an 800×600 desktop resolution), you can change the default Acrobat document size (8 1/2 inches × 11 inches) to match. To modify the page layout of a captured web page, follow the steps below.

NOTE *The default unit of measure for Acrobat is inches. When you capture web pages, you may find it helpful to convert the unit of measure to points by choosing Edit | Preferences, and in the Units section, choose Points.*

1. Open the Web Page Conversion Settings dialog box as outlined previously.
2. Click the Page Layout tab to reveal the Page Layout section, as shown here:

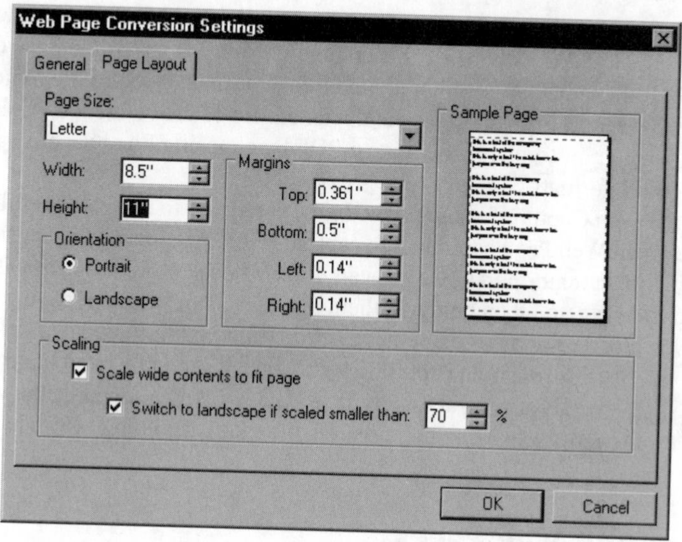

TIP *If the web page you are capturing has no margins, you can duplicate this when you capture the page by entering 0 for each margin setting in the Page Layout section of the HTML Conversion Settings dialog box.*

3. Click the triangle to the right of the Page Size field and choose an option from the drop-down menu. When you select a preset page layout, the values in the Width and Height fields change to reflect your choice.
4. Alternatively, select Custom from the Page Size drop-down menu and specify the page size by entering values in the Width and Height fields or by clicking the spinner buttons to change the values.
5. In the Margins section, accept the defaults or enter your own values in the Top, Bottom, Left, and Right fields.
6. In the Orientation section, choose Portrait (the default) or Landscape.

7. In the Scaling section, you can modify the following options:
   - **Scale Wide Contents To Fit Page** Choose this option and Acrobat resizes the contents of a web page that exceeds the width of the screen to fit the page.
   - **Switch To Landscape If Scaled Smaller Than [ ] %** Accept the default value (70 percent) or enter a value of your own in this field. Acrobat will automatically switch the page layout from Portrait to Landscape if it is necessary to scale the page to a value lower than specified.
8. Click OK to apply the settings and close the Web Page Conversion Settings dialog box.

Save Converted Web Pages

After you convert one or several web pages to PDF format, you can save the document for future use by choosing File | Save. After choosing this command, Acrobat opens the Save dialog box and prompts you for a filename and location to which to save the converted file. After specifying these options, click Save, and Acrobat saves the document for future reference. Alternatively, you can save the document in formats other than a PDF by choosing File | Save As and choosing one of the supported file formats.

After you use the Web Capture feature a few times, you begin to see how useful this feature is. You can use the Open Web Page command to capture a web page with product specifications. If you are contemplating a major purchase, you can download the product specifications of every product you are considering and then compare them at your leisure, without having to wait for the web pages to download or perhaps be bumped off the Internet during peak traffic.

If you use the Internet for research, capturing web pages is a great way to build a reference library. After you save several (or several hundred) web pages as PDF documents, you can use Acrobat Catalog (Professional only) to build a searchable index. Building a searchable index is covered in Chapter 16.

Update Converted Web Pages

If you surf the Internet frequently, you know it is in a constant state of flux. New web sites open, old ones disappear, and web sites are frequently updated. If you specified Save Refresh Commands (Windows) or Save Update Commands (Macintosh) for your web page conversions settings (see "Modify General Conversion Settings" presented earlier in this chapter), you can update a captured web page you saved as a PDF document by doing the following:

1. Launch Acrobat and log onto the Internet.
2. Open the PDF file you captured from a web page.
3. Choose Advanced | Web Capture | Refresh Pages to have Acrobat open the Refresh Pages dialog box, as shown next.

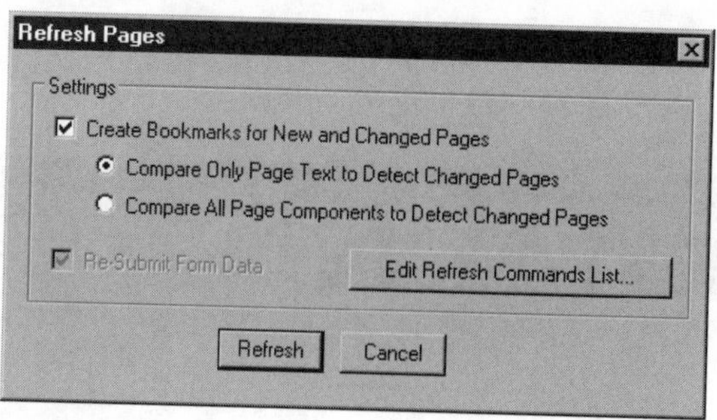

4. Choose Create Bookmarks For New And Changed Pages. When you choose this option, Acrobat creates bookmarks for downloaded pages that have been added to the site or modified since you captured the web page.

5. Choose Compare Only Page Text To Detect Changed Pages, and Acrobat compares the captured page to the web site page and will download the page if the page text has changed.
6. Choose Compare All Page Components To Detect Changed Pages, and Acrobat compares all elements from the PDF document to the web site from which the document was captured. The document will be updated if Acrobat detects a change, such as a new image.
7. If the captured web page has a form in it, the Re-Submit Form Data option is active. This option is enabled by default.

AUTION *When the Re-Submit Form Data option is selected, any data on the form is resubmitted. If you captured a web page with a form you used to purchase an item, a duplicate purchase may result if you enable this option.*

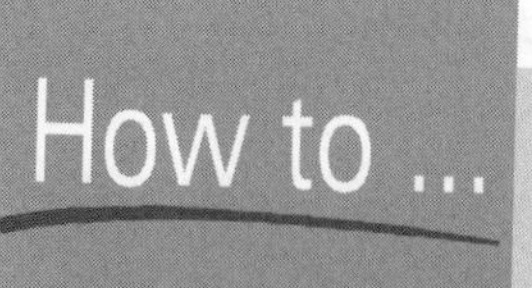

Save a Web Search

If you use Internet Search engines to find web pages that you want to save for reference, after you enter your query, launch Acrobat and choose File | Create PDF | From Web Page and then enter the URL for the results page. After Acrobat downloads the page, you can append the document with the results of your search by clicking a link. Download additional web pages by clicking other links. After you have downloaded all the pages you want to save, you can delete the initial search page by clicking its thumbnail and then choosing Document | Delete Pages. If your search returns pages of URLs, you can save the PDF document and open the document at a later date to peruse the desired URLs at your leisure.

8. Click Edit Refresh Commands List to reveal the Refresh Commands List dialog box, as shown here:

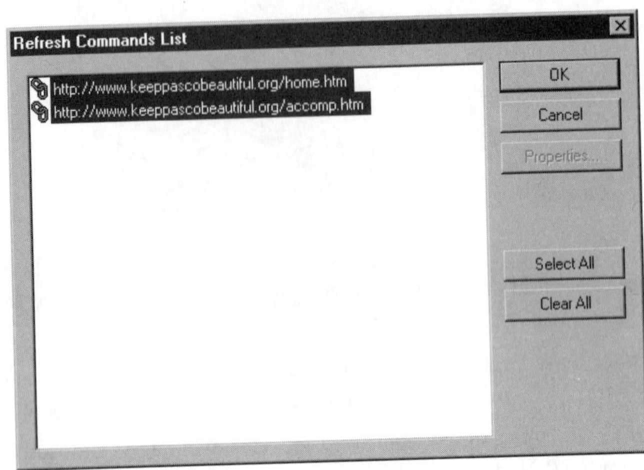

9. To update all links in the list, click OK. Note that all links from the captured page are selected by default. If you want to update all captured pages, you do not need to click the Edit Refresh Commands List button. You need to choose this option only to update specific pages from the captured document by selecting the URLs you want to update from the list in this dialog box. Click a link to select it, or select multiple links while holding down the SHIFT key. Alternatively, you can select all or clear all. After clicking OK, you exit the Refresh Commands List dialog box and are returned to the Refresh Pages dialog box.
10. Click Refresh to have Acrobat search for the changes as specified and download new or changed pages.

Summary

In this chapter, you learned to create PDF documents by capturing with your scanner, your digital camera, and from web pages. Another topic of discussion was the Paper Capture command, which enables you to convert PDFs from scanned documents into searchable text. In the next chapter, you'll learn to create navigation for your PDF documents.

Chapter 7 Create Navigation for PDF Documents

How to...

- Create bookmarks
- Edit bookmarks
- Use thumbnails
- Create links
- Create a navigation menu

When you create a PDF document within an authoring application, navigation devices are added to the document. PDF documents have two types of navigation devices that are created automatically: bookmarks and thumbnails. Bookmarks and thumbnails have their own tabs in the Navigation pane.

When you create a PDF document, one thumbnail is created for each page. Viewers of your PDF documents can navigate to a specific page of the document by clicking its thumbnail, or with a single-page document, navigate to a specific part of the page, as you will learn in this chapter. Bookmarks, on the other hand, may or may not be created depending on how you created the PDF document. If, for example, you use PDFMaker (the Adobe Acrobat plug-in for Microsoft Office) with its default settings to create a PDF file from a Microsoft Word document that contains Heading styles, a bookmark appears for each Heading style used in the document. If you use the Word Print command and choose Acrobat Distiller to create the PDF document, no bookmarks are created. To navigate to a bookmark within a document, viewers just click its name in the Bookmarks tab of the Navigation pane. For more information on the Navigation pane, refer to Chapter 3.

After you open a PDF file in Acrobat, you can modify bookmarks and thumbnails as well as create other navigation devices such as text links or buttons. After you create a link (also known as a *hotspot*), you can assign an action to it that determines what occurs when the link is activated with a mouse click. You can also add actions to bookmarks and links, and assign one or more actions to an individual page that occur when the page opens or closes.

Use the Bookmarks Tab

In Adobe Reader, you use the Bookmarks tab to navigate to bookmark destinations. In Acrobat, you also use the Bookmarks tab to navigate a document as well as to edit existing bookmarks and add new ones. The Bookmarks tab is part of the Navigation pane. To open the Bookmarks tab, click Bookmarks. Figure 7-1 shows the Bookmarks tab for the Adobe Acrobat 6.0 Help document.

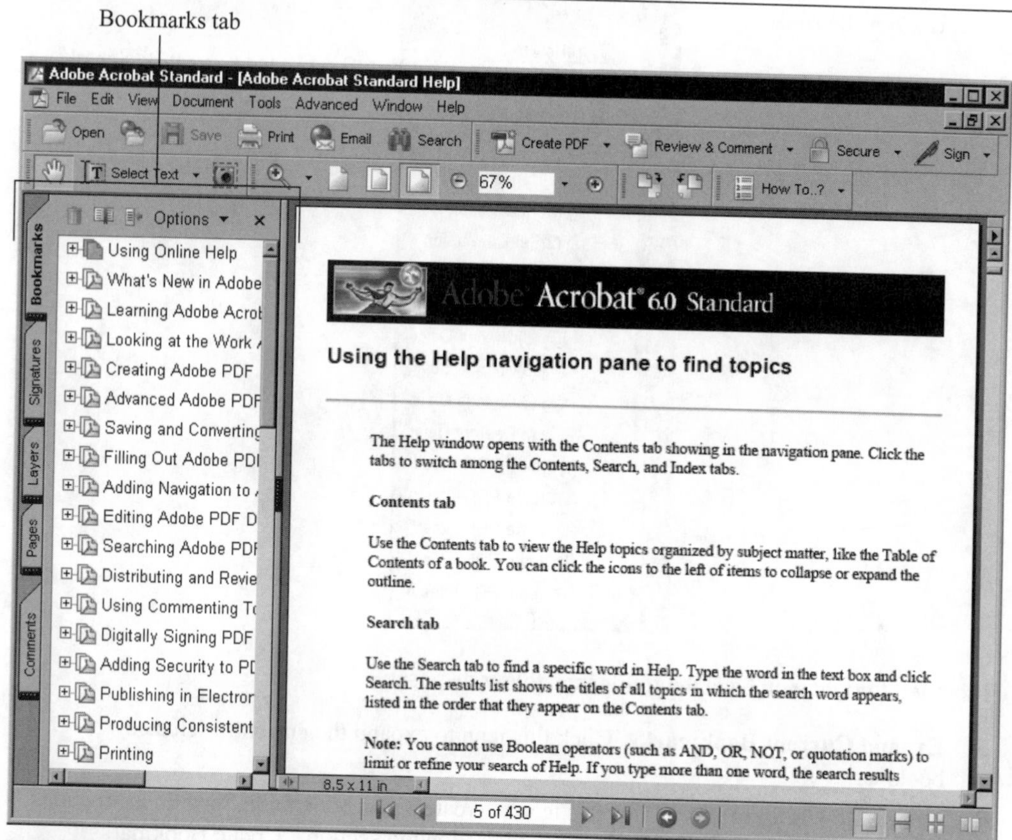

FIGURE 7-1 In Acrobat, use the Bookmarks tab to navigate to, create, and edit bookmarks.

About the Bookmarks Tab Toolbar

Bookmarks are an important part of any multipage PDF document. Viewers of your PDF files would have a hard time finding what they want to view without bookmarks. When you create bookmarks, edit bookmarks, or use bookmarks to navigate within a document, you can use the Bookmarks tab toolbar to streamline your work. The Bookmarks tab toolbar contains three tool icons and one menu icon, as shown here:

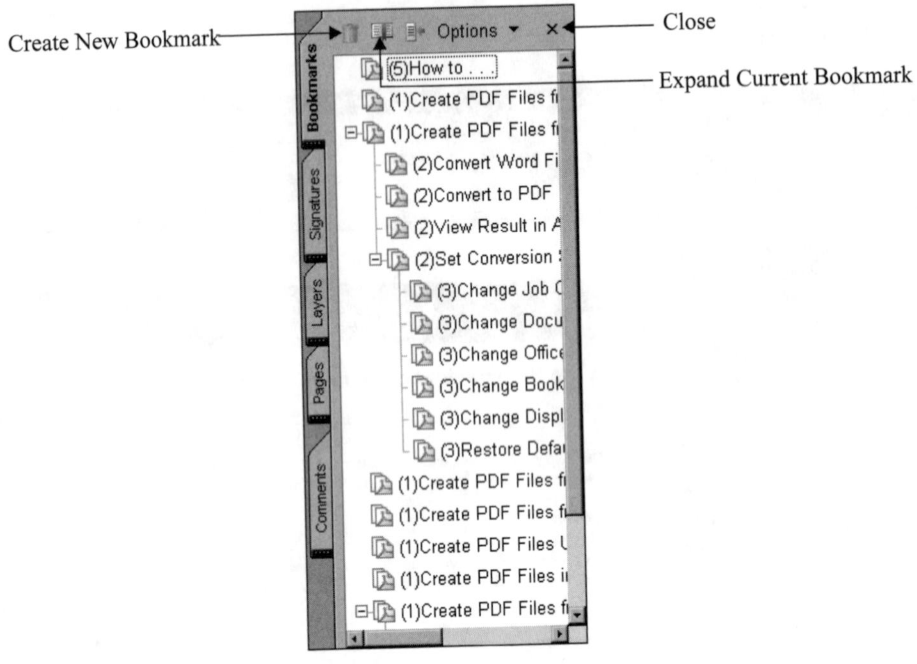

From left to right, you have the following at your disposal:

- **Expand Current Bookmark** Click this icon to expand the currently selected bookmark.
- **Create New Bookmark** Click this icon to create a new bookmark. Specific instructions for creating bookmarks are presented in the following section, "Create Bookmarks."
- **Options** Click the text icon to open the Bookmarks tab Options menu.
- **Close** Click this icon to close the Bookmarks tab.

Create Bookmarks

A bookmark is a text link in the Bookmarks tab of the Navigation pane that viewers of your PDF documents can use to navigate to a specific part of the document. If the bookmarks in the document are created from an authoring application plug-in, the bookmark is linked to a specific part of a document such as a heading, or in the case of a document comprised of captured web pages, a specific web page. Bookmarks can also be configured to link to external PDF documents and other PDF files by modifying the action that occurs when the bookmark is clicked. Figure 7-2 shows the bookmarks the PDFMaker created when the first version of this chapter was converted to a PDF file.

You can, however, create your own bookmarks to draw a viewer's attention to a specific point. You can also use bookmarks to open other PDF documents or other files. To create a document bookmark, do the following:

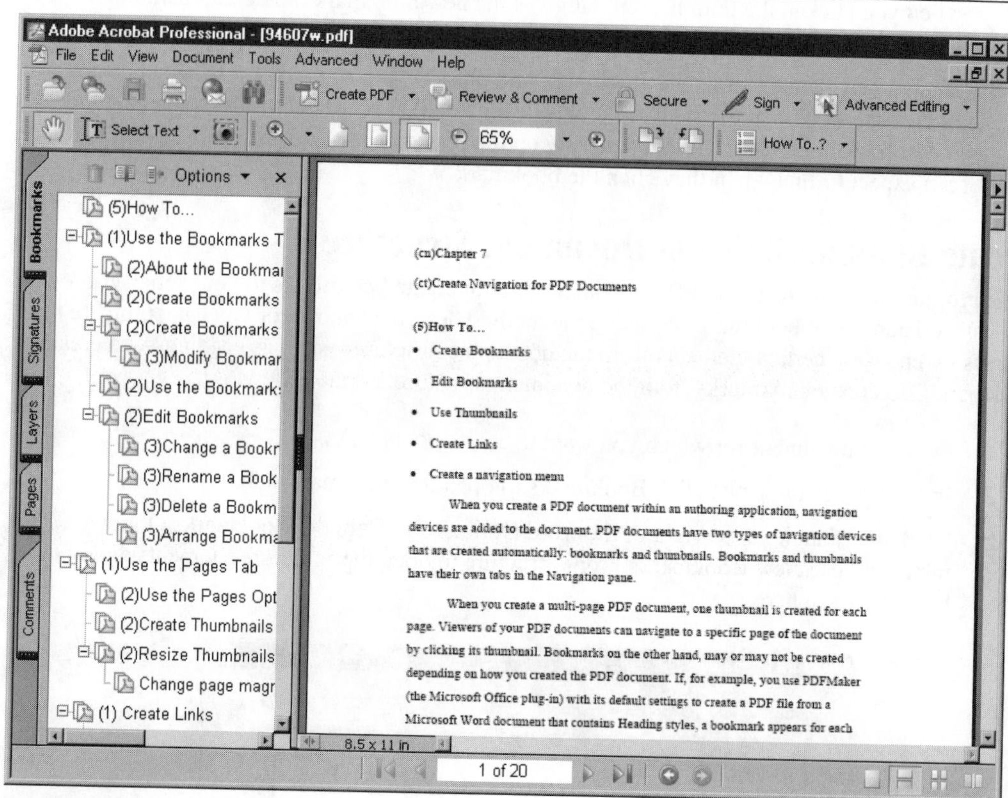

FIGURE 7-2 Use bookmarks to navigate to specific points in a document.

1. Open the Navigation pane and click Bookmarks to open the Bookmarks tab.
2. Click the bookmark above the place where you want the new bookmark to appear. If you do not specify a place for the new bookmark, it is added at the bottom of the list.
3. Use the Hand tool, Viewing tools, or menu commands to navigate to the part of the document where you want the bookmark to link. Note that you can also use existing bookmarks and thumbnails to navigate to desired parts of the document.

OTE *Remember, you can also link to a magnified view of a page to direct the reader's attention. You can magnify the page view by using the Zoom tool.*

4. Click the Create New Bookmark button shown in the previous illustration. Alternatively, click the Options icon and choose New Bookmark from the Bookmarks Options menu. After you do one of the above, the new bookmark appears below the bookmark you selected

when you clicked the button. Acrobat gives the new bookmark the default name of Untitled. The bookmark name is highlighted.

5. Enter a new name for the new bookmark and press ENTER or RETURN. When choosing a name for a bookmark, remember to choose a name that accurately reflects the contents of the bookmark. Your viewers will rely on the bookmark title to get an idea of what they can expect to find when they click the bookmark.

Create Bookmarks from Document Structure

If the program used to create the PDF document did not create bookmarks to your satisfaction, you can add additional bookmarks by using the method described above, or you can automate the process by choosing certain elements from the document structure—such as headings—to create bookmarks. To create bookmarks from the document structure, do the following:

1. Open the document for which you want to create bookmarks.
2. In the Navigation pane, click Bookmarks to open the Bookmarks tab.
3. Click the triangle to the right of the word Options and from the Bookmarks Options menu, choose New Bookmarks From Structure to open the Structure Elements dialog box, as shown here:

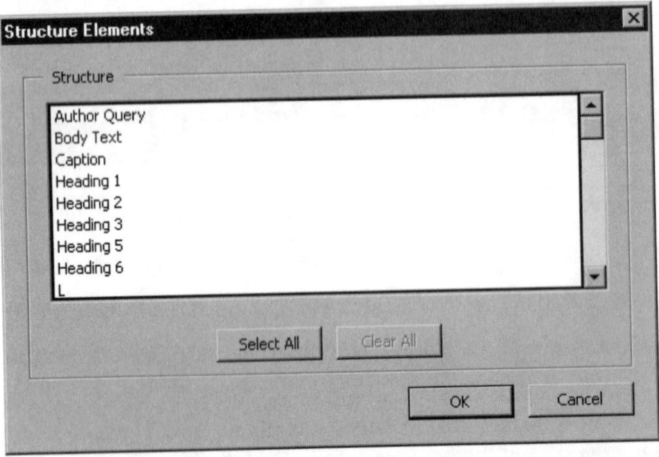

NOTE *The New Bookmarks From Structure command is dimmed out if the document does not have elements Acrobat can use to create bookmarks.*

4. Click a structure element name to select it. To add additional structure elements, hold down SHIFT and click to add contiguous elements, or hold down CTRL and then click to add noncontiguous elements. To select all structure elements, click the Select All button.

5. Click OK, and Acrobat scans the document and creates a bookmark for each selected structure element located. The bookmarks are untitled and nested in tree fashion. Click the plus sign (+) to the left of the top element to expand the first bookmark, as shown in the following illustration. The bookmarks in this illustration were created from a PDF file of this chapter, as created in Word, using the Caption structure element that notes where the figures and illustrations are inserted.

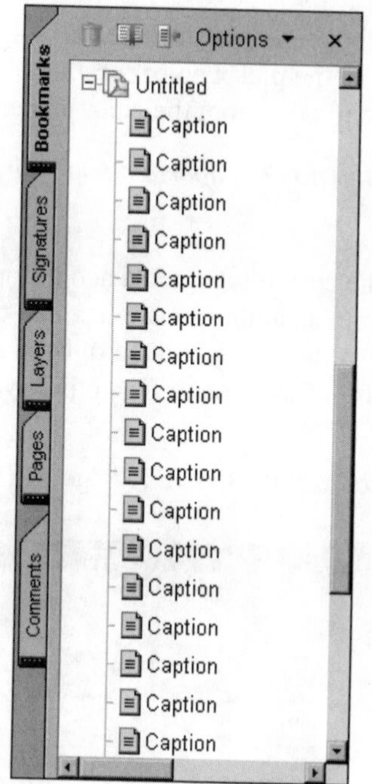

Modify Bookmark Properties

After you create a bookmark, you can modify the bookmark by changing its properties. You can modify the appearance of the bookmark, modify the view of the link destination, and modify the action that occurs when a user clicks the link. To set bookmark properties, do the following:

1. Click the bookmark whose properties you want to modify.
2. Click the triangle to the right of the word Options and from the Bookmarks Options menu, choose Properties to open the Bookmark Properties dialog box, as shown here. Alternatively, you can right- click (Windows) or CTRL-click (Macintosh) a bookmark and choose Properties from the Context menu.

3. When you open the Bookmark Properties dialog box, the Appearance tab is selected by default. You can modify the Appearance properties to change the look of the selected bookmark's text. Click the triangle to the right of Style and choose one of the following from the drop-down menu: Plain (the default), Bold, Italic, or Bold & Italic.
4. Click the color swatch and choose a color from the pop-up palette. You can choose one of the preset colors or click Other Color to create a custom color from the color picker.

TIP *You can direct a reader's attention to important bookmarks by changing the bookmark text style and color.*

5. Click the Actions tab, and the currently selected action for the bookmark is displayed. If the bookmark was created in an authoring application, the action is usually Go To A Page In This Document. Click the triangle to the right of the Select Action field and choose an option from the drop-down menu. The other available actions are discussed in detail in Chapter 8.
6. Click Edit, as shown next, to open the Go To A Page In This Document dialog box:

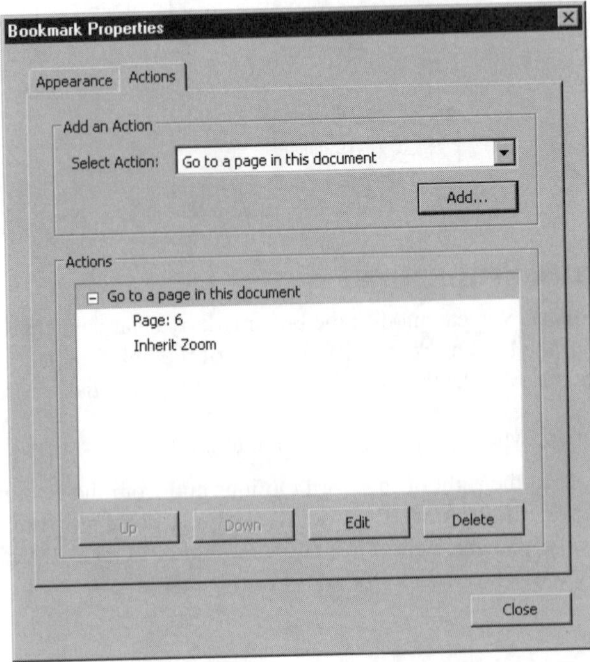

7. Enter the number of the page that you want to open when the bookmark is clicked.

8. Click the triangle to the right of the Zoom field and choose an option from the drop-down menu. For more information on the magnification options, refer to the "Change Zoom Settings" section that appears later in this chapter.
9. Click OK to close the Go To A Page In This Document dialog box and then click Close to exit the Bookmark Properties dialog box and apply your changes.

Use the Bookmarks Options Menu

You use the Bookmarks Options menu to perform functions associated with bookmarks. You can use commands from the Bookmarks Options menu to modify bookmarks, navigate to bookmarks, and maintain the Bookmarks tab. To open the Bookmarks Options menu, follow these steps:

1. In the Navigation pane, click Bookmarks to open the Bookmarks tab.
2. Click Options to open the Bookmarks Options menu, as shown here:

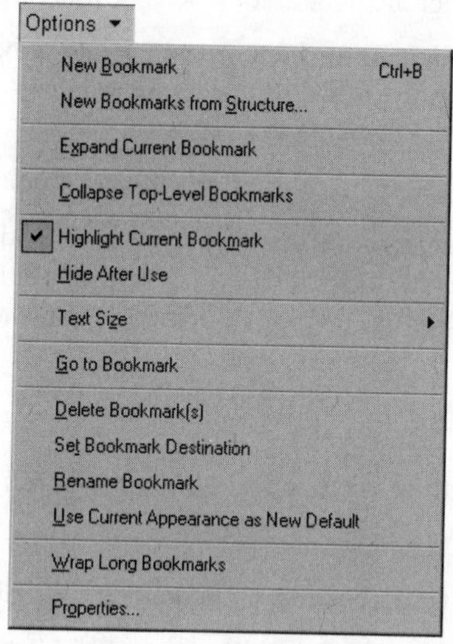

After you open the Bookmarks Options menu, click the menu command you want Acrobat to perform. Some of the commands in this menu have already been presented; others will do the same job as their toolbar counterparts. For example, to expand a bookmark, you can click the plus sign (+) next to a collapsed bookmark, or choose the Expand Current Bookmark command from the Bookmarks Options menu. Detailed information about other relevant Bookmarks Options menu commands are discussed in upcoming sections.

Edit Bookmarks

You can edit existing bookmarks by changing the bookmark destination, renaming the bookmarks, deleting selected bookmarks, and rearranging the hierarchy of bookmarks. When you add new bookmarks to a document, you can specify the bookmark destination and view magnification. However, at times it may be preferable to layout the document structure by creating bookmarks first and then modifying the destination and view of the bookmarks later. You can use the Bookmarks tab toolbar and Options menu to edit bookmarks. You can also right-click (Windows) or CTRL-click (Macintosh) to choose a command from the Bookmarks tab Context menu, which is a watered-down, but still useful, version of the Bookmarks Options menu.

Change a Bookmark Destination

You can change the destination of a bookmark; change its zoom, or both. By modifying the view of a bookmark, you call attention to a specific part of the document. To modify a bookmark destination, follow these steps:

1. In the Bookmarks tab, select the bookmark whose destination you want to modify.
2. In the Document pane, change to the location you want the bookmark to link to by using either the Hand tool, navigation tools, or menu commands. Alternatively, you can click a thumbnail in the Pages tab to navigate to a page.
3. Change the zoom of the document by using the viewing tools or menu commands.
4. Choose Set Bookmark Destination from the Bookmarks Options menu and then click Yes in the Warning dialog box to set the new destination of the link. Alternatively, you can right-click (Windows) or CTRL-click (Macintosh) and choose Set Destination from the Context menu.

Rename a Bookmark

Another edit you may need to perform is renaming a bookmark. You have two methods available to change a bookmark name:

1. Select the bookmark and then click inside the text box to select the bookmark text.
2. Enter a new name for the bookmark and then press ENTER or RETURN.

Alternatively, you can:

1. Select the bookmark.
2. Choose Rename Bookmark from the Bookmarks Options menu to select the bookmark text.
3. Enter a new name for the bookmark and then press ENTER or RETURN.

Delete a Bookmark

You can delete any bookmark. When you delete a bookmark, you do not change the content of a document; you merely remove a link. If you created a PDF document that has several heading levels, you may want to consider deleting a few bookmarks to simplify navigation. To delete a bookmark, follow these steps:

1. Select the bookmark. To add contiguous bookmarks to the selection, press SHIFT and click the bookmark(s) you want to add to the selection. To add noncontiguous bookmarks to the selection, press CTRL and click the bookmark(s) you want to add to the selection.
2. Choose Edit | Delete, press Delete, or choose Delete Bookmark(s) from the Bookmarks Options menu.

There is no warning dialog box before the bookmark is deleted. If you delete a bookmark in error, choose Edit | Undo Delete Bookmark or press CTRL-Z.

Arrange Bookmarks

When you create a PDF document, bookmarks are created in descending order from the first page of the document to the last. Acrobat nests bookmarks when you convert a document with multiple heading levels or if you use the New Bookmarks From Structure command. You can create your own bookmark nests to organize a cluttered Bookmarks tab. To nest a bookmark or group of bookmarks under another bookmark, follow these steps:

1. Select the bookmark(s) you want to nest. You can select contiguous or noncontiguous bookmarks.
2. Click and drag the bookmarks toward the bookmark under which you want to nest them. As you drag the bookmarks towards another bookmark, a left-pointing arrowhead appears.
3. Release the mouse button when you reach the desired bookmark. As soon as you release the mouse button, Acrobat nests the bookmark in its new location. If the bookmark to which you are nesting the bookmark is collapsed, Acrobat expands the bookmark. Collapse the bookmark by clicking the minus sign to its left.

Remove a bookmark from a nested position by doing the following:

1. Expand the bookmark that contains the bookmark(s) you want to remove from a nested position.
2. Click the bookmark(s) you want to move.
3. Drag the bookmarks to the left and position them under the title of the parent bookmark. You know the bookmarks are positioned properly when you see an inverted red triangle under the parent bookmark name next to a left-pointing arrow.

When you select and drag a branch that has children, the children of the parent are moved as well, maintaining the structure of the branch.

4. Release the mouse button, and Acrobat moves the bookmark(s) out of a nested position.

Use the Pages Tab

When you convert a file to PDF format and open the document in Acrobat, thumbnails are automatically generated. Thumbnails are neatly arranged by page order in the Pages tab, which resides in the Navigation pane. You can use thumbnails as navigation devices when reading a document as well as to reorder pages, a technique that is discussed in Chapter 9. Thumbnails are also used to print and change the magnification of pages. To access the Pages tab, choose View | Navigation Tabs | Pages. If the Navigation pane is open but another palette is displayed, click Pages to open the tab. Figure 7-3 shows the Pages tab with the thumbnails enlarged.

Pages tab

Adobe Acrobat Professional - [94607w.pdf]

File Edit View Document Tools Advanced Window Help

Create PDF · Review & Comment · Secure · Sign · Advanced Editing

Select Text · 67% · How To..?

Options

Bookmarks · Signatures · Layers · Pages · Comments

(cn)Chapter 7

(ct)Create Navigation for PDF Documents

(5)How To…

- Create Bookmarks
- Edit Bookmarks
- Use Thumbnails
- Create Links
- Create a navigation menu

When you create a PDF document within an authoring application, navigation devices are added to the document. PDF documents have two types of navigation devices that are created automatically: bookmarks and thumbnails. Bookmarks and thumbnails have their own tabs in the Navigation pane.

When you create a multi-page PDF document, one thumbnail is created for each page. Viewers of your PDF documents can navigate to a specific page of the document by clicking its thumbnail. Bookmarks on the other hand, may or may not be created depending on how you created the PDF document. If, for example, you use PDFMaker (the Microsoft Office plug-in) with its default settings to create a PDF file from a

8.5 x 11 in · 1 of 19

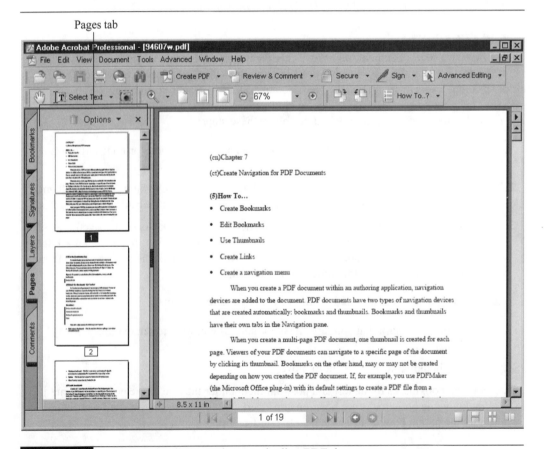

FIGURE 7-3 Use thumbnails to navigate and edit a PDF document.

Use the Pages Options Menu

The Pages tab has a menu that you use to perform tasks in the Pages tab. The menu has commands to edit pages, embed thumbnails or remove embedded thumbnails, and change the size of thumbnails. In upcoming sections, you'll learn to use the commands that pertain to editing thumbnails. In Chapter 9, you'll learn to use thumbnails to edit and reorder document pages. To open the Pages Options menu, do the following:

1. Open the Navigation pane and click Pages.
2. Click the Options icon to open the Pages Options menu, as shown here:

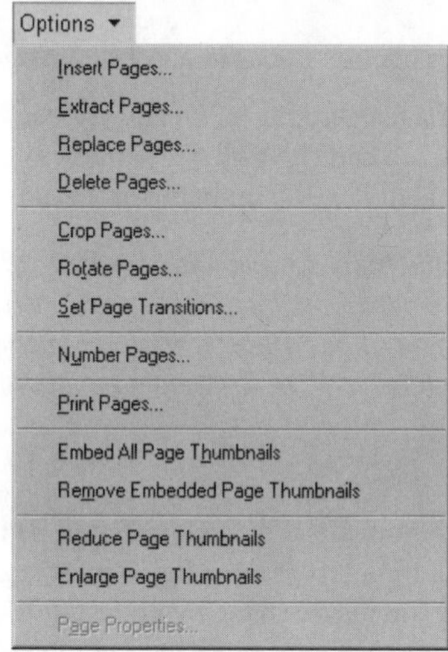

Alternatively, you can right-click (Windows) or CTRL-click (Macintosh) within the Pages tab to open a Context menu. The Pages tab context menu is a watered-down version of the Pages Options menu. However, you may prefer to use the Context menu when you need to access its commands quickly. You can access the complete version of the Pages Options menu by selecting a thumbnail and then right-clicking on a Windows machine, or CTRL-clicking on a Macintosh machine.

Create Thumbnails

When you create a PDF document in an authoring application or using the Adobe PDFMaker plug in, you can modify a setting to embed thumbnails. Thumbnails increase the file size of the published PDF document by approximately 3K or more per thumbnail for a page with images; thumbnails for pages with text are only slightly smaller. The actual size of the thumbnail will vary depending on the amount of graphics in the page from which the thumbnail is generated. When you create a document without embedded thumbnails, Acrobat creates them dynamically when you open the Pages tab. This can take several seconds for a large document. You can choose to embed thumbnails to circumvent the redraw every time you open the palette. You can easily remove embedded thumbnails in the future if desired.

To embed all thumbnails within a document, follow these steps:

1. Open the Navigation pane and click Pages to open the Pages tab.
2. Open the Pages Options menu and choose Embed All Page Thumbnails. Alternatively, you can choose the Embed All Page Thumbnails command from the Pages tab Context menu.

To remove embedded thumbnails from a document, do the following:

1. Open the Navigation pane and click Pages to access the Pages tab.
2. Click Options to open the Pages Options menu and choose Remove Embedded Page Thumbnails. Alternatively, you can right-click (Windows) or CTRL-click (Macintosh) and choose Remove Embedded Page Thumbnails from the Context menu.

TIP

After you remove thumbnails from a document, Acrobat will create them on the fly whenever the Pages tab is opened. As mentioned previously, this may take considerable time with a lengthy document. As a rule, you should remove embedded thumbnails only when the file size of the published PDF document is a factor.

Resize Thumbnails

When you open the Pages tab, all thumbnails are displayed at default size. Unless you resize the width of the Navigation pane, the thumbnails are displayed in a single column. If you prefer, you can display more thumbnails in the Navigation pane by choosing Reduce Page Thumbnails from the Pages Options menu. After you choose this command, thumbnails are displayed at reduced magnification. To return thumbnails to their original size, choose Enlarge Page Thumbnails from the Pages Options menu.

You can use the Reduce Page Thumbnails or Enlarge Page Thumbnails command more than once to arrive at the optimum thumbnail size for your working preference.

Create Links

As you have already learned, when you convert a document into PDF format, navigation devices in the form of thumbnails and bookmarks are created for you. You can, however, exceed the limitations of these rudimentary navigation devices by creating links. When you create a link, you create a hotspot in the document that changes the user's cursor into a pointing hand when a

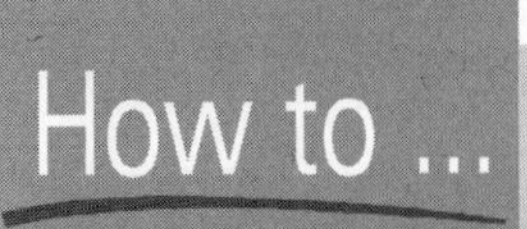

Change Page Magnification with Thumbnails

A black border surrounds each thumbnail. You can change page magnification by clicking and dragging the black rectangle at the thumbnail's lower-right corner. After changing the page magnification, a red rectangle surrounds the current page view from which you can click and drag any borderline to scroll to a different part of the document.

mouse passes over it; the same thing happens for a link on a web page. You can create links for text or images in a PDF document or any other kind of link anywhere in the document. The links you create can be visible or invisible.

7

Links give you tremendous flexibility. You can create links that change the view of a document, load another document, open a web page, load a multimedia element, and more. You can specify the appearance of a link as a visible or invisible rectangle, as well as specify the type of highlight that appears when a user's mouse passes over the link. The first step in creating a link is to define the active area of the link, also known as a *hotspot.*

Create a Hotspot

As it relates to PDF documents, a hotspot is an active area of the document that, when clicked by a user, causes an action to occur. You create a hotspot with the Link tool that is found on the Advanced Editing toolbar. The Link tool looks like two interconnecting links of a chain. Use the Link tool to define the boundary of the hotspot as follows:

1. Choose Tools | Advanced Editing | Link Tool. After you select the tool and move your cursor into the Document pane, it becomes a crosshair. As long as the Link tool is selected, any other links in the document, even invisible ones, are displayed.
2. In the Document pane, click a spot to define one of the hotspot corners and then drag diagonally. As you drag, a dotted bounding box gives you a preview of the area you are selecting.
3. When the bounding box surrounds the area you want to define as a hotspot, release the mouse button.

TIP

To create a text link, select the Link tool, hold CTRL *(Windows) or* OPTION *(Macintosh), and the cursor becomes an I-beam. Click the target text to create a hotspot the exact size of the text.*

After you create the hotspot, the Create Link dialog box appears, as shown here:

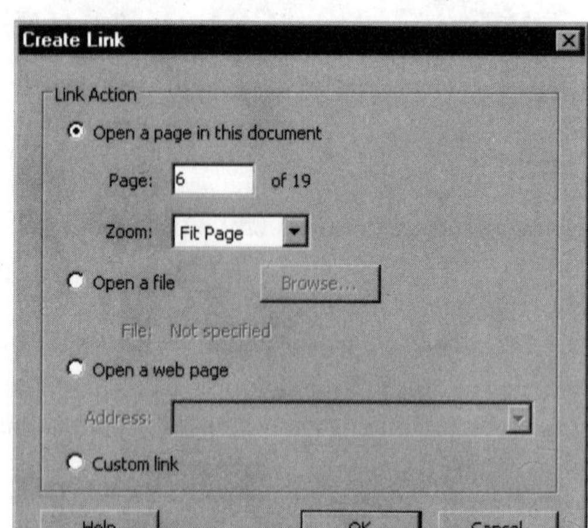

4. Choose one of the following link actions:
   - **Open A Page In This Document** Enables you to specify which page will appear and at what zoom setting when the button is clicked.
   - **Open A File** Loads a file when the link is clicked. If you choose this option, Acrobat creates a link to the file including the relative path of the file. Use this option when the document will only be viewed on the computer that creates the document.
   - **Open A Web Page** Opens a web page when the link is clicked. If you choose this option, the Address field becomes available. In this field enter the URL for the web page you want to open when the link is clicked.
   - **Custom Link** Lets you choose a custom action that will occur when the link is clicked. After choosing this option, the Link Properties dialog box opens and the Actions tab is displayed. Actions are discussed in detail in Chapter 8.
5. In the Appearance tab of the Link Properties dialog box shown in the following illustration, click the triangle to the right of the Link Type field and from the drop-down menu choose one of the following:
   - **Visible Rectangle** This option creates a hotspot with a visible rectangle at its perimeter.

- **Invisible Rectangle** This option creates a hotspot that is not visible. If you choose Invisible Rectangle, the Width, Color, and Style options are not valid and are no longer displayed.

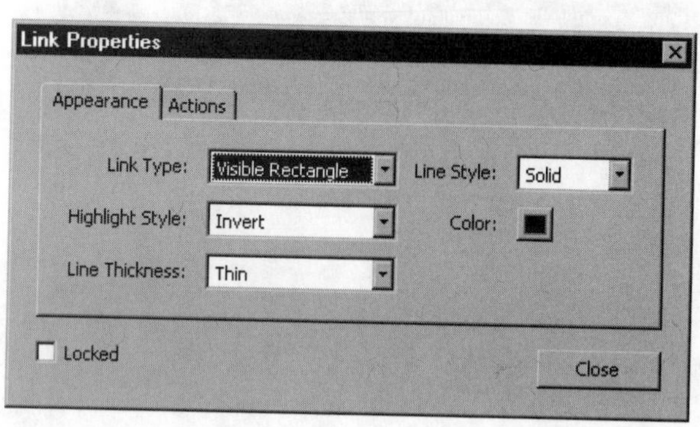

6. Click the triangle to the right of the highlight field and choose one of the following options to determine how the link is highlighted when users click it:
   - **None** No highlight appears when the link is clicked.
   - **Invert** The link is highlighted in black when clicked.
   - **Outline** The link outline color changes when clicked.
   - **Inset** A shadow appears when the link is clicked. This effect is similar to a web page button that appears to recess into the page when clicked.
7. If you choose Visible Rectangle, click the triangle to the right of the Line Thickness field and choose Thin, Medium, or Thick from the drop-down menu. This option defines the thickness of the hotspot border.
8. Click the triangle to the right of the Line Style field and choose Solid, Dashed, or Underline. This option defines the line style for the hotspot border.
9. Click Color and choose the rectangle color from the pop-up palette. To choose a color other than the presets, click Other Color, and choose a color from the system color picker.
10. Click the Actions tab to open the Actions section of the dialog box, which looks identical to the Actions section of the Bookmark Properties dialog box shown previously.
11. The default link action is Go To A Page In This Document. You can choose another action by clicking the triangle to the right of the Select Action field and then selecting an option from the drop-down menu. (Actions are discussed in detail in Chapter 8.) To use

the default link action, click Add to open the Go To A Page In This Document dialog box, shown next:

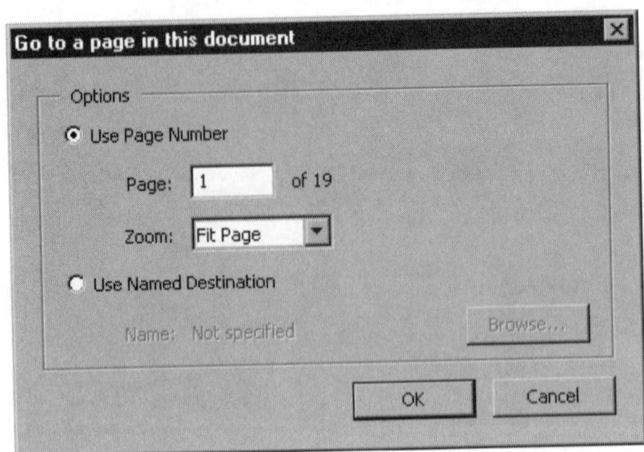

12. To navigate to a page in the document, click the Use Page Number radio button. You can also choose to navigate to a Named Destination in the document. Named Destinations are covered in Chapter 8.
13. In the Page field, enter the page number you want to appear when the link is clicked.
14. Click the triangle to the right of the Zoom field and choose an option. The option you choose determines the magnification of the view connected to the link. Zoom settings are discussed in detail in the following section of this chapter.
15. Click OK to close the Go To A Page In This Document dialog box. You can now add additional actions by selecting them from the Select Action drop-down menu and then clicking Add.
16. Click Close to exit the Link Properties dialog box.
17. Select the Hand tool and click the link to test it. If the link does not perform as you expected, you can edit the link by following the instructions in the upcoming "Edit Links" section.

If you will be adding or editing extensive links in a document, you can save time by choosing Tools | Advanced | Show Advanced Editing Toolbar. This command displays the Advanced Editing Toolbar in the last position in which it appeared in the workspace, giving you easy access to the Link tool.

Change Zoom Settings

When you create or edit a link or bookmark, you can control the magnification setting of the bookmark or link destination. You can change magnification in the Zoom field of the Go To A Page In This Document dialog box, which can be accessed as follows:

1. Select the link or bookmark whose zoom settings you want to modify. Select the bookmark from within the Bookmarks pane. To select a link, choose Tools | Advanced | Links Tool, or choose the Links tool from the Advanced Editing Tools toolbar if available.
2. Right-click (Windows) or CTRL-click (Macintosh) the link or bookmark and choose Properties from the Context menu. After choosing this command, the applicable Properties dialog box appears with the previously used tab displayed. If necessary, click the Actions tab.
3. Select the Go To A Page In This Document action from the list of actions assigned to the link or bookmark.
4. Click Edit to open the Go To A Page In This Document dialog box.
5. Click the triangle to the right of the Zoom field and choose one of the following options:
   - **Fit Page** Choose this option, and the visible contents of the bookmark or link destination are sized to fit the Document pane.
   - **Actual Size** Choose this option, and a selected link or bookmark destination will be displayed at 100 percent magnification, the original size of the document.
   - **Fit Width** Choose this option, and the link or bookmark destination zooms to the current width of the Document pane. If you choose the fit width option, images on the page may be pixelated. An image becomes pixelated when it is enlarged enough to make the individual pixels appear as square blocks of color. At normal magnification, pixels are blended so as not to be visible.
   - **Fit Visible** Choose this option, and when selected, the link or bookmark destination zooms so that all visible elements on the page resize to the current width of the Document pane. Note that this view will differ at different monitor resolutions.
   - **Inherit Zoom** Choose this option, and the bookmark or link destination displays at the viewer-selected magnification level when the bookmark or link is selected.
6. Click OK to close the Go To A Page In This Document dialog box and then click Close to apply the zoom settings to the bookmark or link.

Edit Links

When the need arises, you can edit any property of a link. You can resize the link, change its destination, change the level of magnification, or change the appearance of the link. When you edit a link, the changes apply only to the selected link.

Change Link Properties

To change link properties, do the following:

1. Choose Tools | Advanced Editing | Link tool, or select the Link tool from the Advanced Editing toolbar if available in the workspace.

2. Double-click the link you want to edit and the Link Properties dialog box appears. Alternatively, you can right-click (Windows) or CTRL-click (Macintosh) the link and then choose Properties from the Context menu.
3. Modify the Link Properties as described in the "Create a Hotspot" section earlier in the chapter.

TIP

After you've edited a link and it's performing as you'd like, you can prevent inadvertently moving the link or otherwise editing it by right-clicking (Windows) or CTRL*-clicking (Macintosh) the link with the Link tool, choosing Properties from the context menu, then clicking the Locked check box in the Link Properties dialog box.*

Resize a Hotspot

When you use the Link tool to create a hotspot, the resulting hotspot may not be sized properly. When you create a hotspot, it's better to make it a tad larger than needed, unless, of course, you have several hotspots in close proximity. An oversized hotspot gives your viewer a bigger target area. You can change the size of a hotspot at any time by doing the following:

1. Choose Tools | Advanced Editing | Link Tool, or select the Link tool from the Advanced Editing toolbar if available in the workspace.
2. Click the hotspot that you want to resize. After you click the hotspot, eight handles in the form of solid red rectangles appear on the hotspot perimeter.
3. Click and drag any of the corner hotspots to create a larger hotspot. If you hold down SHIFT while you drag, the hotspot resizes proportionately.
4. Click the handle in the middle of the left or right side of the hotspot and drag left or right to resize the width of the hotspot.
5. Click the handle in the middle of the top or bottom of the hotspot and drag up or down to make the hotspot taller or shorter.

Delete a Link

If you decide a link is no longer needed, you can delete it from the document by doing the following:

1. Choose Tools | Advanced Editing | Link Tool, or select the Link Tool from the Advanced Editing toolbar if available in the workspace.
2. Choose Edit | Delete. Alternatively, select the link, right-click (Windows) or CTRL-click (Macintosh), and choose Delete from the Context menu, or press DELETE.

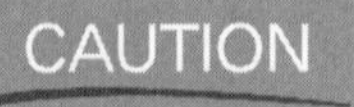

After you press DELETE*, Acrobat does not display a warning dialog box asking you to confirm the action. If you delete a link in error, choose Edit | Undo or press* CTRL-Z.

TIP

If you're editing multiple objects in a document such as links, graphic objects, text objects, and so on, you can use the Select Object tool to select and edit an object. After you select the tool, all objects in the document are highlighted with a black rectangle.

Create a Menu Using Links

When you create a PDF document for a specific purpose, such as an employee manual or product presentation, adding a menu is a great way to direct your readers to specific parts of a document. Of course, you can rely on the Acrobat built-in navigation devices: bookmarks and thumbnails. However, if your intended audience is not familiar with Adobe Reader, your document will be easier to navigate if you create a menu.

If you create a document in a word processing program, you can create a menu page as the first page of the document. On the menu page, list the major parts of the document you want your readers to be able to select by clicking links. Create the rest of the document and then convert it to PDF using the application's Print command and then choosing Adobe PDF as the printing device, or, if the application supports it, convert the document to PDF using the application's Save As or Export command. If you are creating the document in Microsoft Word, you can click the Convert To Adobe PDF button. Open the document in Acrobat and use the Link tool to create a link for each menu item. After you create the links for the menu page, choose File | Document Properties. In the Initial View section of this dialog box, choose Page Only for the Show option. Click OK to close the Document Open Options dialog box and then save the document. When your viewers open the document, the first thing they will see is your menu page with the Navigation pane closed.

Did you know?

You Can Create Links with the Select Text and Select Graphic Tools

You can quickly create a link by selecting text with the Select Text tool or selecting a graphic element such as a logo or photo with the Select Image tool. After selecting an object with either tool, right-click (Windows) or CTRL-click (Macintosh) and then choose Create Link from the context menu. After the Create Link From Selection dialog box appears, follow the instructions from the "Create Links" section of this chapter to finish the process.

Summary

In this chapter, you learned to work with bookmarks and page thumbnails, as well as create links. You learned to use these objects as navigation devices and assign actions to these items to turn them into interactive devices. In the next chapter, you'll learn to work with other navigation elements and specify document Open options.

Chapter 8

Create Interactive PDF Navigation

How to...

- Use actions
- Add JavaScript to documents
- Create articles
- Use named destinations
- Modify Open options

In Chapter 7, you learned to add navigation to your documents by using bookmarks, page thumbnails, and links. You can take PDF navigation up a notch or two when you use Actions. Adding actions to a PDF document lets you open files, play files, navigate to web sites, and more when a link or bookmark is clicked. You can assign multiple actions to a link or bookmark. You can also assign actions to page thumbnails to trigger an action when a page is opened or closed.

In this chapter, you'll learn to work with actions. You'll learn to add them to links, bookmarks, and page thumbnails. You'll also learn to work with JavaScript. Acrobat features extensive JavaScript support. Another topic of discussion is the Article tool, which you use to create linked threads of text and graphics in different parts of the document. *Article threads* are much like magazine articles where the topic of discussion ends on one page and is continued many pages later. You'll also learn to add named destinations to your documents. Toward the end of the chapter, you'll learn how to modify the view of a PDF document when it is opened.

Work with Actions

When you create a link or bookmark, the default action is Go To A Page In This Document. However, Acrobat supplies you with a plethora of actions from which to choose, which enables you to assign different actions to a link or bookmark, as well as add additional actions to these navigation items. You can also apply actions to form fields (Professional only) and individual pages. When you apply an action to a page, the action determines what the viewer sees or what happens when the page is opened or exited.

You set actions for bookmarks and links in their respective dialog boxes within the Select Action field of the Actions tab. You can also add actions to individual pages of the document. For more information on page actions, refer to the upcoming "Set a Page Action" section. To learn more about assigning actions to form fields, refer to Chapter 14. To add interactivity to a link, bookmark, form field, or page, choose from the following actions:

- **Go To A Page In This Document** In most applicable dialog boxes, this is the default action. Use this action to advance to another page or view in the current document or another PDF file.
- **Go To A Page In Another Document** Use this action to advance to a page in another document. When you choose this option, you specify which document opens and which page of the document is displayed. The action is applicable only if the PDF file is viewed with the same machine on which it was created.

- **Go To Snapshot View** Use this action to advance to a view that you have created with the Snapshot tool. You must create the view with the Snapshot tool prior to selecting the action. After selecting this action, Acrobat creates a view based on the snapshot you captured to the clipboard. The snapshot view appears when the action is triggered.
- **Open A File** Use this action to open a file when the action is triggered. The opened file will be viewed in its native application. Use this action only when the PDF file will be viewed with the same machine on which the file was created.
- **Read An Article** Use this action to read an article when the action is executed. After choosing this action, a dialog box appears with a list of articles in the document. For more information on creating articles, refer to the "Create a Thread of Linked Articles" section of this chapter.
- **Execute Menu Item** Use this action to execute a menu command. Even though you can choose any Acrobat command to execute as an action, the most logical choices would be to open another file, choose one of the navigation options from the Document menu, or choose one of the magnification options from the View menu.

NOTE *If you distribute your document to users with Adobe Reader, make sure the Menu command you choose is also an Adobe Reader Menu command.*

- **Set Layer Visibility** Use this action to set the visibility for a layer in the document.
- **Show/Hide A Field** Use this action to toggle the visibility of a form field in the document when the link is clicked.
- **Submit A Form** Use this action with a button to submit data from a form to a URL.
- **Reset A Form** Use this action to clear all previously entered data in a form.
- **Import Form Data** Use this action to specify a file from which to import form data. The imported data is inserted in the active form. For more information on working with forms, refer to Chapter 14.
- **Run A JavaScript** Use this action to run a JavaScript. When you choose this option, you can create or edit a JavaScript within a text editor.
- **Play Media (Acrobat 5–compatible)** Use this action to execute a QuickTime or AVI movie. To use this action, you must have a QuickTime or AVI movie within the document. For more information on adding movies to your PDF documents, refer to Chapter 15.
- **Play A Sound** Use this action to play a sound file. If you add this action to a document, the document must be viewed on the machine that was used to create the PDF file.
- **Play Media (Acrobat 6–compatible)** Use this action to play any Acrobat 6–compatible media. To use this action, you must have the media within the document. For more information on adding Acrobat 6–compatible media to your PDF documents, refer to Chapter 15.
- **Open A Web Link** Use this action when you want to open a web page on the World Wide Web. When you choose this action, you are prompted for the URL of the Web link you want to open when the action executes.

Use Page Actions

You can make your PDF documents more interactive by specifying an action to perform a certain task when a page opens or closes. For example, you can use an action to play a movie when a page opens and play a sound when a page closes.

Set a Page Action

Set a page action to execute one or more actions when a page opens or closes. If you choose multiple actions, you can edit the order in which the actions execute. To set a page action, follow these steps:

1. Choose the page to which you want to assign the action by selecting its thumbnail in the Pages tab.
2. Choose Page Properties from the Pages Options menu to open the Page Properties dialog box and then click the Actions tab to display the Actions section shown in the following illustration. Alternatively, you can right-click (Windows) or CTRL-click (Macintosh) and choose Page Properties from the Context menu. If it's not already open, click the Actions tab.

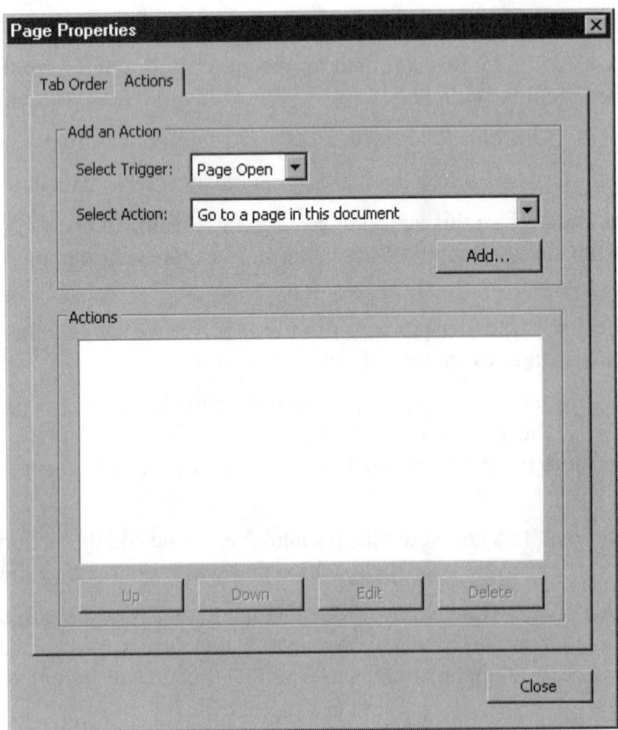

3. Click the triangle to the right of the Select Trigger field and choose one of the following:
   - **Page Open** Executes an action when a page loads.
   - **Page Close** Executes an action when the page closes.
4. Click the triangle to the right of the Select Action field and choose an action from the drop-down menu, as shown here:

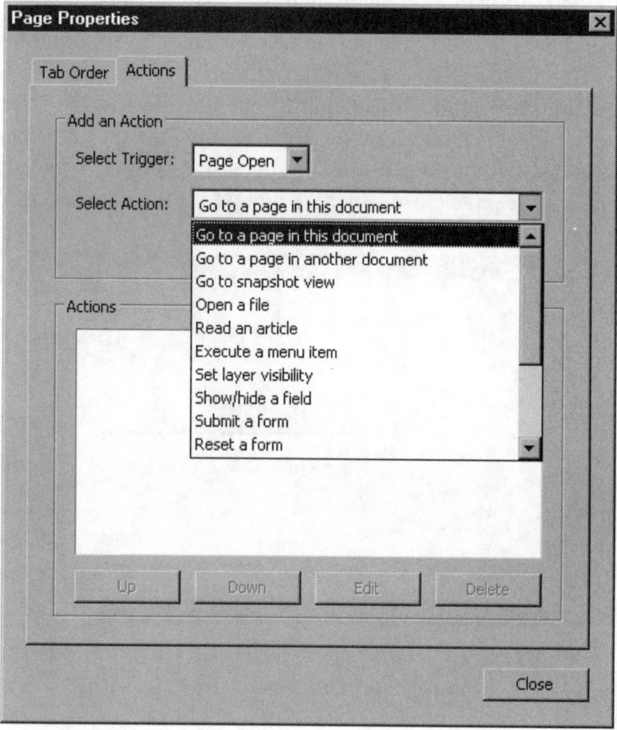

5. Click Add to add the action to the events that occur when the page loads. This opens a dialog box for the selected action in which you set the action's parameters.
6. After setting an action's parameters, click OK to apply the changes and exit the action's dialog box.
7. Repeat Steps 4–6 to add additional actions to the list.
8. Click Close to exit the Page Properties dialog box.
9. Save the document.

The next time you open the document and select the page to which you applied the actions, they execute.

8

Edit Actions

The majority of time, when you assign actions to a bookmark, link, or page, they perform without a hitch. However, sometimes the actions do not execute in proper order, or perhaps you feel an action should be deleted or added. When this occurs, you can easily edit actions by doing the following:

1. Select the bookmark, link, or page thumbnail to which you have applied the actions.
2. Right-click (Windows) or CTRL-click (Macintosh) and choose Properties from the Context menu. The following illustration shows the Page Properties dialog box as it appears when actions are applied to a page. Notice the minus sign (–) next to Page Open and Page Close. The minus sign (–) signifies that one or more actions occur when the page opens and when the page closes. If you assign actions to execute only when the page opens or when the page closes, there is no text for the other event.

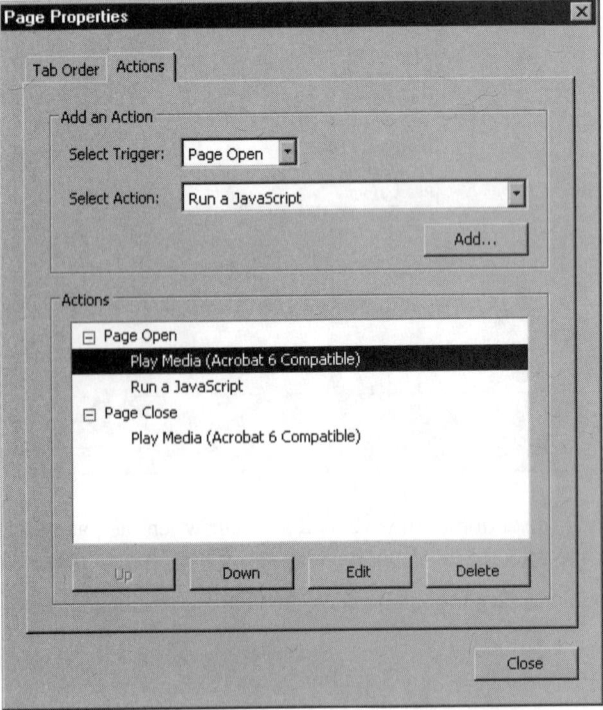

3. In the Actions window, select the event you want to modify.
4. To add an action, select it from the Select Action drop-down menu and then click Add. This opens the selected action's dialog box. Set any parameters for the action as outlined earlier in this chapter.

5. To delete an action, click Delete.
6. To edit an action, click Edit.
7. To rearrange the order in which actions execute, select an action and click Up or Down. If the action is at the top of the list, only the Down button will be available and vice versa if the action is at the bottom of the list. If the action is in the middle of the list, both buttons are available. If there is only one action for a trigger, both buttons are dimmed out.
8. When you have finished editing the actions for the bookmark, link, or page, click Close.

Use JavaScript Actions

You can add functionality and interactivity to your PDF document by using JavaScript to access database information, control navigation, access information from the Internet, and more. In Acrobat 6.0, you have more JavaScript actions to work with than ever before.

JavaScript is an object-orientated programming language. If you have designed web pages, you may be familiar with JavaScript. Each JavaScript object has associated methods and properties. Acrobat JavaScript uses standard JavaScript objects and has its own set of unique objects, such as the Bookmark object. Unfortunately, a detailed discussion of using JavaScript with Acrobat is beyond the scope of this book.

Create a JavaScript Action

You can use the JavaScript Action with form fields (Professional Only), bookmarks, and links, or you can create global JavaScript that can be used for an entire document. When you choose the JavaScript action, you create the actual script in a text editor known as the JavaScript Editor. As previously mentioned, there are myriad uses for JavaScript with PDF documents. The following steps show how to create a link and use JavaScript to navigate to a specific page when a link is clicked:

1. Choose Tools | Advanced Editing | Link Tool, or select the Link Tool from the Advanced Editing toolbar if you have it floating in the workspace.
2. Create a link around the text or image that will trigger the JavaScript. This opens the Link Properties dialog box.
3. Click the Custom Link radio button and then click OK to open the Link Properties dialog box.
4. Click the triangle to the right of the Select Action field, choose Run A JavaScript from the drop-down menu, and then click Add. The JavaScript editor opens.
5. Enter the following JavaScript: **`this.pageNum = x`** where *x* is the page number you want displayed when the JavaScript executes. When you enter the page number for a document, always subtract one from the page number that you want to open when the JavaScript executes. This is because the JavaScript language begins indexing with the

number zero; therefore page one is recognized as zero in JavaScript. The following illustration shows JavaScript to display page 8 when the link is clicked:

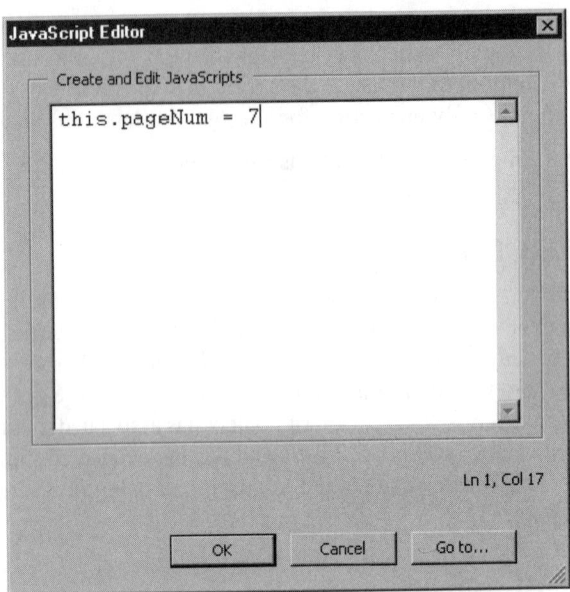

6. Click OK to close the JavaScript Editor and then click Close to exit the Link Properties dialog box. When the link is clicked, the desired page is displayed.

Edit a JavaScript Action

When you create complex, multiline JavaScript code, it's easy to make a mistake. If you have Acrobat Professional, you can put the JavaScript Debugger on the case, but if you own Acrobat Standard, you'll have to unravel your own JavaScript snafus. If you mistype a variable name or choose the wrong method of a JavaScript object, your script will fall flatter than a cake without enough baking powder. When this happens, you need to put on your thinking cap, or perhaps deerstalker cap, as you may have to do a bit of Sherlock Holmes–style deducting to figure out where your script went wrong. To edit a JavaScript action, select the object the JavaScript is assigned to and open the Actions tab of the object's Properties dialog box. Select the JavaScript action, click Edit to reopen the Edit JavaScript dialog box, and then examine the script. Make sure you have chosen the proper JavaScript object and the proper method of the object for the action you want to occur when the script executes. Note that many failed scripts are the result of typographical errors and not choosing the proper case for a JavaScript object. For example, if you refer to pageNum (proper syntax) as pagenum, your script will fail.

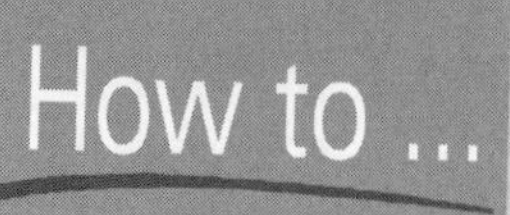

Master JavaScript

JavaScript is a wonderful tool that you can use to make your PDF documents more interactive. However, it does have a learning curve. The good news is that you do not have to know all the JavaScript objects and methods. When you decide to add a JavaScript action to a PDF document, research the Acrobat JavaScript guide (which you can locate at http://partners.adobe.com/asn/acrobat/index.jsp) to find the proper object and method for the result you want to achieve. If you want to master JavaScript, take the advice of a major athletic shoe company slogan and Just Do It. You may also want to consider investing in a good JavaScript book to learn the proper syntax of the JavaScript programming language. Ask your local bookseller for a copy of *JavaScript: A Beginner's Guide* by John Pollock or *JavaScript: The Complete Reference* by Thomas Powell and Fritz Schneider, both published by McGraw-Hill/Osborne. You can also order either book online at http://www.osborne.com.

8

TIP *If you prefer working in a text editor when creating JavaScript, choose Edit | Preferences and then choose JavaScript. In the JavaScript Editor section, choose external editor, then enter the path to the external editor executable (.exe) file. After changing the preference, whenever you edit JavaScript, Acrobat launches the external editor. After you enter the JavaScript, choose the external editor Save command before closing the Properties dialog box for the object to which you have applied the JavaScript.*

Create a Thread of Linked Articles

You create *articles* to link blocks of text within a PDF file. If you are creating an eBook in magazine format (an eMagazine, if you will), an article that begins on page 23 may be divided into sections and the next section begins on page 54. To make it easy for the reader to navigate from one part of the article to the next, define the block of the document that is the start of the article; then define the additional blocks of content that cover the rest of the article.

If you create an eBook for educational purposes, you can use articles to link chapter summaries together, thus making it easy for the student to skim through the book and locate desired information.

Create an Article

You define articles in a PDF document by using the Article tool to define the boundary of each block of content in the article. Note that an individual article can be a combination of text and graphics. The content area for different parts of the article are linked, and the viewer can easily navigate the article. To create an article in a PDF document, do the following:

1. Choose Tools | Advanced Editing | Article Tool, or select the Article tool (as shown in the following illustration) from Advanced Editing tool group if you have it floating in the workspace.

2. Click and drag the tool around the area you want to define as the first part of the article. As you drag the tool, a rectangular bounding box gives you a preview of the area you are selecting. When the bounding box surrounds the desired content, release the mouse button to have Acrobat define the first block of the article, as shown in the following illustration. Notice the article numbering system at the top of the article box. The 1-1 designates that article 1, block 1 has been created.

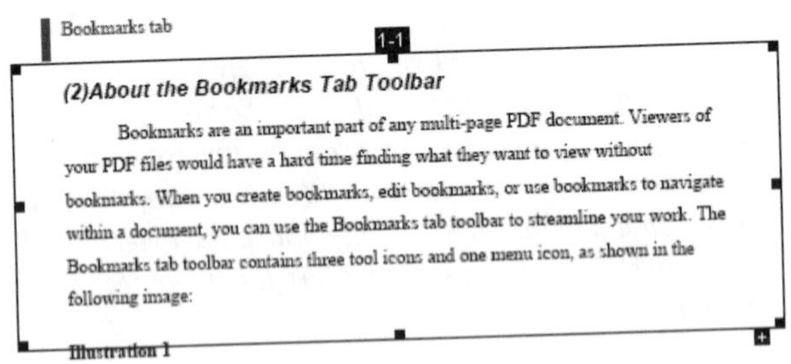

3. After you create the first block of an article, your cursor changes to two lines forming a right angle around the Article tool icon, which means that Acrobat is ready for you to define the next content area in the article. Navigate to the section of the document that contains the next portion of the article.
4. Click and drag the Article tool until it encompasses the next area of the article.
5. Continue in this manner until you have defined all blocks of content in the article and then press ENTER or RETURN to open the Article Properties dialog box, as shown here:

6. Enter the title, subject, and author of the article, plus any other keywords you want associated with the article, and click OK to close the dialog box.

Use the Articles Tab

After you create one or more articles, you can use the Articles tab to test your handiwork. Readers of your document also use the Articles tab to select an individual article to read. To open the Articles tab, as shown in the following illustration, choose View | Navigation Tabs | Articles:

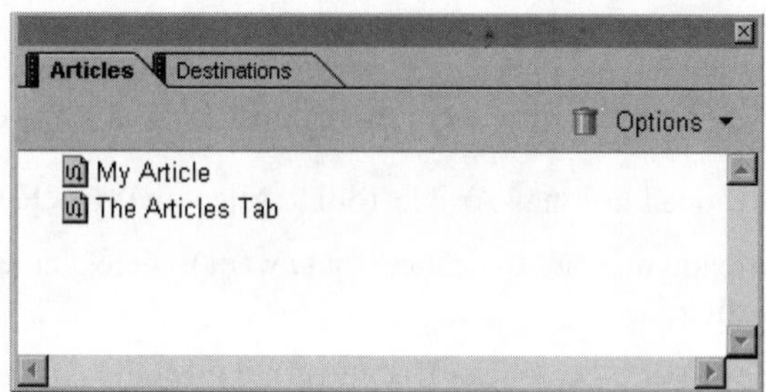

To read an article, double-click its title and Acrobat displays the first block of text in the article. After the first block of text is opened, your cursor becomes a hand with a down-pointing arrow in its palm.

Click to navigate to the next thread in the article. When you reach the last text block of the article, a line appears underneath the arrow, which signifies you've reached the end of the article. Click within the current article thread to return to the start of the article.

Add a Thread to an Article

After you review the article, you may find it necessary to add additional text blocks to the article. You can easily do this by following these steps:

1. Choose Tools | Advanced Editing | Article Tool. After you select the Article tool, Acrobat displays the bounding box and number of all articles in the PDF document.
2. Click the text block after which you want the new text block to appear. After you select the text block, a plus sign (+) appears at the lower-right corner of the box, as shown here:

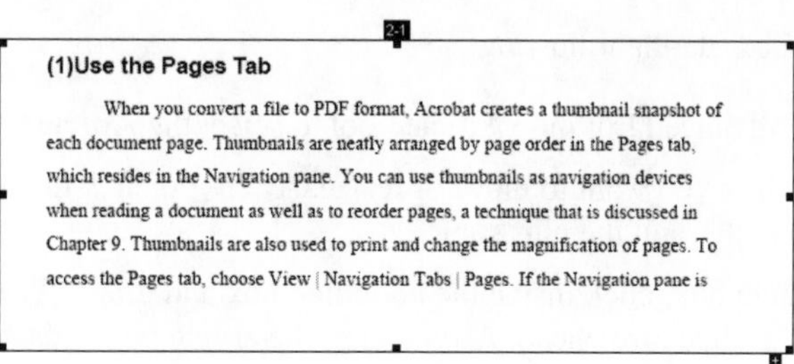

3. Click the plus sign and then navigate to the text block you want added to the article thread.
4. Click and drag to define the boundary of the box; when the bounding box encompasses the text, release the mouse button.
5. Add additional threads to the article or deselect the Article tool to finish editing the contents of the article. When you add threads to an article, Acrobat automatically renumbers the other threads in the order they appear in the article.

Delete an Article

After previewing the document, you may decide that certain parts of an article thread are not needed. You can easily delete an entire article or article thread by doing the following:

1. Choose Tools | Advanced Editing | Article Tool to select the Article tool.
2. Click the article thread you want to delete. If you want to delete an entire article, click any thread in the article.
3. Right-click (Windows) or CTRL-click (Macintosh) to open the Article Context menu.
4. Choose Delete and Acrobat displays the dialog box shown here:

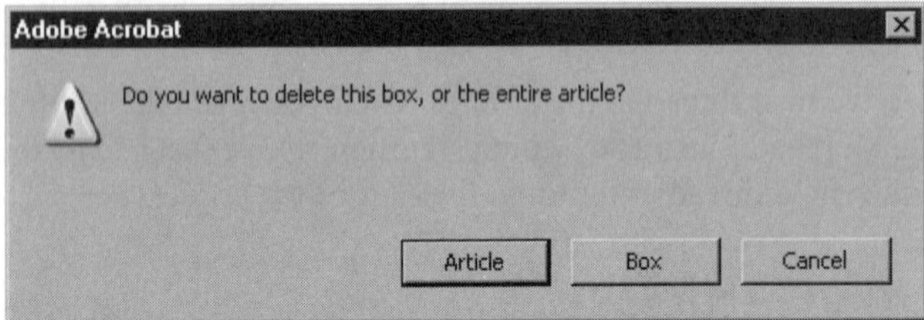

5. Click Box to delete the article thread or Article to delete the article. When you delete a thread, Acrobat renumbers the remaining threads in the article in their proper order.

Move or Resize an Article Box

When your article thread is viewed, Acrobat magnifies the view to fit the confines of the article box. If, after reviewing the document, you decide the position or size of an article box is off, you can move or resize it.

To move the article box, do the following:

1. Choose Tools | Advanced Editing | Article Tool to select the Article tool.
2. Click the article box you want to move or resize. After you click the box, Acrobat displays eight handles and the plus sign.
3. To move the article box, click inside the bounding box and drag. When you click, your cursor becomes a filled arrowhead. As you drag the article box, a dashed bounding box

gives you a preview of the position of the box. When the bounding box is where you want the article box to be, release the mouse button.

To resize the article box, do one of the following:

- Click one of the corner handles and drag to resize the entire article box. Hold down the SHIFT key to resize the box proportionately. Release the mouse button when the box is the desired size.
- Click the handle in the middle on either side of the box and drag away from the box to make it wider or drag towards the center of the box to make it narrower. Release the mouse button when the box is the desired width.
- Click the handle in the middle of either the top or bottom of the article box and drag up or down to change the height of the box.

NOTE *When you grab a handle to change the width or height of the box, only the handle you select is changed; the opposite side is unaffected.*

Edit Article Properties

After you create an article, you can change the title or any other article properties by doing the following:

1. Choose Tools | Advanced Editing | Article Tool to select the Article tool.
2. Click any thread of the article whose properties you want to modify.
3. Right-click (Windows) or CTRL-click (Macintosh) and choose Properties from the Context menu to display the Article Properties dialog box.
4. Modify the article properties as needed and then click OK.

Work with the Destinations Tab

When you create a complex PDF document, you may find it helpful to work with named destinations. A named destination links to a specific point in a document. When you work with multiple documents, as is often the case when creating a multimedia presentation, you can simplify cross-document navigation by linking to a named destination. When you link to a named destination, the link remains active even when pages are added or deleted from the target document.

You use the Destinations tab to display and sort named destinations within a document. You also use the tab to rename destinations. To display the named destinations within a document, do the following:

1. Choose View | Navigation Tabs | Destinations to open the Destinations tab.

2. Click the Scan Document button to display a list of destinations within the document, as shown here:

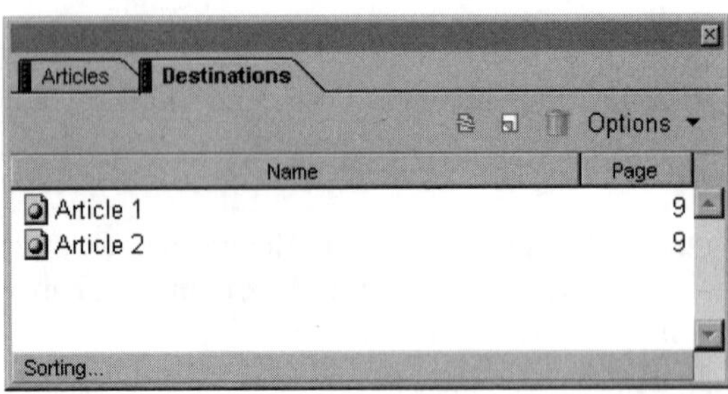

3. To sort the destinations alphabetically, click the Name bar near the top of the tab.
4. To sort the destinations by page number, click the Page bar near the top of the tab.
5. To go to a named destination, double-click its name. Alternatively, you can right-click (Windows) or CTRL-click (Macintosh) and choose Go To Destination from the Context menu.
6. To delete named destinations, select them and press DELETE. Alternatively, you can click Delete Selected Destinations (which looks like a garbage can), or choose Delete from the Context menu.
7. To rename a destination, select it and right-click (Windows) or CTRL-click (Macintosh), choose Rename from the Context menu, and enter a new name for the destination.
8. To create a named destination, navigate to the document page you want added to the named destination list, set the magnification of the page, and click the Create New Destination button. Alternatively, you can choose New Destination from the Context menu. A new listing with the default name of Untitled appears in the Destinations tab.
9. Before creating a new destination, enter a name for the new destination.

You must scan the document prior to adding a new destination. If you open the Destinations tab, the Create New Destination button is dimmed out until you scan the document, as outlined in Step 2.

Summary

In this chapter, you learned to enhance your navigation by assigning one or more actions to a link or bookmark. You learned to assign actions to a page that determine what occurs when a page opens or closes. You also learned to create a thread of articles and to work with named destinations. In the next chapter, you'll find out how to edit your PDF documents.

Part III

Edit PDF Documents

Chapter 9

The Basics of Editing PDF Documents

How to…

- Edit visually with thumbnails
- Edit with menu commands
- Append PDF documents
- Add page transitions
- Touch up a PDF document

After you create a PDF document, you can easily edit it. Within Acrobat, you can add, delete, reorder, and renumber pages. You can also edit individual objects within the PDF document.

You edit PDF documents by using tabs, tools, and menu commands. Many of the edits you perform with Acrobat tools can also be accomplished using menu commands or by selecting commands from the appropriate tab Options menu or Context menu. In this chapter, you'll learn to edit PDF documents as well as add pages to PDF documents. When you're editing a PDF document that's used for a presentation, you can create some interesting effects by applying page transitions.

Edit Visually with Thumbnails

Thumbnails are miniature images of each page in a PDF document. Each thumbnail displays with a page number below it. In previous chapters of this book, you have seen thumbnails used as navigation devices. You can also use them to edit your documents. You can use thumbnails to insert pages, delete pages, and change the order of pages. Thumbnails are located in the Pages tab, as shown in Figure 9-1.

The Pages tab is part of the Navigation pane and can be opened by clicking Pages or by choosing View | Navigation Tabs | Pages. The Pages tab has its own Options menu, a Context menu, and one solitary tool.

Use the Pages Tab Options Menu

You use the Pages tab Options menu to access certain menu commands to edit a document and work with thumbnails. To open the Pages tab Options menu, as shown next, click Options near the upper-right corner of the tab.

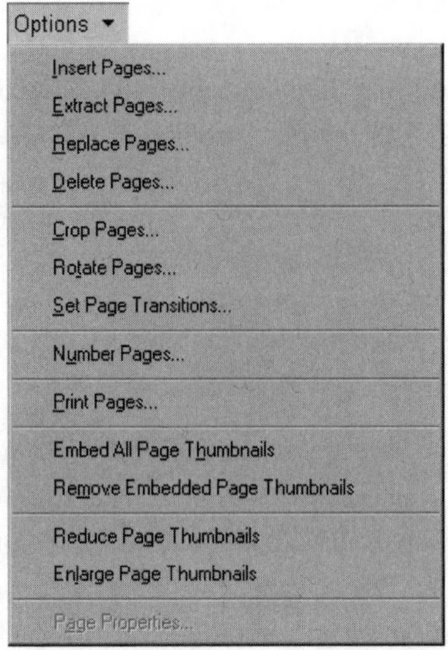

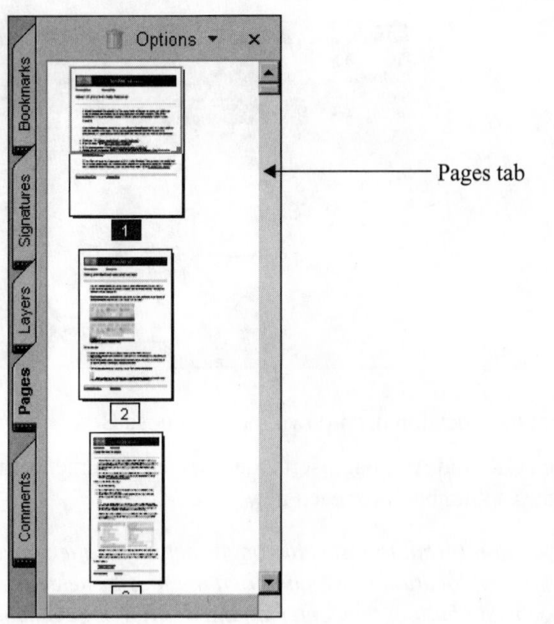

FIGURE 9-1 You can edit pages with the Pages tab.

Use the Pages Context Menu

Many of the commands you use to edit PDF documents can be found on the Pages Context menu. To access the Pages Context menu, select a thumbnail and right-click (Windows) or CTRL-click (Macintosh).

Insert Pages

You can insert pages from within the Pages tab. From within the tab, you click a thumbnail to select a page and then insert pages before or after the selected page. To add one or more pages to your document, follow these steps:

1. Click a thumbnail to select the page before or after the place where the new pages will be inserted.
2. Choose Insert Pages from the Pages tab Options menu or Context menu to open the Select File To Insert dialog box.
3. Select the page(s) you want to insert and click Select to open the Insert Pages dialog box, as shown here:

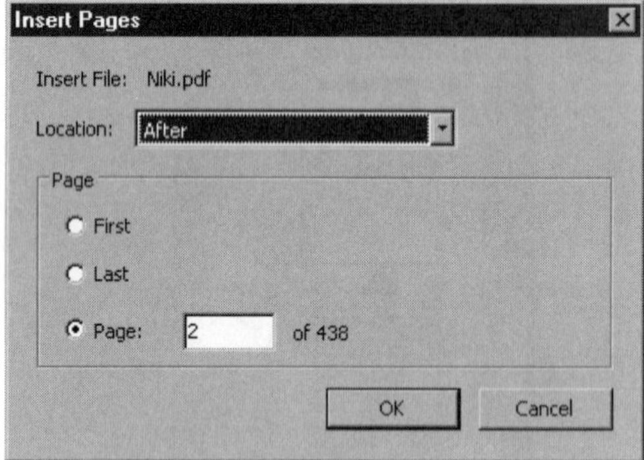

4. From the Location drop-down menu, choose Before or After.
5. Click OK, and Acrobat inserts the selected documents in the location specified and creates a thumbnail for each new page.

NOTE *If you don't want to insert the pages before or after the current page, you can specify a different location in which to add the files by selecting a location option, clicking the Page radio button, then entering the desired page number in the text field.*

Delete Pages

You can also use thumbnails to delete one or more pages. To delete pages from within the Pages tab, do one of the following:

- To delete a single page, click its thumbnail and then click the Delete Selected Pages button, which looks like a trash can. Acrobat displays a warning dialog box. Click OK to delete the page or Cancel to stop the operation.
- To delete contiguous pages, click a thumbnail that corresponds to a page you want to delete and then, while pressing SHIFT, click contiguous thumbnails to add them to the selection. When you have finished selecting thumbnails, click the Delete Selected Pages button. Click OK to close the warning dialog box and delete the pages.
- To delete noncontiguous pages, click a thumbnail that corresponds to a page you want to delete and then, while pressing CTRL, click additional thumbnails to add them to the selection. Click the Delete Selected Pages button to delete the pages from the document. Click OK to accept the deletion of the pages.
- You can also delete pages by selecting thumbnails and choosing Delete Pages from the Pages tab menu or Context menu. When you choose this command, Acrobat displays the following dialog box, which gives you the opportunity to change the pages that will be deleted when you execute the action:

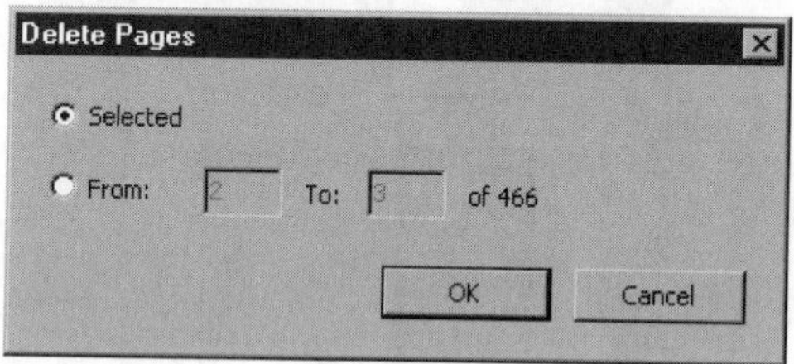

9

Drag-and-Drop Editing

The Pages tab not only gives you a visual representation of each page in your document, but can also be used to edit the document by dragging-and-dropping thumbnails. You can use the Pages tab to change the order in which pages display and to import pages from other documents.

Reorder Document Pages

You can use thumbnails to change the order in which pages appear in a PDF document. To move a single page or a selection of pages to a new position in the document, select them and then drag-and-drop them to a new location. To change the order of document pages, follow these steps:

1. Open the Pages tab and select the thumbnail that corresponds to the page you want to move. You can move more than one page at a time by selecting contiguous or noncontiguous thumbnails, as discussed previously.

TIP *To view several thumbnails at once, choose Reduce Page Thumbnails from the Pages tab Options menu or the Pages tab Context menu. You can also display more thumbnails by clicking the vertical border between the Navigation pane and the Document pane and dragging it to the right.*

2. Click and drag the thumbnails up or down. As you drag the selected thumbnails, your cursor becomes a filled arrow attached to a document, and a solid blue line appears below each thumbnail to indicate the current position of the thumbnail, as shown in the following illustration. If the Navigation pane is sized so more than one column of thumbnails is visible, the blue line appears to the side of each thumbnail.

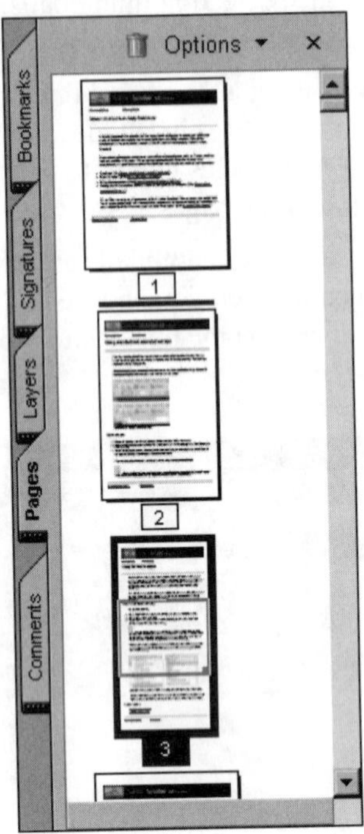

3. Release the mouse button when the selected thumbnails are where you want them. Acrobat moves the selected pages to their new location and renumbers the thumbnails.

Copy Pages from Other Documents

If you have more than one document open, you can use the Pages tab to copy pages from one document to another. Copying pages is an excellent way to build a document when working with a team of PDF authors. To copy pages from one document to another, follow these steps:

1. Open the source document and target document.

2. Choose Window | Tile and then choose Vertically or Horizontally. Alternatively, you can choose Cascading, but you will have to rearrange the documents so each document Pages tab is visible.
3. If they are not already visible, open the Pages tab of each document by choosing View | Navigation Tabs | Pages while the respective document is selected.
4. In the Pages tab of the source document, select the thumbnail for the page you want to copy. You can select more than one thumbnail if necessary.
5. Click and drag the thumbnails from the Pages tab of the source document to the Pages tab of the target document.
6. As your cursor moves into the Pages tab of the target document, the cursor becomes an angled arrow attached to a document with a plus sign (+) in it.
7. In the Pages tab of the target document, drag the thumbnail to the desired position and release the mouse button. After you release the mouse button, Acrobat copies the selected pages to the target document, and then creates numbered thumbnails for the copied pages.

TIP *You can move a page from one document to another by clicking its thumbnail in the source document Pages tab, pressing CTRL, then dragging it to the Pages tab of the target document. An icon that resembles a document page appears under your cursor, signifying that you are moving and not copying a page.*

Edit with Menu Commands

Many of the menu commands that are discussed in the following sections are exact copies of Pages tab Options menu and Pages tab Context menu commands. When you use these commands in the Pages tab, you work with a single thumbnail or selection of thumbnails. When you use a menu command, you can specify any page in the document. The previous sections dealt with using editing commands in a specific manner within the Pages tab. The following sections show you how to use menu commands to edit selected pages within your documents.

Insert Pages

You can add existing documents to any PDF document using the Insert Pages command. With the Insert Pages command, you specify the exact location within the document where the pages are to be added. To append an existing PDF document using the Insert Pages command, follow these steps:

1. Open the PDF document that you want to add pages to.

2. Navigate to the document page that is before or after the place where you want to insert the pages. This step is optional. You can specify the exact location to add the pages in the Insert Pages dialog box.
3. Choose Document | Pages | Insert to open the Select File To Insert dialog box.
4. Choose the file(s) you want to insert and then click Select to open the Insert Pages dialog box.
5. From the Location drop-down menu, choose After or Before.
6. In the Page section, the Page option is selected by default with the current page listed. You can change this by choosing First or Last, or by entering a different page number in the Page field.
7. Click OK, and Acrobat inserts the selected pages at the specified location and creates a thumbnail for each added page.

Delete Pages

You can modify a PDF document by deleting unwanted pages. To do this, you use the Delete Pages command. This command enables you to delete a single page, a range of pages, or selected pages. To remove pages from a PDF document, follow these steps:

1. Open the document you want to remove pages from.
2. Select the pages you want to delete by clicking their thumbnails in the Pages tab. This step is optional. You can specify which pages you want to delete after invoking the command.
3. Choose Document | Pages | Delete to open the Delete Pages dialog box, as shown previously. Alternatively, you can select pages you want to delete by clicking their thumbnails and then choosing Document | Delete Pages.
4. If you selected the pages to delete, click OK; otherwise, enter the range of pages to delete and then click OK. After you click OK, Acrobat displays a warning dialog, asking you to confirm that you want the pages deleted.
5. Click OK and Acrobat deletes the specified pages and their thumbnails, then renumbers the remaining thumbnails.

Replace Pages

You can update a document by replacing a page or a selection of pages. This option is useful when you have a multi-page PDF document that needs only minor revisions. Create the pages you need to replace in an authoring application, convert them to PDF format, and then use the Replace Pages command. You can also replace a specific number of pages from one document with a specific number of pages from another document. Acrobat replaces pages on a one-to-one basis. For example, you cannot replace 3 pages with 50 pages. To replace pages in a PDF document, follow these steps:

1. Open the document that contains the pages you want to replace.
2. Open the Pages tab by clicking Pages in the Navigation pane or by choosing View | Navigation Tabs | Pages.
3. Click the thumbnails that correspond to the pages you want to replace. Note that you can only select contiguous thumbnails. If you select non-contiguous thumbnails, Acrobat will insert a range of pages from the first selected thumbnail to the last.
4. Choose Document | Pages | Replace to open the Select File With New Pages dialog box.
5. Locate the PDF file with the pages that will replace the selected ones and click Select to open the Replace Pages dialog box, as shown here:

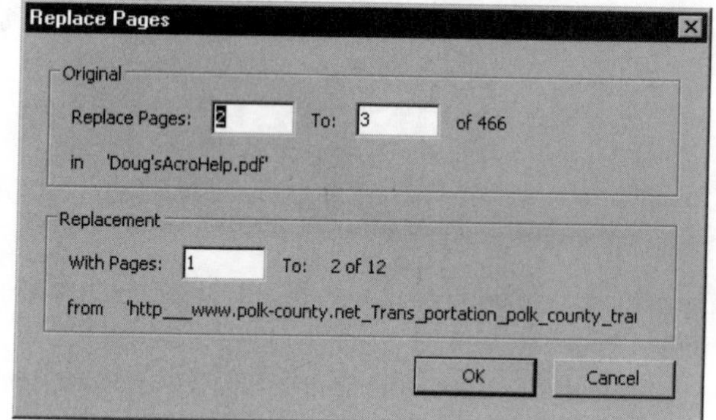

6. If you have already selected the pages you want to replace, go to Step 7; otherwise, in the Replace Pages field of the Original Pages section, enter the number of the first page you want replaced and then in the To field, enter the number of the last page you want replaced.
7. In the With Pages field of the Replacement section, enter the number of the first replacement page of the PDF file you selected. Acrobat automatically calculates the ending page based on the number of pages selected in the original document. If you do not specify a page number, Acrobat will replace the first specified page in the target document with the first page of the replacement document.
8. Click OK, and Acrobat replaces the pages and generates thumbnails for the replaced pages.

Extract Pages

You can extract pages from an existing PDF document and use them as the basis for a new PDF document. When you extract pages, you can preserve the extracted pages in the original document or delete them. To extract pages from a PDF document, follow these steps:

1. Open the PDF document that contains the pages you want to extract.
2. Open the Pages tab by clicking Pages in the Navigation pane or by choosing View | Navigation Tabs | Pages.
3. Click the thumbnails that correspond to the pages you want to extract. Alternatively, you can enter the range of pages to extract in the Extract Pages dialog box. Note that if you select non-contiguous pages, Acrobat extracts a range of pages from the first selected page to the last.
4. Choose Document | Pages | Extract to open the Extract Pages dialog box, as shown here:

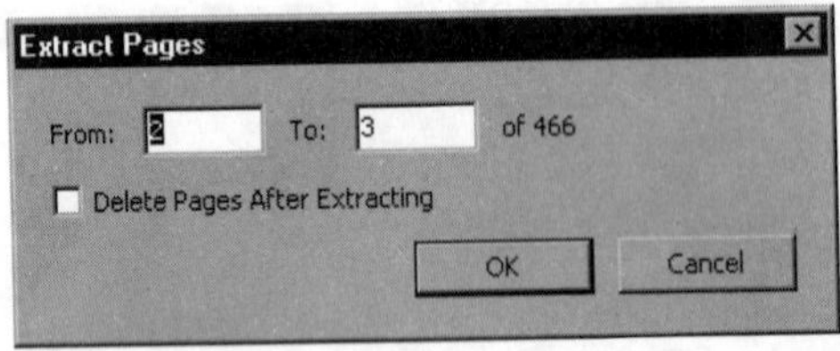

5. If you already selected thumbnails, go to Step 6; otherwise, specify a range of pages by entering page numbers in the From [ ] and To [ ] fields.
6. Choose the Delete Pages After Extracting option to have Acrobat delete the pages from the original document when they are extracted.
7. Click OK to extract the pages, and Acrobat opens the extracted pages as a new document.
8. Choose File | Save As and then specify a filename and location where you want the extracted pages saved.

Crop Pages

If you create a PDF document and you find that one or more of the document pages have excessive margins, you can trim (crop) the margins. You can also use this command to crop out extraneous material from a PDF document, for example, a banner in a PDF document created from a Web page. You crop pages by using a menu command or a tool. To crop pages, follow these steps:

1. Open the document whose pages you want to crop. Select a range of pages to crop by clicking thumbnails in the Thumbnails tab. Alternatively, you can specify which pages to crop by selecting a range in the Crop Pages dialog box.
2. Choose Document | Pages | Crop to open the Crop Pages dialog box, as shown next.

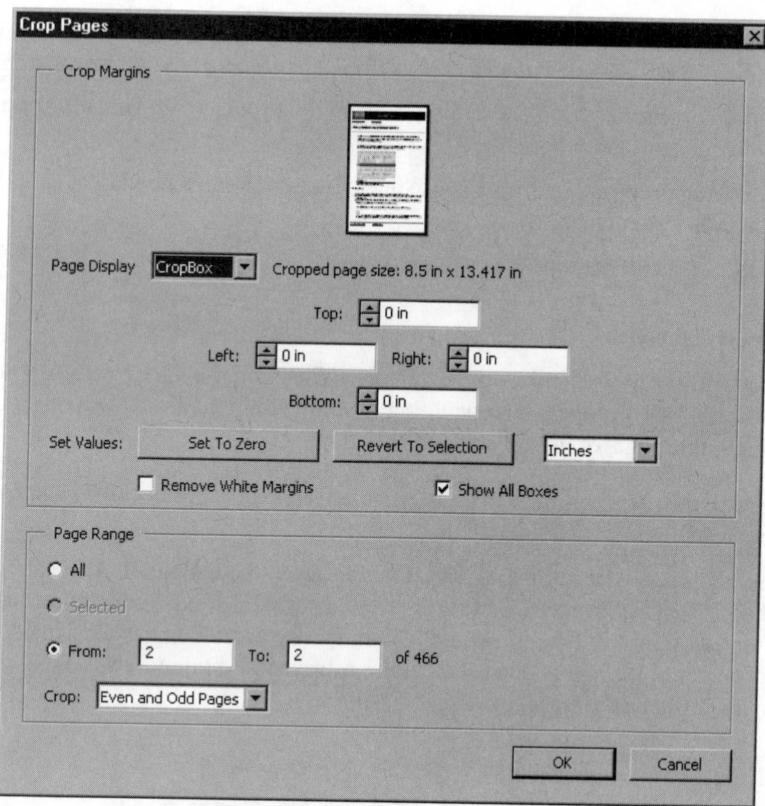

3. In the Crop Margins section, enter a value to crop in any or all of the following fields: Top, Left, Right, and Bottom. For example, to crop 1 inch from the top margin, enter **1** in the Top field. Alternatively, you can click the spinner buttons to select a value. Press SHIFT while clicking a spinner button to make the values change in greater increments. As you modify the margin values, a black rectangle around the thumbnail in the center of the Crop Margins section changes to reflect the size of the document with the modified margin settings.
   - Click Set To Zero to reset the margin values to zero.
   - Click Revert To Selection to reset the margins to the previous cropping rectangle. This button resets the margins to zero unless you use the Crop tool to define the cropping rectangle and then modify one of the margins.
   - Enable the Remove White Margins option to crop the side margins to the document contents, thus eliminating a white border.
4. In the Page Range section, choose one of the following:
   - Choose All to have Acrobat crop all pages to the specified size.

- Choose Selected to have Acrobat crop only selected pages to the specified size. This option is dimmed out if you have not selected pages by clicking their thumbnails.
- Choose the From option and enter a value in the From and To fields to specify a range of pages to crop.

5. From the Crop drop-down menu, choose one of these: Even And Odd Pages, Odd Pages Only, or Even Pages Only.
6. Click OK and Acrobat crops the page(s) to the sizes you specified.

Use the Crop Tool

You can also manually crop a page with the Crop tool. When you use the Crop tool, you define the area you want the page cropped to by dragging the tool within the Document pane. Use this method to crop a single page, or multiple pages, as follows:

1. Navigate to the page you want to crop. Alternatively, you can select the page by clicking its thumbnail.
2. Choose Tools | Advanced Editing | Crop tool to select the Crop tool. Alternatively, you can choose Tools | Advanced Editing | Show Advanced Editing Toolbar and choose the Crop tool, as shown in the following illustration. If you are doing extensive editing of PDF documents, it's a good idea to float the Advanced Editing toolbar in the workspace, or display it and dock it in a convenient position.

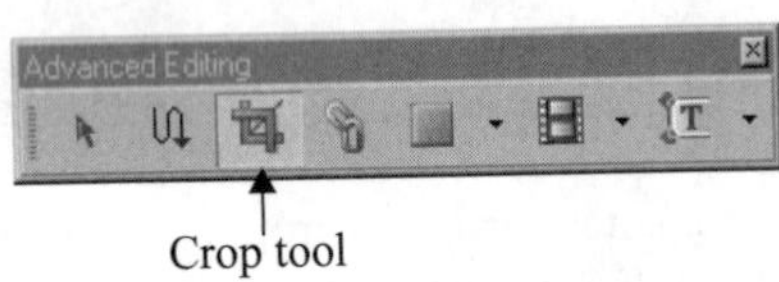

3. Click the point that will define one of the outer boundaries of the cropped page and then drag the tool diagonally. As you drag, a bounding box appears, giving you a preview of the area you are defining. When the area is the desired size, release the mouse button and Acrobat defines the area. There are square resizing handles at the corners of the bounding box.
4. With the Crop tool still selected, you can modify the cropping rectangle by doing one of the following:
   - To move the cropping rectangle, click inside the rectangle and drag it to a new position. Release the mouse button when the rectangle is in the desired position.
   - To change the height of the cropping rectangle, click one of the handles and drag up or down.

- To change the width of the cropping rectangle, click one of the handles and drag left or right.
- To change the size of the cropping rectangle, click one of the handles and drag diagonally. To resize the rectangle proportionately, press SHIFT while dragging.

5. When the cropping rectangle is the desired size, double-click anywhere inside the rectangle, or press ENTER or RETURN to reveal the Crop Pages dialog box. By default, when you select a single page and use the Crop tool, the current page is selected in the Page Range section. If desired, you can modify the range of pages to crop or fine-tune the margins by changing the values in the Crop Margins section, as discussed in the "Crop Pages" section.
6. Click OK and Acrobat crops the page(s) as specified.

Rotate Pages

When you create a PDF document by combining several documents, you often end up with different page sizes and orientations. For example, when you create a multi-page PDF document, you may end up combining pages with both landscape and portrait orientation. When this happens, you can rotate pages as needed by following these steps:

1. Open the document whose pages you want to rotate.
2. To select specific pages, open the Pages tab and click the thumbnails for the pages you want to rotate. You can select noncontiguous pages to rotate. Alternatively, you can navigate to a specific page or specify a range of pages in the Rotate Pages dialog box.

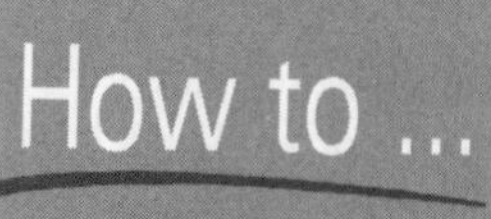

Restore Keyboard Shortcuts

If you're an Acrobat veteran, you've probably noticed the absence of keyboard shortcuts. For example, in Acrobat 5.0, you could select the Hand tool by pressing H, the Crop tool by pressing C, the Links tool by pressing L, and so on. With the release of Acrobat 6.0, Adobe decided to remove the keyboard shortcuts, but if you like the convenience of keyboard shortcuts, you can restore them by choosing Edit | Preferences to open the Preferences dialog box. Click General in the left-hand window to open the General section of the dialog box and then enable the Use Single-Key Accelerators To Access Tools option. Click OK to exit the dialog box. After enabling this option, each tool's keyboard shortcut is displayed in a tooltip with your cursor over the tool. After a while, the shortcuts for the tools you commonly use will become second nature and you'll be able to quickly access a tool by pressing the proper key.

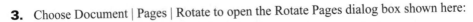

3. Choose Document | Pages | Rotate to open the Rotate Pages dialog box shown here:

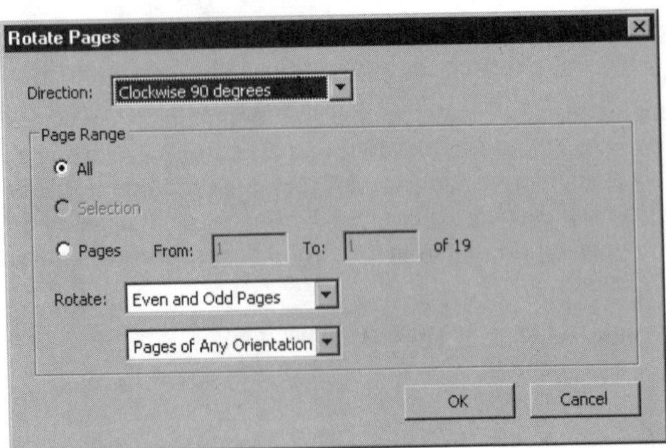

4. Choose one of the following options from the Direction drop-down menu: Counterclockwise 90 Degrees, Clockwise 90 Degrees, or 180 Degrees.
5. In the Page Range section, choose one of the following options:
   - **All** Choose this option, and Acrobat rotates all pages in the direction specified.
   - **Selection** This option is available if you selected pages by clicking their thumbnails; otherwise, it is dimmed out.
   - **Pages** This option is selected if you navigate to a specific page before invoking the Rotate Pages command. You can accept the page range (the page you navigated to) or modify the range by entering a page number in the From [ ] and To [ ] fields.
6. In the Rotate section, click the triangle to the right of the first field and from the drop-down menu, choose one of the following: Even And Odd Pages, Even Pages Only, or Odd Pages Only.
7. In the Rotate section, click the triangle to the right of the second field and from the drop-down menu, choose one of these options: Landscape Pages, Portrait Pages, or Pages Of Any Orientation.
8. Click OK, and Acrobat rotates the specified pages to the desired orientation.

Number Pages

When you create a PDF document, Acrobat automatically numbers the pages. When you add pages, move pages, or delete pages, Acrobat updates the page numbers to reflect the order in which the pages appear. Acrobat uses a default integer numbering system, starting with 1 for the first page of the document, and so on. If the document you create has a title page, copyright pages, or similar front matter pages, you can modify the numbering style by following these steps:

1. In the Pages tab, select the thumbnails of the pages you want to renumber. Alternatively, you can specify a range of pages to renumber in the Page Numbering dialog box.
2. Click Options to open the Pages tab Options menu and then choose Number Pages to display the Page Numbering dialog box shown here:

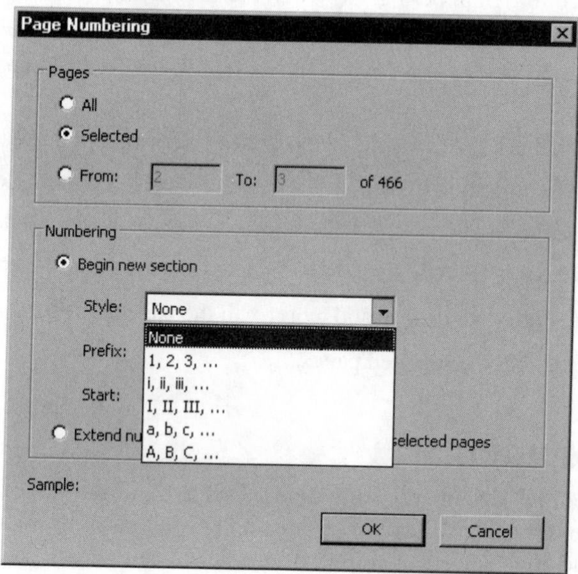

3. In the Pages section, choose one of the following options:
   - **All** Choose this option to have all pages renumbered.
   - **Selected** This option is available and selected by default when you create a selection of pages by clicking their thumbnails.
   - **From [ ] To [ ]** Choose this option to renumber a range of pages. To specify the range of pages you want to renumber, enter the desired page numbers in the From [ ] and To [ ] fields.
4. In the Numbering section, choose one of the following options:
   - **Begin New Section** Choose this option to begin a new numbering sequence. Click the triangle to the right of the Style field and choose an option from the drop-down menu. To add a prefix to the page numbers, enter the desired prefix in the Prefix field. In the Start field, enter the beginning value for the page sequence.
   - **Extend Numbering Used In Preceding Section To Selected Pages** Choose this option to have Acrobat renumber the selected pages using the same sequence as the preceding pages, numbering the first selected page with the next page number in the sequence.

5. Click the triangle to the right of the Style menu and choose an option from the drop-down menu. After you choose a style, a preview appears in the Sample section of the dialog box. You can renumber selected pages using any of the styles shown here:
   - **None** Choose this option and a number will not appear below the thumbnails you have selected for renumbering. However, the document page number information is still displayed in the small Navigation window below the Document pane.
   - **1, 2, 3** Use this style for the pages that comprise the content of a document or eBook.
   - **i, ii, iii** Use this style to display the selected pages as lowercase Roman numerals.
   - **I, II, III** Use this style to display the selected pages as uppercase Roman numerals.
   - **a, b, c** Use this style to display the selected pages as lowercase letters.
   - **A, B, C** Use this style to display the selected pages as capital letters.
6. Enter text in the Prefix window to add a prefix to the page number.
7. Click OK to renumber the selected pages.

Append PDF Documents

You can add pages to a PDF document at any time by using the Insert Pages command, as discussed previously in this chapter. You can *append* a PDF document by adding existing PDF documents, images, and other supported formats to the document.

To add existing files to a PDF document, follow these steps:

1. Open the PDF document to which you want to add files. If desired, you can open more than one PDF document to combine the open PDF documents with other file types.
2. Choose Create PDF | From Multiple Files to open the Create PDF Document From Multiple Files dialog box.
3. Make sure the Include All Open PDF documents option is selected.
4. Click Browse and choose the file(s) you want to add to the document.

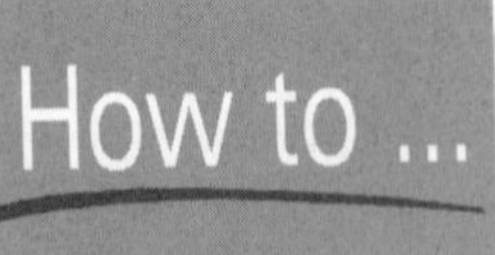

Combine Two PDF Documents

You can combine two PDF documents by opening one PDF document and choosing Document | Pages | Insert. Select the PDF file and choose the proper options to insert the new PDF file before or after the current PDF file.

5. Use the buttons in the Arrange Files section to arrange the files in the desired order. The PDF document(s) to which you are adding the files appears at the top of the list.
6. Choose OK, and Acrobat converts the selected files to PDF format and adds the new pages to the document. For more information on the Create PDF From Multiple Files command, refer to the "Create PDF from Multiple Files" section in Chapter 4.
7. Choose File | Save As, and in the Save As dialog box specify a filename and the location where you want the appended document saved; then click OK.

Adding Page Transitions

If you're creating a PDF document as part of a presentation, you can add a bit of panache by adding a transition between pages. When you add a transition, the PDF document looks similar to a PowerPoint presentation or a slide show. Transitions will only be displayed when the document is viewed in Full Screen mode. You can set a document to display in Full Screen mode by setting Window Options in the Initial view section of the Document Properties dialog box. To add transitions between pages, follow these steps:

1. Choose Document | Pages | Set Page Transitions to open the Set Transitions dialog box shown next:

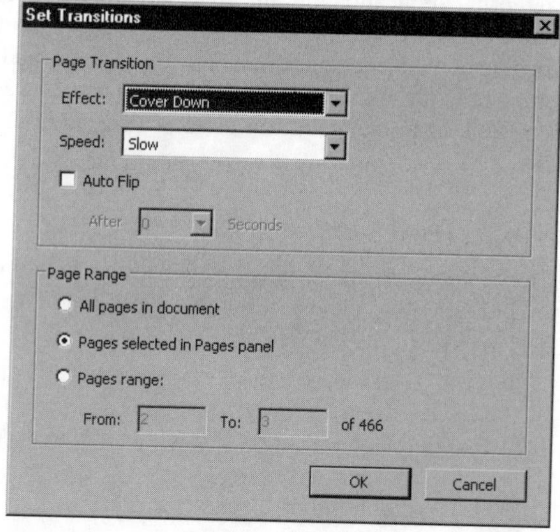

2. Click the triangle to the right of the Effect field and choose one of the presets from the drop-down menu. The effects are very similar to those found in PowerPoint and other presentation programs.
3. Click the triangle to the right of the Speed field and choose one of the following: Slow, Medium, or Fast.
4. Choose the Auto Flip option to turn the pages automatically. When you choose this option, the After [ ] Seconds field becomes available. Enter a value for the number of seconds you'd like each page displayed or choose a preset from the drop-down menu.

5. In the Page Range field, choose one of the following options:
   - **All Pages In Document** Applies the selected transition to all pages in the document.
   - **Pages Selected In Pages Panel** Applies the selected transition to the pages corresponding to the thumbnails you selected from the Pages tab. This option is dimmed out if no thumbnails are selected.
   - **Pages Range** Applies the selected transition to a range of pages. When you choose this option, enter values in the From and To fields to specify the page range.
6. Click OK to apply the transition to the selected pages.
7. Save the document.

TIP *When creating a presentation, it's a good idea to stick with one transition type for the entire presentation. Mixing transitions can be jarring and looks unprofessional.*

Touch Up a PDF Document

As you know, PDF documents originate in authoring applications where they are converted to the PDF format using the authoring application plug-in, an export command, or by using the application Print command and choosing Adobe PDF. The converted document retains the look and feel of the original. When you open the document in Acrobat, you can add interactivity to the document but cannot perform wholesale edits to the document. You can, however, perform minor edits using the TouchUp tools. You can also touch up the order of a tagged PDF document. Tagged PDF documents are discussed in Chapter 14.

Use the TouchUp Text Tool

You use the TouchUp Text tool to perform minor edits to text within a PDF document. You can use the tool to change a word or letter, copy a line of text to the clipboard, fit text within an existing selection, and more.

Edit Text

When you select the TouchUp Text tool, you can select text within a PDF document and delete or replace the text.

To edit text with the TouchUp Text tool, follow these steps:

1. Choose Tools | Advanced Editing | TouchUp Text tool. If you will be editing text and other elements in the document, you can choose Tools | Advanced Editing | Show Advanced Editing Toolbar and then choose the TouchUp Text tool, as shown next.

TouchUp Text tool

2. Click a block of text to select it. Click the sentence or paragraph you want to edit and Acrobat selects all text on the page. After you select the text, Acrobat surrounds it with a black rectangle and your cursor becomes an I-beam, as shown here:

> The How To area works a little like a limited Web browser. Both have Back and Forward buttons you can use to navigate among the pages you've viewed in your current session. Both the How To area and Web browsers display pages that can contain links to other pages. The How To display even has a home page, which appears by default when you choose View > How To Window to open the How To area.
>
> The How To home page contains links to How To pages that are organized into various categories. In some How To task pages, there are "Do it for me" links that automatically launch specific features in the application itself. Other links are cross references that open either another How To page or a related topic in Complete Acrobat 6.0 Help. (See Using Complete Acrobat 6.0 Help.)

3. To change a letter or word in a text selection, click and drag the tool over the letter or word you want to change. As you drag the tool, your selection is highlighted. Release the mouse button when you have selected the characters you want to change.
4. Enter new text, and Acrobat applies the edit to the selected text. If the embedded font is not installed on your system, Acrobat displays a warning dialog box to this effect. Click Yes to remove font embedding. If the unembedded single-byte font is not present in your system encoding, you receive an error message saying you cannot edit the font.

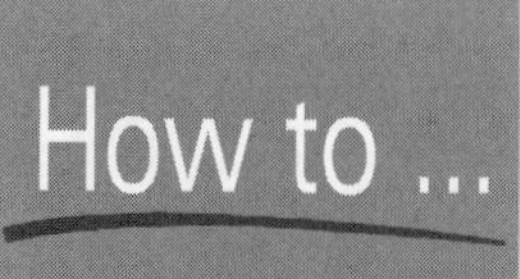

Look Up the Meaning of a Word

If you are connected to the Internet while working in Acrobat, you can look up the meaning of any word in a text object. Acrobat 6.0 has a powerful option equivalent to having a dictionary on demand. To look up the meaning of a word, access the Select Text tool, select the word for which you want to find the meaning. Right-click (Windows) or CTRL-click (Macintosh), then choose Look Up "selected word" where selected word is the word you highlighted with the Select Text tool. After selecting the command, Acrobat launches your Web browser and the meaning for your selected word is displayed.

Even though a single-byte font may be present in your system, legally you must own a licensed version of the actual font or have it installed on your system to change the text.

Change Text Appearance

After you select a block of text with the TouchUp Text tool, you can change the font style, font size, font color, and more. To change text appearance, follow these steps:

1. Select the TouchUp Text tool as outlined previously.
2. Click a block of text to select it.
3. Click and drag to select a single character, word, or the entire line of text. Alternatively, you can place your cursor before a word and double-click to select a single word.
4. Right-click (Windows) or CTRL-click (Macintosh) and choose Properties from the Context menu to open the TouchUp Properties dialog box shown next. Note that this dialog box has two additional tabs that are present in Acrobat Professional only:

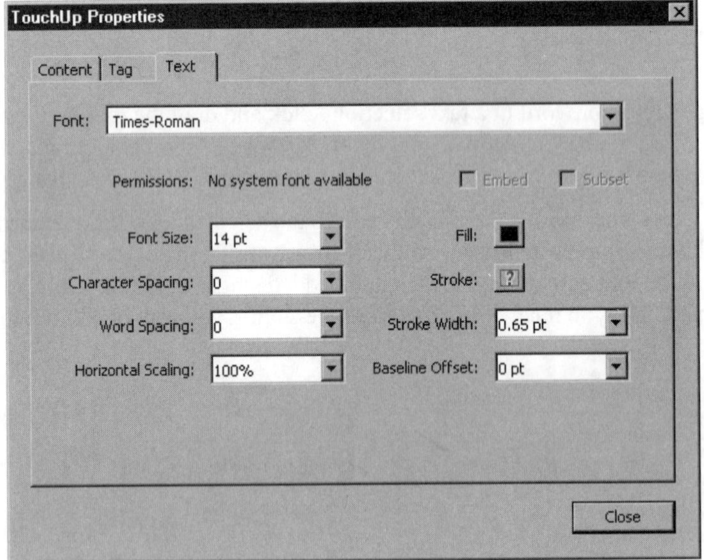

TIP

As you change text parameters in the dialog box, the text updates in real time. If the dialog box covers the text, click and drag the dialog box title bar to move the dialog box to a new location.

5. To change the font style, click the triangle to the right of the Font field and choose a font style from the drop-down menu.

6. If a licensed version of the font you choose is present on your system, you will see "Can Embed Font" to the right of the Permissions field. If you choose to embed the font, you have two options:
   - **Embed Font** Embeds the entire font set, even characters not used in the selected text.
   - **Subset** Embeds a subset of the font type to cover all characters used in the text selection. If another party attempts to edit the document, they will have to un-embed the subset.
7. To change the font size, click the triangle to the right of the Font Size field and choose a size from the drop-down menu.

NOTE *If you use Acrobat on a computer with limited processing power, it may take a while for Acrobat to render your font changes, especially when you significantly enlarge the font size or make changes within large blocks of text.*

8. To change spacing between the characters of the selected text, click the triangle to the right of the Character Spacing field and choose a value from the drop-down menu. Alternatively, you can enter a value between –100 and 200.
9. To change spacing between selected words, click the triangle to the right of the Word Spacing field and choose a value from the drop-down menu.
10. To change the horizontal scale of the selected text, click the triangle to the right of the Horizontal Scaling field and choose a value from the drop-down menu. This option changes the proportion between the width and height of the selected text.
11. To change the baseline shift of the selected text, click the triangle to the right of the Baseline Offset field, and choose a value from the drop-down menu. Alternatively, you can increase or decrease the baseline shift by clicking the spinner buttons or by entering a value between –32768 points and 32767 points. This option determines where the text appears in relation to the baseline. For example, if you select one word from a sentence and increase the baseline shift, the word appears above the other words in the sentence.
12. To change the font fill color, click the Fill button and choose a color from the pop-up palette. Alternatively, you can choose a color not listed on the palette by clicking the Other Color icon and choosing a color from the system color picker. To display only an outline around the selected text, click the No Color icon.
13. To change the font stroke (outline) color, click the Stroke button and choose a color from the pop-up palette. Alternatively, you can click the Other Color icon and choose a color from the system color picker. To display the text with no stroke, click the No Stroke icon.

NOTE *If you choose No Stroke and No Fill, the selected text will not be visible.*

14. Close the dialog box.

TIP *If you do extensive modifications to a document and it is not turning out as you planned, you can eliminate all of your modifications by choosing File | Revert. When you choose this command, Acrobat reverts to the* last saved version *of the document.*

Use the TouchUp Object Tool (Professional Only)

You use the TouchUp Object tool to perform minor edits to an image or to edit the image in a supported external image-editor. The TouchUp Object Context menu has several commands that allow you to perform other tasks with embedded graphics. You can use the TouchUp Object tool to delete or remove an object by performing the following steps:

1. Choose Tools | Advanced Editing | TouchUp Object tool. If you're going to be touching up several objects in a document, choose Tools | Advanced Editing | Show Advanced Editing Toolbar to display the toolbar in the workspace. You then have ready access to the TouchUp Object tool, as shown here:

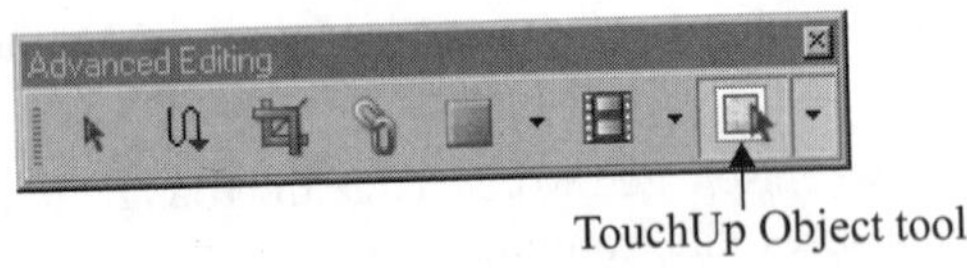

2. Click the object you want to edit. You can select graphic images or entire blocks of text with the TouchUp Object tool. To select more than one object, select the first object, and then click additional objects while holding down the SHIFT key. After selecting the object(s), do one of the following:
   - Drag the object to a new location.
   - Delete the object by choosing Edit | Delete. You can either press DELETE to remove the selected object from the document or choose Delete from the TouchUp tool Context menu.

Use the TouchUp Object Tool Context Menu

When you select the TouchUp Object tool, you have additional options available through the Context menu of the tool. Right-click (Windows) or CTRL-click (Macintosh) to open the TouchUp tool Context menu, as shown next.

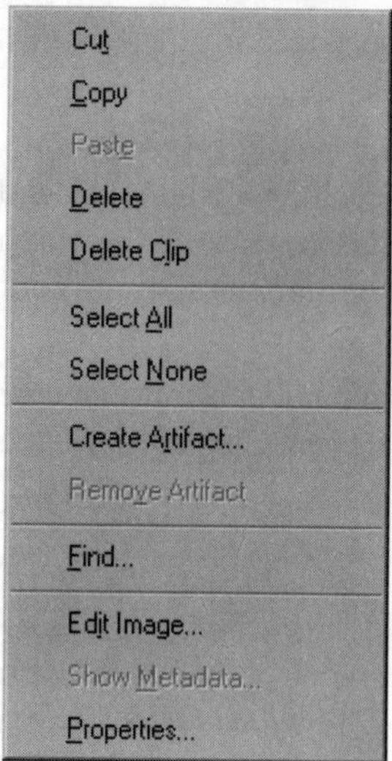

The available Context menu commands will vary depending on previous actions you have performed with the tool. The following list shows all of the tasks you can perform from the TouchUp Object tool Context menu:

- **Cut** Use this command to cut the selected object from the document and place it on the clipboard.
- **Copy** Use this command to copy the selected object to the clipboard while preserving it in the document.
- **Paste** Use this command to paste an object from the clipboard to the document. The command pastes the object in the exact location it was copied from. To move the pasted object, select the object with the TouchUp Object tool and drag it to the desired location.
- **Delete** Use this command to remove the selected object from the document. Alternatively, you can press DELETE to remove selected objects from the document.
- **Delete Clip** Use this command to delete any objects that are clipping the selected objects. For example, if you modify the size of a text object and some of the characters are clipped, choosing this command reveals the clipped text.
- **Select All** Use this command to select all graphic objects, including text blocks, from the page.
- **Select None** Use this command to deselect selected graphics.
- **Create Artifact** Use this command to add an artifact to the selected object. Artifacts are used as elements in tagged documents.
- **Remove Artifact** Use this command to remove an unwanted artifact from a PDF file.

- **Find** Use this command to launch the Find Element dialog box and search for a document element such as an artifact, unmarked link, and so on.
- **Edit Image** Use this command to launch the supported image or illustration editing application. To specify an external editor, choose Edit | Preferences | General and click the TouchUp title. You can then choose PhotoShop for an image editor and Illustrator for a page/object editor. As of this writing, these are the only applications that support this command.
- **Show Metadata** Use this command to display any metadata associated with the object. This command is dimmed out if there is no such metadata.
- **Properties** Use this command to open the Properties dialog box, which supplies information about the selected object.

You can use the TouchUp tool to copy objects from one document to another. Open two documents and then choose Window | Tile (or if you prefer, Window | Cascade). Use the TouchUp tool to select an object, and then choose Copy from the Context menu. Click anywhere in the second document, and then choose one of the Paste options from the Context menu.

Summary

In this chapter, you learned how to edit your PDF documents by adding pages, deleting pages, and extracting pages. You learned how to accomplish these tasks using the Pages tab, menu commands, and tools. You learned how to remove unwanted elements from pages with the Crop tool and Crop Pages menu commands. If you create PDF documents for presentations, you learned how to add a touch of professionalism using page transitions. In the next chapter, you'll learn how to add comments to and review PDF documents.

Chapter 10 Review PDF Documents

How to...

- Use the Comments tab
- Add comments
- Use the Note tool
- Add audio comments
- Use the File Attachment tool

When you use Acrobat in a corporate environment, you can share information with colleagues in faraway locales. You can send documents via e-mail or a corporate intranet for review and approval. Team members or clients can mark up the PDF document with audio comments, notes, highlighted phrases, shapes to highlight items, text boxes, and more. If you ever have sent out an original document for review and a team member altered the original by adding comments to the text or modifying the formulas of a spreadsheet, you will appreciate how easy it is to create a PDF document from the original and use the copy to share and receive comments with colleagues using the Acrobat annotation tools.

When you mark up a document, you often need to identify the object you want modified and then create a note or other annotation to reflect the desired change. You can use shapes to identify the object, highlight the object, or point to the object with an arrow, straight line, or squiggly line drawn with the Pencil tool. In this chapter, you'll learn how to use the annotation tools to mark up a document, add comments to a document, and more.

Initiate an E-Mail Review

When you create a PDF document that you want other colleagues to review, you can easily do so by initiating an e-mail review. When you start an e-mail review and send the document to selected reviewers, Acrobat sends an *FDF* (Forms Data Format) file that contains setup and configuration information, as well as a copy of the PDF document you want reviewed. Your reviewers can open the file attachment—which opens the document in Acrobat—add their own comments to the document, then send the comments back to you. To initiate an e-mail review, follow these steps:

1. Open the document you want to send for review.
2. Choose File | Send By Email For Review. Acrobat displays the Send By Email For Review dialog box.
3. Enter the e-mail addresses of your reviewers in the To field. Separate each e-mail address with a comma.
4. Send copies of the e-mail review to other recipients by entering e-mail addresses in the CC and BCC fields. E-mail addresses you enter in the BCC field will not be displayed in the e-mail header.
5. Accept the default Subject title or enter a different title.

6. Accept the default Message For Reviewers or modify it with additional information. The default message gives reviewers detailed instructions on how to conduct the review and return their comments to you.
7. Click Send. Acrobat sends the document for review.

NOTE *Certain e-mail applications generate error messages saying the temporary file for the document isn't available when you try to send a PDF document for review. It this occurs, refer to your e-mail application Help menu, or select another e-mail application such as Microsoft Outlook Express, which will send the document with no errors.*

You'll receive comments from your reviewers as FDF files. Open the file, and Acrobat opens the original file you sent for review while adding the reviewer's comments. You can keep track of your reviews using the Review Tracker (see the following section).

Use the Review Tracker

You use the Review Tracker to keep tabs on the documents you send out for review. When you use the Review Tracker, it appears on the right side of the interface, the same area that the How To...? and Search pane occupy when in use. To use the Review Tracker, follow these steps:

1. Click the triangle to the right of the Review & Comment button and from the drop-down menu, choose Track Reviews. The Review Tracker opens, as shown in Figure 10-1. In the Showing All window, you'll see a list of the documents you've sent for review. When you click a document title, information about the review appears in the lower half of the dialog box. Reviews are listed as Active or Completed.
2. Select a review in the Showing All window and then click Open to view the document and reviewer's comments in the Document pane.
3. Select a completed review and then click the Remove button to remove it from the tracker.
4. Click the Manage button and choose one of the following options:
   - **Email All Reviewers** Launches your e-mail application with the Subject and e-mail addresses of your reviewers already entered. You can modify the Subject with your own follow-up message and send the e-mail. (The default reads "Follow up to" and the filename of the document you sent for review.)
   - **Send Review Reminder** Launches your e-mail application with the Subject and e-mail addresses of your reviewers already entered. You can modify the Subject, which by default reads "Follow up to" and the filename of the document you sent for review. The default message reminds reviewers to respond to your review if they have not already.
   - **Invite More Reviewers** Launches your e-mail application with the FDF attachment. The FDF attachment contains instructions to the reviewer as well as the PDF file you want reviewed. Enter the e-mail addresses of the new reviewers and send the message.
   - **Go Back Online** Opens the document in a Web browser when you are participating in a browser-based review.

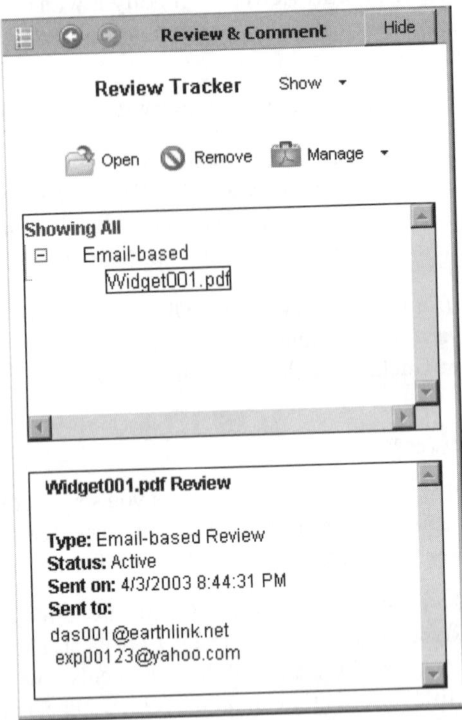

FIGURE 10-1 You can keep track of Email reviews with the Review Tracker.

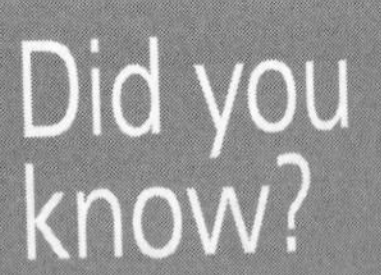

You Can Launch Browser-Based Reviews

If your organization has a Web server, you can institute a browser-based review. Before doing this, you'll have to add your server settings to the Online Commenting section of the Preferences dialog box. After setting up your server information, select the document you want to review and then choose File | Upload For Browser-Based Review. You'll be prompted for the e-mail addresses of the colleagues with whom you want to review the document. After completing the dialog, the PDF document is uploaded to your server and an FDF file is sent to your reviewers. To review the document, your reviewers must be online. When they open the FDF file attachment, the review document opens in their browser. They can then comment online and upload the comments or download the document for review offline.

Use the Comments Tab

When you open a document with comments, each comment is noted in the Comments tab. The Comments tab lists the title of each comment and the page number on which the comment can be found. You can configure the Comments tab to display comments by Author, Date, Page, or Type. The Comments tab has several tools and an Options menu that you can use to import comments, export selected comments, find comments, and delete comments. You also use the Comments tab to navigate to comments and change comment properties. To open the Comments tab, as shown in Figure 10-2, open the Navigation pane and click Comments. Alternatively, you can choose View | Navigation Tabs | Comment.

Navigate to a Comment

The Comments tab has been completely revised for Acrobat 6.0. The Comments tab title still resides on the left side of the Navigation pane, but when you click the title, the tab opens at the

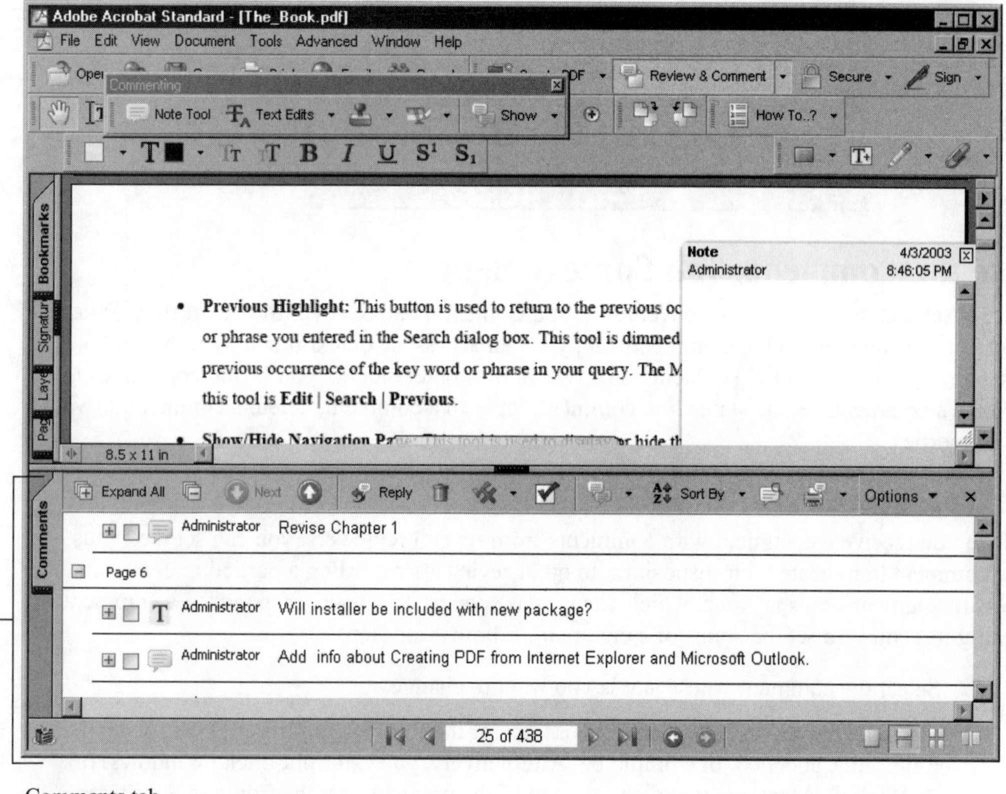

FIGURE 10-2 You use the Comments tab to navigate to document comments.

bottom of the Document pane, as shown in Figure 10-2. Comments are referred to by their icon types, or if a document have been annotated with an attached file, the comment is referred to by its filename and extension. If there are several comments attached to a page (or authors, types, or dates, depending on how you configure the tab to display comments), there is a plus sign (+) next to the heading. Click the plus sign to expand the comment group. After you expand a comment group, a minus sign (–) appears to the left of the comment group heading. Click it to collapse the group to the heading. To navigate to a comment, click the comment icon or the comment title.

Use the Comments Options Menu

You use the Comments Options menu to perform various tasks related to comments such as importing comments, exporting comments, summarizing comments, and so on. To open the Comments Options menu, shown in the following illustration, click the Comments icon near the upper-right corner of the tab:

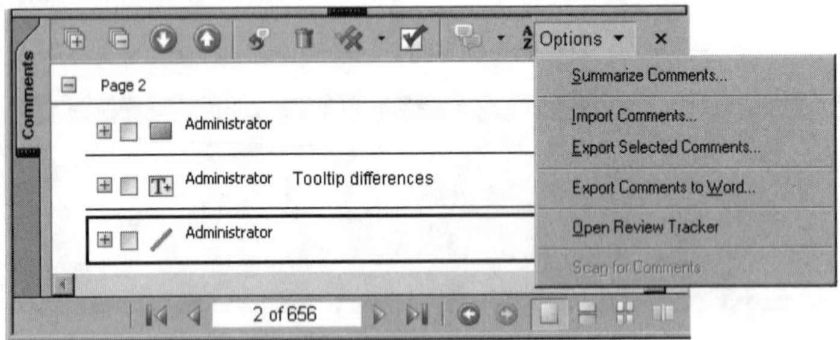

Use the Comments Tab Context Menu

Many Acrobat users prefer the convenience of a Context menu to streamline workflow. When you select a comment in the Comments tab, you can access a Context menu by right-clicking (Windows) or CTRL-clicking (Macintosh). Within the context menu, you'll find commands to expand a comment, set the status of a comment, reply to a comment, delete a comment, or view its properties.

Set Comment Status

When you receive a document with comments from several reviewers, you can set the status of the comment to indicate your disposition to other reviewers regarding a particular comment. The default comment status is None, which changes as soon as a reviewer responds to a comment by setting its status. To set the status of a comment, follow these steps:

1. Select the comment whose status you want to change.
2. Click the Set Status button and choose one of the following options: None, Accepted, Rejected, Cancelled, or Completed. Alternatively, you can right-click (Windows) or CTRL-click (Macintosh) and choose one of the previous options from the Set Status drop-down menu.

TIP

You can mark comments with a checkmark by selecting a comment and then clicking the Checkmark icon on the Comments tab toolbar, or by clicking the check box next to a comment icon. Marking a comment in this manner is your reminder that you've already reviewed the comment. When you mark comments in this manner, the checkmarks are saved with your copy of the document; however, other reviewers will not be able to see them.

Sort Comments

By default, Acrobat sorts all comments by the page number they appear on. You can, however, change the way Acrobat sorts comments. For example, if you work with a team of authors on a document, you can sort comments by author. To change the way comments in the document are sorted follow these steps:

1. In the Navigation pane, click Comments. Alternatively, you can choose View | Navigation Tabs | Comments.
2. Click the Sort By icon and from the drop-down menu, choose one of the following:
   - **Type** Acrobat sorts the comments by type. When you choose this option, Acrobat creates one heading in the Comment tab for each type used in the document.
   - **Page** Acrobat creates a heading for each page that has comments (this is the default).
   - **Author** Acrobat creates a heading for each author that added comments to the document.
   - **Date** Acrobat sorts comments by date, creating a heading for each date on which a comment was created. Acrobat displays the earliest date at the top of the tab. Dates are displayed in *mm/dd/yyyy* format.
   - **Color** Acrobat creates headings that are square color chips. This option sorts the comments by the icon color of the tool used to create them. For example, if you click a yellow color chip, you'll see comments created with the Note tool, Text Box tool, and Highlight tool, all of which have yellow as the primary color for their tool icon.
   - **Checkmark Status** Acrobat creates two headings: Unmarked and Marked. If you have no Unmarked comments, Acrobat does not create an Unmarked heading, and vice versa. Note that the checkmarks created by other authors are not saved with the document. This feature enables the current viewer of the document to check a comment after reading it.
   - **Status By Person** Acrobat creates headings for each status you assign a comment. As an example, you'll see separate headings for comments you have accepted, rejected, cancelled, and so on.

Use the Show Comments Menu

When you are reviewing a PDF document with multiple comments, you can decide which comments are displayed and which comments are not. For example, you can choose to show only comments created by a certain reviewer or show only comments created with the Note tool. To specify which comments are displayed, follow these steps:

1. Click Comments to open the Comments tab. Alternatively, choose View | Navigation Tabs | Comments.
2. Click the Show icon, and choose one of the following options from the drop-down menu:
   - **Hide Comments List** Closes the Comments Tab.
   - **Hide All Comments** Hides all comments in the document and the Comments tab. After invoking this command, the Show Comments command appears on the drop-down menu. Choose the Show Comments command to display comments again.
   - **Show By Type** Displays a drop-down menu with a list of all comment types. Select a comment type and only comments of that type are displayed in the documents and Comments tab. You can select more than one comment type.
   - **Show By Reviewer** Displays a drop-down menu listing all reviewers. Select one or more reviewers whose comments you want to display or select All Reviewers.
   - **Show By Status** Displays a drop-down menu of status types. Select one or more comment status types you want to display or select All Status.
   - **Show By Checked State** Displays a drop-down menu from which you can choose to display checked comments, unchecked comments, or both.
   - **Open All Pop-Ups** Opens all pop-up notes in the document.
   - **Close All Pop-Ups** Closes all pop-up notes in the document.
   - **Show Connector Lines** Displays a connector line between an open pop-up note and its icon in the document when your mouse hovers over the icon.
   - **Align New Pop Ups By Default** Aligns a pop-up note with the right border of the document, no matter where you click the Note tool inside the document.

TIP *If the default Comments preferences don't suit your working habits, click the Show icon discussed in the preceding steps and choose Commenting Preferences from the drop-down menu. This opens the Commenting section of the Preferences dialog from which you can change the default comment font type, font size, pop-up opacity, and several other commenting options.*

Search Comments

When you're reviewing a document with multiple comments, you can search for specific information by entering a word or phrase in a field. To search comments, follow these steps:

1. Click Comments in the Navigation pane to open the Comments tab. Alternatively, choose View | Navigation Tabs | Comments.
2. Click the Search Comments icon. The Search pane appears to the right of the Document pane. This is a watered down version of the pane that appears when you choose the Search command.
3. Enter the word or phrase you want to find within the document's comments. You can fine-tune your search by selecting the Whole Words Only option and/or the Case Sensitive option.
4. Click the Search Comments button. Acrobat displays a list of all instances of the word or phrase you entered in the text field. Each keyword is a link to the comment.
5. Click a keyword to view a comment.

TIP *To print a copy of all comments in a document, click the Print Comments icon and choose to print a comments summary on a device printer or create a PDF comments summary.*

Delete Comments

When a comment has outlived its usefulness, you can delete it. When you delete comments, you decrease the file size of the document and eliminate having to deal with comments that are no longer pertinent. To delete a comment, follow these steps:

1. In the Navigation pane, click Comments.
2. Select the comment you want to delete and do one of the following:
   - Press DELETE.
   - Choose Edit | Delete.
   - Choose Delete from the Comments Options menu.
   - Choose Delete from the Context menu.

Modify Comments

You can modify comment appearance and change the author and subject information. You can change the color of any comment as well as change the default icon used to display a comment created with the Note tool; however, the icons for many of the other annotation methods are set by default. To modify a comment, follow these steps:

1. In the Navigation pane, click Comments
2. Select the comment you want to modify.

3. Right-click (Windows) or CTRL-click (Macintosh) and then choose Properties from the Context menu to open the Properties dialog box. Note that the dialog box name varies to reflect the comment type you select. The following illustration shows the Note Properties dialog box:

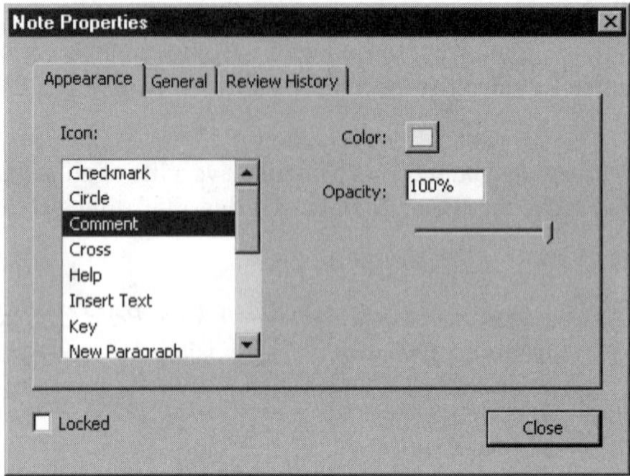

4. Modify the comment as desired and then click OK to close the dialog box.

If Acrobat Security has been applied to the document and commenting is not allowed, you will not be able to edit comments unless the settings are changed. If Acrobat Certificate Security has been assigned to the document, you will be able to edit comments if the document author grants you permission to edit comments. For more information on Acrobat security, see Chapter 11.

Reply to Comments

When you receive documents for review, you can reply to comments other reviewers have added to the document. If you set the status for a comment, you can add a reply to let the reviewer know why you chose a particular status or just add a general reply to add your two cents' worth to the review. To reply to a comment, follow these steps:

1. Open the Comments tab, as outlined previously, in "Navigate to a Comment."
2. Select the comment to which you want to respond.
3. Click Reply. Acrobat opens a text field to the right of the comment title. Alternatively, you can right-click (Windows) or CTRL-click (Macintosh) and choose Reply from the Context menu.
4. Enter your reply and then press ENTER or RETURN. Note that if you enter a lengthy comment, Acrobat will wrap the text to a new line and a minus sign (–) appears to the left of the comment title. Click the minus sign to collapse the reply to a single line.

When other reviewers see your reply, they can continue the thread by clicking your comment and then clicking Reply.

To edit a reply, move your cursor over the reply until it becomes an I-beam, click to open the text window, and then apply your edits. To delete a reply, select it and press DELETE.

Add Comments

When you receive a PDF document or send a PDF document, you can add comments to the document. Comments are a handy way to communicate between team members or clients. Comments are readily accessible in the Comments tab and can easily be added with the click of a mouse. You can add notes (the PDF equivalent of a yellow sticky note) or audio comments, or create comments in text boxes.

TIP

If the document you are viewing is part of a review, you can display any changes made to an annotation created with a commenting tool. To do so, select the comment, right-click (Windows) or CTRL-click (Macintosh), and choose Properties from the context menu. After the comment's Properties dialog box appears, click the Review History tab to view a list of any changes to the document.

Use the Note Tool

Use the Note tool when you want to add a quick comment that is specific to a certain part of the document. When you use the Note tool to create a comment, you can accept the default option and leave the note open so a reviewer can read it when the page opens, or collapse the note to an icon that when clicked, opens the note in a window. When you create a comment with the Note tool, you can define the size of the window and the type and color of the note icon, as well as enter your comments. To add a comment to a PDF document with the Note tool, follow these steps:

1. Navigate to the point in the document where you want to add the note.
2. Choose Tools | Commenting | Note Tool. Alternatively, you can click the Review & Comment button to display the toolbar in the following illustration and then select the Note tool:

3. Click the point in the document where you want the note to appear. When you create a note in this manner, Acrobat opens a blank note window of the default size. When you use the default window size, scroll bars are provided for use when reading lengthy notes. After you create the window, a blinking cursor appears in the window, signifying that Acrobat is ready for you to enter some text.

TIP

To size the note window while creating it, click a point in the document where you want the note to appear and then drag diagonally. As you drag, a bounding box appears and defines the size of the window you are creating. Release the mouse button when the window is the desired size. To constrain the window to a square, press SHIFT while dragging. Acrobat sizes the note window as you specify when the document is next opened.

4. Enter the comments you want to appear in the window.
5. Click the X in the upper-left corner of the note window to close it. Alternatively, you can leave the note open by not clicking the X.

Reviewers of your document read a closed note by clicking its icon. After you create a note, you can modify the appearance of the note icon and its colors by changing its properties.

Set Note Properties

The default icon for a note looks like a sticky note, and in keeping with that paradigm, the Acrobat designers gave the icon a default color of bright yellow. If you don't like bright yellow for your virtual sticky notes, you can change the characteristics of the icon by following these steps:

1. To select the note you want to modify, click its name in the Comments tab, as discussed previously, or click the actual note in the document. You can select the note with either the Hand tool or the Note tool.
2. Right-click (Windows) or CTRL-click (Macintosh) and choose Properties from the Context menu. The Note Properties dialog box appears.
3. In the Appearance tab, choose an icon from the list in the Icon window.
4. Click the Color button and choose a color from the pop-up palette. Alternatively, click the Other Color icon and choose a color from the system color picker. When you choose colors from the system color picker, they may not look the same when viewed cross-platform.
5. Enter a value in the Opacity field or drag the slider to specify note opacity. This determines how much of the document is visible through the note icon. The note icon is totally opaque at the default setting of 100 percent.
6. Click the General tab, as shown next. In this section, you can enter text to change the author name or the note subject. By default, Acrobat uses the registered owner of Acrobat for the author information. Notice there is a time stamp at the bottom of this section. After you modify the note properties, the time stamp updates to reflect the time the properties were changed.

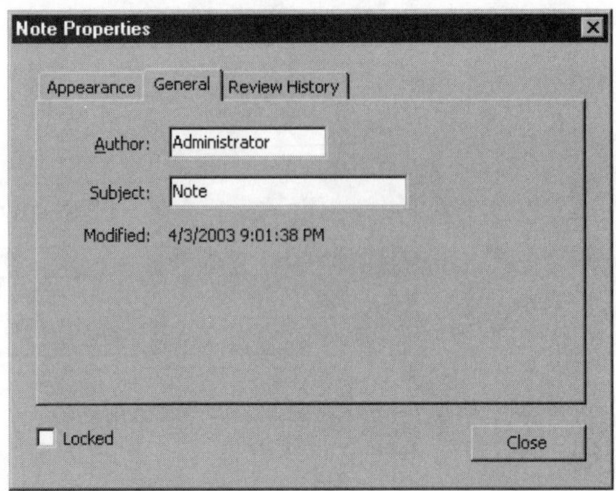

7. Click the Locked check box to lock the position of the note in the document and prevent any property changes until the note is unlocked by once again clicking the check box.

NOTE *Even though you lock a comment, another reviewer can unlock and modify it unless you add security to the document and disallow commenting.*

8. Click OK to close the Note Properties dialog box and Acrobat applies the changes to the note.

Modify Note Text

In addition to modifying a note's properties, you can also modify the text in a pop-up note, which is the electronic equivalent of a sticky note. As mentioned earlier, you can display pop-up notes or hide them. Hidden pop-up notes can be displayed when users double-click a note icon, or an annotation made with any of the other commenting tools. Text for pop-up notes is displayed in the Comments tab as well. You can change the font color, size, and style. To change text in a pop-up note, follow these steps:

1. Select the note whose text you want to modify. The easiest way to do this is to click the note icon in the document to open the pop-up note. If the note is already open, this step is not necessary.
2. Click inside the note and then drag to select the text you want to modify. Note that you can modify a single character, word, sentence, or the entire text.

TIP *To select all text in a pop-up note, place your cursor inside the note and then press CTRL-A (Windows) or COMMAND-A (Macintosh).*

3. Choose View | Toolbars | Properties Bar to open the Properties bar, as shown in the following illustration:

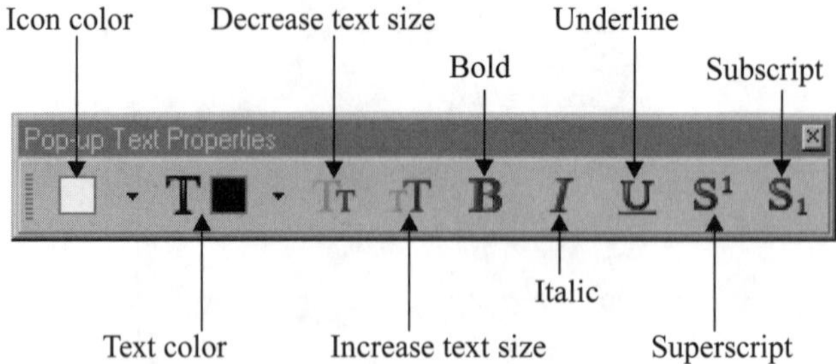

4. Click the triangle to the right of the Color icon and choose a color from the pop-up palette. This determines the color displayed for the note's icon in the document, as well as the title bar of the note when popped up.
5. To change the color of the pop-up note text, select the text in the note, and then in the Properties bar, click the triangle to the right of the Text Color icon and choose a color from the pop-up palette. Alternatively, you can click Other Color and choose a color from the system color picker.
6. To decrease the size of selected note text, click the Decrease Text Size icon. You can click the icon repeatedly; however, Acrobat stops decreasing the text size when it reaches 6 points.
7. To increase the size of selected note text, click the Increase Text Size icon. You can click the icon repeatedly; however, Acrobat stops increasing text size when it reaches 18 points.
8. Click the applicable icon to boldface, italicize, underline, subscript, or superscript the selected text.

Edit Notes

In addition to changing the properties of a note, you can change the position of a note, edit its contents, or delete it. In a previous section, you learned to delete a note from within the Comments tab. In this section, you'll learn to edit a note from within the document. To edit a note within the document, select it with either the Hand tool or the Note tool and perform one of the following tasks:

- To delete a selected note, choose Edit | Delete. Alternatively, press DELETE or choose Delete from the Context menu.
- To move a selected note, click the title bar of the note and then drag it to a new location.

- To change the contents of a selected note, double-click its icon to open the note, edit the contents, and then click X to close the window. If the note is already open, place your cursor inside the note and perform your edits.
- To resize the window of a selected note, double-click its icon, and then click and drag the lower-right handle of the pop-up note window. To resize the window proportionately, press SHIFT while dragging. If the note is already open, click and drag the handle to resize the note window.

Add Audio Comments

If you prefer the spoken word to a written comment, you can record a comment and add it to a document. Audio comments can often be more effective than written comments. You can convey excitement and enthusiasm with a recorded comment.

You record the audio comments through a microphone attached to your computer or choose an audio file stored on your system. Whichever method you use, the sound is embedded with the document. In order to record comments with your PDF documents, your computer must have a sound card and software capable of recording from a microphone. Acrobat relies on your system recording software to create the comment that is embedded with the PDF document. To record an audio comment for a PDF document, follow these steps:

1. Choose Tools | Advanced Commenting | Attach | Attach Sound. Alternatively, you can choose the Attach Sound tool that looks like a speaker from the Advanced Commenting toolbar if available in the workspace.
2. Click the spot in the document where you want to add the audio comment and the Sound Recorder dialog box appears, as shown next. This is the Windows version of the recorder. The Macintosh version is slightly different.

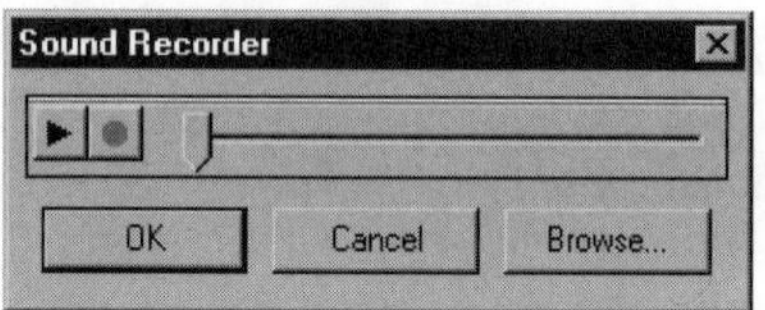

3. Click the Record button (the red circle) and speak into the microphone. Alternatively, click the Browse button to navigate to a folder on your computer that contains a pre-recorded sound you want to attach to the document.
4. Click the Stop button (the filled-in circle) to stop the recording. Acrobat displays the Sound Attachment Properties dialog box.
5. In the General tab accept the default information for Author, Subject, and Description fields, or enter different information.

6. Click the Appearance tab and accept the default icon type (Sound) or choose a different one from the list, as shown here:

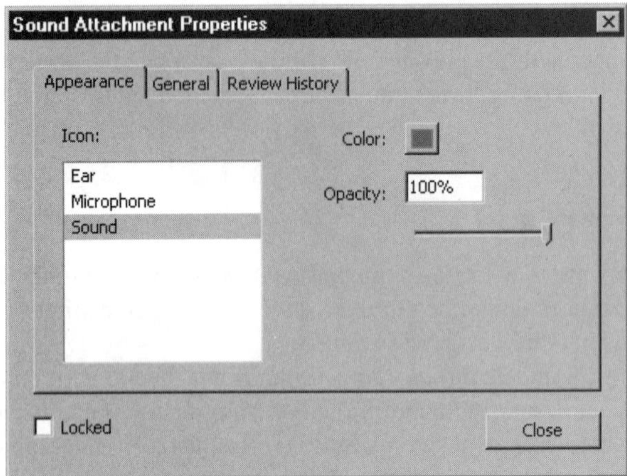

7. Accept the default Sound Attachment icon color (blue) or click the Color button to choose a different color from the pop-up palette. Click the Other Color icon to choose a color from the system color picker.
8. Click OK to embed the sound in the document.

After you finish the recording, Acrobat designates the audio comment with the default speaker icon or the icon specified by the audio comment's speaker. To play the recording or sound file, double-click the icon. Alternatively, right-click (Windows) or CTRL-click (Macintosh) the icon and choose Play File from the context menu.

You can modify the properties of an audio comment by selecting it and then choosing View | Toolbars | Properties Toolbar, which enables you to change the comment icon, color, and opacity. Click the More button for other information such as the comment author, description, and so on.

Create Text Annotations

You have another Acrobat tool at your disposal for adding comments to a document: the Text Box tool. When you use the Text Box tool, you can add text notes with borders, and if you desire, a solid color background. When you annotate a document, with the Text Box tool, you create a static note that occupies space in the document whereas a Note tool annotation can be collapsed to an icon and popped up when needed. You can specify the font type, size, and style. Figure 10-3 shows the Text Box tool used to point out a change a reviewer wants made.

Text Box annotation

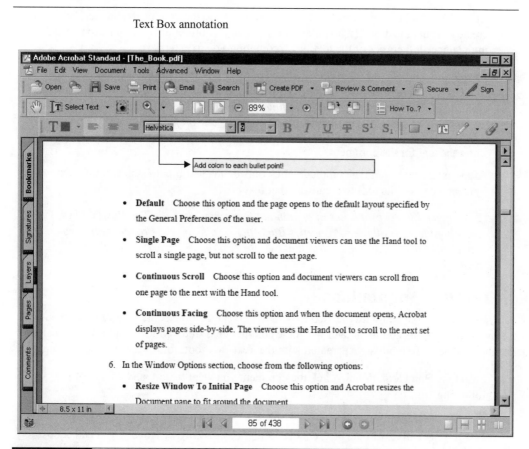

FIGURE 10-3 You can use the Free Text tool to create a comment.

Use the Text Box Tool

You can create a comment using the Text Box tool at any location in the document. When you create a comment with the Text Box tool, the comment appears on top of the actual elements in the PDF document.

To add a comment with the Text Box tool, follow these steps:

1. Choose Tools | Advanced Commenting | Text Box tool. Alternatively, choose the Text Box tool from the Advanced Commenting toolbar (shown here) if you have previously displayed the toolbar.

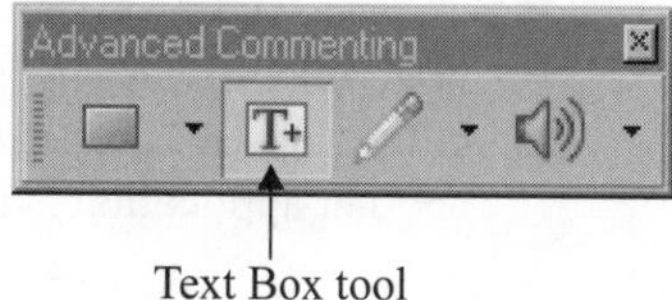

Text Box tool

2. Click the point in the document where you want to add the comment, and Acrobat creates a square text box (with default dimensions). A blinking cursor positions itself in the upper-left corner of the text box, prompting you to enter text.

TIP

If you find the default size of the Text Box tool text box is not to your liking, you can size the box while creating it by clicking in the document and then dragging diagonally. As you drag the tool, a rectangular bounding box gives you a preview of the text box size. Release the mouse button when the box is sized to your preference.

3. Enter the text for the comment.
4. After you have written the comment, click outside the text box to stop entering text. You can now use the tool to create another text box.

You can modify the properties of an annotation created with the Text Box tool by choosing View | Toolbars | Properties Bar. After displaying the Properties bar, you can change the background color, font type, text color, text size, text justification, and text style.

Edit Text Box Annotations

When you create a comment with the Text Box tool, you can edit the contents of the comment, move the location of the comment, and when the comment has outlived its usefulness, you can delete the comment. To modify text created with the Text Box tool, follow these steps:

1. Select the Hand tool, double-click the comment you want to edit, and do one of the following:
   - To select text, click and drag your cursor over the text characters you want to select.
   - To select all text in the box, choose Edit | Select All. Alternatively, you can choose Select All from the Context menu.
   - To modify the selected text, enter new text from your keyboard.
   - To delete selected text, press DELETE. Alternatively, choose Edit | Delete or choose Delete from the Context menu.
   - To copy selected text to the clipboard, choose Edit | Copy. Alternatively, you can choose Copy from the Context menu.
   - To cut selected text to the clipboard, choose Edit | Cut. Alternatively, you can choose Cut from the Context menu.
   - To paste text from the clipboard into a selected comment, place your cursor at the point you want to display the text and choose Edit | Paste. Alternatively, you can choose Paste from the Context menu. Note that any formatting applied to the text in another application is lost when it is pasted into a Text Box comment.

You can also change the position and size of a comment created with the Text Box tool. To move a comment, select the comment with the Hand tool and then drag it to a new location.

To resize the text box, follow these steps:

1. Select the text box with the Hand tool and four rectangular handles appear, one at each corner of the box.
2. Click and drag a handle to resize the box. To resize the box proportionately, press SHIFT while dragging. As you drag, Acrobat draws a rectangular bounding box, which gives you a preview of the current size of the box. Note that this does not change the size of the text.
3. Release the mouse button when the box is the desired size.

You can spell check your comments before saving the document by choosing Edit | Check Spelling | In Comments And Form Fields.

Attach Files to Document

You can attach any file to a document for use by another reviewer or colleague. When you use the Attach File tool to attach a file to a document, it becomes embedded in the document. Reviewers will need software associated with the file installed on their computer to be able to view the file. To attach a file to a document, follow these steps:

1. Choose Tools | Advanced Commenting | Attach | Attach File Tool. Alternatively, you can select the Attach File tool from the Advanced Commenting toolbar if you have previously displayed the toolbar.
2. Click the spot in the document where you want the File Attachment icon to appear, and Acrobat opens the Select File To Attach dialog box.
3. Navigate to the file you want to attach and click Select, and Acrobat opens the File Attachment Properties dialog box shown here:

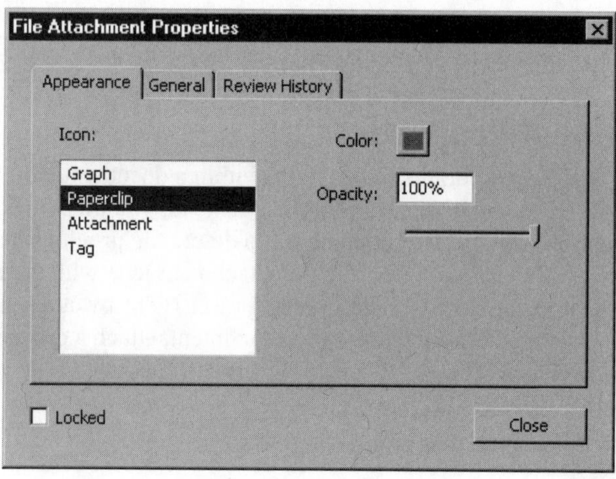

4. In the Icon section of the Appearance tab, select the icon you want to appear in the document. By default, the file attachment icon is a paper clip. However, you can choose a different icon if you feel it is a better representation of the type of document you want to attach. For example, you may want to use the graph icon when attaching a spreadsheet.
5. Click the Color button and select a color from the pop-up palette or click the Other Color icon to choose a color from the system color picker.
6. Enter a value in the Opacity field, or drag the slider to determine the opacity of the text box background. The background is totally opaque at the default setting of 100 percent.
7. Click the General tab and accept the default information, or enter new information in the Author, Subject, and Description fields. If desired, click the Lock check box to lock the position of the file attachment icon.
8. Click close to exit the dialog box and attach the file to the document.

Attaching a file to a document may considerably increase the document file size. Since Acrobat stores additional information with the embedded (attached) file, the final document file size will be above and beyond the file size of the original document, combined with the file size of the attached file.

Open a File Attachment

When you receive a PDF document with a file attachment, you open the file by double-clicking the file attachment icon. After you double-click the icon, Acrobat displays a warning dialog box saying that the attached file may contain programs or macros with viruses. If you received the document from a trusted source, click Open to view the file. If you do not know the author of the PDF document, or have reason to believe the attachment may in fact have a virus, click Do Not Open, close the document, exit Acrobat, and then check the PDF document with your virus scanning software. If you decide to open the file, Acrobat launches the application on your computer associated with the file type. When you open an attached file, your operating system creates temporary files, the location of which will vary depending on the operating system you use.

Edit File Attachment Properties

When you use the File Attachment tool to embed a file within a document, you cannot change the embedded file with the File Attachment Properties. Instead, you must make and save changes to the file before attaching it to a document. To delete the previous version of an attached file and embed a different one, select the file attachment icon with the Hand or Attach File tool and delete it by choosing Edit | Delete, pressing DELETE, or by choosing Delete from the Context menu. After you delete the incorrect file attachment, attach a different file using the steps outlined in the previous section.

You can't change the file attached to a document by editing its properties in the File Attachment Properties dialog box. However, if unlocked, you can change the position of the file attachment icon by clicking it with either the Hand or File Attachment tool, and then dragging it to a different location. You can also edit the properties of the file attachment icon by clicking the attachment icon and then choosing Properties from the Context menu to open the File Attachment Properties dialog box shown previously. Modify the properties, as outlined in the previous section, and then click Close to exit the dialog box.

TIP

You can save an embedded file to your hard drive by clicking the file attachment icon and then choosing Save Embedded File To Disk from the Context menu. Even if you know the author of the file, it's a good idea to run a virus scan on the file before you open it, especially if it's a Word or Excel file that may contain macros, which can harbor viruses that can be harmful to your system.

Apply a Stamp

When you receive a PDF document for review, you can literally apply a stamp of approval to the document. You apply a stamp to a PDF document using the Stamp tool, the virtual equivalent of a rubber stamp minus the messy inkpad. You can use one of the Acrobat preset stamps on a document or create your own custom stamp. An Acrobat stamp as it appears when applied to a document is shown here:

INITIAL HERE

Use the Stamp Tool

You use the Stamp tool to apply a stamp to a PDF document. You can choose from a large selection of preset stamps. After you stamp a document, you can change the color, size, and location of the stamp. You can even attach a note to a stamp. To annotate a document using the Stamp tool, follow these steps:

1. Choose Tools | Commenting | Stamp Tool, and then choose a preset from one of these categories: Dynamic, Sign Here, and Standard Business. When you choose one of these categories, a drop-down menu with that category's presets appears. Move your cursor over the preset title to display a preview of the stamp. Alternatively, you can click the Stamp tool from the Commenting toolbar if present in the workspace and then choose a preset.
2. Click the preview of the desired stamp to select it.
3. Click the location inside the document where you want the stamp to appear.

To move the stamp, select it with the Hand tool and drag it to another location. To resize the stamp, select it and then move your cursor toward one of the rectangular handles at each corner of the stamp. Click the handle, and drag in or out to resize the stamp. Press SHIFT while dragging to constrain the stamp to its original proportions.

You Can Create Custom Stamps

If your organization has a need for stamps other than the robust set of presets that come with Acrobat, you can create your own. In your favorite image-editing program, create a graphic approximately 2.00 inches × 1.5 inches. In Acrobat, choose Tools | Commenting | Stamps | Create Custom Stamp. Follow the prompts in the dialog box to locate the graphic you created in your image-editing program. You'll be prompted for a category name and a name for the stamp. When you close out of the dialog box, your custom stamp is available for immediate use.

You can attach a pop-up note to a stamp. For more information, refer to the upcoming "Attach a Pop-Up Note" section.

Edit Stamp Properties

You can edit the properties of any stamp in a PDF document. You can change the appearance of the stamp as well as the author name. The ability to change the appearance of a stamp comes in handy when there are several stages in a review process. For example, if you are the head of the review team and you decide the document is ready for final publication, you can change a stamp appearance from Draft to Final. To edit stamp properties, follow these steps:

1. In the document, use the Hand tool to select the stamp whose properties you want to change. Alternatively, you can select a stamp annotation by clicking its icon in the Comments tab.
2. Right-click (Windows) or CTRL-click (Macintosh) and then choose Properties from the Context menu to display the Stamp Properties dialog box.
3. In the Appearance tab, you can choose a different color for the Stamp icon as it appears in the Comments tab or change the opacity of the stamp in the document.
4. Click the General tab and enter new text to change the author or subject information. By default, Acrobat uses the name of the registered owner of the software for Author, and the name of the stamp for Subject.

Delete a Stamp

To delete a stamp, select it with the Hand tool and then choose Edit | Delete. Alternatively, you can press DELETE or choose Delete from the Context menu.

Mark Up a Document

In addition to annotating your documents with notes, stamps, text boxes, and attached files, you can also highlight, strikethrough, and underline text to create annotations. You can also create graphic elements to mark up a document. You can use a circle, rectangle, line, or pencil to highlight areas of the document.

TIP *You can also mark up text by choosing Tools | Commenting | Text Edits and then choosing a tool from the drop-down menu. These tools are labeled Insert Text At Cursor, Replace Text At Cursor, and so on. These tools don't actually change the document text; rather, the text is marked with a proofreading symbol that corresponds to the desired action, and a note is attached to the mark-up in which you enter the desired changes.*

Highlight Text

You can call another reviewer's attention to text that needs to be changed within a document by using one of the Highlight tools. Figure 10-4 shows the three text annotation methods (Highlighter, Cross-Out Text, and Underline Text) being used in a single paragraph.

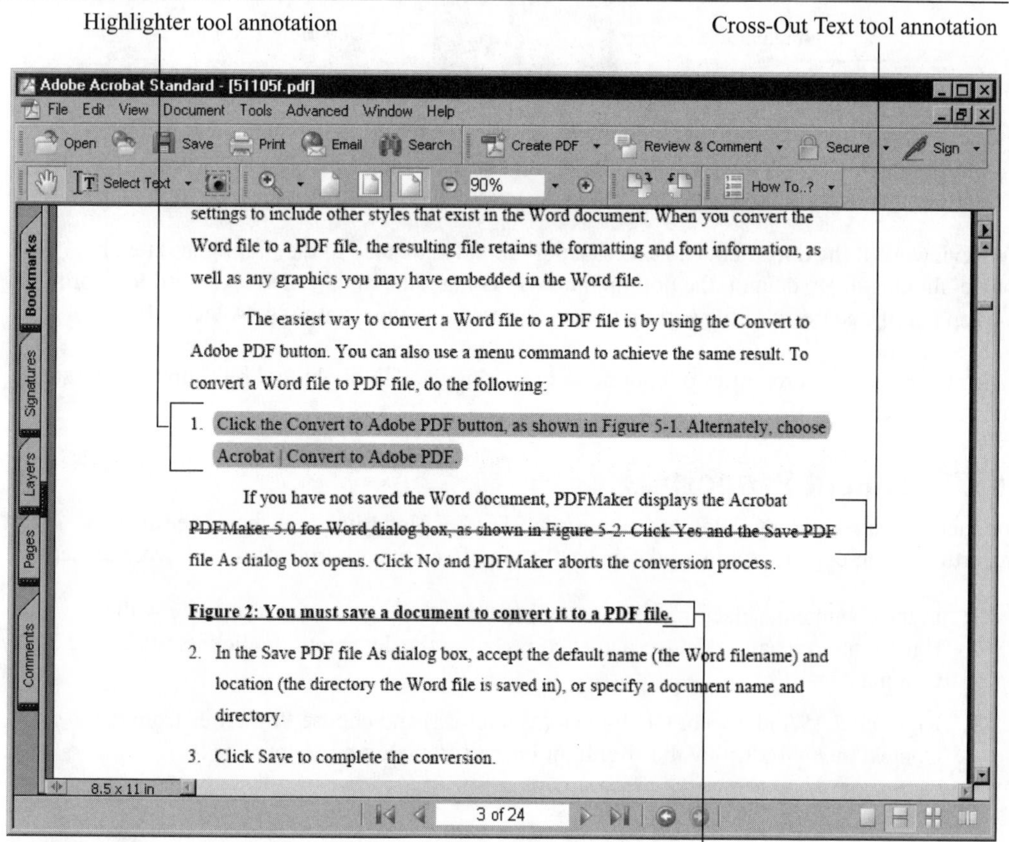

FIGURE 10-4 You can draw a reviewer's attention to text using one of three tools.

Use the Highlight Tools

When you want to draw attention to a block of text that needs to be changed in a paper document, you use a highlighter. Acrobat gives you similar tools you can use to draw attention to text: the Highlight tools. You have three from which to choose: Highlighter tool, Cross-Out Text tool, and Underline Text tool. The steps involved in using each tool are the same, as discussed in the following steps.

1. Choose Tools | Commenting | Highlight and select the desired tool from the drop-down menu. Alternatively, you can choose Tools | Highlighting | Show Highlighting toolbar to display the toolbar shown here:

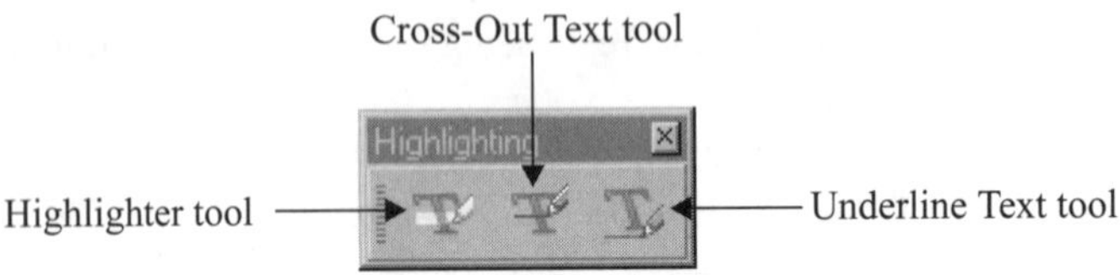

2. Select the desired tool and then move the selected tool into the Document pane and highlight text by clicking and dragging. After you select a single word with the tool, it automatically snaps to the end of the next word over which you move your cursor.

Reviewers of the document can access a pop-up note attached to the highlighted text by double-clicking it. By default, the pop-up note will contain the highlighted text word for word. You can edit the contents of the pop-up note as described in the upcoming "Attach a Pop-Up Note" section.

You can also edit properties of comments created with a Highlight tool by following the steps in the next section.

Edit Comment Properties

Comments created with the Highlight, Cross-Out Text, or Underline tool share the same properties: color, opacity, author and subject. To modify comment properties, follow these steps:

1. In the document, select the comment whose properties you want to modify with the Hand tool. You can select the actual comment in the document or click its title in the Comments tab.
2. Right-click (Windows) or CTRL-click (Macintosh) and choose Properties from the Context menu to display the Highlight Properties dialog box shown next.

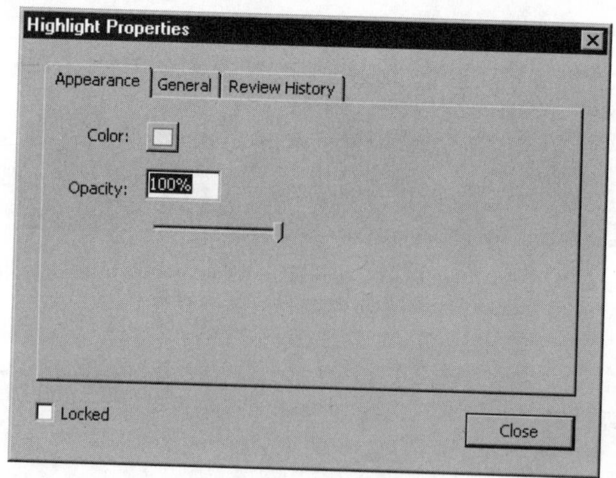

3. In the General tab, you can modify the Author and Subject information by entering new text or editing the existing text. By default, Acrobat lists the registered owner of Acrobat as the author and the tool name as the Subject.
4. Click the Appearance tab and then click the Color button to choose a color from the pop-up palette. This changes the color of the annotation in the document and the Comments tab. Alternatively, you can click Other Color and choose a color from the system color picker.
5. Enter a value in the Opacity field. Alternatively, drag the Opacity slider to specify the level of opacity for the comment as it appears in the document.
6. Click Close to exit the dialog box and apply the property changes.

10

When you change a comment's properties, this does not automatically change the default properties for the tool as it did in previous versions of Acrobat. When you next use a tool, it reverts to its default settings.

Use Graphic Elements

Some reviewers prefer to use graphic elements to mark up a document. You can create graphic elements to mark up a document with one of the tools on the drawing toolbar or the Pencil tool. When you mark up a document with one of these tools, you can attach a pop-up note, as outlined in the upcoming "Attach a Pop-Up Note" section.

Some PDF reviewers prefer to mark up a document with a combination of graphic elements and text created with the Text Box tool. For example, you can use the Circle tool to highlight a

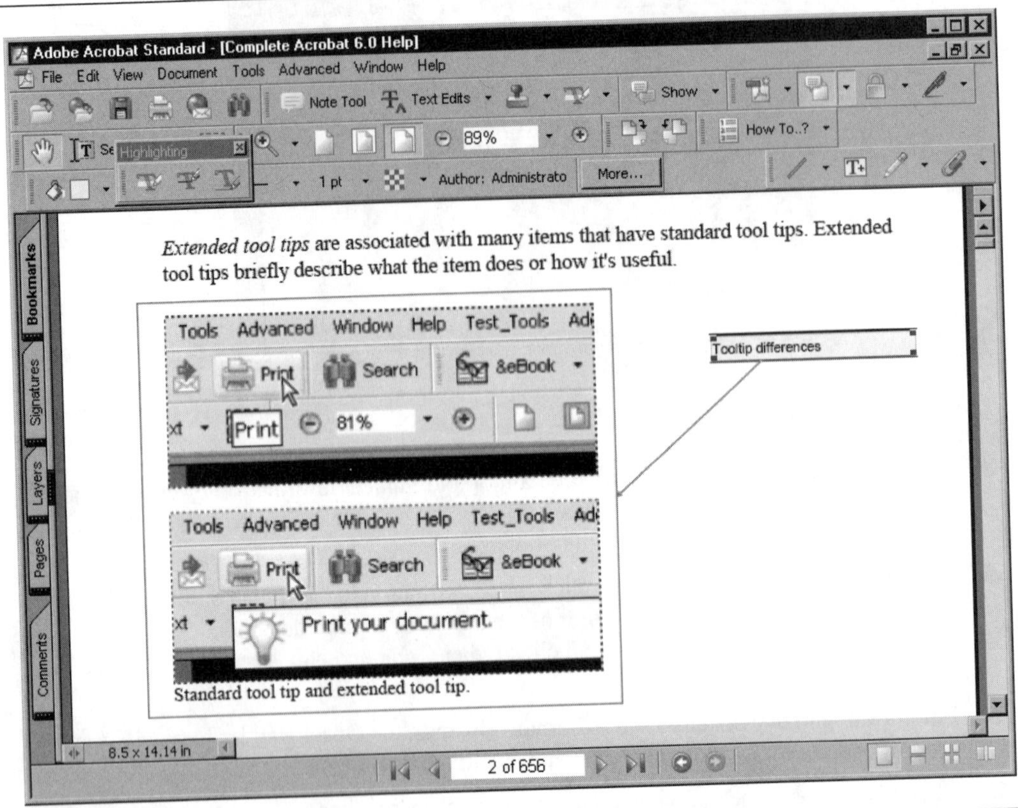

FIGURE 10-5 You can use a combination of comment tools to mark up a document.

graphic element that needs to be modified and then use the Arrow or Line tool to point to text created with the Text Box tool. In Figure 10-5, the Rectangle tool is used to draw attention to a graphic in the Acrobat 6.0 Help document. The Text Box tool was used to create the "Tooltip Differences" annotation, while the Arrow tool is used to associate the annotation with the graphic highlighted by the Rectangle tool.

Use the Pencil Tool

If you are a card-carrying member of Pocket Pals anonymous, the Pencil tool is right up your alley. You can use it to create expressive squiggles to direct another reviewer's attention to an element you feel needs correcting. When you mark up a document with the Pencil tool, Acrobat smoothes out the rough spots; however, it is not possible to constrain the tool to a perfectly straight line—for that you use the Line tool. To mark up a document with the Pencil tool, follow these steps:

1. Choose Tools | Advanced Commenting | Pencil Tool. Alternatively, you can select the Pencil tool from the Advanced Commenting toolbar (shown here) if you've previously displayed it.

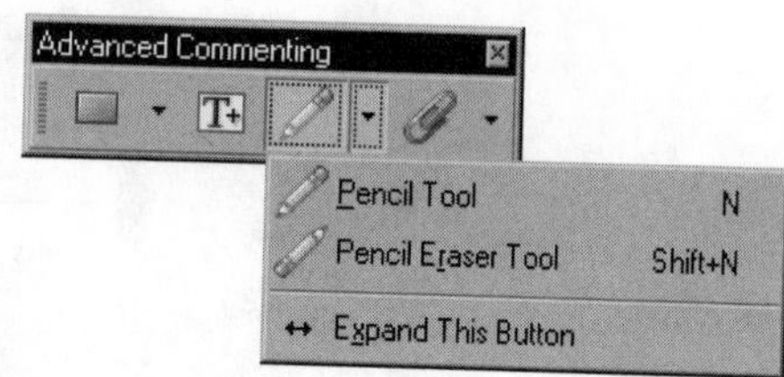

2. Click anywhere inside the Document pane and drag to create a line.
3. Release the mouse button to finish drawing with the Pencil tool.

Edit a Pencil Tool Markup

After you create a markup with the Pencil tool, you can move or resize it. You edit a Pencil tool markup with the Hand tool. You could edit it with the Pencil tool, but if you inadvertently click outside of the markup you want to edit, you create another line. You can edit a Pencil tool markup by doing one of the following:

- To move the markup, select it with the Hand tool and drag it to another location.
- To resize the markup, click it with the Hand tool; then click and drag one of the rectangular handles at the corners of the markup bounding box. To resize proportionately, press SHIFT while dragging.
- To erase part of the markup, choose Tools | Advanced Commenting | Pencil Eraser Tool and drag the tool across the markup to erase the unwanted portion. Alternatively, you can choose the Pencil Eraser tool from the Pencil Tool drop-down menu on the Advanced Commenting toolbar if you've previously displayed it.

10

Modify Pencil Properties

You can change the color, opacity, and thickness of a line created with the Pencil tool, as well as change the author and the subject of the comment. To modify the properties of a line drawn with the Pencil tool, follow these steps:

1. Select the Hand tool.
2. Select the line whose properties you want to change.
3. Right-click (Windows) or CTRL-click (Macintosh) and choose Properties from the Context menu to open the Pencil Mark Properties dialog box.
4. In the General tab, you can modify the default listing for Author and Subject by entering new text in the appropriate field.

5. Click the Appearance tab to display the appearance parameters for the comment, as shown next:

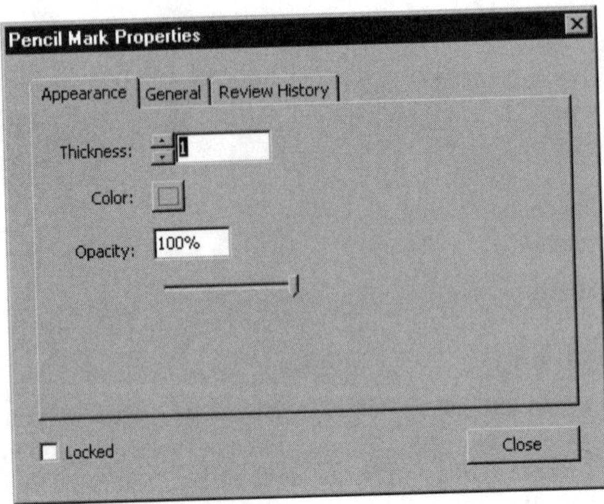

6. Click the spinner buttons to the left of the Thickness field to increase or decrease the thickness of the line. Alternatively, you can enter a value between 0 and 12 points.
7. To change the color of the line, click the Color button and choose a color from the pop-up palette or click the Other Color icon to choose a color from the system color picker.
8. To change the opacity of the line, enter a new value in the Opacity field. Alternatively, you can drag the Opacity slider to set the value.
9. Click Close to exit the dialog box and apply the changes.

After changing the properties of a comment made with any tool, you can apply the new properties (except Author and Subject) to all future comments created with the associated tool. Before deselecting the comment, open the Context menu and then choose Make Current Properties Default.

Use the Drawing Toolbar

You can use shapes to draw attention to certain parts of a document. When you annotate a PDF document with shape tools, you can select them by using menu commands or select them from the Drawing toolbar. If you're annotating a large document with shapes from the Acrobat Standard drawing toolbar (shown next), it's more convenient to display the toolbar by choosing Tools | Advanced Commenting | Drawing | Show Drawing Toolbar.

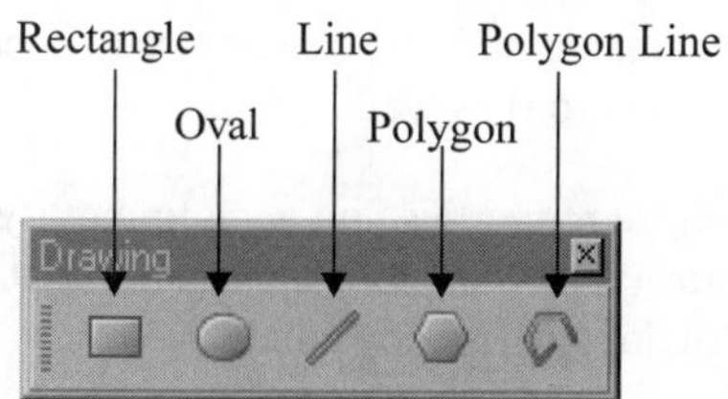

All of the tools function in a similar manner. The following steps describe the process of commenting with one of the Drawing tools:

1. Select a drawing tool from the Drawing toolbar or by choosing Tools | Advanced Commenting | Drawing and then selecting the desired tool from the drop-down menu.
2. Click the spot in the document where you want the comment to appear and do one of the following:
   - **Rectangle tool** Click and drag diagonally to create the shape. Hold down the SHIFT key while using the tool to create a square.
   - **Oval tool** Click and drag diagonally to create the oval. Hold down the SHIFT key while dragging to create a circle.
   - **Line tool** Click the spot where you want the line to begin, and then drag. Hold down the SHIFT key while dragging vertically or horizontally to create a vertical or horizontal line. Hold down the SHIFT key while dragging diagonally to constrain the line to 45 degrees.
   - **Polygon tool** Click to create the first point and then click to add additional points to the shape. Double-click to close the shape.
   - **Polygon Line tool** Click to create the first point and then click to add additional points to the line.
   - **Cloud tool (Professional Only)** Click to create the first point and then click to create the additional points that define the cloud's shape. Double-click to close the shape.
   - **Arrow tool (Professional Only)** Click and drag to create a line with arrowheads. Hold down the SHIFT key while dragging to constrain the line to 90-degree increments while dragging vertically or horizontally or 45-degree increments while dragging diagonally.

10

Editing a Drawing Tool Comment's Properties

As you know from reading previous sections of this chapter, comments have properties that you can modify. Comments created with the drawing tools are no exception. The following steps show how to modify the properties of a comment created with the Rectangle tool. These steps follow suit for comments created with the other closed-shaped commenting tools (Cloud [Professional Only], Oval, and Polygon) as well.

1. Select the comment whose properties you want to modify, right-click (Windows) or CTRL-click (Macintosh) and then choose Properties from the Context menu. The Rectangle Properties dialog box is shown here:

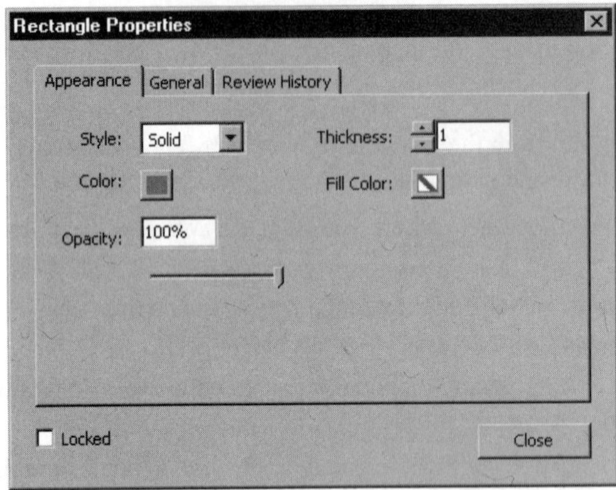

2. Click the triangle to the right of the Style field and choose an option from the drop-down menu. This option determines the appearance of the shape's border (or line).
3. Click the spinner buttons to the right of the Thickness field to specify line thickness. Alternatively, you can enter a value between 0 and 12 points.
4. Click the Color button and then choose a color from the pop-up palette. The selected color determines the color of the shape's border. Alternatively, click Other Color to select a color from the system color picker.
5. Click the Fill button and then choose a color from the pop-up palette. This determines the color of the inside of the shape. Accept the default no-color option to create an outline of a shape.
6. Enter a value in the Opacity field to determine the comment's opacity. Alternatively, you can click and drag the Opacity slider to set this value.
7. Click the General tab to modify the Author and Subject information by entering new information in each field.
8. Click Close to exit the dialog box and apply the changes.

TIP *If you own Acrobat Standard, you can still create arrowheads. Create a line with the Line tool and then edit the comment's properties as discussed in the previous step. Select Closed or Open from the Start drop-down menu to add an arrow to the start of the line, or select Closed or Open from the End drop-down menu to add an arrow to the end of the line. You can also choose from other shapes such as a diamond or circle.*

Attach a Pop-Up Note

You can attach a pop-up note to an annotation created with a tool from the Drawing or Highlight toolbar. When you attach a pop-up note, with the exception of the default pop-up color, the note window looks identical to one created with the Note tool. When you attach a note to an annotation, it is viewable by double-clicking the comment or by selecting the comment and choosing Open Pop-up Note from the Context menu. To add a pop-up note to an annotation made with a commenting tool from the Drawing or Highlight toolbar, follow these steps:

1. Select the Hand tool and then double-click an annotation created with a tool from the Drawing or Highlight toolbar. Acrobat opens a pop-up note with a flashing cursor, as shown here:

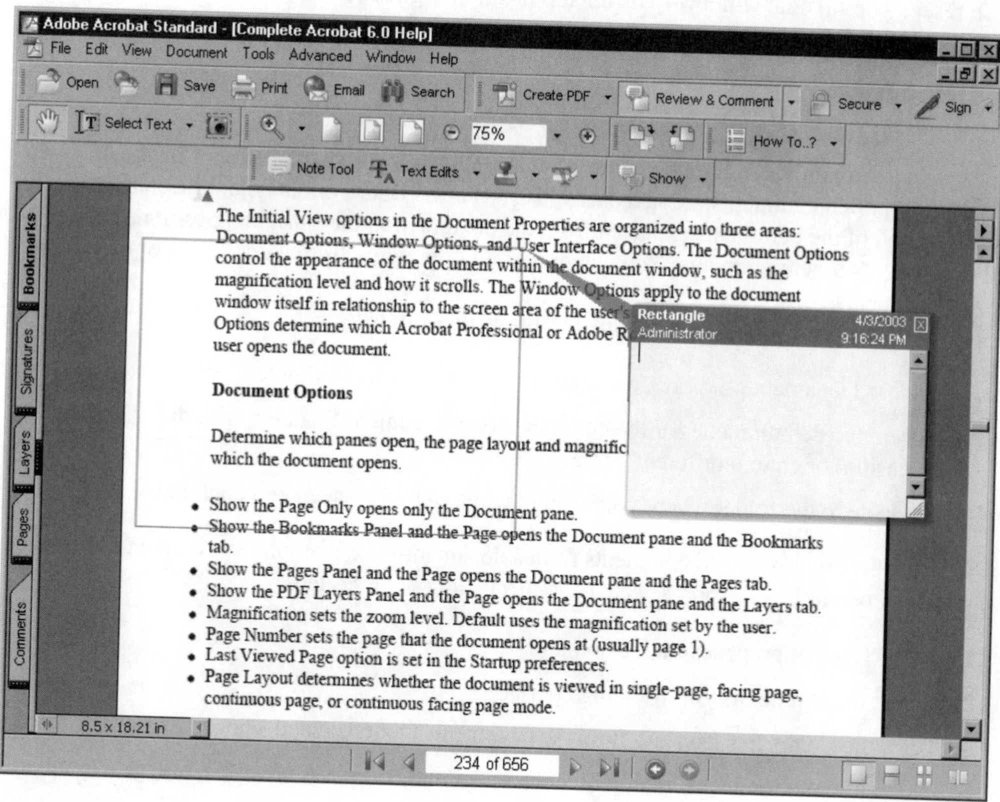

2. Enter the text for the note and then click the X in the upper-left corner of the note to close the note. Alternatively, you can leave the pop-up note open.

TIP *If you leave a pop-up note open, select it and then move it away from the annotation to which it is referring. Use the Line tool (Standard), or Arrow tool (professional) to create a line from the pop-up note to the annotation.*

Edit a Pop-Up Note

You can edit a pop-up note attached to an annotation by moving it to a new position or changing the text of the pop-up note. You can also reset a pop-up note to its default position. To edit a pop-up note, double-click the comment the note is attached to and do one of the following:

- Click the Note title bar and drag it to a new location.
- Select text to edit and enter new text.
- Select text to delete and then press DELETE or choose Edit | Delete.

To reset a pop-up note window to its default position, right-click (Windows) or CTRL-click (Macintosh) and choose Reset Pop Up Note Location from the Context menu.

Export Comments

You can export comments from one document and use them in another version of the same document. Exported comments are saved as an FDF (Forms Data Format) file. The comment file contains all of the comments exported from the document in their original positions but not the actual document elements. You can export all comments from a document or export selected comments.

To export all comments from a document, follow these steps:

1. Choose Document | Export Comments to open the Export Comments dialog box.
2. Accept the default name for the comments (the document filename with the FDF extension) or enter a different name.
3. Navigate to the folder where you want the comment file saved and click Save.

You can also export selected comments from a document—for example, all comments created by a particular reviewer. To export selected comments, follow these steps:

1. In the Navigation pane, click Comments.
2. Select the comments you want to export.
3. Click the Comments icon and from the Comments Options menu, choose Export Selected.
4. In the Export Comments dialog box enter a name for the comment file, navigate to the folder you want to save the file in, then click Save.

TIP *You can also export comments as a Word document by choosing Document | Export Comments to Word. Note that you must have Word 2002 or newer installed on your system to use this feature.*

mport Comments

You can import a comment file into a different version of a document. The imported comments appear in their original positions. If you receive several versions of the same document marked up by different reviewers, you can collate each reviewer's comments in a single document. First, export the comments from each document, as outlined in the previous section. Second, open the master copy of the document into which you want to collate the comments. Third, follow these steps:

1. Choose Document | Import Comments to open the Import Comments dialog box. You can now import comments by having Acrobat strip comments from a PDF file or by importing an FDF file.
2. Click the triangle to the right of the Files Of Type field and choose PDF to import comments directly from a PDF file or choose FDF to import an FDF comment file.
3. Choose the file and then click Select.

After you invoke the command, Acrobat imports the comments and places them in the exact location they appeared in the document they were extracted from. If you choose to import comments from a PDF file, this may take a while if the document is large and contains many comments.

OTE *If you own Acrobat Professional, you can compare two versions of the same document by choosing Document | Compare Documents. After you choose the documents to compare, you can choose to compare visual differences and textual differences and have Acrobat generate a report that annotates the differences with a side-by-side comparison.*

ımmary

In this chapter, you learned to generate an e-mail review. You also learned to keep tabs on the review with the Review Tracker. Other chapter topics showed you how to annotate a PDF document with notes, shapes, and text as well as display comments from other reviewers using the Comments tab. You also learned how to reply to a comment. In the next chapter, you'll learn to add security to the PDF documents you create.

Part IV

Add Security and Distribute PDF Documents

Chapter 11

Add Digital Signatures and Document Security

How to...

- Use digital signatures
- Modify signature appearance
- Use the Signatures tab
- Use Acrobat Password Security
- Use Acrobat Certificate Security

When you create a document for use in a corporate environment with several team members, you can keep track of who did what to a document with digital signatures. When a reviewer or team member digitally signs a document, Acrobat acknowledges the reviewer and creates a time stamp. All changes to the document are noted as being performed by the digital signer. When more than one person digitally signs a document, you can compare different versions of the document.

Documents created in a corporate environment are often confidential. When this is the case, you can assign security to a document. When you add security to a document, you limit a viewer's access to the document. When you use Acrobat Password Security, you can assign a password to the document. Before a document can be viewed, the user must enter the proper password. You can also assign a permissions password to the document. If a permissions password is assigned to a document, it must be entered in order for the user to modify any of the security settings. When you use Acrobat Certificate Security, you limit access to the document to certain team members. With Acrobat Certificate Security, you can create different user permissions for each member of your team. For example, you can disallow editing and printing for certain team members, while giving other team members full access to the document.

About Digital Signatures

With Acrobat, documents can be digitally signed. A digital signature is like an electronic thumbprint; it identifies the signer of the document. It also records any changes made by the signer and stores information about the signer with the document.

When you add Acrobat Certificate Security to a document, the only way the document can be viewed is by a team member with an authorized digital signature. Acrobat users with digital signatures select their digital ID while working on documents. Secure documents will open without password verification if an authorized user has selected his or her digital ID prior to opening the document.

If you use Acrobat to send contracts to clients, digital signatures can be used to approve contracts. If both parties accept a digital signature as an electronic facsimile of a handwritten signature, a digitally signed contract may be legally binding. Before you accept a digital signature as legally binding authorization to proceed with a contract, it is best to seek the advice of legal counsel. Figure 11-1 shows a document that has been digitally signed.

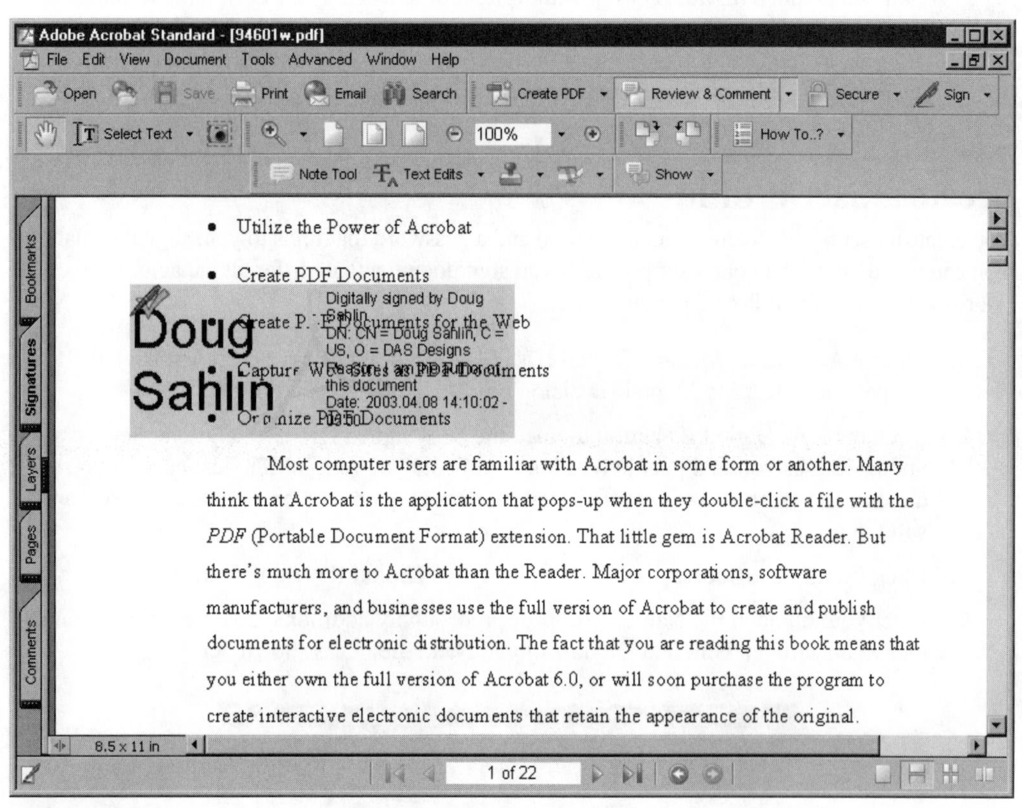

FIGURE 11-1 You can use digital signatures to identify recipients of your documents and limit access to your documents.

Use Digital Signatures

When you decide to use digital signatures to verify the identities of users modifying your documents, you can use the default Acrobat Certificate Security or specify a third-party plug-in to handle digital signatures. After you decide on a signature handler, you need to create a digital ID. Your digital ID stores information about you. You can use the default Acrobat graphic for a digital signature or customize the digital signature with a photo or other graphic, such as a logo. When you create a digital ID, you can create a list of *trusted identities*. Trusted identities are digital signature files in FDF format that are used to verify digital signatures. You can request digital IDs of colleagues via e-mail and share your certificate with other colleagues so that your digital signature can be verified.

Documents can be signed multiple times by multiple authors. Whenever a document is digitally signed, Acrobat records the changes made since the document was last digitally signed. When you open a document with multiple signatures, you view the most current version of the document. You can view earlier versions of a digitally signed document and compare different versions.

TIP *You can create a digital ID from within Acrobat and send your certificate to other parties in order to verify your signature. If you intend to distribute the document widely, this can be tedious. You can, however, secure a digital ID from a trusted Adobe party, which will enable any user of Adobe Reader 6.0, Acrobat Standard, or Acrobat Professional to verify the document.*

Create a User Profile

You create a user profile to create identification and a password that links to your digital signature. You can create more than one user profile if you sign documents in different capacities. To create your first user profile, follow these steps:

1. Choose Advanced | Manage Digital IDs | My Digital ID Files | Select My Digital ID File to open the Select My Digital ID dialog box.
2. Click the New Digital ID button to open the Self-Signed Digital ID Disclaimer. This dialog advises you that people wishing to validate your digital ID must contact you directly and creating a digital ID in this manner may not be appropriate for third-party validation.
3. Click Continue to access the Create Self-Signed Digital ID dialog box.
4. Enter your name in the Name field. If desired, supply additional contact information in the Organizational Unit and Organizational Name fields, as shown here:

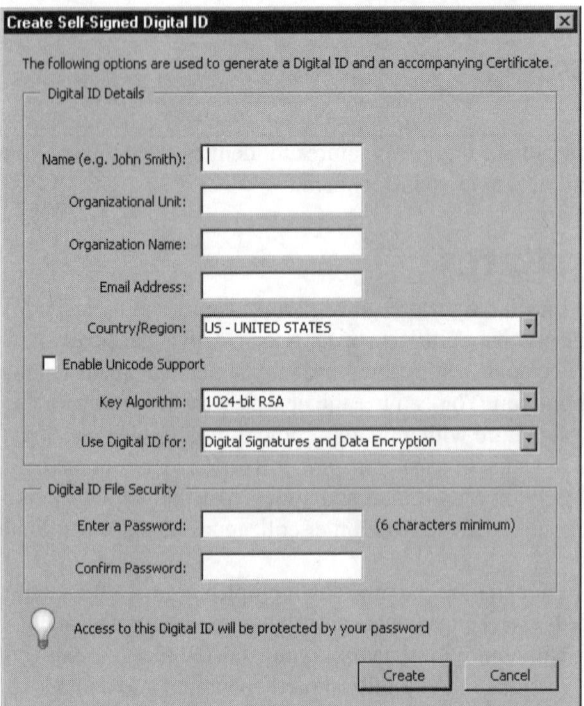

How to ... Create a Secure Password

When many people choose a password, they create one that is easy to remember, such as their birthday, a relative's birthday, or a combination of initials from their name and their spouse's name. Passwords such as these are easy to decipher. When you need to create a secure password, create one with at least eight characters. Create a combination of alphabetic characters interspersed with numeric characters such as *j87ty91w*. After creating the password, make sure you archive a hard copy of the password in a remote location. You may also want to consider saving a digital copy of your password to your PDA (Personal Digital Assistant) if it is secure.

5. Enter your e-mail address in Email Address: field.
6. Click the Enable Unicode Support check box if you want to include Unicode information with the certificate. Unicode standard provides a unique number for every character, that is cross-platform. The Unicode standard for most English documents is UTF-8. If you choose this option, Unicode fields appear to the right of your contact information. Enter the appropriate Unicode information in the desired fields.
7. Click the triangle to the right of the Key Algorithm field and choose 1024-bit US or 2048-bit US. The latter choice offers better security but may not be available to all users.
8. Click the triangle to the right of the Use Digital ID For and then choose an option from the drop-down menu. The default option allows you to use the digital ID for signing documents and encrypting. Alternatively, you can choose Digital Signatures or Data Encryption to limit your use of the digital ID.
9. Enter and confirm your password. Your password must be at least six characters and cannot contain any of the following symbols: !@#$%^&*,|\<>_ or double quotation marks.
10. Click Create to complete the process and exit the dialog box.

Modify Signature Appearance

When you digitally sign a document, Acrobat uses a default text-only signature with the Acrobat logo in the background. You can change the appearance of your digital signature by creating a file in a graphics program and converting it to PDF format. For that matter, you can choose File | Import | Scan, and then scan a copy of your actual signature and save it as a PDF file. After you create a PDF file with the graphic you want to use for your digital signature, follow these steps:

1. Choose Edit | Preferences to open the Preferences dialog box.
2. Click Digital Signatures and then click New to open the Configure Signature Appearance dialog box.

3. In the Title field, enter a name for the signature configuration.
4. In the Configure Graphic section, within the Show options, choose No Graphic, Imported Graphic, or Name. If you choose Imported Graphic, click the PDF File button to open the Select Picture dialog box. Click the Browse button and navigate to the PDF file that contains the image for your digital signature and then click Select. Acrobat displays a sample of the image in the Preview window. If the image is acceptable, click OK to close the Select Picture dialog box. If the desired image is not a PDF file, click the triangle to the right of the Files Of Type field and select an option from the drop-down menu, which contains all the image file types supported by Acrobat; then navigate to and select the desired graphic.

NOTE *If you're using an image for a digital signature graphic, make sure the image has been optimized for the smallest possible file size. If you use an image with a large file size for a digital signature, every time you sign the document, the file size of the PDF increases as well.*

5. Click OK to exit the Select Picture dialog box.
6. In the Configure Text section, choose the options you want to appear with your digital signature. Every option is selected by default. As you change the options, Acrobat updates the preview in real time, as shown here:

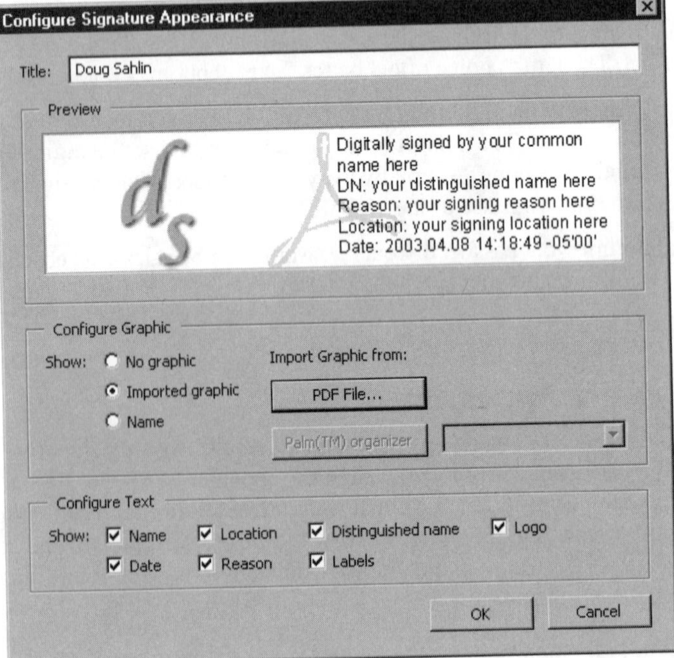

7. Click OK to close the dialog box and Acrobat adds your custom signature to the list, as shown in the following illustration. Notice that when you select the signature, there are options to edit, copy, and delete the custom signature.

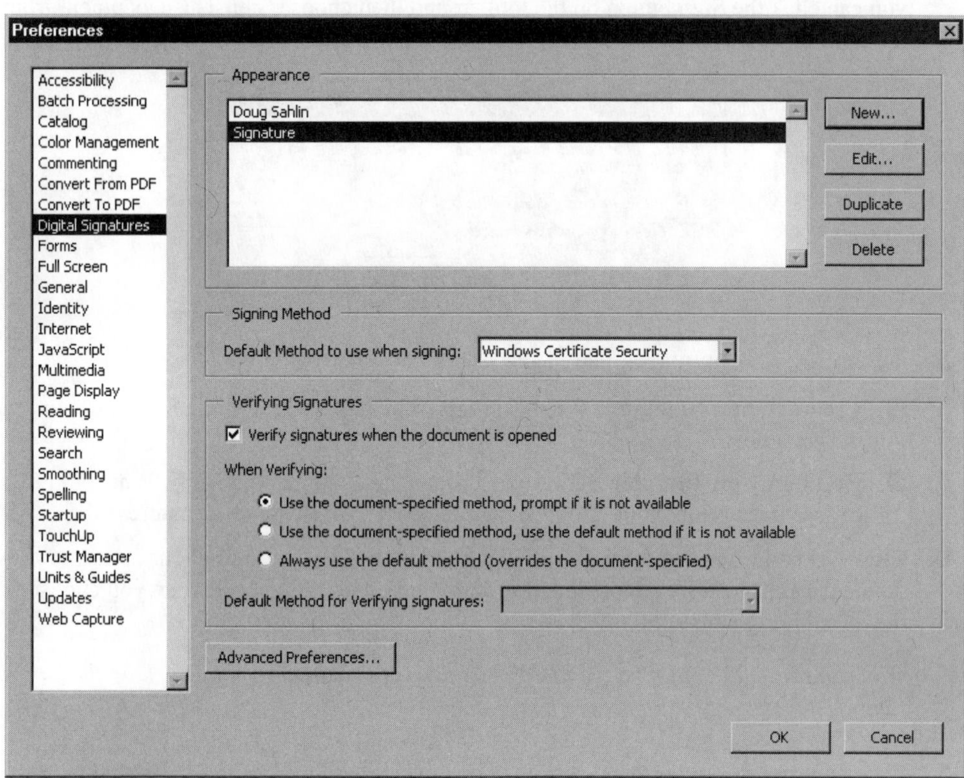

8. Click OK to exit the Preferences dialog box.

Sign a Document

After you create a user profile, you can digitally sign documents. When you digitally sign a document, you are required to save it. When you save the document for the first time, Acrobat saves it in an *append only* format. From this point forward, you will not be able to do a full save as the Save option is not available for a digitally signed document. After you sign a document, your signature appears in the Signatures tab, which is discussed in a "Use The Signatures Tab" section of this chapter. To digitally sign a document, follow these steps:

1. Finalize all of your required changes prior to signing the document. If you digitally sign the document and make additional changes, the document will be marked as modified since your digital signature.

2. Choose Document | Digital Signatures | Sign This Document. Acrobat displays a warning dialog telling you the document is not certified.
3. Click Continue Signing to open the Sign Document dialog box, shown next. Alternatively, you can click the Sign button on the toolbar and then choose Sign This Document from the drop-down menu.

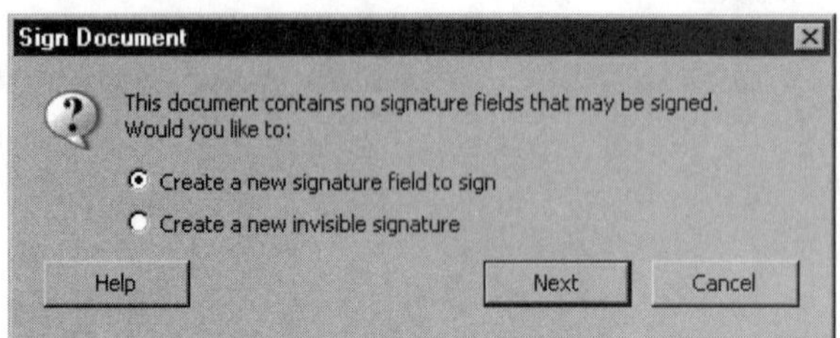

4. Choose one of the following options:
   - **Create A New Signature Field To Sign** Creates a visible digital signature in the document.
   - **Create A New Invisible Signature** Signs the document invisibly. When you choose this option, your digital signature is noted only in the Signatures tab.
5. Click Next and Acrobat displays a dialog box instructing you to use your mouse to define the signature area. Note that this dialog box does not appear when you choose the invisible signature option.

You can prevent the instruction dialog box from appearing again by clicking the Do Not Show This Message Again check box.

5. Drag your mouse across the area of the document where you want your signature to appear. Note that if you designate a small area, Acrobat displays a warning dialog to that effect.
6. After you release the mouse button, the Apply Digital Signature—Digital ID Selection dialog box appears. All of your digital IDs are listed in this dialog box.
7. Select the digital ID with which you want to sign the document and then click OK to display the Apply Signature To Document dialog box, shown next.

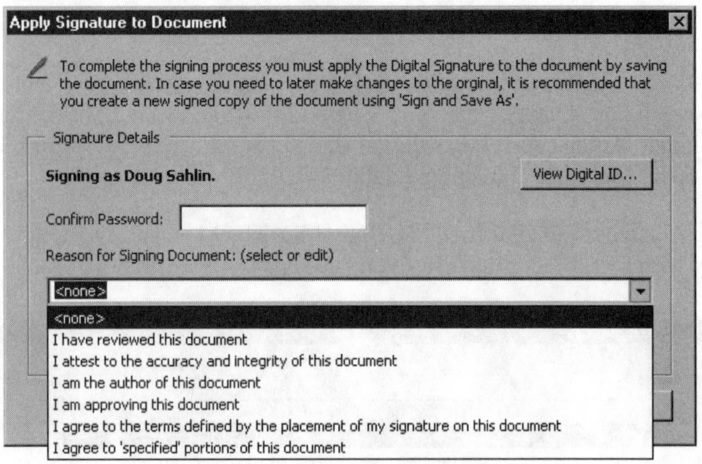

8. In the Confirm Password field, enter your password.

NOTE *If you're using Windows Certificate Security when you install Acrobat, this becomes the default signing method and you will not be prompted for a password. If you're using Acrobat in a corporate environment and will vacate your workstation while using Acrobat, it is recommended that you use Acrobat's Default Certificate Security, whereupon you will be prompted for a password whenever you digitally sign a document. To switch to Default Certificate Security, choose Edit | Preferences and then click Digital Signatures. In the Signing Method section, choose Default Certificate Security from the drop-down menu.*

9. Click the triangle to the right of the Reason For Signing Document: (Select Or Edit) field and choose an option from the drop-down menu. Alternatively, you can enter text that describes why you are signing the document.
10. Click the Options button to display additional digital signature parameters. Note that the Options button is hidden in the above illustration in order to display the choices for Reason For Signing Document.
11. In the Signature Appearance section, accept the default Standard Text signature, or click the triangle to the right of the field and from the drop-down menu, choose a signature you have created. If you choose a custom signature, you can change the signature by clicking the Edit button. If you do not want to use any of the available signature appearance options, you can create a new signature by clicking the New button and following the steps described previously in the "Modify Signature Appearance" section.
12. If desired, enter information in the Location field and the Your Contact Information field.
13. Click the Sign And Save button to save the document with its current filename. Alternatively, click Sign And Save As to save the document with a different filename. If you choose the Sign And Save As option, to continue the review process, you will have to save this version of the document because your digital signature and changes will not appear on the original document. After you save the document, Acrobat displays a dialog box alerting you that the document has been signed successfully.

Choose a Digital ID

If you launch Acrobat for the purpose of reviewing documents with digital signatures, you'll need to choose the digital ID with which you'll be reviewing and signing the documents. When you choose a digital ID, you can validate digital signatures from your list of trusted identities as soon as you open a document. To choose a digital ID, follow these steps:

1. Choose Advanced | Digital IDs | My Digital ID. The Manage My Digital IDs dialog box appears with a list of all digital IDs you have created, as shown here:

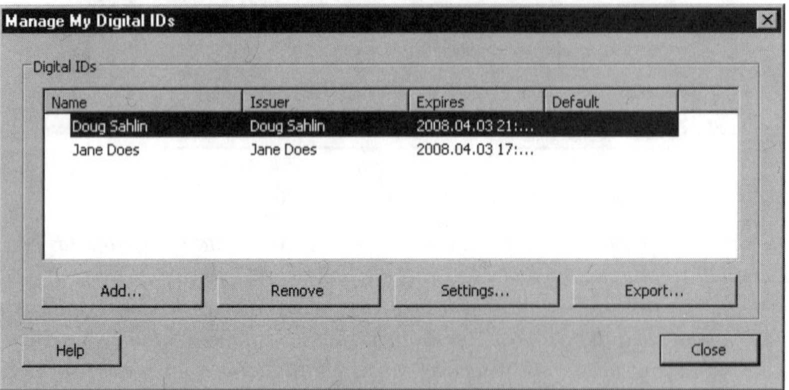

2. Select the desired digital ID.
3. Click Close to log in with the selected digital ID.

After selecting a digital ID, you can sign documents with the digital ID and validate signatures, as shown in upcoming sections.

From within the Manage My Digital IDs dialog box, you can add additional IDs and remove selected IDs, as well as view the settings for selected digital IDs. You can also export a copy of your digital ID to a folder in your hard drive. The exported digital ID serves as a backup if you ever have to reinstall Acrobat.

Change Digital ID Password

If you feel that security has been breached, you can change the password for your digital ID. To change your digital ID password follow these steps:

1. Choose the digital ID whose settings you want to modify as outlined previously.
2. Choose Advanced | Manage Digital IDs | My Digital ID Files | My Digital ID File Settings to access the Digital ID File Settings dialog box shown next.

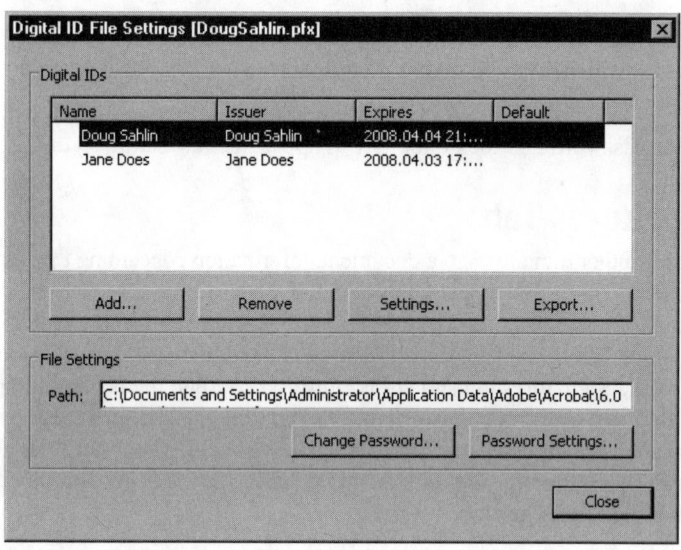

3. Click Change Password to open the Change Password dialog box.
4. Enter your current password in the Old Password field.
5. Enter your new password in the New Password field, and then confirm your new password.
6. Click OK to close the Change Password dialog box.
7. Click Close to exit the Digital ID File Settings dialog box.

Change Password Settings

By default, you are required to enter your password every time you sign a document. This feature prevents other people from using your digital signature on a document when you temporarily vacate your workstation while using Acrobat. You can, however, change password settings to prevent entering your password every time you digitally sign a document. To change password settings, follow these steps:

1. Choose the digital ID whose settings you want to modify, as outlined previously.
2. Choose Advanced | Manage Digital IDs | My Digital ID Files | My Digital ID File Settings to access the Digital ID File Settings dialog box shown previously.
3. Click Password Settings to open the Password Settings dialog box.
4. Choose the Require Password To Access When Signing. This option is selected by default and requires a password every time you digitally sign a document. You can deselect this option if you are a sole entrepreneur or you secure your computer when not at your workstation.

5. Click the After button and then click the triangle to the right of the field to choose a time interval after which you will be required to enter your password when digitally signing a document.
6. Enter your password and then click OK to apply the new settings.

Use the Signatures Tab

After you or another author digitally sign a document, information concerning the signature appears in the Signatures tab. You can select a signature in the tab and find out when the document was signed, who the author was, the validity of the signature, and the reason for signing the document. You use the Signatures tab to manage the signatures in the document as well as perform other functions. To open the Signatures tab shown in Figure 11-2, open the Navigation pane and click Signatures. Alternatively, you can choose View | Navigation Tabs | Signatures.

The Signatures tab has an extensive Options menu with commands pertaining to digital signatures. To open the Signatures Options menu, as shown in the following illustration, click the Options icon in the Signatures tab:

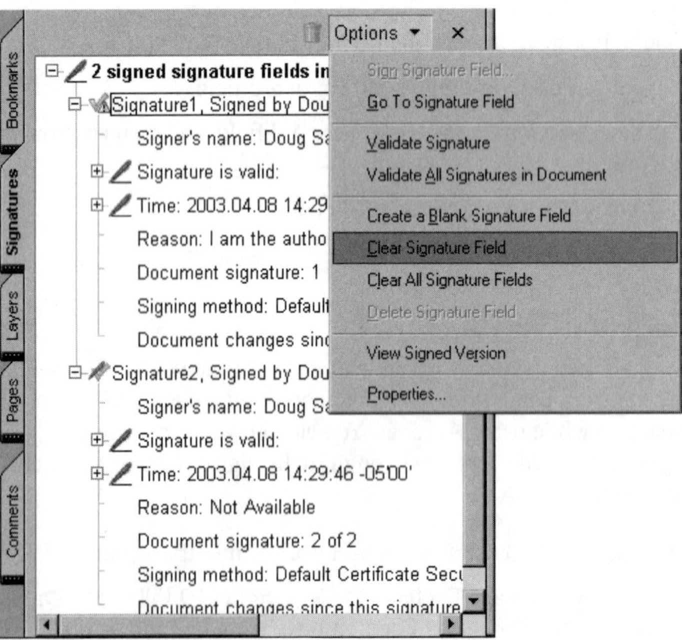

Signatures tab

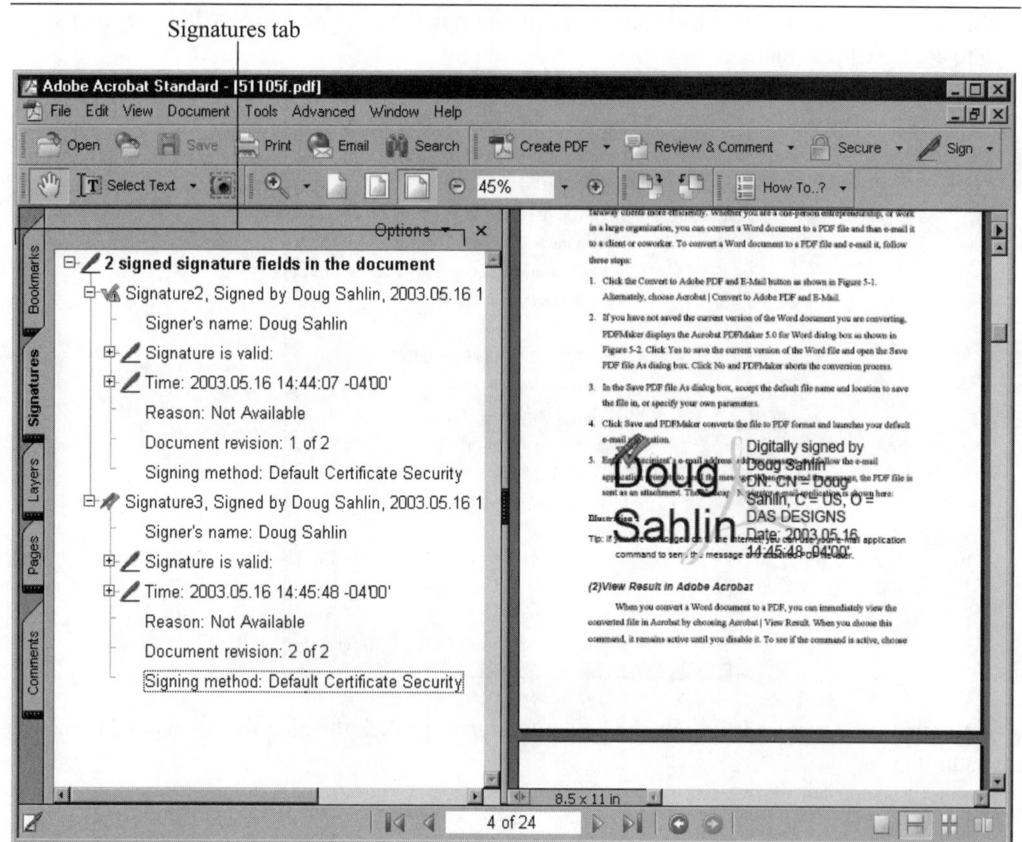

FIGURE 11-2 You use the Signatures tab to manage digital signatures in a document.

In the sections that follow, you'll learn how to use commands from this menu to sign signature fields, clear and delete signature fields, verify signatures, view different versions of the document, and more.

View Digital Signatures

After you open the Signatures tab, you'll see a single listing for each signature in the document. The listing notes the author's name, the verification status of the signature, and the date the signature was added to the document. Verifying signatures is discussed in an upcoming section of this chapter. To the left of the signature is a minus sign (–), as shown here. Click the minus sign to collapse the signature.

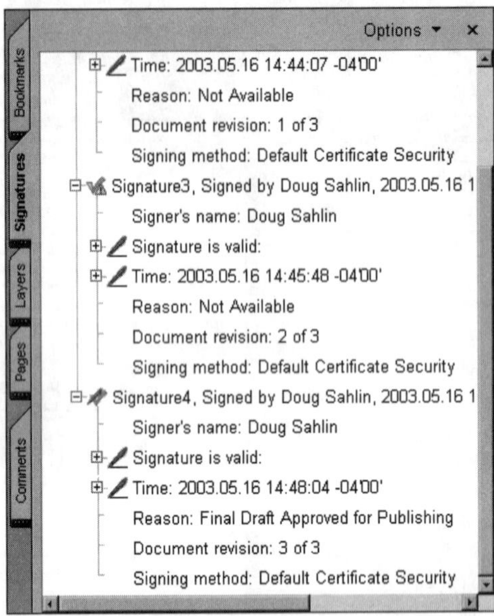

A collapsed signature is designated by a plus sign (+). Click the plus sign to expand the signature.

Sign Signature Fields

When you create a document with a digital signature field, you can sign the field in one of two ways: one, click the field with the Hand tool within the document; or two, select the signature field in the Signatures tab and then choose Sign Signature Field from the Signatures tab Options menu. After you choose to sign the field using one of these methods, follow the previously discussed steps to sign the signature field. For more information on creating signature fields, refer to the upcoming "Create a Blank Signature Field" section.

Clear Signature Fields

When you or another author digitally signs a document, you create a field that contains a digital signature. You can also clear a digital signature field for use by another reviewer by following these steps:

1. In the Navigation pane, click Signatures to open the Signatures tab.
2. Click the name of the digital signature whose field you want to clear.

3. Choose Clear Signature Field from the Signatures Options menu.
4. Click OK to clear the signature field.

To clear all signature fields, choose Clear All Signature Fields from the Signatures tab Options menu.

After you clear a signature field, it is signified in the Signatures tab with a signature icon followed by a title. In the document, the cleared signature is signified by the signature icon in the upper-left corner of an opaque rectangle. You can sign a blank signature field by selecting it in the Signatures tab and then choosing Sign Signature Field from the Signatures tab Options menu or by clicking it with the Hand tool.

Validate Signatures

When you open a document with digital signatures, they are verified by default. Acrobat checks the authenticity of the signature to see if the document or signature has been changed since the signing. If you select a digital ID prior to opening a document, Acrobat checks all signers' digital IDs against the list of trusted identities in your user profile. If the signature matches one of the certificates, or if the document or signature has not been modified since last signing, Acrobat verifies the signature. You can verify selected signatures or all signatures.

To verify selected signatures, do one of the following:

- Click a signature in the document with the Hand tool.
- Open the Signatures tab, select the signatures you want to verify, and then choose Validate Signatures from the Signatures tab Options menu.

Acrobat verifies the signature of a member of your trusted identities list by replacing the question mark icon with a green checkmark. If Acrobat finds that the document has not been modified since the signature and finds the signature in your trusted identities list, Acrobat displays the dialog box shown here:

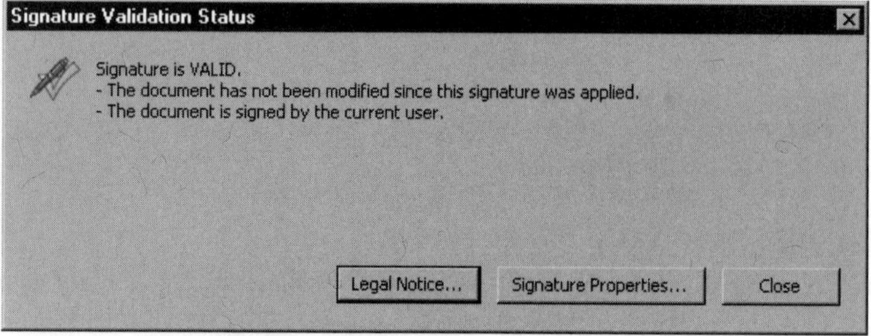

To accept the verification and continue working, click the Close button.

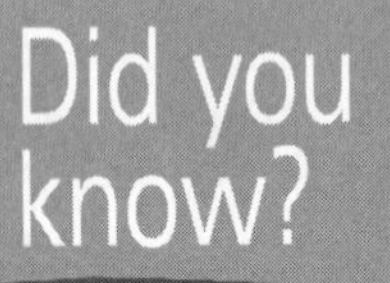

You Can Compare Signed Versions of Documents

If you own Acrobat Professional, choose Document | Compare Documents. This opens a dialog box that enables you to choose which signed versions of the document you want to compare. After selecting two versions, click OK and Acrobat Professional creates a side-by-side comparison (or detailed report if you choose that option) of each page of the document. You can see differences between versions by scrolling through the pages. By default differences are highlighted in pink rectangles unless you choose a different color.

TIP *To verify all signatures in a document, click the Sign button and then choose Validate All Signatures In The Document from the Sign drop-down menu.*

View Document Version

When a document is digitally signed, Acrobat remembers the exact contents of the document at that stage of the revision process. You can use the Signatures tab or menu commands to view any version of the document. To view a signed version of the document, follow these steps:

1. In the Navigation pane, click the Signatures tab.
2. Click the digital signature that corresponds to the version of the document you want to view.
3. Choose View Signed Version from the Signatures tab Options menu. Alternatively, you can choose Document | Digital Signatures | View Signed Version.
4. After you invoke this command, Acrobat re-creates a version of the document as it appeared at that stage of the revision process, and displays it in another window. You can view as many signed versions of the document as needed. You can compare signed versions to the original by following the previous steps to re-create previous versions of the document, choosing Window | Tile, and then choosing Horizontally or Vertical.

TIP *To navigate to a signature field location within the document, open the Signatures tab, select the signature you want to navigate to, and then choose Go To Signature Field from the Signatures palette menu.*

View Digital Signature Properties

You can learn everything you want to know about a digital signature by viewing its properties. When you view a digital signature's properties, you can verify the signature and get information about the author of the digital signature. To view the properties of a digital signature, follow these steps:

1. In the Navigation pane, click Signatures to open the Signatures tab.
2. Click a digital signature to select it.
3. Choose Properties from the Signatures tab Options menu to open the Signature Properties dialog box, as shown here:

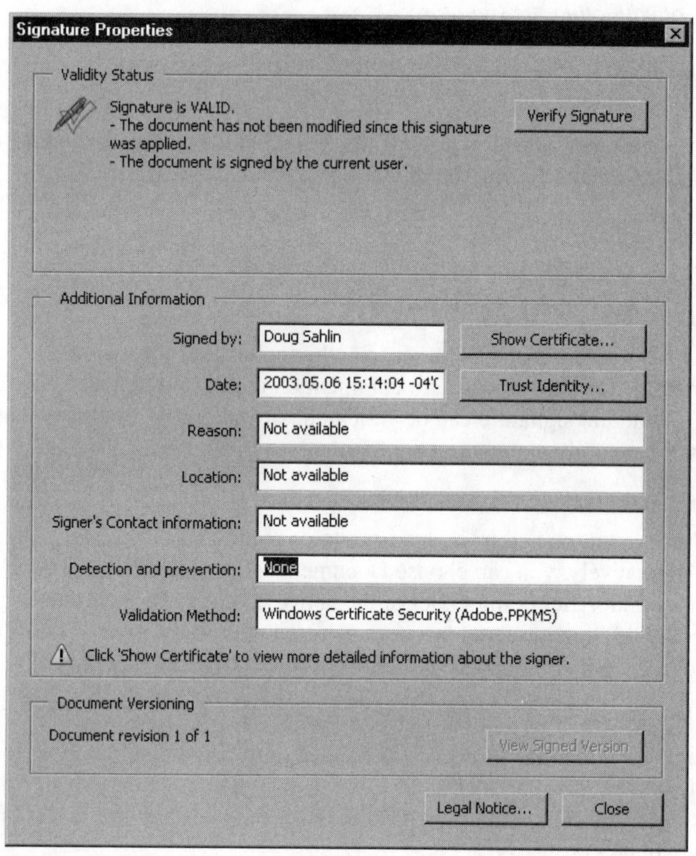

4. With the dialog box open, you can perform the following operations:
   - Click the Verify Signature button to verify the digital signature.

- Click the Show Certificate button to display the Certificate Attributes dialog box. Click Close to exit the Certificate Attributes dialog box.
- Click the Trust Identity button to open the Trust Identity dialog box. If the owner of the certificate is not on your trusted identities list, you have the option to add the owner. After verifying the identity of the signer, close the dialog box.

CAUTION *If you choose to add a signature to your list of trusted identities, a dialog box appears warning you against adding a certificate from a document with good reason as you have no way of validating the signature.*

- Click the View Signed Version button to view the document as it appeared when the digital signature was created.

5. Click the Legal Notice button to view the Legal Notice dialog box, which contains additional information about the digital ID and a disclaimer.
6. Click Close to exit the Signature Properties dialog box.

Create a Blank Signature Field

When you create a document that will be sent to other colleagues for review, you can request their digital signature after they review and comment on the document. When the document is returned to you, the digital signature can be validated. Any alterations to the document after the field is signed will be readily apparent in the Signatures tab. To create a signature field, follow these steps:

1. Click the Sign button and from the drop-down menu choose Create A Blank Signature Field. Alternatively, you can choose Document | Digital Signatures | Create A Blank Signature Field. After doing either of the above, Acrobat displays a dialog box telling you the Digital Signature tool has been selected with instructions on how to create the field.
2. Click OK.
3. Click and drag diagonally to define the shape of the digital signature field. As you drag the tool, Acrobat displays a bounding box, showing you the current size of the signature field. Release the mouse button when the field is the desired size to display the Digital Signature dialog box.
4. Click the General tab to display the General tab of the Digital Signature Properties dialog box, shown next.

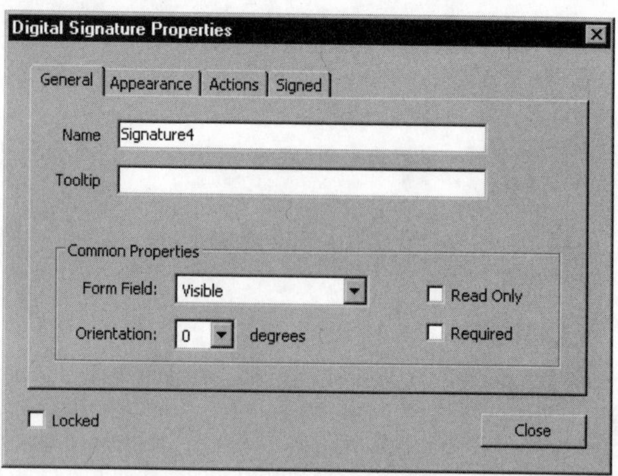

5. Accept the default Name (signature followed by the next available signature number) or enter a different name.
6. If desired, enter instructions or other information in the Tooltip field. This information will be displayed when a user's mouse hovers over the signature field.
7. Click the triangle to the right of the Form Field window and choose one of the following: Visible, Hidden, Hidden But Printable, or Hidden But Does Not Print.

NOTE *If you choose Hidden, make sure you enter information in the Tooltip field or leave other instructions for reviewers, as they will not be able to see the signature field in the document.*

8. Click the triangle to the right of the Orientation field and choose an option from the drop-down menu. This option determines how the field is oriented to the document.
9. Click the Required check box and the field is marked as required. If you distribute the document with a Submit button and the Submit button is clicked when the field is still blank, Acrobat displays a warning to that effect.

NOTE *There is also an option to make signature fields read only. If a signature field is read only, it cannot be signed unless JavaScript is created to change the field status when an authorized user accesses the document. Unfortunately, the JavaScript involved is beyond the scope of this book.*

10. Click the Appearance tab. Within this tab you can set the color and line type of the signature field border, fill color, and the font type used to display the digital signature.
11. Click the Actions tab. Within this tab, you can assign one or more actions that occur when the field is digitally signed. For more information on actions, refer to Chapter 8.

12. Click the Sign tab. Within this tab you'll find options to create JavaScript that executes when the document is signed. For more information on using JavaScript in PDF documents, refer to Chapter 8.
13. Click the Locked check box, and the signature field cannot be moved until this option is deselected.
14. Click Close to exit the dialog box and complete the creation of the blank signature field.

About Acrobat Security

When you assign security to a document, you can limit user access to the document. For example, you can prohibit printing of the document and copying elements from the document. You have two versions of Acrobat Security: Acrobat Password Security and Acrobat Certificate Security.

With Acrobat Password Security, you can password-protect a document and require a permissions password in order to change the document password or security settings. When you use Acrobat Password Security, the same permissions level is granted to all recipients of the document. Acrobat Password Security is available with 40-bit encryption for Acrobat 3.x or Acrobat 4.x and is available with 128-bit encryption for Acrobat 5.x and 6.0.

If you need to assign different levels of permission for different recipients of your document, use Acrobat Certificate Security. When you secure a document with Acrobat Certificate Security, the document can only be opened if the user's digital signature appears on your list of trusted identities. You can assign differing levels of permission for each user on your trusted identities list, as discussed in the upcoming "Use Acrobat Certificate Security" section.

Certify a Document

When you certify a document, you digitally sign it to verify its contents. Other reviewers will be able to fill in form fields and digitally sign the document, but if they attempt to change any of the other document attributes—such as links, editing text, and so on—the document is no longer listed as certified. To certify a document, follow these steps:

1. Choose the digital ID with which you want to certify the document, as discussed previously, in "Choose a Digital ID."
2. Choose File | Save As Certified Document. Acrobat displays a dialog box with information about certifying documents. You also have the option of clicking the Get Digital ID From Adobe Partner button, which transports you to a Web page on the Adobe Web site where you can procure a third-party digital ID. Third-party digital IDs may be easier for recipients to validate if you widely distribute the document.
3. Click OK to display the Save As Certified Document—Choose Allowable Actions dialog box.
4. Click the triangle to the right of the Allowed Actions field and choose one of the following options:

- **Disallow Any Changes To The Document** Prevents any document changes by future viewers.
- **Only Allow Form Fill-In Actions On This Document** Enables future viewers of the document to fill in form fields.
- **Only Allow Form Commenting And Form Fill-In Actions On This Document** Allows future viewers of the document to create annotations with any of the commenting tools, as well as fill in form fields.
- **Lock The Certifying Signature So It Can't Be Cleared Or Deleted By Anyone** This option is available when you allow viewers to change the document. Click the check box, and future viewers will not be able to clear the field in which your signature appears.

5. Click Next. Acrobat displays a warning dialog if you have any items that may compromise document security if they are not removed; for example, actions that open URLs with their associated browsers.
6. Click Next to display the Save As Certified Document—Select Visibility dialog box. Choose one of the following options:
   - **Show Certification On Document** Displays a blue-ribbon icon on the certified document
   - **Do Not Show Certification On Document** Does not display the certification icon on the certified document
7. Click Next. Acrobat displays instructions for using your mouse to create the area where the certification icon will be displayed.
8. Click OK. Acrobat displays the Data Exchange File—Digital ID selection dialog box.
9. Click the triangle to the right of the Digital ID file and choose the digital ID with which you want to sign the document.
10. Click Sign And Save to certify the document with its current filename. Alternatively, choose Sign And Save As to certify the document with a different filename.

Use Acrobat Password Security

In today's economy, corporations often have branches in different counties, states, and countries. Before the advent of e-mail, corporations had to send documents via courier, a very expensive way to communicate. With e-mail, corporate documents can be sent as e-mail attachments. However, anyone with a bit of computer savvy can access an e-mail message and, with the proper software, can view sensitive communications. When you use Acrobat Password Security, you can assign a password to open the document. When a user tries to open a password-protected document, Acrobat prompts the user for a password. When the user enters the correct password, Acrobat opens the document. When you password-protect a document, you can assign permissions—

for example, whether a viewer with Acrobat can edit the document or not. To limit access to a document with Acrobat Password Security, follow these steps:

1. Choose Document | Security |Restrict Editing And Opening to access the Password Security—Settings box dialog box, as shown here:

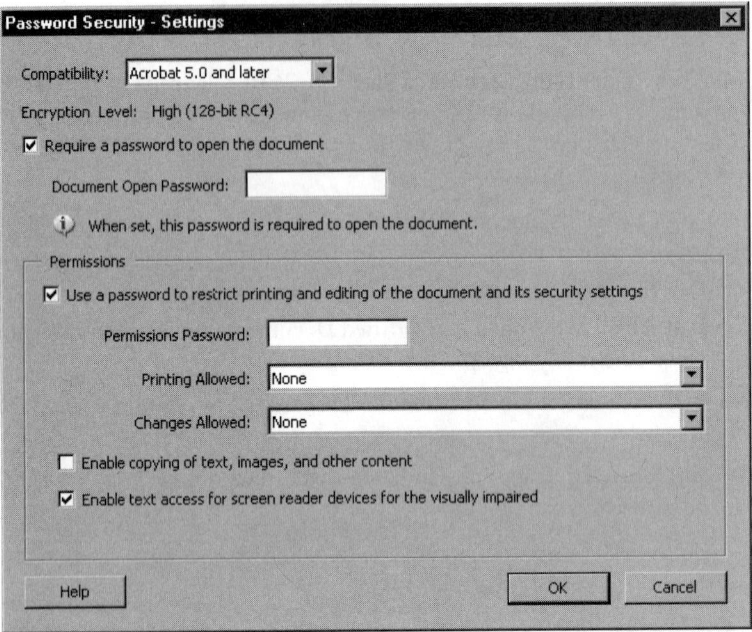

2. Click the triangle to the right of the Compatibility field and choose one of the following: Acrobat 3.0 or later, Acrobat 5.0 or later, or Acrobat 6.0 or later. Choosing 5.0 or 6.0 gives you the best security, but the document will be available only to users with the applicable version of Acrobat, Adobe Reader, or Adobe Reader 6.0.
3. To assign a password to the document, choose the Require A Password To Open The Document option. After choosing this option, the Document Open Password field becomes available.
4. In the Document Open Password field, enter the password that will be required to open the document. As you type each letter of the password, an asterisk appears to prevent prying eyes from seeing the password you enter.
5. To assign a permissions password to the document, choose the Use A Password To Restrict Printing And Editing Of The Document And Its Security Settings option and the Permissions Password field becomes active. When you assign a permissions password to a document, a user who enters the proper document open password cannot change the document open password or permissions without entering the permissions password.

6. In the Permissions Password field, enter the password that must be entered to change document passwords or permissions. As you enter text in the Permissions Password field, each letter appears as an asterisk. The document open password and permissions password must be unique. For security reasons, it is a good idea to use dissimilar passwords.

TIP *To prevent against being locked out of a document you created, consider copying your document passwords in a safe place, for example, your PDA if you use one.*

7. Click the triangle to the right of the Printing Allowed field and choose an option from the drop-down menu. The options vary depending on the compatibility you choose. If you choose Acrobat 5.0 or 6.0, your options are None, Low Resolution (150 DPI), or High Resolution (300 DPI). If you choose low resolution and a document viewer chooses Acrobat Distiller as the printing device, the resulting PDF file is also printed at low resolution, which prevents the user from pirating a high-resolution copy of the document.
8. Click the triangle to the right of the Changes Allowed field and choose an option. If you choose Acrobat 5.0 or 6.0, choose one of the following options:
   - **None** Viewers will not be able to make any changes to the document.
   - **Inserting, Deleting, And Rotating Pages** Viewers will only be able to add, remove, and rotate pages.
   - **Filling In Form Fields and Signing** Viewers of the document will be able to fill in and sign form fields but will not be allowed to create them.
   - **Only Document Accessibility** Viewers will be permitted to insert, delete, and rotate pages as well as be able to create bookmarks and thumbnails.
   - **Commenting, Filling In Form Fields, And Signing** Viewers will be able to add comments to the document, as well as be able to fill in and sign the document, but not create or otherwise alter form fields.
   - **Any Except Extracting Of Pages** Viewers of the document have full access to the document, with the exception of extracting pages.
9. Choose the Enable Copying Of Text, Images, And Other Content to allow Acrobat users to use the applicable tools to copy content to the clipboard for use in other PDF documents or applications.
10. Choose the Enable Text Access For Screen Reader Devices For The Visually Impaired option to allow the visually impaired to read the document with their screen readers. They will not be able to copy or extract objects from the document.
11. Click OK to set document security and a warning dialog appears telling you that security settings may not be supported by third-party products and that users of these products may be able to bypass your security settings.

TIP *To prevent the third-party security settings warning from appearing, click the Do Not Show This Message Again check box.*

12. Click OK to exit the warning dialog. If you password-protected the document, the Password Security dialog box appears.
13. Confirm the document password and click OK. If you assigned only a document open password to the document, the Password Security dialog box closes. If you assigned a permissions password to the document as well, the Password Security dialog box appears again, prompting you to confirm the permissions password. Confirm the permissions password, and the Password Security dialog box closes.
14. Choose File | Save. When the document opens again, the security measures you selected are assigned to the document.

TIP

If changes in your organization prompt a change in document security settings, you can easily do so by opening the document whose security settings you need to change and then choosing Document | Security | Restrict Editing And Opening. You'll be prompted for the document open password, after which you'll be able to access the Password Security—Settings box dialog box and change security settings.

Use Acrobat Certificate Security

When you use Acrobat Certificate Security, you have complete control over who is permitted to open the document and who is permitted to edit the document. You can assign varying degrees of permission as well, which is useful if you create a document that will be distributed in a corporate environment. You can allow complete access to some team members and varying degrees of access to others. For example, if the document needs to be available to a recent hire, you can disable editing, printing, and extracting elements from the document. When you assign Acrobat Certificate Security, you choose the users who have access to the document from your list of *trusted identities.*

Build a List of Trusted Identities

Before you can assign Acrobat Certificate Security to a document, you need to build a list of trusted identities. Trusted identities are Acrobat users who have sent you their *certificate.* When users create a digital ID, they have the option to export the certificate associated with their digital ID to file. You can exchange certificates with other members of your team via e-mail, as discussed in the following section.

Exchange Certificates

The first step in building a list of trusted identities is to exchange certificates. You can import certificates received from other team members or you can request a certificate from a recipient via e-mail. To exchange certificates via e-mail, follow these steps:

1. Select a digital ID, as outlined previously.
2. Choose Advanced | Manage Digital IDs | Trusted Identities to access the Manage Trusted Identities dialog box.

3. Click the triangle to the right of the Display field and choose Certificates to display a list of your trusted identities, as shown here:

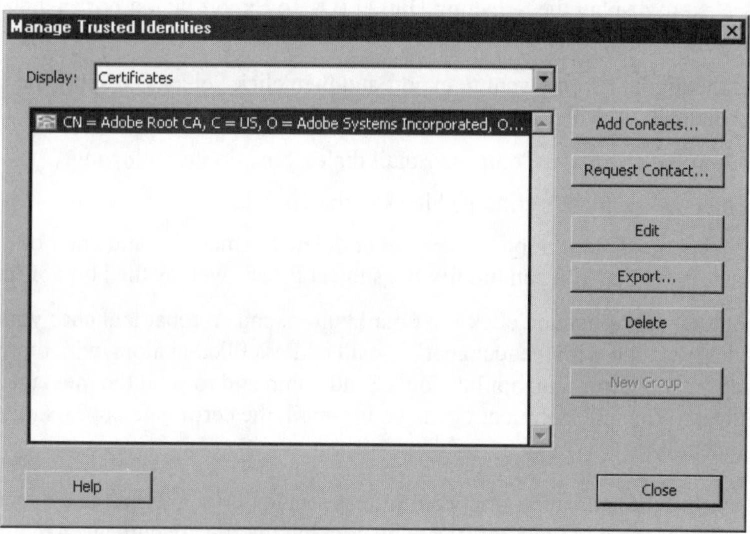

4. Click Request Contact to display the Email A Request dialog box.
5. Enter your name in the My Name field, and your Email address in My Email Address field, as shown here:

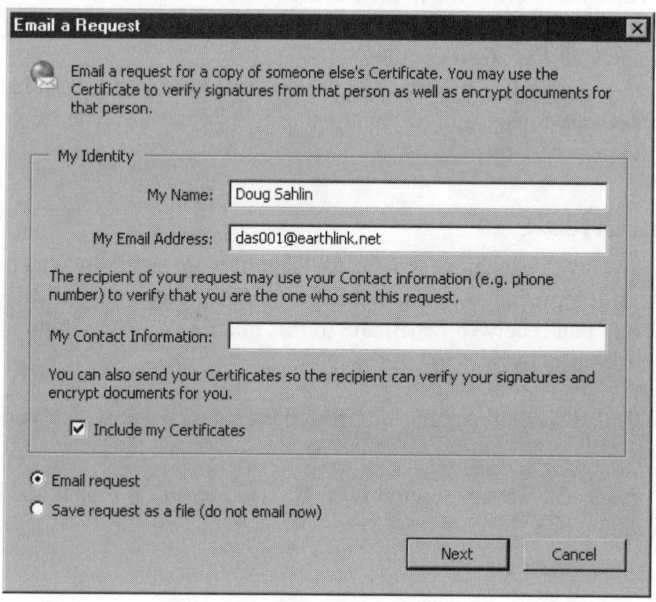

6. If desired, enter information in the My Contact Information field. For example, you may want to enter a phone number that recipients can use to verify your certificate.
7. Click Next to display the Selecting Digital IDs To Export dialog box, which contains a list of your digital IDs.
8. Select the digital ID you want to export and then click Select to display the Compose Email dialog box. Note that you can select only one digital ID to export.
9. After Acrobat opens the Compose Email dialog box, do the following:
   - Enter the recipient's e-mail address in the To field.
   - Accept the default Subject message or delete the message and enter one of your own. Note that you can modify the subject title as well as the body of the message.
10. Log on to the Internet and click the Email button, and Acrobat launches your default e-mail application with the recipient's e-mail address filled in along with the subject and message. Use your e-mail application's Send command to send the message and certificate. When the recipient opens your e-mail, the certificate appears as an attachment.

After you click the Email button, your certificate is sent to the recipient as an e-mail attachment. Your e-mail recipient can add your certificate by clicking the file attachment. After clicking the attachment, Acrobat launches and displays the Data Exchange File—Request and Contact dialog box, as shown in Figure 11-3. Note that a certificate comprises two components: a public key and a private key. The public key can be viewed by someone who intercepts a certificate you send via e-mail. However, the private key will not be visible and cannot be reverse engineered.

Recipients can add your certificate to their trusted identities list by clicking the Set Contact Trust button and following the prompts. If you requested a return certificate, the user can send it by clicking the Email Your Certificate button.

When you receive a return certificate, open the e-mail attachment, double-click the file extension as described previously, and follow the prompts. Make sure you select the digital ID you want the certificate saved to.

Import a Certificate

E-mail is an efficient way to exchange certificates. The files are small and can be sent quickly with even the slowest Internet connection. However, you may receive certificates on floppy disk or other media. When you receive a certificate in this manner, you can import it. To import a certificate, follow these steps:

1. Select the digital ID that contains the trusted identities list to which you want to import a certificate.
2. Choose Advanced | Manage Digital IDs | Trusted Identities to open the Manage Trusted Identities dialog box.

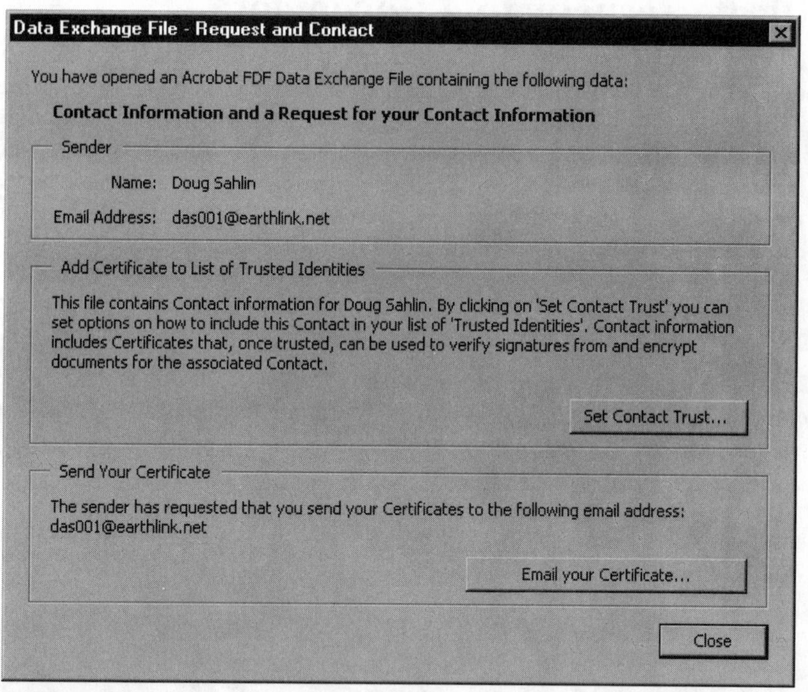

FIGURE 11-3 Use the dialog box to add a certificate to your list or e-mail your certificate to an associate.

3. Click the triangle to the right of the Display field and choose Certificates.
4. Click Add Contacts to open the Select Contacts To Add dialog box.
5. Click Browse For Certificate, navigate to the folder where the certificate you want to add to the list is stored, select it, and then click Open.
6. Click Add To Contacts List to add the issuer of the digital ID to your list of contacts.
7. Click OK to exit the Select Contacts To Add dialog box.
8. Click Close to exit the Manage Trusted Identities dialog box. Acrobat adds the certificate to your list of trusted identities, and your contacts list if you performed Step 6.

Add Certificate Security to a Document

After the members of your team are added to your list of trusted identities, you can begin to secure your documents with Acrobat Certificate Security. When you set up Certificate Security, you do not have to enter passwords. Each team member's password information is stored with his or her own certificate. All you need to do is determine which members of your list of trusted identities have access to the document and the level of permissions each team member will have. You then create a list of recipients that will have the same privileges and then add security. To add Acrobat Certificate Security to a document, follow these steps:

1. Choose Document | Security | Encrypt For Certain Identities Using Certificates to open the Document ID—Digital ID Selection dialog box.
2. Choose the digital ID with which you want to encrypt the document and then click OK to open the Restrict Opening And Editing To Certain Identities dialog box. If you neglect to choose a digital ID, you may not be able to open the document after encrypting it.
3. Enter your password and click OK to display the Document Security—Digital ID selection.
4. Select the digital ID with which you want to encrypt the document to access the Restrict Opening And Editing To Certain Identities dialog box shown here:

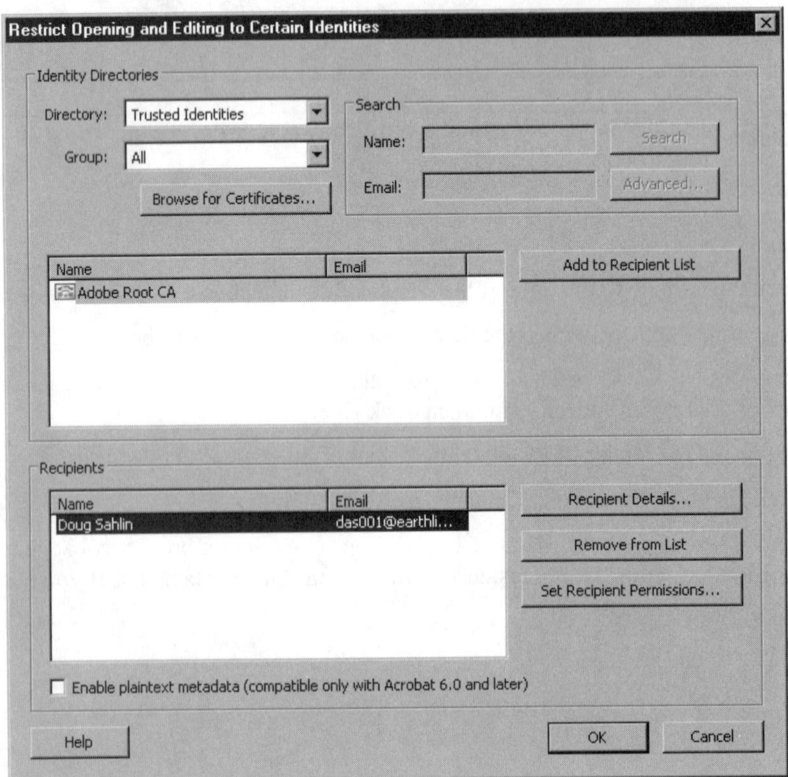

5. In the Recipients window, select the names of the users that you want to have access to the document.
6. Click Set Recipient Permissions and Acrobat displays a warning that viewers using third-party products to display the document may be able to bypass some of your settings.
7. Click OK after you have read the warning to open the Recipient Permission Setting dialog box shown next. By default, users have complete access to the document until you modify the settings.

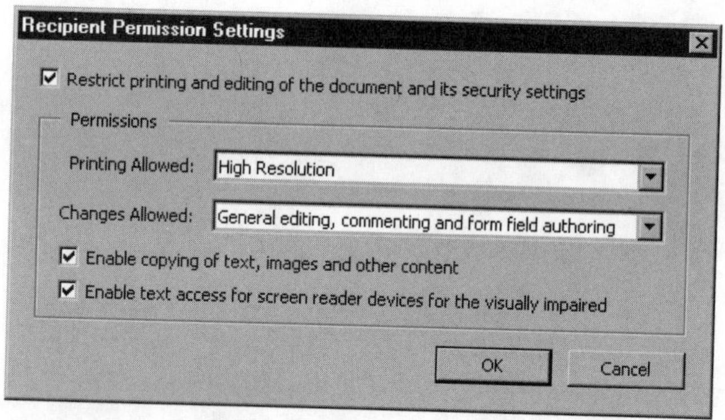

8. In the Recipient Permissions Settings dialog box, modify the parameters for the selected recipients. These options are the same as Acrobat Password Security, as discussed previously in the "Use Acrobat Password Security" section of this chapter.
9. Repeat Steps 7 and 8 for the other recipients on your list. Remember, you can assign different permissions for each user, which is what makes Acrobat Certificate Security such a powerful tool.
10. Click OK to close the Recipient Permissions Settings dialog box, and then click OK to close the Restrict Opening And Editing To Certain Identities dialog box. When you save the document, the security is set.

Summary

In this chapter, you learned how to add your digital signature to a document, add signature fields to a document, and verify other colleagues' digital signatures. Certifying a document was another topic of discussion. You also learned to restrict a document by adding password security or certificate security to it. In the next chapter, you'll learn to optimize PDF documents for specific destinations.

Chapter 12 Optimize PDF Documents

How to...

- Optimize documents for the visually impaired
- Optimize documents for print
- Optimize documents for CD-ROM applications
- Optimize documents for the Web
- Customize Distiller conversion settings

When you create a PDF document, you can optimize it for a specific or for several destinations. If you create a document in an authoring application and (if available) use the PDF export feature of the application, or use Adobe PDF to print the file, you can modify the output settings for an intended destination. You modify output settings by changing the Adobe PDF Settings. When you change Adobe PDF Settings, you can specify how Acrobat Distiller compresses the images in your document and how it adjusts color settings for the intended destination of the document, and specify whether or not fonts are embedded.

In previous chapters, you learned to use preset Adobe PDF Conversion Settings to convert documents into PDF format. In this chapter, you'll learn to fine-tune Adobe PDF Conversion Settings to suit the intended destination of the document. Fonts are an important consideration when you create a PDF document. In this chapter, font considerations are discussed as well as when it is necessary to embed fonts. You'll learn specific strategies for optimizing your documents for an intended destination. You'll also learn how to create a document that can be reflowed for easier reading in devices with different monitor sizes, as well as learn to modify a document for the visually impaired.

About Tagged Documents

When you create a document that will be distributed to users who view the document on devices with a limited viewing area, you can create a tagged document that can be reflowed to any window size. When a user *reflows* a document, the font size stays unchanged so it is legible, even on a smaller viewing device. Images, however, reduce in size to accommodate reduced viewing area. If your tagged PDF document will be viewed on devices such as a PalmPilot or some of the smaller eBook readers, viewers with Adobe Reader or Acrobat can reflow the document to fit the smaller viewing area.

Create a Tagged Document

You can create a tagged document by converting Web pages to PDF format or by creating a document within a Microsoft Office application and then using Acrobat PDFMaker to convert the document to PDF. To create a tagged document from a Microsoft Office application, you modify the Object Level Compression option in the General section of the Adobe PDF Settings dialog box, as detailed in the upcoming "Set General Options" section.

To create a tagged document from Web pages and HTML documents, follow these steps:

1. Choose File | Create PDF | From Web Page.
2. In the URL field, enter the URL of the page you want to convert to a tagged document. Remember, you can also capture an HTML document located on your computer by entering the relative path to the file.
3. Click the Settings button to open the Web Page Conversion Settings dialog box.
4. Choose the Add PDF Tags option and then click OK to close the dialog box.
5. Click Download, and Acrobat captures the Web page with PDF tags. For more information on converting Web pages to PDF documents, refer to Chapter 6.

Reflow a Tagged Document

The recipients of a tagged document can reflow the document to fit the viewing area of the device they use to view the document. Tagged PDF files are optimized for accessibility, making them available to viewers using screen-reader devices. To reflow a document with Acrobat or Adobe Reader, choose View | Reflow.

Optimize Documents for the Visually Impaired (Professional Only)

When you create a document that will be viewed by visually impaired people using onscreen readers, a different challenge presents itself to you—the document will be viewed at varying degrees of magnification. Creating a tagged document eliminates the problem of reflowing the document, but there is still the issue of images in the document. When a document is greatly magnified, only a portion of the image will be rendered. In order to offset this difficulty, you must provide a way for visually impaired readers to identify what the image is. To accomplish this, provide alternate text for tagged, non-text elements in the document using the Tags tab.

TIP *You can optimize a document for the visually impaired in Acrobat Standard or Acrobat Pro by choosing Advanced | Accessibility | Full Check.*

Use the Tags Tab (Professional Only)

You use the Tags tab to view the logical order of a tagged document. When you open the Tags tab, you'll see the logical structure of the document, which is a visual representation of the organization of the document elements. You can use the Tags tab to modify tags in a document. For example, many onscreen readers can take advantage of alternate text for a tagged element. The alternate text tells the visually impaired person what the element is about. You can also use tag information to specify the text language of the document. To open the Tags tab shown next, choose View | Navigation Tabs | Tags. If the document is not tagged, No Tags Available displays at the top of the tab.

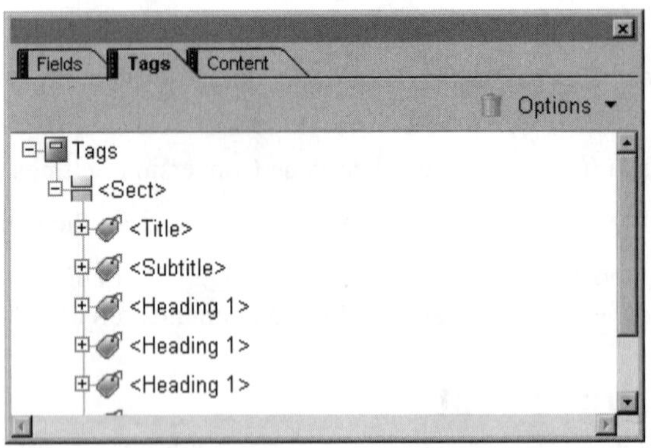

If you open the Tags tab and see No Tags Available, you can add tags in Acrobat Professional by choosing Advanced | Accessibility | Add Tags To Document.

If the document you create will be viewed with onscreen reading devices that have limited graphics capabilities, you can add an alternate tag that describes what the image is about. To add an alternate tag to a non-text element, follow these steps:

1. Open the Tags tab, as previously outlined.
2. Select the tag that denotes the image in the PDF document. If you have a hard time determining which tag is associated with which element in the text, click the Options icon in the upper-right corner of the tab and choose Highlight Contents. When you enable this option, Acrobat highlights the element in the document when you select the corresponding tag. Also note that graphic elements have different icons in the Tags tab.
3. Click the Options icon and choose Properties from the Tags tab Options menu to open the TouchUp Properties dialog box. Alternatively, you can right-click (Windows) or CTRL-click (Macintosh) and choose Properties from the Context menu.
4. In the Alternate Text field, enter a description of the image. For example, if the image depicts the Eiffel Tower you might enter the following: **This image is an illustration of the Eiffel Tower**.
5. Click OK to assign the alternate text to the tag.

Optimize Documents for Print

When you create a PDF document for print, you modify the Press Quality conversion settings to match the intended output device. If the document is to be printed by a service center, check with the service center technicians to get the necessary information about the printing device with which your documents will be printed. This is the information you need to modify conversion settings—in particular, when modifying the color and advanced settings of the Press Quality conversion settings. You should also pay careful attention to image resolution. If the document is for print only and file size is not a concern, you can disable all compression options to maintain maximum image quality. If you create documents that will be printed by a service center, or on a printer attached to a different computer, embed all fonts to ensure the document prints properly.

The default resolution of 2400 dpi is fine for most commercial printing devices; however, it is higher than needed for most laser printers. You can change the resolution setting to match your laser or DeskJet printer in the General section of the Press Quality Conversion Settings dialog box. Modifying conversion settings is discussed in detail in the upcoming "Customize Distiller Conversion Settings" section of this chapter. Alternatively, you can also choose the Press Quality conversion settings as the basis for documents you print in-house on laser or DeskJet-type printers.

Optimize Documents for CD-ROM Applications

When you optimize a document for a CD-ROM application, use the Standard conversion settings as a starting point. This option has compression settings with higher resolutions than those generally needed for screen viewing, but when you create a CD-ROM, file size is generally not an issue. If you stick with the High option for image quality, your viewers will be able to zoom in on document images with little or no loss in quality. In fact, you may want to use the Maximum quality setting and increase the resolution if your CD-ROM presentation has many intricate images, such as maps that beg to be examined at higher magnification settings.

Optimize Documents for the Web

When you optimize documents for viewing over the Internet, begin with the Smallest File Size conversion settings. The default settings of this conversion setting resample document images to 100 ppi. The resulting file is a compromise between file size and image quality. You can decrease the size of the file if you modify the settings in the Compression section of the Smallest File Size conversion settings dialog box. Experiment with the Low and Minimum settings. If the images in the original document were high quality, you may be able to produce an acceptable document using the Low or Minimum image quality compression settings. You can create a document using the default Smallest File Size conversion settings and then create another document using the Smallest Files Size conversion settings with modified image quality compression settings. Compare the two documents in Acrobat arranged in tile format and you will be able to see the difference in image quality between the different compression settings.

By default, documents created with Smallest File Size conversion settings are optimized for *byteserving* (sending a document to a Web browser a page at a time) over the Web. A document optimized for fast Web viewing downloads a page at a time if the Web-hosting service supports byteserving.

Customize Distiller Conversion Settings

When you create a document for a specific destination using Acrobat Distiller or Adobe PDFMaker, you can use one of the preset Adobe PDF Settings to convert the file. You can also customize preset conversion settings by modifying the parameters to suit your needs. When you modify an Adobe PDF setting, you begin with one of the presets, apply the needed changes, and then save the Adobe PDF setting with a different filename. After you save the modified Adobe PDF settings, the modification appears on the Default Settings menu in Acrobat Distiller and the Conversion Settings menu in Microsoft Office applications.

Each Adobe PDF Settings dialog box is comprised of five tabbed sections in Acrobat Standard, six in Acrobat Professional. You can modify as many or as few sections as needed to create the optimal conversion for your document(s). To create a custom conversion setting in Acrobat Distiller, follow these steps:

1. Click the triangle to the right of the Default Settings field and choose a conversion setting from the drop-down menu.
2. Choose Settings | Edit Adobe PDF Settings to open the Adobe PDF Settings dialog box, as shown in Figure 12-1. Note that the dialog box in Figure 12-1 is for the Standard—Adobe PDF Settings as viewed in Acrobat Professional. The title of the dialog box changes depending on the conversion setting you are modifying; for example, if you modify Press Quality Adobe PDF Settings, the dialog box title reads Press Quality—Adobe PDF Settings.

When you modify a conversion setting from within a Microsoft Office application, you are modifying an Adobe PDF Settings option. Adobe PDF Settings created in Acrobat Distiller can be used to convert a document to PDF in a Microsoft Office application and vice versa. To modify an Adobe PDF Settings option from within a Microsoft Office application, follow these steps:

1. Choose Adobe PDF | Change Conversion Settings.
2. Click the triangle to the right of the Conversion Settings field and from the drop-down menu, choose a conversion setting to modify.
3. Click the Advanced Settings button to open the Adobe PDF Settings dialog box, as shown in Figure 12-1.

After you open the Adobe PDF Settings dialog box, modify the conversion settings by making changes in each section. To access the settings in each section, click the section tab. In following sections of this chapter, conversion settings you can modify are discussed in detail.

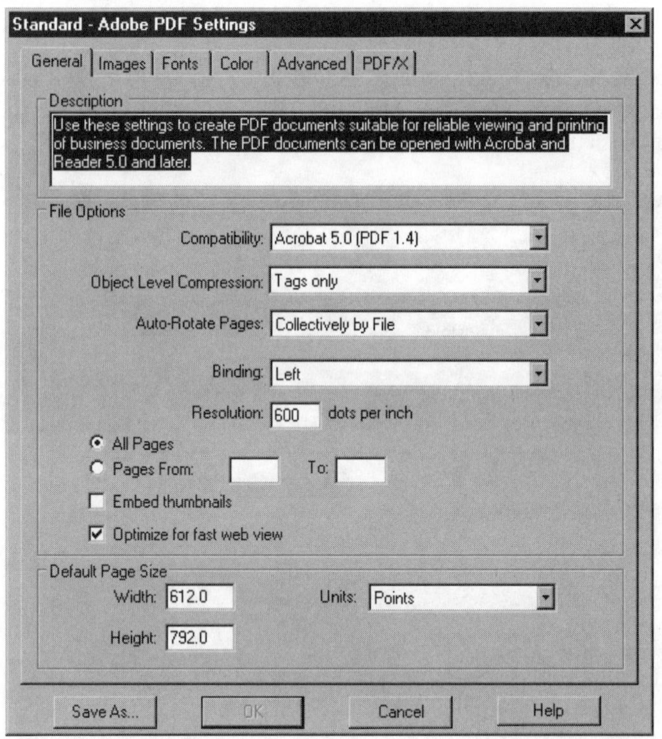

FIGURE 12-1 Modify Adobe PDF Settings within this dialog box.

Acrobat Distiller defaults to the last conversion setting used. Before converting a document to PDF with Acrobat Distiller or using Adobe PDF as a printing device or using PDFMaker in a Microsoft Office application, choose the desired PDF Setting from the Conversion Settings menu and your document will be created with the new conversion settings.

Set General Options

In the General section of the Adobe PDF Settings dialog box, you determine which version of Acrobat is compatible with the published document. Also, you can optimize the file for fast

Web viewing, set the document resolution for printing, and set the page size of the published document. To set General job options, follow these steps:

1. Choose a conversion setting to modify and open the Adobe PDF Settings dialog box, as discussed previously. When you click the Advance Settings button, Acrobat opens to the General section by default, as shown here:

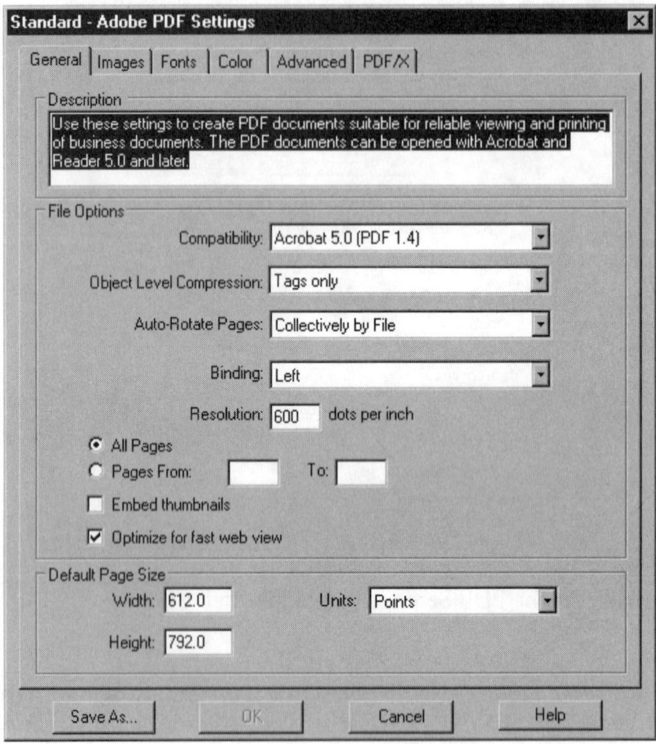

2. In the File Options section, click the triangle to the right of the Compatibility field and from the drop-down menu, choose the version of Acrobat that you want the published document to be compatible with. You can choose from Acrobat 3.0 (PDF 1.2), Acrobat 4.0 (PDF 1.3), Acrobat 5.0 (PDF 1.4), or Acrobat 6.0 (PDF 1.5). Choose the version of Acrobat that supports the features in the document you have created. Remember to take into account which version of Acrobat the majority of your target audience is likely to have.

3. After you choose the version of Acrobat that documents created with this conversion setting will be compatible with, you can modify the following settings:

   - **Object Level Compression** Choose this option to apply tags to the structure of a PDF document.

- **Auto-Rotate Pages** Choose this option to have Acrobat automatically rotate document pages when the page should be rotated for viewing without scrolling. You can choose Individually to rotate each page based on the page orientation or Collectively By File to rotate all pages based on the majority orientation of pages within the document.
- **Binding** Choose either Left or Right binding to determine how Acrobat displays the document in Continuous-Facing viewing mode and how thumbnails are displayed when the thumbnails are resized so they can be viewed side-by-side. Thumbnails are arranged from left to right when you choose Left binding; right to left when you choose Right binding.
- **Resolution** Enter a value that matches the resolution of the device the document will be printed on. When you create a PDF file with Acrobat Distiller, or Acrobat Distiller in the guise of Adobe PDF, the device is actually printing a PostScript file for display in PDF format. The value you enter for resolution emulates the resolution setting of a printing device. If you choose a higher resolution, recipients of your document can print the file on a high resolution device but the file size will be larger.
- **All Pages** This default option converts all pages in the document to PDF.
- **Page From** Choose this option to have Acrobat convert all pages within a document to PDF or specify a range of pages by entering the first page to convert in the Pages From field and the last page to convert in the To field.
- **Embed Thumbnails** Choose this option to have Acrobat Distiller embed a thumbnail for each page of documents converted to PDF with this conversion setting. Remember that this will increase the file size of the published document. If you choose not to select this option, Acrobat automatically generates thumbnails on the fly when the document viewer opens the Thumbnails tab. If, however, you are creating large PDF documents with hundreds of pages, you may want to consider embedding thumbnails, as generating hundreds of thumbnails every time the Pages tab is open can severely tax the system resources of the computer used to view the document.
- **Optimize For Fast Web View** Choose this option if you create a document to view over the Internet. When you choose this option, Acrobat converts documents created with this job option for page-at-a-time downloading (byteserving) from the host Web server. Note that this option is chosen by default with all Adobe PDF Settings options.

4. In the Default Page Size section, enter values in the Width and Height fields; then choose a unit of measure. The settings you enter here determine the dimensions of the files Acrobat creates with this conversion setting. Enter dimensions that match the sizes of documents you create in the authoring application, which you use as the basis for PDF files created with this conversion setting. Remember that if you use Adobe PDF to convert a Microsoft Office file to PDF format, you must configure Acrobat Distiller to match the page dimensions specified in the Conversion Settings setting; otherwise,

Adobe PDF (which is actually using Acrobat Distiller to print the PDF file) reverts to the default dimensions for Acrobat Distiller. For more information on configuring Acrobat Distiller page size, refer to Chapter 5.

After you modify the General settings of the Adobe PDF Setting, you can click a tab to modify other settings or save the Adobe PDF Settings option, as described in the later "Save Conversion Settings" section.

Conversion Settings Images Options

When you choose a specific conversion settings option to create a PDF document, Acrobat compresses the document text, line art, and images using settings deemed optimal for the conversion setting. You can, however, modify the compression settings to suit documents you create for specific applications. You can modify the settings to reduce file size or enhance the quality of the published document. With a bit of experimentation, you can modify compression settings for optimal file size while still maintaining a high level of detail in the published document.

Acrobat Distiller Compression Methods

The compression method you choose will greatly affect the overall quality of the images in your published document. When you modify compression settings, you can have Acrobat Distiller automatically choose the compression method deemed right for the images in the document, or you can choose one of following Acrobat Distiller compression methods:

- **ZIP** Use the ZIP (Adobe's variation of the ZIP filter as derived from the zlib package of Jean-loup Gailly and Mark Adler) method of compression on images with large areas of solid color, such as GIF images. This method of compression works well with simple images created in painting applications such as Windows Paintbrush or Corel Painter. It also works quite well with artwork created in vector-based drawing programs, such as Adobe Illustrator. If the vector images in your document contain complex gradients, choose the JPEG compression method. You can use ZIP compression with 4-bit and 8-bit color depth. If you choose 4-bit color depth on an 8-bit image, you end up with a smaller file size but degrade image quality because you lose data when the image compresses.
- **JPEG** Use the *JPEG (Joint Photographic Experts Group)* method of compression on full-color or grayscale images, such as photographs. When you use JPEG compression, you can control the size of the file by telling Acrobat how much compression to apply to the images. You can modify the settings to create a PDF document with high-quality images at the expense of a larger file size, or you can apply a higher level of compression and your published PDF file will be smaller but the images will not be as detailed due to the data lost during compression. JPEG compression is also known as *lossy* compression because data is lost when the document images are compressed. Acrobat Distiller has five JPEG compression options. JPEG compression is best suited for photographs. If you

have images with large areas of solid color such as GIF images in your document, use ZIP compression.

- **CCITT** Use the *CCITT (Consultative Committee for International Telephone & Telegraph)* method of compression for 1-bit black and white images, such as faxes. When you use the CCITT method of compression, no data is lost. Use the CCITT Group 4 method for general-purpose compression of monochrome images; use the CCITT Group 3 method for faxed documents.
- **Run Length** Use this option when your document contains images with large areas of solid black or white. Run Length is a loss-less compression method.

Acrobat Distiller Resampling

When Acrobat Distiller compresses images, it also *resamples* them. When you use software to resample an image, pixels are either added or removed from the image to change the resolution (pixels per inch, or *ppi*) the image displays at. When pixels are added to an image to increase resolution, image degradation generally occurs as you ask the software to interpolate between neighboring pixels in order to create new pixels. It is always best to start out with a high-resolution image and then downsample the image when converting it to PDF. You can specify one of the following interpolation methods to resample images:

- **Average Downsampling** Choose this method to have Acrobat Distiller create new pixels at the specified resolution using the average color of *neighboring* pixels within a given area.
- **Bicubic Downsampling** Use this interpolation method to yield the highest quality images. When you specify bicubic downsampling, Acrobat Distiller creates new pixels at the specified resolution using a weighted average to determine pixel color. In other words, the resulted color is weighted toward the dominant color in each *area* Acrobat Distiller samples. This is the slowest method but will give you the best results.
- **Subsampling** Choose this method of interpolation to have Acrobat Distiller create new pixels at the specified resolution using the color of a pixel in the *center* of the sampled area. Because this method of interpolation uses a single pixel to create new pixels, subsampling is the quickest interpolation method but can lead to images with harsh transitions between adjacent pixels.

Set Images Settings

Each Adobe PDF Settings option has a specific set of compression options that you can modify for documents you create. You modify compression settings to determine the quality of the text, line art, and images in the published PDF document. To modify an Adobe PDF Settings Images setting, follow these steps:

1. Choose a Conversion Settings option to modify and open the Adobe PDF Settings dialog box, as discussed previously.

2. Click the Images tab to open the Adobe PDF Settings Images section, as shown here:

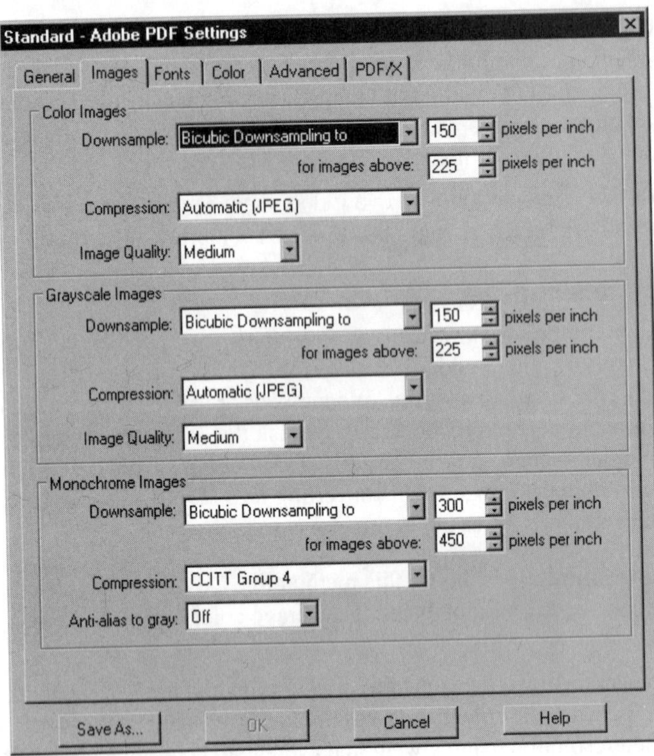

3. In the Color and Grayscale Images sections, click the triangle to the right of the Downsample field and choose an option from the drop-down menu.
4. In the Color and Grayscale Images sections, choose a compression method. By default, Acrobat Distiller compresses and automatically chooses the compression option it deems best for the color and grayscale images in the document. You can choose Off to have Acrobat Distiller convert the file to PDF without compressing it. To choose a compression method other than Automatic (JPEG), click the triangle to the right of the Compression field and choose the desired method from the drop-down menu.
5. In the Color and Grayscale Images sections, to the right of the Downsample field, enter the dpi value to which you want Acrobat Distiller to downsample color and grayscale images.

6. In the Color and Grayscale Images sections, enter a value in the For Images Above fields. When you use this job option, Acrobat Distiller downsamples all images above the resolution you enter in this field to the lower output resolution you entered in Step 5.
7. In the Color and Grayscale Images sections, click the triangle to the right of the Image Quality field and choose an option from the drop-down menu. This setting varies depending on the Adobe PDF Settings option you are modifying. Choose High or Maximum to create a better-looking document with a larger file size, or choose Minimum or Low to create a PDF document with a smaller file size and less detailed images.
8. In the Monochrome Images section, click the triangle to the right of the Downsample field and choose an option from the drop-down menu.
9. In the field to the right of the Downsample field, enter the ppi value to which you want Acrobat Distiller to downsample monochrome images.
10. In the For Images Above field, enter the value above which you want Acrobat Distiller to downsample images to the value entered in Step 9.

NOTE *If a PDF document converted with applied downsampling does not properly display black-and-white images, modify the Adobe PDF Settings option and choose Off for the Monochrome Downsample option.*

11. Click the triangle to the right of the Compression field and choose an option from the drop-down menu.
12. Click the triangle to the right of the Anti-Alias (blend neighboring pixels of different colors to avoid jagged edges) to Gray field and choose Off (the default options), 2-bit, 4-bit, or 8-bit. This option determines how many levels of gray are used to smooth the image. Choose 8-bit (256 levels of gray) for the best results.

Set Fonts Options

When you want to ensure that a document appears exactly as you created it, you embed the font set with the document. When you embed fonts with a document, the document will display and print correctly, even if the user's computer does not have the font installed. Acrobat Distiller can embed Roman Type 1 fonts and True Type fonts. Specify which fonts to embed when you convert documents to PDFs by modifying an Adobe PDF Settings' Font settings as follows:

1. Choose a conversion settings option to modify and open the Adobe PDF Settings dialog box, as discussed previously in "Customize Distiller Conversion Settings."

2. Click the Fonts tab to reveal the Fonts section of the Adobe PDF Settings dialog box, as shown here:

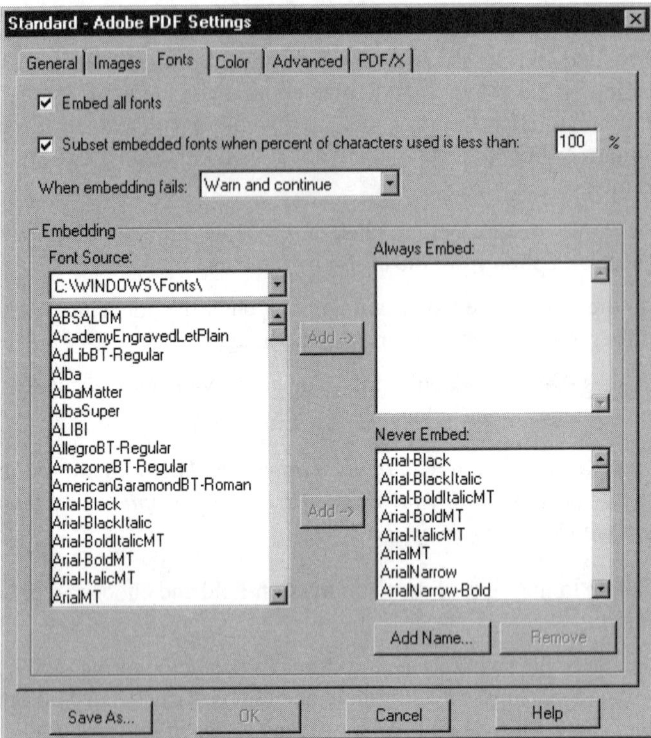

3. Enable the Embed All Fonts option to embed all fonts used to create the document.

4. Enable the Subset Embedded Fonts When Percent Of Characters Used Is Less Than [ ] % option and enter a percentage value. When you choose this option, Acrobat Distiller embeds only the characters used to create the document when the percentage of characters used from the font set falls below the value you specify. For example, if you enter a value of 60, Acrobat Distiller embeds only characters used to create the document when less than 60 percent of the font set is used.

5. Click the triangle to the right of the When Embedding Fails field and from the drop-down menu choose one of the following: Ignore, Warn And Continue, or Cancel Job.

6. To select a different font list, click the triangle to the right of the Font Source window and select a font folder from the drop-down menu.
7. If you always want to embed a certain font set with documents created using this Conversion Settings option, select the font(s) from the left window and click the Add button to the left of the Always Embed window to add the fonts to the Always Embed list.
8. To add a font to the Never Embed list, select the font from the left window and click the Add button to the left of the Never Embed window. To remove a font from the Never Embed List, select the font from the Never Embed list and click the Remove button.

NOTE *Licensing issues prohibit you from embedding certain fonts in a document. If you select a font with licensing issues, Acrobat Distiller displays a key icon before the font name and a warning at the bottom of the dialog box.*

After you change the conversion settings fonts parameters, click another tab to modify different settings or save the job option by following the steps in the upcoming "Save Conversion Settings" section.

TIP *When you install Acrobat, the install utility locates every folder in your system that contain fonts. If you add a new font folder to your system, launch Acrobat Distiller and choose Settings | Font Locations to open the Acrobat Distiller—Font Locations dialog box. Click the Add button, navigate to the folder that contains the fonts you want to use with Acrobat Distiller, select the folder, click OK, and then close the Font Locations dialog box. The next time you launch Acrobat Distiller, the font folder will be available.*

Set Color Options

When you convert a document to PDF format using Acrobat Distiller or PDFMaker, you can modify the color options. You can choose a color-management settings file and let Acrobat Distiller manage the color of the images during conversion or you can modify the color settings to suit a specific output device. To set color options, follow these steps:

1. Choose a Conversion Settings option to modify and open the Adobe PDF Settings dialog box, as discussed previously.

2. Click the Color tab to open the Color section of the Adobe PDF Settings dialog box, as shown here:

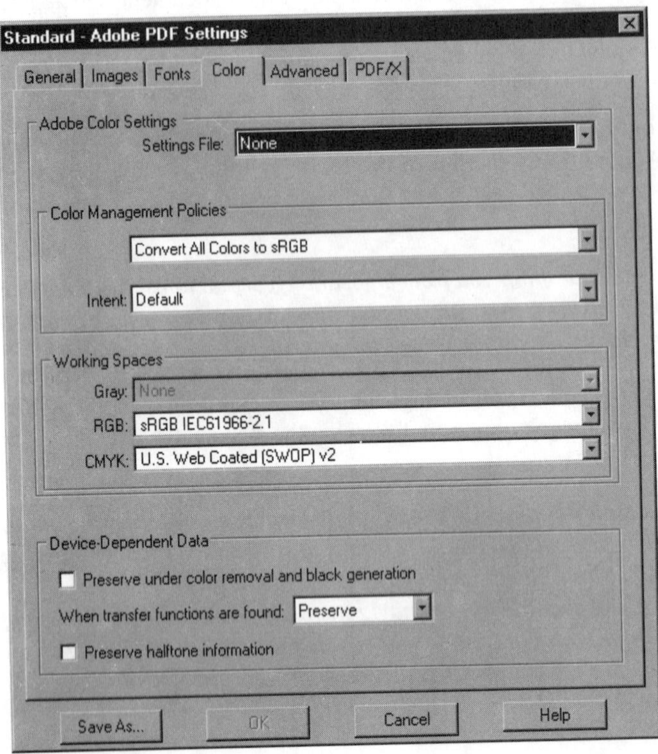

3. To use a preset color settings file, click the triangle to the right of the Settings File field and choose an option from the drop-down menu. When you choose one of the color-management setting files, all the color options are dimmed out. You can choose None (the default) for no color management, Color Management Off (for documents that will be displayed on a monitor), or one of the Prepress defaults: Emulate Acrobat 4, Emulate Photoshop 4, Photoshop 5 Default Spaces, Europe Prepress Defaults, Japanese Prepress Defaults, U.S. Prepress Defaults, or Web Graphic Defaults.

4. If you accept the default settings option (None), click the triangle to the right of the Color Management Policies field and choose one of the following:

   - **Leave Color Unchanged** Choose this option, and Acrobat Distiller does not modify device-dependent colors; rather, Distiller processes device-independent colors to the nearest match in the resulting PDF. Use this option if the file will be printed by a color-calibrated device that specifies all color management.

- **Tag Everything For Color Management** When you choose this option and specify Acrobat 4.0, 5.0, or 6.0 compatibility in the General Adobe PDF Settings tab, Acrobat Distiller embeds an *ICC (International Color Consortium)* color profile with the document. The ICC color profile calibrates image color and makes the colors in the converted PDF document device-independent. When you choose this option and specify Acrobat 3.0 compatibility in the General Options section, the option becomes Convert Everything For Color Management, and Acrobat Distiller does not embed an ICC color profile with the document. Device-dependent colors in the original files (RGB, Grayscale, and CMYK) are converted to device-independent color spaces (CalRGB, CalGrayscale, and LAB) in the resulting PDF file. (*Cal* in these examples stands for calibrated.)
- **Tag Only Images For Color Management** Choose this option with Acrobat 4.0, 5.0, or 6.0 compatibility so that when Acrobat Distiller converts a document to PDF format, it embeds ICC color profiles with document images but not with text or line art. When you specify Acrobat 3.0 compatibility, this option becomes Convert Only Images For Color Management, and Acrobat Distiller does not embed an ICC color profile with document images; however, device-dependent colors in the document images convert to device-independent color spaces (CalRGB, CalGrayscale, and LAB) in the resulting PDF file, leaving line art and graphics unchanged.
- **Convert All Colors to sRGB** When you choose this option with Acrobat 4.0 or 5.0 compatibility and Acrobat Distiller converts the file, all images with RGB and CMYK colors convert to sRGB. If you specify Acrobat 3.0 compatibility, the option becomes Convert All Colors To CalRGB and Acrobat Distiller converts all RGB and CMYK image colors to CalRGB.

5. Click the triangle to the right of the Intent field to specify how Acrobat Distiller maps color between the color spaces. Choose from the following options: 12

    - **Default** Choose this option, and the output device specifies the intent, not the PDF file. The majority of output devices use the Relative Colormetric intent.
    - **Perceptual** Choose this option, and the original color values of the document images are mapped to the gamut of the output device. This method preserves the visual relationship between different colors; however, color values may change.
    - **Saturation** Choose this option, and the file that Acrobat Distiller produces will maintain the same relative color saturation as the original image pixels. Choose this method when document color saturation is more important than maintaining the visual relationship between colors of the original document.
    - **Absolute Colormetric** Choose this option, and Acrobat Distiller disables the black and white point matching when converting colors in the document. This option is not recommended unless your intent is to preserve specific colors used in a trademark or logo.
    - **Relative Colormetric** Choose this option, and Acrobat Distiller preserves all colors within the output device gamut range. Colors in the original document that are out of the printing device gamut range convert to brightness values within the printer gamut.

6. If you choose any Color Management Policies option other than Leave Colors Unchanged, then in the Working Spaces section you will be able to choose an ICC profile for managing Grayscale, RGB, and CMYK color conversion.
   - **Gray (Grayscale)** Choose None from the drop-down menu, and Acrobat Distiller does not convert grayscale colors. The default option is determined by your operating system: Gray Gamma 2.2 for Windows, Gray Gamma 1.8 for Macintosh. Alternatively, you can choose one of the Dot Gain options (10 percent to 30 percent). Choose a lower dot gain value to lighten the image, a higher value to darken the image.
   - **RGB** Choose a color management profile from the drop-down menu. The available options are the color profiles installed on your computer. If you are uncertain which profile to choose, the default option (sRGB IEC61966-2.1) will yield good results. Choose None, and Acrobat Distiller does not convert colors in RGB images when distilling them to PDF.
   - **CMYK** Choose one of the options from the drop-down menu to specify how Acrobat Distiller handles colors in CMYK images when converting them to PDF format. If in doubt, choose the default (U.S. Web Coated [SWOP] v2). Choose None and Acrobat Distiller does not convert colors in CMYK images when distilling them to PDF.
7. In the Device-Dependent Data section, choose from the following options that pertain to the device that the converted documents will be printed with. These options have no effect on screen viewing:
   - **Preserve Under Color Removal And Black Generation** Choose this option if the documents you want to convert with this job option are PostScript files that contain Color Removal and Black Generation settings.
   - **When Transfer Functions Are Found** Click the triangle to the right of the field and choose one of the following options:
     - **Preserve** Choose this option to preserve transfer functions if they are present in the original file. Transfer functions are traditionally used to compensate for dot gain or dot loss when an image transfers to film.
     - **Apply** Choose this option and Acrobat Distiller applies the transfer functions to the file. This option changes the colors in the file.
     - **Remove** Choose this option and Acrobat Distiller removes all applied transfer functions when converting the file to PDF. You should choose this option unless the resulting PDF file will be printed on the same device the PostScript file was created for.
8. Choose the Preserve Halftone Information option, and the resulting file that Acrobat Distiller produces preserves halftone information embedded in the original PostScript document. Halftone screens control the amount of ink deposited in specific locations

when the file prints. By varying the dot size, halftone screens simulate the illusion of flowing color and varying shades of gray. CMYK images have four halftone screens, one for each color (Cyan, Magenta, Yellow, and Black).

After you modify the Conversion Settings Color settings, click another tab to modify another setting or save the job option, as outlined in the upcoming "Save Conversion Settings" section.

Set Advanced Options

The last tab in the Adobe PDF Settings dialog box allows you to modify Document Structuring Convention (DSC) comments that appear in the original PostScript file as well as other options that affect the conversion from PostScript to PDF. To modify job option Advanced Options settings, follow these steps:

1. Choose a Conversion Settings option to modify and open the Adobe PDF Settings dialog box, following the steps presented earlier in this chapter.
2. Click the Advanced Options tab to reveal the Advanced Options section of the Adobe PDF Settings dialog box, as shown here:

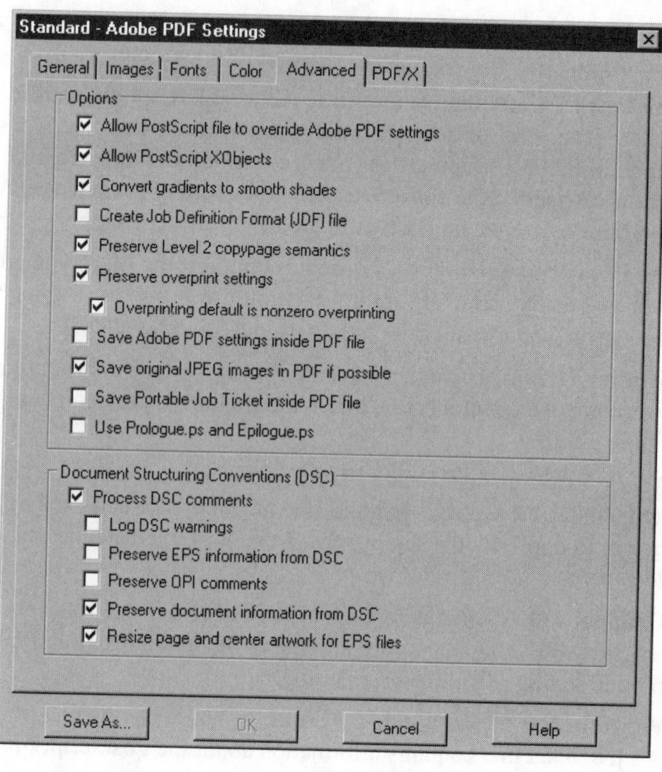

3. In the Options section, choose from the following:
   - **Allow PostScript File To Override PDF Conversion Settings** Choose this option if you are reasonably certain the PostScript files you convert with this job option contain the necessary information for the intended output device. Deselect this option if you want conversion settings to take precedence over any settings embedded in the PostScript files that you intend to convert with this job option.
   - **Allow PostScript XObjects** Choose this option and Acrobat Distiller creates XObjects (eXternal Objects) that store information that appears on multiple pages of the same file. This can result in faster printing but requires more printer memory as the XObjects are stored in printer memory and called when needed.
   - **Convert Gradients To Smooth Shades** Choose this option if the files you distill to PDF with this job option have Acrobat 4.0 compatibility or greater. When you choose this option, Acrobat Distiller smoothes gradients from the original files creating a seamless blend. This option has no effect on how the document appears onscreen; however, if you print the converted file to a PostScript 3 device, you will notice a marked improvement in quality. Note that if you choose this option, it may take longer for Acrobat to render the gradient onscreen.
   - **Create Job Definition Format (JDF) File** Choose this option and Acrobat Distiller creates an XML file that contains information for the printer.
   - **Preserve Level 2 Copypage Semantics** Choose this option, and Acrobat Distiller uses the copypage editor defined in LanguageLevel 2 PostScript instead of LanguageLevel 3 PostScript. Do not choose this option if printing to LanguageLevel 3 PostScript devices. If the converted file will be sent to a service center, check with the technicians to see which PostScript level their devices support.
   - **Preserve Overprint Settings** Choose this option if the PDFs you create with this job option originally had overprint information. An *overprint* is when two or more colors are printed on top of each other to produce another color.
   - **Overprinting Default Is Nonzero Overprinting** Choose this option, and files with overprints that contain zero CMYK information will not prevent underlying colors from printing.
   - **Save Adobe PDF Settings Inside PDF File** Choose this option, and Acrobat Distiller includes the settings, as a file attachment can be accessed by other applications to duplicate the settings that were used to create the file within the PDF document.
   - **Save Original JPEG Images In PDF If Possible** Choose this option, and Acrobat Distiller saves JPEG images from the original file in the resulting PDF file with the compression settings from the original file.
   - **Save Portable Job Ticket Inside PDF File** Choose this option and Acrobat Distiller creates a job ticket that contains information about the PostScript file used to create

the PDF document. The job ticket includes information such as page size and orientation, resolution, halftone information, and so on. Disable this option if the PDF documents you create with this job option are strictly for screen viewing.

- **Use Prologue.ps And Epilogue.ps** Choose this option to send a prologue and epilogue file with each document Acrobat Distiller converts with this job option. Epilogue files can be edited to append information to the PDF file. Prologue files can be edited to resolve procedure problems with PostScript files. Sample Prologue.ps and Epilogue.ps files are located in the Distiller folder. Neither file contains data but you can use them as templates. Unless you are familiar with creating PostScript code, it is suggested you disable this option.

4. In the Document Structuring Conventions (DSC) section, enable the Process DSC Comments option to have Acrobat Distiller preserve DSC information from the original PostScript file. With this default option, you can include any of the following:
   - **Log DSC Warnings** Choose this option, and Acrobat Distiller displays warning messages about troublesome DSC comments in the original PostScript file and creates a text file log of these errors. Choose this option if the files you process with this job option contain DSC comments.
   - **Preserve EPS Information From DSC** Choose this option when processing EPS files with DSC comments and the DSC comments will be preserved when the file converts to PDF.
   - **Preserve OPI Comments** Choose this option, and when Acrobat processes files with FPO (For Placement Only) images or comments, they will be replaced with the high-resolution image located on servers supporting OPI (Open Press Interface) versions 1.3 and 2.0.
   - **Preserve Document Information From DSC** Choose this option and Acrobat Distiller includes the title, creation date, and time information when you use this job option to convert files to PDF. When the PDF file opens, this information appears in the Document Summary and can be accessed by choosing File | Document Summary.
   - **Resize Page And Center Artwork For EPS Files** Choose this option when processing EPS files, and Acrobat Distiller resizes the page to the document artwork and centers the artwork.
5. After setting the Advanced Options, you can click another tab to modify different settings or save the job option file, as covered in the following section.

Set PDF/X Options (Professional Only)

If you own Acrobat Professional, you have an additional tab from which you can modify PDF/X settings. PDF/X (Portable Document Format Exchange) is an ISO standard that combines all criteria for the PDF document in a single file. To set PDF/X options for a conversion setting, follow these steps:

1. Choose a Conversion Settings option to modify and open the Adobe PDF Settings dialog box, following the steps presented earlier in this chapter.
2. Click the PDF/X tab to open the PDF/X section of the Adobe PDF Settings dialog box shown here:

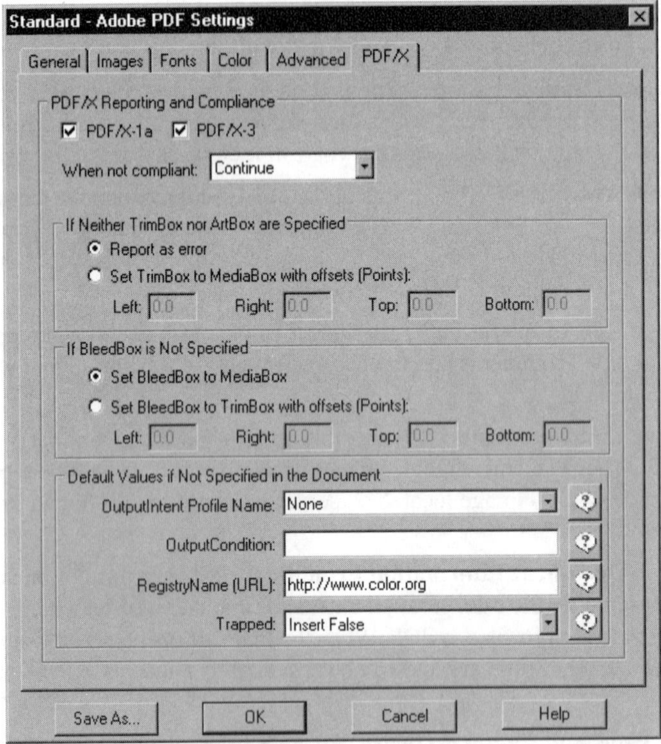

3. Choose PDF/X-1A, PDF/X-3, or both. This option produces a report that determines whether the document is compliant with the selected option. When you choose both, a single report combining both PDF/X options is produced.
4. Click the triangle to the right of the When Not Compliant field and choose one of the following options:
   - **Continue** Creates the PDF file anyway and lists the compliancy issues in the report.
   - **Cancel Job** Aborts creation of the PDF file when there are compliancy issues. If both options are selected and the PostScript is only compliant with one PDF/X option, a PDF file is created for the PDF/X option with which the original file is compliant. The problems with the other PDF/X option are noted in the report.

5. In the If Neither TrimBox Nor ArtBox Are Specified section, choose from the following options:
   - **Report As Error** If neither option is specified in the PostScript document, this is reported as an error.
   - **Set TrimBox To MediaBox With Offset(Points)** Choose this option and four fields become available, enabling you to enter the desired values. The TrimBox is always the same size, or smaller than the MediaBox.
6. In the If BleedBox is Not Specified section, choose one of the following options:
   - **Set BleedBox To MediaBox** Sets the BleedBox dimension equal to the MediaBox dimensions.
   - **Set BleedBox Offset To TrimBox(Points)** Enables four fields that let you set the offset from BleedBox size to TrimBox size. The BleedBox is always the same size or larger than the TrimBox.
7. Click the triangle to the right of the OutputIntentProfile name field and choose an option. This option is required and indicates the printing condition under which the document will be printed if this option is not included with the PostScript file from which the PDF document is being created.
8. Enter text in the OutputCondition field (optional) to describe the intended printing condition.
9. In the RegistryName(URL): field, accept the default entry or enter a URL for the web site associated with the ICC profile associated with the document. A URL is provided by default for the ICC registry names associated with the document. More information about the ICC registry can be found at the URL provided.
10. Click the triangle to the right of the Trapped field and choose an option for color trapped state. This is required for PDF/X compliance. Choose from Leave Undefined (when the PostScript document specifies this option), Insert True, or Insert False.

12

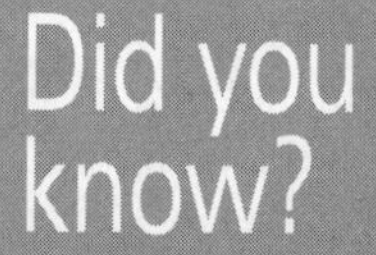

Understanding Gradients

When graphic designers create illustrations in programs like Adobe Illustrator, Macromedia FreeHand, or CorelDraw, they often blend two or more colors to create a colorful blend. The gradient can be linear, rectangular, or conical to conform to the contours of the object the gradient is being used to fill. Gradients often use a large number of steps for blending to create an eye-pleasing shape with no banding. If you use PostScript files that were created by graphic designers using illustration software, choose the Convert Gradients To Smooth Shades option as outlined in the "Set Advanced Options" section of this chapter; otherwise, the image may appear banded when converted to PDF format.

Save Conversion Settings

After you modify an Adobe PDF Settings option, you can save it for future use. To save a conversion setting and close the Adobe PDF Settings dialog box, follow these steps:

1. Click the Save As button to open the Save Adobe PDF Settings As dialog box. By default, the Adobe PDF Settings option you use to create the new setting is appended by the next available number—for example, Standard(1).
2. Accept the default filename or enter a different name. Choose a name that reflects the intended source of documents you create with this conversion setting. For example, if the documents you create with this job option will be included on a CD-ROM, enter **CD-ROM**.
3. Click Save.

After you save the new job option, it appears on the Acrobat Distiller Default Settings menu. If you use Microsoft Office applications, the job option appears on the Adobe PDF Conversion Settings menu.

PDF Font Considerations

When you create a document in an authoring application, a little time spent choosing fonts will produce a better-looking document. Try to avoid highly stylized fonts with long swooping curves. They may look great printed, but oftentimes they do not display properly on monitors. If you choose a large bold font, the center of characters such as *a, o,* and *p* fill in and are not legible unless the user greatly magnifies them when viewing them as a PDF file. When you are in doubt whether a particular font style will display well in Acrobat, create a test document in the authoring application using every character from the font set in both upper and lowercase. Convert the document to PDF format and view the document in Acrobat at 100 percent magnification. One look and you will know whether to use the font or not.

You should also be careful of mixing fonts. If you create a document with multiple fonts, make sure the finished document is aesthetically pleasing. A document with multiple fonts can be hard to read. The actual number of fonts you can safely include in a document is a matter of personal taste and document size. For example, creating a single-page document with more than two fonts would not be a good idea. Also, when you create a document with multiple fonts and embed those fonts, the file size of the document increases dramatically.

When you create a document for print, a service center charges you for every color you use. However, this is not an issue when you create a document for viewing onscreen. You can add a little bit of color to text headings to draw a viewer's attention and spice things up. The tasteful use of color with text can dramatically increase the effectiveness of your document. If you create a document for viewing over the Web, make sure you choose your text colors from the 216-color Web-safe palette.

When you create a PDF document, you view the output on your computer and everything looks as you planned. The images are crystal clear, and the text is sharp and stylish. However, if your intended audience does not have the fonts used in the document installed on their computer, the document will look quite different. When you do not embed fonts and viewers do not have the document fonts installed on their system, Acrobat substitutes either the AdobeSansMM font or the AdobeSerifMM font. *MM* is an acronym for Multiple Master. Through the use of these fonts, Acrobat tries to create a reasonable facsimile of the original font while maintaining the width of the original font to preserve line breaks from the original document.

Embed Fonts

When you embed fonts, you can rest assured that viewers of your document will see the document as you intended. Embedding several fonts, however, can dramatically increase the file size of the document. You can embed fonts when you set Adobe PDF Settings for Acrobat Distiller. Make sure you do not violate any font licensing agreement when you decide to embed a specific font. For more information on embedding fonts when setting Adobe PDF Settings, refer to the "Set Fonts Options" section of this chapter.

You should embed fonts whenever you need the published document to look identical to the original. If, for example, your clients use a font as part of their corporation identity package, embed the font. If you use a stylized font that is difficult for Acrobat to re-create with a MM font, then embed the font.

Subset a Font

When you embed a font, you can reduce the file size by *subsetting* the font. When you subset a font, you embed only the characters used in the document. You can have Acrobat subset a font when the percentage of characters used drops below a certain value. By default Acrobat subsets a font when the percentage of characters used drops below 100 percent. To subset a font, click the Fonts tab in the Adobe PDF setting you are modifying, choose the option to subset fonts, and then specify the value that Acrobat uses as its signal to embed the entire font set or subset the font set.

The only disadvantage to subsetting a font is when you edit a document with subset fonts. If you do not have the font set installed on your computer, you have to unembed the font before you can use the text tools to edit the document.

Preview an Unembedded Font in Acrobat

If you have any question as to whether you should embed a font or not, create a test document in an authoring application and view it in Acrobat without using *local fonts*. When you view a PDF document in Acrobat without using local fonts, fonts installed on your system are disregarded and Acrobat goes into font substitution mode. To preview an unembedded font in Acrobat, follow these steps:

1. Create a document in an authoring application using every character of the font set in both upper- and lowercase.

2. Choose Adobe PDF from the application Print command, or, if you are in a Microsoft Office application, choose AdobePDF to convert the document to PDF format.
3. Edit the conversion settings, and in the Fonts section, deselect the Embed All Fonts option, as outlined previously in the "Set Fonts Options" section of this chapter.
4. Convert the document to PDF format.
5. Launch Acrobat and open the document.
6. Choose Advanced | Use Local Fonts.

When this option is deselected (unchecked), Acrobat substitutes document fonts using MM fonts. You see what the document looks like on a viewer's system without the document fonts installed. When you deselect Use Local Fonts, you can also print a copy of the document using the Adobe substituted fonts. If the test document is not satisfactory, embed the fonts when you create the final document. Figure 12-2 shows two PDFs with several lines of different fonts

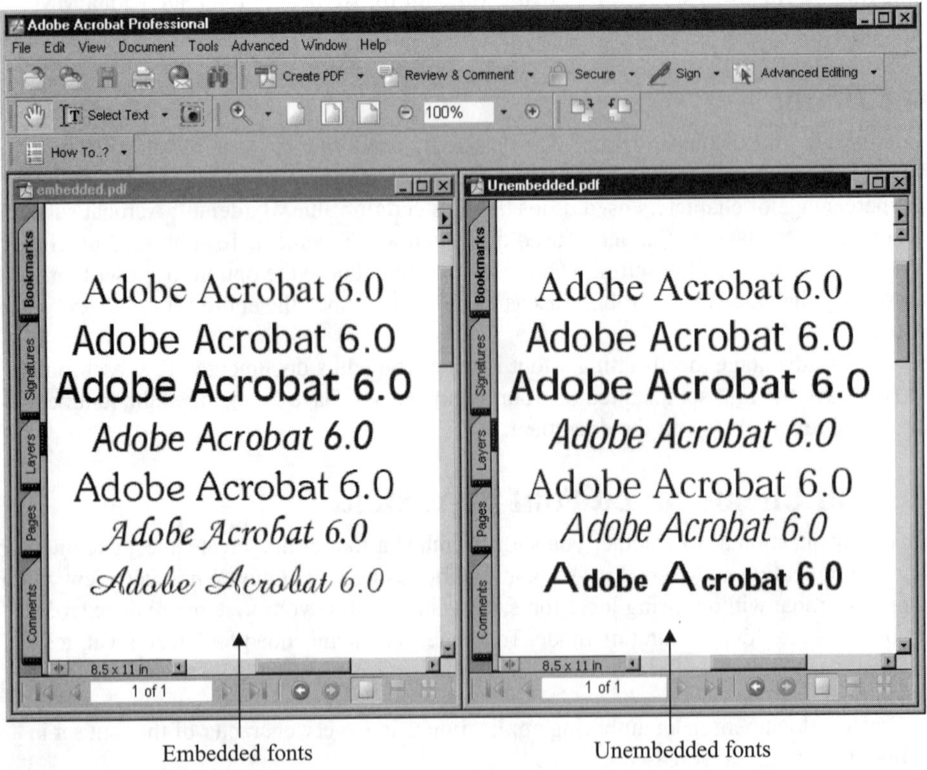

FIGURE 12-2 Decide whether or not to embed a font by deselecting the Use Local Fonts option.

viewed side-by-side in Acrobat. All fonts used in the document in the left window were embedded when the file was converted to PDF; the fonts of the document in the right window were not embedded when the file was converted to PDF. When this screenshot was created, the Use Local Fonts command was in effect.

Summary

In this chapter, you learned about tagged PDF documents and how to optimize documents for intended destinations. You also learned to modify default Adobe PDF settings to suit the documents you create and save the new settings. The topic of fonts and whether to embed them was also presented. In the next chapter, you'll learn to create PDF documents for the Web.

Chapter 13 Create PDF Documents for the Web

How to...

- View PDF documents in a Web browser
- Use the Acrobat plug-in
- Prepare PDF documents for the Internet
- Create links to web sites
- Work with comments online
- Use PDF forms on the Internet

The power of Adobe Acrobat is not limited to distributing documents within an organization or sharing documents with clients. You can also use Adobe Acrobat to create documents for a web site. With Adobe Acrobat, you can create a PDF document for product brochures, product manuals, and other types of presentations. After you optimize the document for fast Web viewing and post it on your or your client's web site, visitors can view the document in their Web browsers. Adobe has an Acrobat plug-in that is compatible with most popular Web browsers. If a visitor to a Web browser does not have the Acrobat plug-in, he or she can download it for free from the Adobe web site.

In this chapter, you'll learn how to view PDF documents within a Web browser as well as prepare PDF documents for use on the Internet. Also covered are Web browser considerations and information about the Acrobat plug-in. You'll also learn how to work with PDF forms and edit documents in a Web browser.

View PDF Documents in a Web Browser

When you view non-HTML documents from a web site, your Web browser detects the document type and loads the necessary helper application so you can view the document in the Web browser. Depending on the type of document you view, the helper application (or *plug-in* as it's known to Web designers) may load within the browser or externally. Some applications give Web designers the freedom to embed a document and call up the plug-in interface within the HTML document or open it in an external window. When you view PDF documents from web sites, Acrobat appears in your Web browser. Figure 13-1 shows Acrobat as it appears in the Internet Explorer 6.0 browser. Notice the difference in the available tools and the absence of the Acrobat menu bar.

To open a PDF within a Web browser, you must specify the path to the document, which consists of the URL and the filename of the document, such as http://www.mysite.net/catalog.pdf. If the file is in the same domain or folder as the HTML document, you can specify a relative URL with just the folder name and the document name. For example, "pdfdocs/catalog.pdf," where *pdfdocs* is the folder name and *catalog.pdf* is the file that opens when the link is clicked.

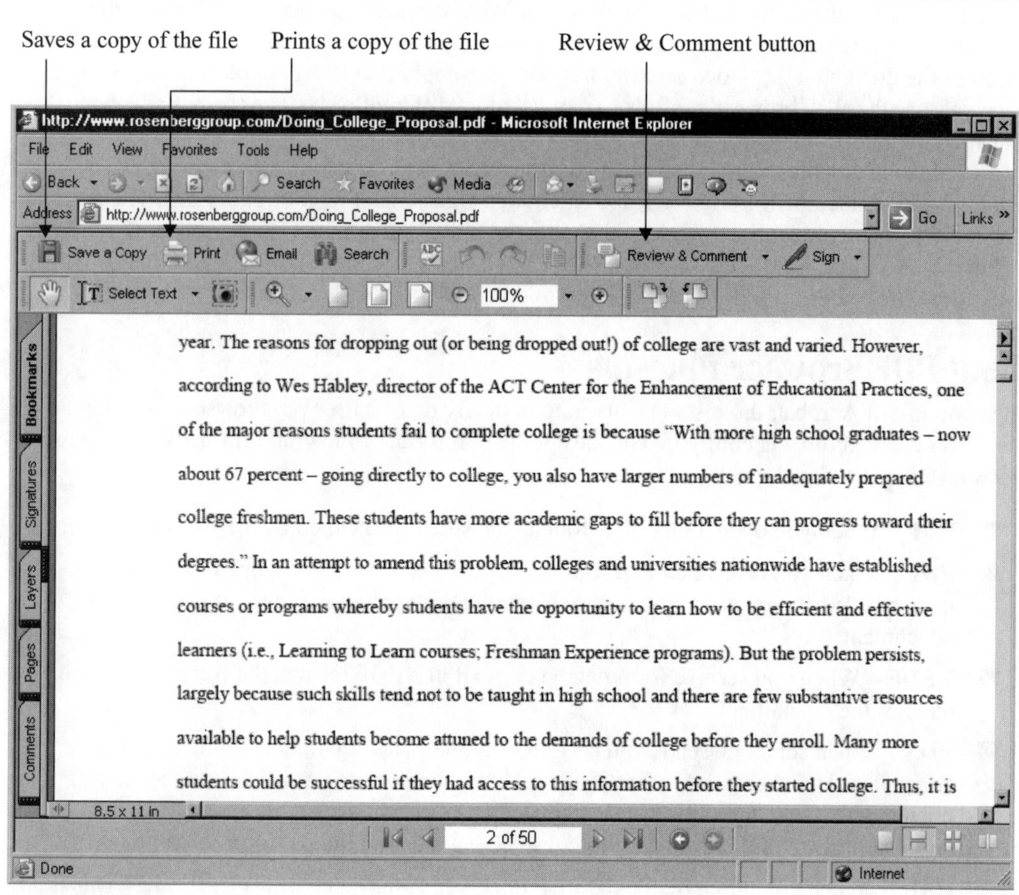

FIGURE 13-1 When you view a PDF document from a web site, you can view it within a Web browser.

When you view documents online, Acrobat provides you with a slightly different set of tools, as shown previously in Figure 13-1. You can select objects from the document, review and comment on the document, and digitally sign the document. Also notice that there are no menu commands, only the Acrobat tools and the Web browser controls. You only have tools to view the document, save a copy of the document, and annotate the document. The tools and menus in your Web browser, however, do not change. If you use the browser Print command to print the PDF document, it will not print correctly as the browser cannot interpret the binary format of the PDF. To print the PDF document, use the Print button in the Acrobat plug-in, previously shown in Figure 13-1.

After you have the document open within your Web browser, you can save a copy of the document for future use. After you save a copy of the document, you can use the Acrobat toolset to modify the document, provided security has not been applied to it. After you finish viewing a document, use the Web browser controls to navigate to a different web site or back to the page that called the PDF document.

You can also download PDF documents directly from the Internet to your hard drive. To download a PDF document using Netscape Navigator, right-click (Windows) or CTRL-click (Macintosh) the document link and then choose Save Link As from the Context menu. If you use Internet Explorer, right-click (Windows) or CTRL-click (Macintosh) the link and then choose Save Target As from the Context menu to download a PDF document.

About PDF Browser Plug-ins

When you install Acrobat, the install utility automatically detects the Web browsers installed on your system and Acrobat is configured as the application for the following *MIME (Multipurpose Internet Mail Extension)* types:

- **PDF** When you open a PDF file from a web site, it is handled by the Acrobat plug-in.
- **FDF** When you receive an FDF file as an e-mail attachment and open it, Acrobat launches. When you send your digital signature certificate via e-mail, it is an FDF attachment.
- **XFDF** When you receive form data via e-mail in XFDF format, the Acrobat program handles the attachment.
- **PDX** When someone sends you an Acrobat index via e-mail, double-clicking the attachment launches the Acrobat program. The Acrobat program also launches if you open a PDX file from within the Web browser. You cannot search a PDX file with the Acrobat plug-in as there is no option to select an index in the plug-in Search pane.
- **RMF** When you purchase locked PDF documents, the seller sends RMF files. This is the licensing information Web Buy uses to unlock the document.

If you install Acrobat on a new system, be sure to install your Web browser first. If you install Acrobat first, in order to view PDF documents in a Web browser, you have to manually configure each Web browser on your system or reinstall Acrobat and perform a custom installation choosing only the Web browser plug-in.

Download Adobe Reader

A large majority of Internet users already have a version of Adobe Acrobat, or the new Adobe Reader installed on their systems. If, however, you post a PDF document at your web site or at a client's web site whose visitors do not have Adobe Reader, they will not be able to view your document. In order to accommodate web site visitors who do not have a copy of Adobe Reader, you can include a link to the Adobe Web page where visitors to the web site can download a free copy of Adobe Reader. The following URL takes the viewer to the Adobe Reader: http://www.adobe .com/ products/acrobat/readstep2.html

Distribute Adobe Reader

You can post Adobe Reader on a company intranet or local network. You can also distribute the Adobe Reader installation software on a CD-ROM, provided you accept the conditions of the Acrobat electronic *EULA (End User License Agreement)* and the Supplement to Permit Distribution. When users install the Adobe Reader, they will also be prompted to accept the conditions of the EULA.

You cannot distribute Adobe Reader from a web site. Adobe requires that any third-party web site must include a link to the Adobe Reader download page at http://www.adobe.com/ products/ acrobat/readstep2.html. You can include an Adobe Get Reader logo or an Adobe PDF logo, as shown in the following illustration. Download both logos after you read the information contained in the Get Adobe Reader and Adobe PDF logos section at http://www.adobe.com/ products/acrobat/distribute.html.

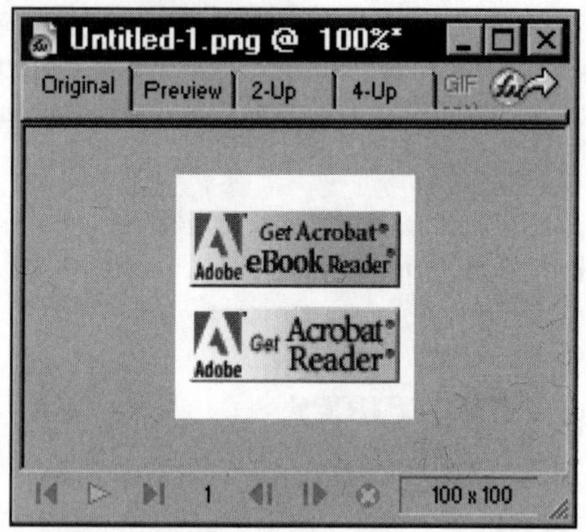

Reviewing Documents Online (Windows Only)

When you initiate a browser-based review, you can upload a PDF document for review to a Web server or use an existing PDF document at a Web server as the basis for a review. After choosing the document for review, you send an e-mail message to your reviewer that contains an FDF setup file. Reviewers open the FDF attachment, which opens a copy of the PDF document in the reviewer's browser and configures the review settings. Reviewers cannot open the PDF document at the Web server and participate in the review.

Reviewers can annotate the document online or download the PDF for review offline. Comments can only be modified by the original author, but reviewers using Acrobat Standard or Acrobat Professional can respond to comments. To set up a browser-based review, follow these steps:

1. Specify the server for the browser-based review as outlined in the upcoming "Configure Reviewing Preferences" section.
2. Open the PDF document and then choose File | Upload for Review.
3. In the Upload for Review dialog box, specify the URL for the browser-based review or the server folder to which you want the document saved and then click Upload.
4. In the Start Browser-Based Review dialog box, enter the e-mail addresses of your reviewers, modify the subject description and message text as desired, and then click Send.

After you start a browser-based review, an FDF file is sent to each reviewer. The default instructions tell your reviewers to open the attachment, which opens in the reviewer's Web browser, the PDF document you uploaded to the server. After the document opens, Acrobat is configured for review.

NOTE *If the document you want to review is already on the server, open the document in your Web browser and then choose Review & Comment | Invite Others To Review.*

Configure Reviewing Preferences

You configure Reviewing preferences to designate the type of server the PDF documents download from. To configure preferences for sharing comments online, follow these steps:

1. Choose Edit | Preferences to open the Preferences dialog box.
2. Choose Reviewing to open the dialog box, as shown next.

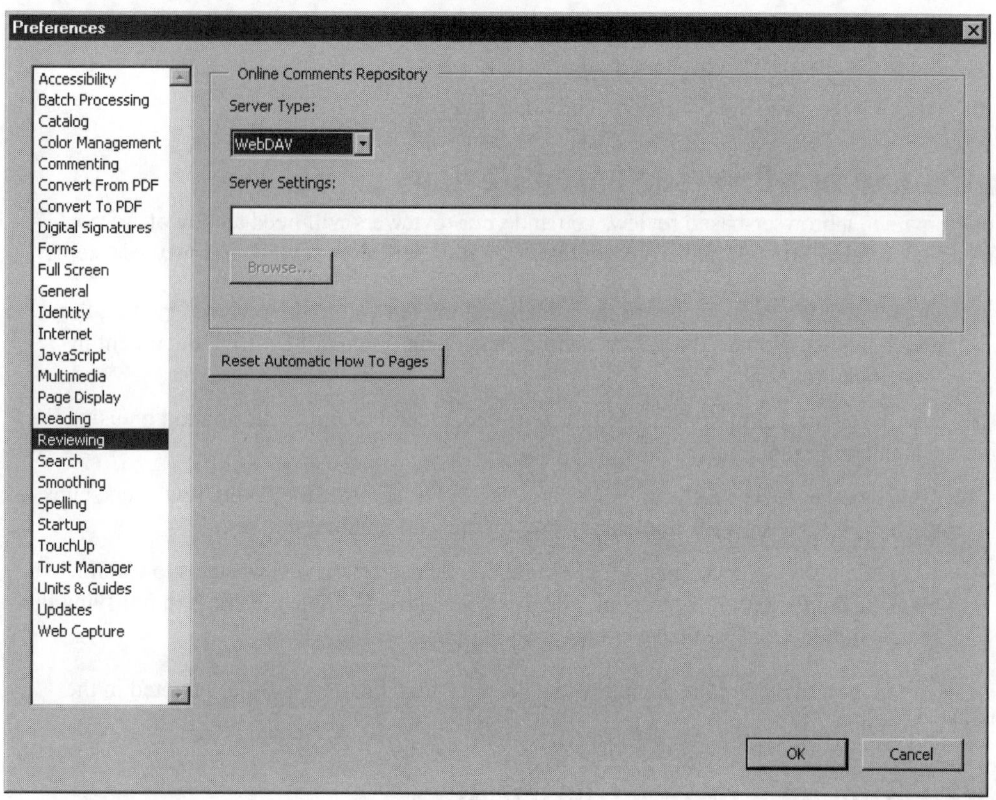

3. Click the triangle to the right of the Server Type field and choose the option that matches your server type. If you use Acrobat with the Windows platform, you have five choices: Database, Network Folder, None, Web Discussions, and *WebDAV (Web-based Distributed Authority and Versioning)*. If you use the Macintosh version of Acrobat, you have three choices: Network Folder, None, and WebDAV. If you choose an option that requires an Internet connection, the Server Settings field becomes available. If you use Web Discussions, you have to configure Internet Explorer as well. If you choose Network Folder, the Browse button becomes available. Click the button and navigate to the network folder that contains the documents for review.

4. Enter the URL in the Server Settings field. If your online collaboration is handled via a Web server, contact the administrator to see which server type is used. You will also need the URL if the connection requires a Web address. Furthermore, if you use Database,

WebDAV, or Web Discussions, these server types have additional parameters that require the assistance of the Web server administrator.

5. Click OK to close the dialog box and apply the changes.

Participate in a Browser-Based Review

To participate in a browser-based review, you and your reviewers will need a copy of Acrobat Standard or Acrobat Professional. To participate in a browser-based review, follow these steps:

1. Open the FDF attachment with the e-mail that invited you to the review. Opening the attachment configures the review settings and opens a copy of the PDF document in your Web browser.
2. Use the Commenting tools to mark up the document. For more information on using the Commenting tools, refer to Chapter 10.
3. To view other reviewers' comments or to send your comments to other reviewers, click the Send And Receive Comments button on the Commenting toolbar.
4. After adding your comments to the document, you can set the review status to Completed by choosing Review & Comment | Set Review Status | Completed and then notifying the review initiator that you have completed your phase of the review.

If desired, you can add your comments to a browser-based review offline, as noted in the following section.

Work Offline in a Browser-Based Review

If you prefer to use the full version of Acrobat Standard or Acrobat Professional to add comments to a document you have been invited to review, you can do so by working offline. When you work offline, you have the full resources of Acrobat at your disposal. After commenting offline, you log onto the Internet and send your comments to the server. To add your comments to a browser-based review offline, follow these steps:

1. After opening the attachment to launch the online review, click the Save And Work Offline button to open the Save And Work Offline dialog box.
2. Navigate to the folder in which you want the document saved and then click Save.
3. Launch Acrobat and open the saved document.
4. Add your comments to the document.
5. After marking up the document, click the Go Back Online button in the Commenting toolbar to open the document in your default Web browser.
6. Click the Send And Receive Comments button to add your comments to the server.

Prepare PDF Documents for the Internet

When you prepare a document for the Internet, the first step is to optimize the document in the authoring application, as discussed in Chapter 12. The most important consideration in optimizing a document for the Internet is to get the file size as small as possible. Remember to resample all images to a resolution of 72 dpi and enable Fast Web View (the default option with all conversion settings) when converting the document to PDF format. If you modify the converted document, you have to use the Save As command to enable Fast Web View, as outlined in the upcoming "Save the Document for the Internet" section.

You should also consider document security issues, document description information, and the view by which the first page of the document opens when a viewer downloads it. If you include document description information, the web site visitor can get an idea of the information included in the document. Add document security if you want to prevent web site visitors from extracting content from the document or printing the document. If you assign security to the document, be sure to include a permissions password. For more information about Acrobat Security, refer to Chapter 11. For more information on modifying the document description and document open options, refer to Chapter 4. Note that if you choose the Open option of Open In Full Screen Mode, the document will not be displayed in full-screen mode when viewed in a Web browser.

But that's only the beginning of your task. After you convert the original document to PDF format, you apply the finishing touches in Acrobat.

How to ... Create Links to Web Sites

When you create PDF documents for viewing from a web site, you may need to create one or more links to other web sites. If you have several interlinked PDF documents, you'll also need to create some sort of link back to the HTML pages of the web site. You can ask visitors to rely on the Back button of the Web browser. However, if a viewer has navigated through several documents, clicking the Back button several times to exit Acrobat and return to the HTML portion of the web site can be annoying. You can create a link to a web site using the Links tool. Define the area of the document that will link to an external web site with the Links tool, and for the link action choose Open A Web Page. Enter the URL for the web site to which you want to link and you're good to go.

Add a Base URL to the Document

If all the Web links in a document are within the same web site, you can enter the relative path for the Web link. However, if all of your links point to another site, you need to enter the absolute path to the URL. If all of your Web links are to the same external site, you can simplify matters by adding a base URL to the document. When you add a base URL, you only need to enter the relative path to the document you want to open; Acrobat automatically links the relative path to the base URL. To specify a base URL for the document, follow these steps:

1. Choose File | Document Properties | Advanced to open the Advanced section of the Document Properties dialog box.
2. Enter the base URL of the document in the Base URL field, as shown here:

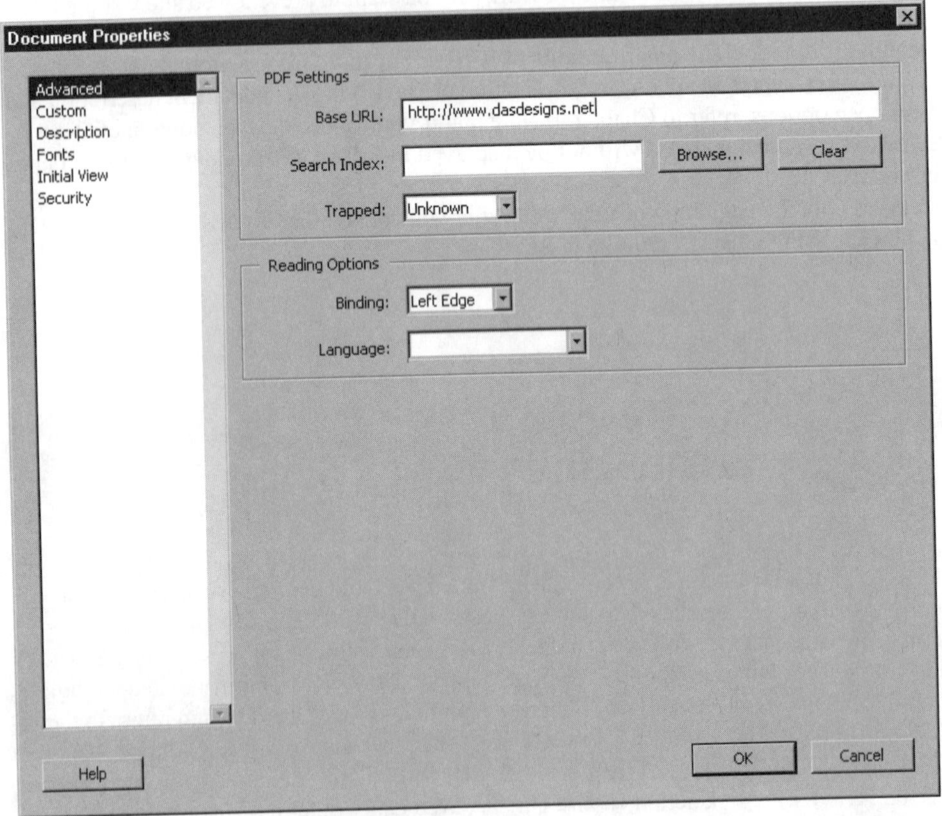

3. Click OK to close the dialog box.

After you set the base URL for the document, whenever you use the Open A Web Page action to set a URL for a link or button, enter the relative URL for the Web page you want to open, and Acrobat adds the base URL to the Web link using the proper HTML nomenclature. For example, if your base URL is http://www.mysite.com and you want to open the about.htm page, enter **about.htm** to have Acrobat add the base URL when you save the document. In this case, the relative path to the document in the directory structure at the Web server is **about.htm** and the absolute path to the document is **http://www.mysite.com/about.htm**, which is how Acrobat configures the link when you add the base URL to the document.

Create Named Destinations and Links

When you create links from an HTML document to a PDF document, the link destination can be the document itself or a named destination within the document. A *named destination* is a named link to a specific location within a PDF document. When you create a destination, you can change the view to zoom in on a specific image or paragraph within a document.

You can link to a named destination from within an HTML document. Create a named destination for each part of the PDF document that you want to link to from within an HTML document. For example, if you post a PDF product manual on the Web, you can create a named destination for each product. Remember to use proper naming conventions for Web browsers as you will be using each destination name as part of a Web link. With this in mind, use standard DOS conventions when specifying a name for the destination. In other words, the destination name should be eight characters or less with no spaces. Remember, before you can create a named destination, you must first scan the document for existing destinations, as outlined in Chapter 8. For more information on creating a link to a named destination, refer to the "Create HTML Hyperlinks to Named Destinations" section of this chapter.

You should also create a link within the document that takes viewers back to the HTML page after they have perused the information. You may also need to create links from within the document to other Web pages. You can create text links or use images within the document as links. If you own Acrobat Professional, you can also create a button in the PDF document that acts as a link. However, if you create several buttons within a document, you increase the file size, which is not a desirable outcome when creating documents for the Web. For more information on creating links, refer to Chapter 7. 13

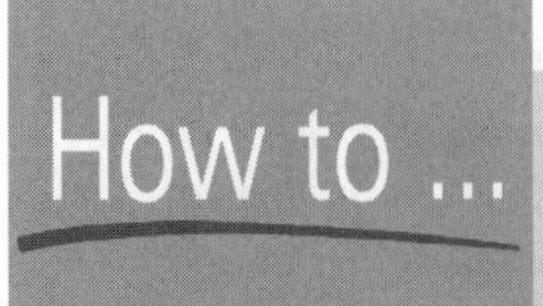

Create an E-Mail Link

When you create a PDF document for a web site, you can create an e-mail link within a PDF document. When viewers of your PDF document click the e-mail link, their default e-mail application opens with a blank message window addressed to the e-mail address of your choice. To create an e-mail link in a PDF document, select the Link tool and define the target for your e-mail link. In the Create Link dialog box, click the Open A Web Page radio button and in the Address field enter **mailto:** followed by the desired recipient's e-mail address—for example: **mailto:JoeSmith@Webserver.com**.

Create a Welcome Page

If you have a large collection of PDF documents at a web site, you can link the documents together using PDF navigation. When you do this, create a welcome page in PDF format that explains what the document collection is about. On the welcome page you can create a menu using the Link tool to create links to the other PDF documents. When you create a welcome page in this manner, as long as the other PDF documents are in the same folder, you can use the Open File action to open a specific document when the user clicks the link.

You can also create a welcome page using HTML. Create hyperlinks on the welcome page for each document, as outlined in the upcoming "Create HTML Hyperlinks to PDF Documents" section of this chapter.

NOTE

When you create navigation for a large PDF document collection at a web site, after the viewers have followed several links within the document collection, they may have a hard time navigating back to the HTML section of the site. Remember to include a link in each PDF document back to the web site home page or create a PDF navigation menu with links to the major areas of the web site.

Use PDF Forms on the Internet

You can use PDF forms to get feedback from visitors of a web site, to conduct an online opinion poll, to build a customer database, and much more. When you use Acrobat Professional to create a PDF form for the Internet, create a Submit button to forward the information to the site Webmaster or site owner.

After filling in the form, the user clicks the Submit button to submit the information to the server. Some Web-hosting services have preformatted CGI scripts that you can modify to forward form results. CGI scripts can be used to password-protect web sites, create guest books, and much more. In this case, you need a CGI script that collects the information from the PDF form and forwards it to a specified person. In Acrobat Professional, create a Submit button that links to the Web server script. With most Web servers, CGI scripts are stored within a folder named CGIbin. Check with the Web hosting service's technical support staff for the relative path to the forwarding CGI script. For more information on creating PDF forms with Acrobat Professional, refer to Chapter 14.

TIP

In lieu of using a CGI script, you can forward the form results to an e-mail address. After you create the Submit button in Acrobat Professional, choose the Submit Form action. Click the Add button and instead of entering the URL to a Web page, enter ***mailto:*** *followed by the e-mail address of the recipient. When a visitor to the web site fills in the form and clicks the Submit button, the viewer's default e-mail application opens. The viewer can add a message or send the e-mail as is. When the recipient receives the e-mail, the form results will be attached as an HTML, FDF, XFDF file, or the complete PDF document, depending on which option you selected with the Submit Form action.*

Save the Document for the Internet

Before you upload the document to a web site, double-check your work. Make sure all links function properly. If any of the document links are to a web site, make sure you have the correct URL. There's nothing more frustrating for a Web visitor than trying to open a link and getting a Not Found error. Remember to test your links in a browser; otherwise, Acrobat will append the current document with the Web page specified in the link.

If all the links are formatted properly, choose Advanced | PDF Optimizer. With PDF Optimizer, you can remove any bookmarks or links with invalid destinations and reduce the file size by specifying compression settings for images in the document and removing unused objects. If you created any named destinations that you intend to use as link destinations from an HTML or other PDF document, disable the Remove Unused Named Destinations option in the Clean Up tab of the PDF Optimizer, shown here:

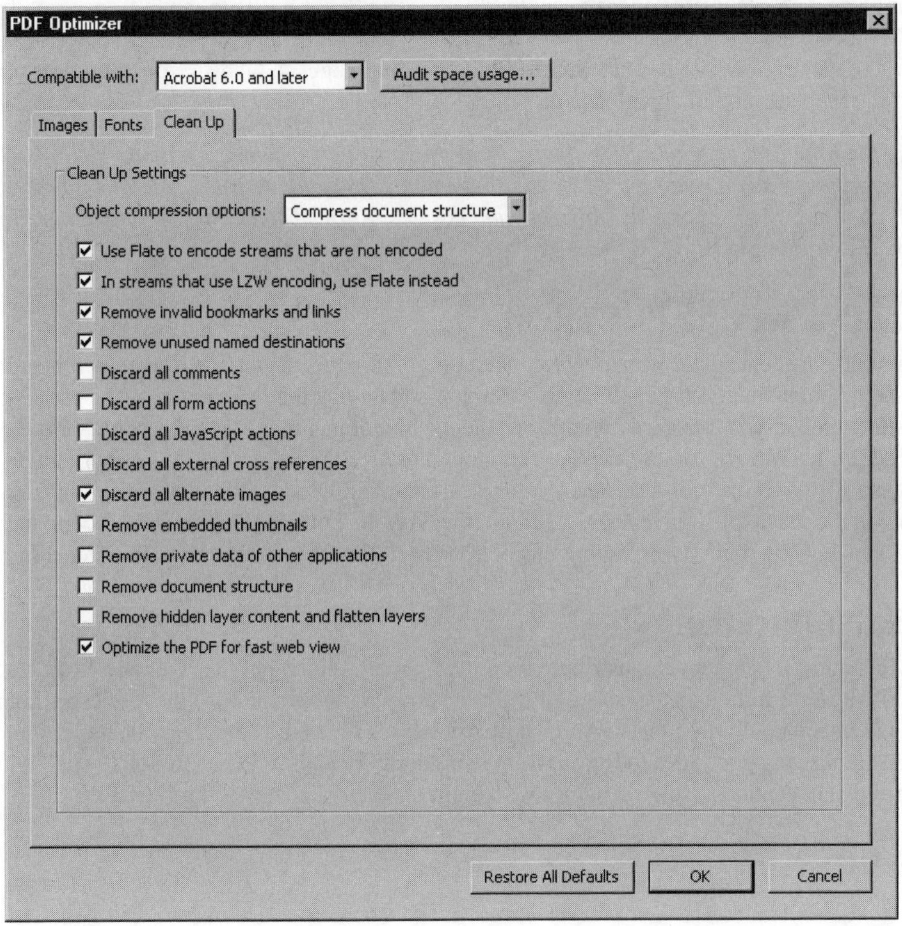

After you finalize the document in Acrobat, save it optimized for fast Web viewing with a Web-hosting service that supports *byteserving,* as outlined in the upcoming "Create Byteserving PDF Files" section of this chapter.

About Byteserving

When you view a PDF document optimized for fast Web viewing from a web site that supports byteserving, you see a page load almost immediately. If you have ever waited for a 350-page PDF document to download before viewing a single page, you realize the value of fast Web viewing. When you optimize a document for fast Web viewing, you create a document that can be downloaded a page at a time, provided the hosting service of the web site supports byteserving. The web site visitor does not have to do anything different to have the pages served up one at a time. Unless the user has disabled the Allow Fast Web View option in the Internet section of Acrobat Preferences, Acrobat or Adobe Reader communicates directly with the Web server. If, for example, a web site visitor opens a lengthy PDF document, it opens to the link specified from the HTML document or linking PDF document. If the viewer enters **page 50** in the Navigation window, the viewer does not have to wait for the preceding pages to load; Acrobat requests page 50 from the Web server and downloads it.

After the first page of a PDF file optimizes for fast Web viewing downloads, Acrobat continues downloading the rest of the document by default. To disable this option choose Edit | Preferences | Internet and deselect Allow Speculative Downloading In The Background.

Create Byteserving PDF Files

Even though you specify fast Web viewing when optimizing the conversion of the document to PDF from within an authoring application, after you add navigation links and other interactive features in Acrobat, you must once again save the document in a manner that produces a file optimized for the Web. If you use the Save command to save the document to file, Acrobat does not create a file optimized for fast Web viewing. To create a PDF document optimized for fast Web viewing, choose File | Save As. By default, the Save As command optimizes a document for fast Web viewing unless you disable this option by editing Acrobat General Preferences.

Name the Document

When you name a document for distribution on the Internet, remember that Web browsers react differently. Refrain from using spaces within a filename and always include the .pdf extension. Web browsers are configured to use Acrobat or Adobe Reader as the default application to view PDF files. It is also a good idea to refrain from using long filenames. When in doubt, stick with DOS naming conventions using filenames with eight characters or less and no spaces.

TIP *When you create a document for the Internet and you want the smallest possible file size, choose File | Reduce File Size. This opens a dialog box in which you choose the version of Acrobat for which you want the file optimized. Choosing an earlier version of Acrobat will result in a smaller file size. Do not choose an earlier version of Acrobat if you have added features such as page transitions, which are supported in Acrobat 6.0 only.*

Combine HTML and PDF Files

When you create PDF documents that will be viewed from a web site, use HTML pages as the basis for the web site and create links from within the HTML pages to a PDF document. After you create the HTML pages for your web site, you need to create the links that will open the PDF document in the web site visitor's browser. You can link directly to a PDF document or you can link to a named destination within a PDF document. You can also create links from within PDF documents to web sites.

Create HTML Hyperlinks to PDF Documents

After you create your Web pages, you then need to create hyperlinks to open the PDF documents within the web site visitor's browser. As long as the PDF documents are stored at the same web site as the HTML documents, you need to enter only the relative path to the document when creating the hyperlink. If the PDF documents are in the same folder as the HTML pages, your hyperlink is equal to the filename of the PDF document followed by the .pdf extension. The following example shows a text link to a PDF document. Refer to your HTML editing software documentation for more information on creating hyperlinks.

```
<a href="empman.pdf">Employee Manual </a>
```

Create HTML Hyperlinks to Named Destinations

If the PDF documents you create for Web viewing have named destinations, you can create links that open directly to the named destination. When the viewer clicks a link to a named destination, Acrobat launches in the viewer's Web browser, and the document opens to the named destination rather than the first page of the document. To create a link to a named destination, follow these steps:

1. Create the HTML page in your HTML editor.
2. Create a hyperlink to the named destination. You format a hyperlink to a named destination the same way as a link to a bookmark within an HTML page. The hyperlink (href) is equal to the filename of the document followed by the extension, which is then followed by the number sign (#) and the name of the destination exactly as it appears in the PDF document. Refer to your HTML editing-software user manual for more

information on creating hyperlinks. The following example shows a text hyperlink to a named destination (Cat1) within a PDF document (mydoc.pdf). When you create the hyperlink, make sure you use the proper case for the named destination; otherwise, the document will open at the first page rather than the named destination. Also refrain from using any spaces when entering a name for a named destination that will be used on the Web. For more information on named destinations, see Chapter 8.

```
<a href="mydoc.pdf#Cat1">Catalog Number 1 </a>
```

Linking to a named destination is not supported by some browsers. If your viewing audience is likely to have older Web browsers or Web browsers tailored for an Internet Service Provider, add a note telling viewers which Web browsers the document is optimized for and provide a link where viewers can download the Web browser. Also, tell your viewers they will need Adobe Reader 4.0 or better to view the document properly and provide a link to download the proper version.

Create and Distribute PDF Documents via E-Mail

As you have learned throughout the course of this book, Acrobat PDF documents can be shared with anyone who has Acrobat or Adobe Reader installed. PDF documents are often referred to as *e-paper,* or electronic paper, if you will. What better way to share an electronic document than sending it via electronic mail (e-mail). In Chapter 5, you learned to convert a document from a Microsoft Office application to PDF format and e-mail it to an associate. You can also e-mail any document that you create or append within Acrobat. After you digitally sign a PDF file and add your comments or otherwise mark up a PDF document, you can send it via e-mail without leaving Acrobat by following these steps:

1. Log on to your Internet Service Provider.
2. From within Acrobat, choose File | EMail. After choosing this menu command, Acrobat launches your system default e-mail application.
3. Within the e-mail composition window, enter any message to accompany the file and then send it. Acrobat automatically sends the PDF document as an e-mail attachment.

It is a smart idea to save the document before e-mailing it. Acrobat uses a good bit of your system resources. Adding the e-mail application to the tasks the system is already processing may exceed the limits of your processing power and lock up your computer.

Summary

In this chapter, you learned to work with PDF documents for the Internet. You learned to create a browser-based review and participate in an online review by adding comments online, as well as while working offline. You learned to prepare documents for the Internet, create links to named destinations, save documents for fast Web viewing, and reduce file size of PDF documents. In the next chapter, you'll learn to create PDF forms with Acrobat Professional.

Part V

Create Enhanced PDFs with Acrobat Professional

Chapter 14 Create Forms

How to...

- Add form fields
- Define form properties
- Validate form fields
- Create form buttons
- Submit forms

Acrobat Professional makes it possible for you to add form fields to your PDF documents. You use form fields to retrieve information from readers of your PDF documents. You can also create forms for orders and questionnaires, and for getting viewer feedback from a web site. You can create forms that tally the results of an online purchase and then submit the order to the online seller.

In this chapter, you learn to use the basic Acrobat form elements to create your own forms. A *PDF form* is a compilation of form fields that you use to accumulate data from users. The fields can be used to collect text and numeric data. You can specify the field format to control the type and look of the data entered. Your form can be a combination of text boxes, check boxes, combo boxes, list boxes, radio buttons, and signature fields. You can create buttons for the users to submit the data or reset the form. If you create a form for Web use and the Web-host server supports *CGI (Common Gateway Interface)* scripting, you can have the form results forwarded to a web site or entered into a database.

Create a PDF Form

When you create a PDF form, you can scan an existing paper form into Acrobat and then use the tools from the Forms toolbar to create interactive form fields in the same position as the fields in the scanned document. When you create a form in this manner, you have the look and feel of the original form along with the interactivity of the Acrobat form fields. You can also create a form from scratch by creating the textual and graphic elements in an authoring application, converting the document to PDF format, and then using one of the tools from the Forms toolbar to create interactive form fields and elements. Figure 14-1 shows an IRS form that was created by scanning the document into Acrobat and then creating the individual form elements in Acrobat with the Forms tools.

Fill Out a PDF Form

When users decide to fill out a form, such as the one shown in Figure 14-1, they click inside a field with the Hand tool. When the user clicks inside the form field, the cursor becomes an I-beam indicating that data can be entered from the user's keyboard. To navigate to another field, the user can either click inside another field with the selected Hand tool or press TAB to advance to the next field. The user can correct an entry error by clicking inside the field with the Hand tool, clicking and dragging to select a word or letter that needs to be changed, and then entering

FIGURE 14-1 You can create PDF forms to collect data.

the new data. If the form is equipped with a properly programmed Reset button, the user can start over by clicking the button.

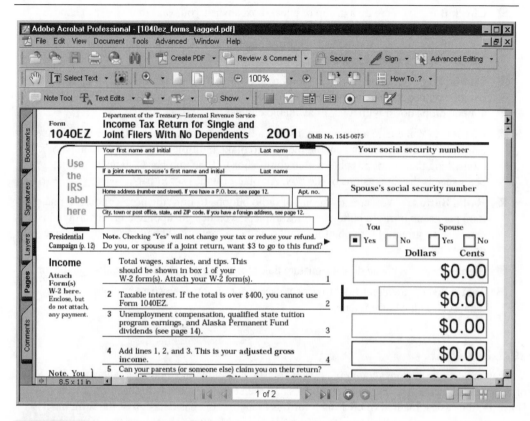

About Acrobat Form Fields

You use a tool from the Forms toolbar or choose Tools | Advanced Editing | Forms and then choose the desired tool to create fields in your PDF forms. Your choice of tool specifies what the field does or what type of data it accepts. You can assign actions to form fields to create a desired result when a user interacts with the form field. In Acrobat Professional, you can create any of the following types of form fields:

- **Button** You can create a text-only button, an icon-only button, or a button with both an icon and text. You can create an invisible button and place it over an existing graphic on a form that you scanned and converted to PDF format, which gives the appearance that the graphic is actually executing the action instead of the form field.

- **Check Box** You create a group of check boxes when you want to the user to choose from a set of options. For example, if you create a PDF questionnaire, you can create a series of check boxes for the user to select one or more items, such as the publications the he or she frequently reads.
- **Combo Box** When you create a combo box, you give the user a choice of options. A combo box is designated by a downward-pointing triangle. When the triangle is clicked, a menu drops down with a list of available choices.
- **List Box** You create a list box to display a list of available choices for the user. You can specify parameters that enable the user to make multiple selections from a list box (something that is not possible with a combo box). If the number of items in the list box exceeds the dimensions of the box, Acrobat provides scroll bars.
- **Radio Buttons** You create a group of radio buttons to limit the user's choice to one item per group of radio buttons. For example, if you design an online order form, you can create a group of radio buttons with credit card options. The user chooses the one option that applies.
- **Signature** You create digital signature fields for authorized users to digitally sign the form.
- **Text** You create a text field to accept user input or you can use a text field to display data, such as the current date.

Design a Form

You can create a form from scratch in any existing PDF document. Create the labels for all of your fields by creating read-only text boxes and then create the fields for user input data. However, the easiest method of creating a form is to lay out the basic design of the form in an authoring application and then to convert the file to PDF format. Then open the PDF file in Acrobat to add and format the form fields. Another alternative is to scan an existing form into Acrobat and create the necessary form fields.

Use the Layout Grid

Whether you decide to create your form from an existing document or lay out one from scratch, you can use the Layout Grid to provide a visual reference while creating and aligning form fields. To enable the grid shown in Figure 14-2, choose View | Grid.

Use the Snap To Grid Command

When you enable the Layout Grid, you can visually align and size items to intersecting grid points. Use any of the Viewing tools to zoom in on your work. For exact alignment and sizing, choose View | Snap To Grid. When you use this command, the Layout Grid develops a magnetic personality, and any object you create snaps to the grid points.

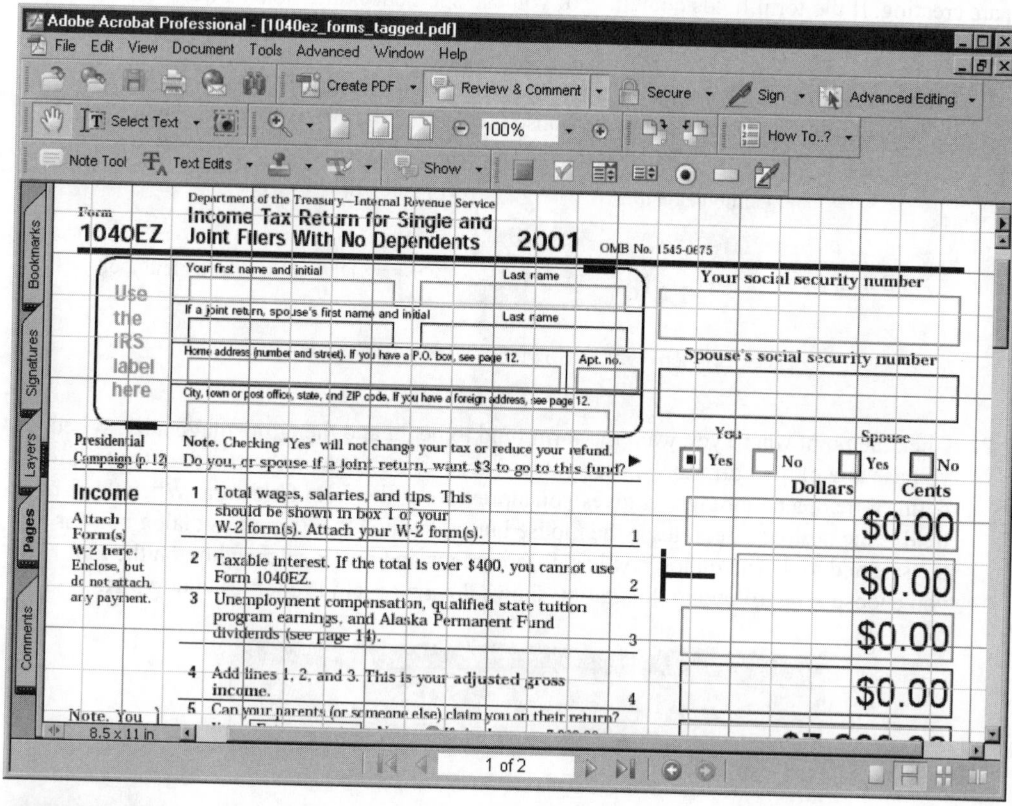

FIGURE 14-2 Use the Layout Grid to place and size form field elements precisely.

TIP *The default color and grid spacing work well in most instances; however, you can modify the color and spacing if they're not suited to your preferences. Choose Edit | Preferences and then click Units And Guides. Within this dialog box, you'll be able to modify grid spacing, color, width between lines, and so on.*

Create Form Fields

After you create the PDF document that is the basis for your form, you are ready to start creating interactive form fields. You create form fields by selecting the desired tool and defining the field area with the selected tool. After you define the field area, the properties dialog box for the selected form tool appears. From within this dialog box you name the field and define parameters. Each field type has its own parameters that you use to modify the field to suit the needs of the form you are creating. If the form fields contain text, you can spell check the field as well. To create a form field, follow these steps:

1. Select a tool from the Forms toolbar shown in the following illustration, or choose Tools | Advanced Editing | Forms and then choose the desired tool from the drop-down menu.

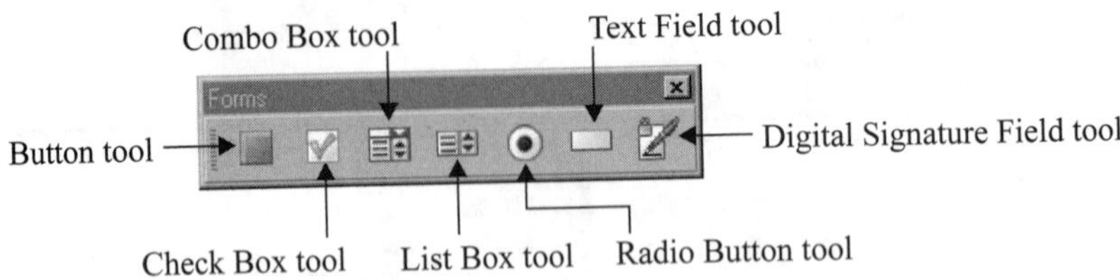

2. Click the point where you want the form field to begin and then drag diagonally. When you use one of the Form tools, your cursor becomes a crosshair. As you drag the tool to define a field, a bounding box gives you a preview of the form field area. When the form field is the desired size, release the mouse button to open the Properties dialog box for the selected tool. The dialog box has different tabs and options depending on the tool you choose. The following illustration shows the Text Field Properties dialog box:

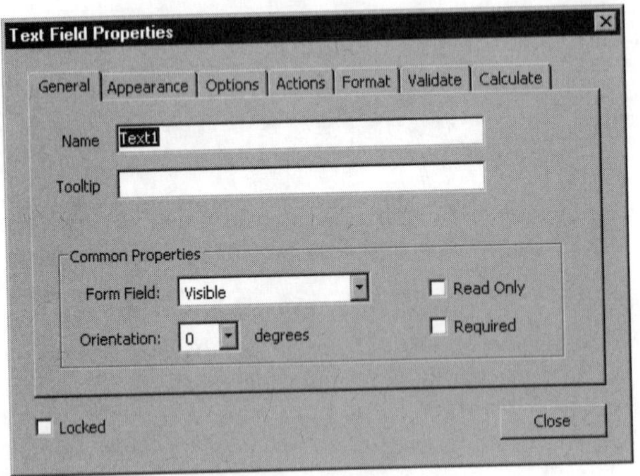

3. In the General tab Name field, enter a name for the field.
4. In the Tooltip field, enter any text you want displayed as a tooltip when a user holds the mouse over the form field. This step is optional.
5. In the Commons Properties section, click the triangle to the right of the Form Field window and choose one of the following options: Visible, Hidden, Visible But Doesn't Print, or Hidden But Printable.

6. Click the triangle to the right of the Orientation field and choose one of the following options: 0, 90, 180, or 270. This determines how the field data is oriented in degrees to the document.
7. Click the Read Only check box to make the field read only. When you choose this option, users will be able to see the content of the form field but will not be able to interact with the form field.
8. Click the Required check box if users are required to interact with the form field. For example, if you choose this option on a text field, users are required to enter information in the field. If the document in which the text field in included has a Submit button and the user attempts to submit the form without filling in a required field, a warning dialog appears telling the user the required field was found empty during export.
9. Click the Appearance tab and select appearance options for the field. For specific instructions on setting appearance parameters, refer to the upcoming "Specify Field Appearance" section.
10. Click the Options tab and specify the options for the field. The choices in this tab differ for each field type and are discussed in detail in upcoming sections.
11. Click the Actions tab, choose an action from the Select Action drop-down menu, and then click the Add button. Actions were discussed in detail in Chapter 8 and will be presented in this chapter as they apply to individual field types.
12. Select the mouse event that will trigger the action. Choose from the following:
    - **Mouse Up** The action executes when the user releases the mouse button (the upstroke of a mouse click).
    - **Mouse Down** The action occurs when the user presses the mouse button (the downstroke of a mouse click).
    - **Mouse Enter** The action occurs when the user passes the mouse over the field boundaries.
    - **Mouse Exit** The action executes when the user moves the mouse beyond the field target area.
    - **On Focus** The action occurs when the field is selected, either through a mouse action or tabbing.
    - **On Blur** The action occurs when the field is deselected as a result of a mouse action or tabbing.
13. Click OK to complete the creation of the form field.

Specify Field Appearance

When you create a PDF form, you can change the appearance of a field to suit the document. You can choose to have a border or not, choose to have a background or not, and, if applicable, specify border and background colors. You can also control text attributes. To specify the appearance of a form field, do the following:

1. Create a form field, as outlined in the previous section.
2. Click the Appearance tab to reveal the dialog box shown here:

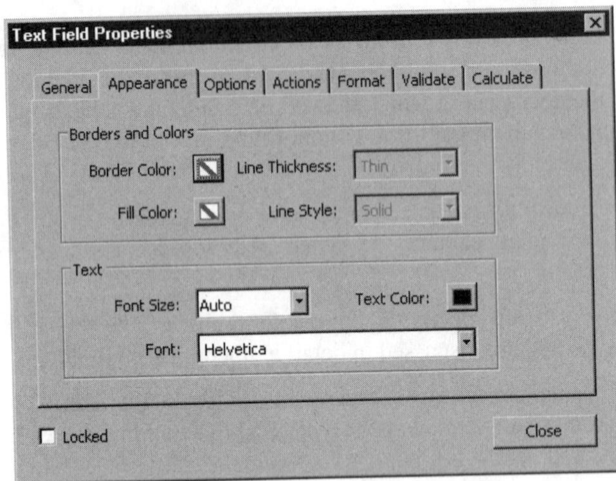

3. In the Borders and Colors section, click the Border Color swatch to choose to choose a color for the field border and then click the Background Color swatch to choose a color for the field background. By default, each swatch has a diagonal red line through it signifying no color. You can choose a color for border and background, either, or none.
4. Click the triangle to the right of the Line Thickness field and from the drop-down menu choose Thin, Medium, or Thick. You use this option to specify the width of the border.
5. Click the triangle to the right of the Line Style field and from the drop-down menu choose Solid, Dashed, Beveled, Inset, or Underlined.
6. If the field type you choose has text, click the triangle to the right of the Font Size field and choose a size from the drop-down menu. Alternatively, you can enter a value no smaller than 2 pts (points) and no larger than 300 pts. If you select Auto, Acrobat sizes the text to fit the field with the exception of a text field that is set to display multiple lines. For a text field with multiple lines, the Auto option sizes the text to fit the field as the user enters it.
7. Click the Text Color button and choose a color from the pop-up palette. Alternatively, you can click the Other Color button to create a custom color from the system color picker.
8. Click the triangle to the right of the Font field and choose a font from the drop-down menu. Note that if you select a font not available on the user's system, the field font reverts to the user's default system font, or, if able, Acrobat renders a reasonable facsimile of the

original font. You can always embed the font, but be aware that font licensing issues may be involved and embedding fonts will bloat the file size.

After you set appearance options for the field, click the other tabs, choose the parameters that apply, and then click OK to complete the field.

TIP *After you create a field, align it, and set up all the parameters, you can prevent accidentally moving or otherwise editing the field by locking it. To lock a field, click the Lock check box from within the form field Properties dialog box.*

Create a Button Field

You can use buttons for many things in Acrobat. You can use them for navigation devices and to submit forms or initiate an action. When you create a button, you can assign different actions to each state of the button. For example, you can have a sound play when the user rolls the mouse over the button. You can even change the appearance of the button based on the interaction of the user's mouse with the button. To create a button field, follow these steps:

1. Select the Button tool from the Forms toolbar and define the boundaries of the field.
2. Click the Appearance tab and specify the applicable appearance options, as outlined previously in the "Specify Field Appearance" section.

If you select the Read Only option, the button will not be interactive and any action you assign to it will not execute.

3. Click the Options tab.
4. Click the triangle to the right of the Layout field and from the drop-down menu choose one of the following options: Label Only; Icon Only; Icon Top, Label Bottom; Label Top, Icon Bottom; Icon Left, Label Right; Label Right, Icon left; or Label Over Icon.
5. Click the triangle to the right of the Behavior tab and from the drop-down menu, choose one of the following:
   - Choose Invert, and the button colors invert when the button is clicked.
   - Choose None, and the button appearance does not change when clicked.
   - Choose Outline, and the button outline is highlighted when clicked.
   - Choose Push, and you can change the button face in the Up, Down, and Rollover states.
6. In the Icon and Label section, if you choose a layout with text, enter the button text in the Label field. If you choose a layout with an icon, click the Icon button and select an image for the button face.
7. If you choose Push for the Behavior option, click one of the three states (Up, Down, or Rollover), and in the Icon and Label section specify the text and icon decoration for the button when it is in this state.

How to ... Create a Multistate Rollover Button

You can pique viewer interest by choosing the Push behavior and then using a different icon for each button state: Up (the default state when a user is not interacting with a button), Down (when the button is clicked), and Rollover (when a user rolls a mouse over a button). All you need to do is create three icons that are the same size in your favorite image-editing program and then specify a different icon for each state. When the user views the document, they'll see different icons when they interact with the button.

8. Click the Actions tab and specify the actions you want to occur when the user interacts with the button. Remember, you can apply multiple actions to the button for each state. For example, on Mouse Enter, you can have a sound play and a tooltip appear; on Mouse Exit, you can hide the tooltip and mute the sound. When you specify different actions and use the Push highlight option, you create highly interactive buttons that pique user interest. Use a small file when you add a sound file to a button; otherwise, the timing may be off as Acrobat has to load the sound and the necessary libraries to play it. For more information on mouse events, refer to the "Create Form Fields" section earlier in this chapter.
9. Click Close to complete the creation of the button.

After creating the button, you can forge ahead to the next field you need to create for the form. However, it is a good idea to select the Hand tool and test the button to make sure it has the functionality you desire.

Rescale a Button Icon

After you test the button, you may find that you need to fine-tune the button face. You can modify the way Acrobat scales the image to the button face by doing the following:

1. With the Button tool, select the button you want to modify.
2. Right-click (Windows) or CTRL-click (Macintosh) and choose Properties from the Context menu.
3. Click the Options tab and then click the Advanced button to open the Icon Placement dialog box, as shown next.

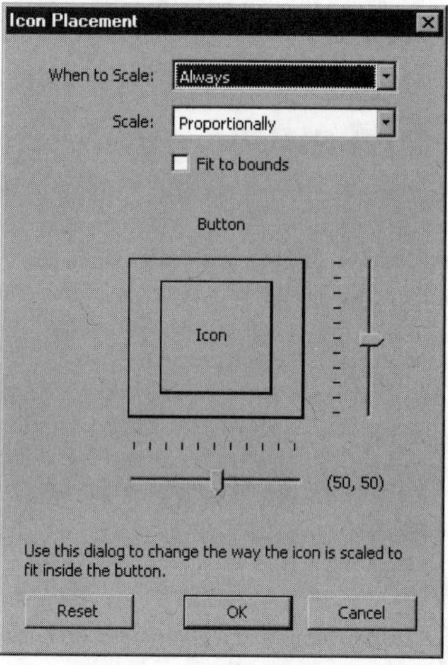

4. Click the triangle to the right of the When To Scale field and choose one of the following options:
   - **Always** Acrobat always scales the icon to fit, regardless of its size in relation to the form field.
   - **Never** Acrobat inserts the icon as originally sized. If the icon is too large for the field, it is clipped from top-left to bottom-right.
   - **Icon Is Too Big** Acrobat resizes the icon to the form field if it is larger than the form field dimensions.
   - **Icon Is Too Small** Acrobat resizes the icon to the form field if it is smaller than the form field dimensions. Note that if the icon is considerably smaller than the field size, the image will be pixelated.
5. Click the triangle to the right of the Scale field and choose one of the following options:
   - **Proportionally** Acrobat preserves the proportion of the original image when resizing it to fit the form field.
   - **Non-Proportionally** Acrobat resizes the icon to the proportions of the form field.
6. Drag the sliders in the Button window to determine icon placement in relation to the form field. By default, equal margins are preserved around the button. To modify the margin on sides of the icon, drag the horizontal slider left or right. To modify the margin on the top and bottom of the icon, drag the vertical slider up or down.
7. Click OK to apply the parameters to the button icon.

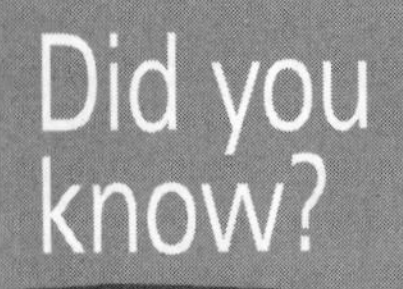

You Can Use Button Fields for Navigation

When you create a multi-page PDF document, readers can use Acrobat navigation tools to find their way around the document. However, if you distribute the document to casual Acrobat users who are not familiar with all the navigation bells and whistles, your readers may not be able to navigate the document. To solve this problem, create three buttons at the top of the page and label them Back, Next, and Home. Remember to assign a unique name to each button in the General tab. Assign the Execute Menu Item to each button. For the Back button, choose View | Go To | Next Page. For the Next button, choose View | Go To | Previous Page. For the Home button, choose View | Go To | First Page. Duplicate the buttons on all pages as outlined previously. On the first page of the document, delete the Back and Home button, and on the last page of the document delete the Next button. You now have a document that can be navigated by anyone.

TIP *When you're creating a form in Acrobat, you can choose a tool by using a menu command. For example, when you need the Text Field tool choose Tools | Advanced Editing | Forms | Text Field Tool. However it's much easier to simply select the tool from the Forms toolbar, which you can display by Tools | Advanced Editing | Forms | Show Forms Toolbar.*

Create a Check Box

You use check boxes to give the user the opportunity to choose more than one option. For example, if you create a questionnaire, you can use check boxes to collect information about which magazines the user reads. The user selects each applicable magazine and the results are sent to the location you specify when the form is submitted. To create a check box, follow these steps:

1. Select the Check Box tool from the Forms toolbar and define the area and position of the field. Generally, you want to create a square form field for a check box. Remember, you can always enable the Layout grid and choose the Snap To Grid option for assistance when creating form fields. After releasing the mouse button, the Check Box Properties dialog box appears.
2. In the General tab Name field, enter a name for the check box and modify the other parameters, as outlined previously in the "Create Form Fields" section.
3. Click the Appearance tab and modify the parameters, as outlined previously in the "Specify Field Appearance" section.
4. Click the Options tab.
5. Click the triangle to the right of the Check Box Style field and from the drop-down menu, choose Check, Circle, Cross, Diamond, Square, or Star. This option determines

what the check box looks like when selected. Note that some of these options may not render properly on different platforms. If possible, test the document on every platform your intended audience may use. When in doubt, Check is usually the best choice.

6. In the Export Value field, Yes is entered by default. This means that the value of "Yes" will be exported when users select the check box. Enter different text to export a different value when users select the check box.
7. Select Check Box Is Checked By Default, and the check style you choose appears in the check box when the document loads; otherwise, the check box is empty.
8. Click Close to complete the check box.

If you create a series of check boxes that are different options for a form element, such as a question, choose the same name for each check box but specify a different Export Value. For example, if you are creating check boxes to gather a response for a simple question, you create two check boxes for each question and give one a "Yes" export value and the other a "No" export value.

Create a Combo Box

You can use a combo box to display a list of items. Create a combo box when you want the user to select only one item from the list, and if you desire, accept input from the user. A combo box functions like a drop-down menu; by clicking a small triangle, the first item on the list displays and users can access the menu. To create a combo box, follow these steps:

1. Select the Combo Box tool from the Forms toolbar and define the area of the field in the PDF document. After releasing the mouse button, the Combo Box Properties dialog box appears.
2. In the General tab Name field, enter a name for the field and then modify other parameters as outlined in the "Create Form Fields" section.
3. Click the Appearance tab and adjust the parameters to suit the style of your form, as previously outlined in the "Specify Field Appearance" section.
4. Click the Options tab.
5. In the Item field, enter the first item in your list.
6. In the Export Value field, enter the export value for the item. If no value is entered, the item is exported with the value listed in the Item field.
7. Click Add to add the item to the combo box.
8. Repeat Steps 4 through 6 to add additional items to the list.
9. After adding all the items to the list, you can select the following options:
   - **Sort Items** Acrobat sorts the items numerically and then alphabetically.
   - **Allow User To Enter Custom Text** Users can enter their own value for the combo box.

- **Check Spelling** Users can spell check the custom text they enter. This option is selected by default.
- **Commit Selected Value Immediately** Users' selections are saved immediately; otherwise, the value is saved when the form is submitted. This option is handy when the value will be used by another field in the form.

10. If you did not choose the Sort Items option, you can manually reorder the list. Select a list item and click the Up button to move the item one position higher in the list; click the Down button to move the item one position lower in the list. If the item is at either extremity of the list, the applicable button is dimmed out. Alternatively, you can click the Delete button to delete a selected item from the Combo Box list.
11. Click the Validate tab to restrict the range of data that can be entered in the combo box. For more information on this option, refer to the later "Validate Form Fields" section.
12. Click the Calculate tab if you want to use items from the combo box to perform a mathematical calculation. For more information on creating a calculating form field, refer to the "Calculate Form Fields" section later in this chapter.
13. Click Close to complete the creation of the combo box. The following illustration shows a completed combo box:

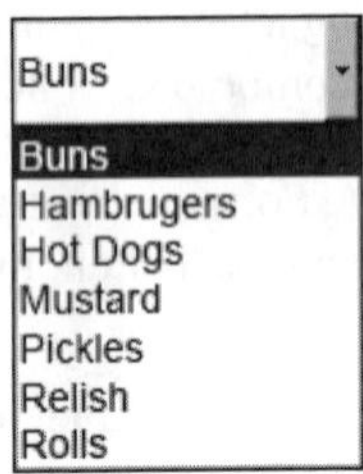

Create a List Box

You create a list box when you want to give users the capability of selecting multiple items. When you create a list box, users can scroll through the list as opposed to opening a drop-down menu with the combo box. Users cannot edit items in a list box, but they can select multiple items from the list whereas only one item can be selected from a combo box. You can use JavaScript to create a custom action when users change the list box selection. To create a list box, follow these steps:

1. Select the List Box tool from the Forms toolbar and define the area and position of the list box in the document. When you release the mouse button, the List Box Properties dialog box appears.
2. In the General tab Name field, enter a name for the field and then modify the other parameters as outlined in the "Create Form Fields" section.
3. Click the Appearance tab and define the appearance parameters for the list box, as discussed previously in the "Specify Field Appearance" section.

4. Click the Options tab.
5. In the Item field, enter a name for the first item in the list.
6. In the Export Value field, enter the export value of the item. If you leave this field blank, the item name becomes the export value.
7. Click the Add button to add the item to the list box.
8. Repeat Steps 5 through 7 to add additional items to the list.
9. After you complete adding items to the list, you can choose the following options:
   - **Sort Items** Acrobat sorts the list items in numerical and alphabetical order.
   - **Multiple Items** You will be able to make multiple selections from the list.
   - **Commit Selected Value Immediately** Users' selections are saved immediately; otherwise, the value is saved when the form is submitted.
10. If you did not choose the Sort Items option, the Up and Down buttons are active. To move a selected item up one position in the list, click the Up button; to move a selected item down one position in the list, click the Down button. Alternatively, you can click the Delete button to remove a selected item from the list.
11. Click the Selection Change tab and, in the When The List box Selection Changes section, choose one of the following options:
    - **Do Nothing** This is the default option and true to its word—nothing other than the selection change happens when you change a selection.
    - **Execute This Script** Choose this option, and the Edit button becomes active. Click the Edit button to open the JavaScript Edit dialog box. Create the script that will execute when a list box item changes and click OK to close the dialog box.
12. Click Close to complete the creation of your list box.

Create a Radio Button

When you create a radio button, you create a form device that enables users to make a selection. When you create a group of radio buttons for users to choose an option, only one button can be selected from the group, thus limiting users to one selection from the group. When you create a group of related radio buttons, each button has the same name but a different *export value*. The export value is used by the CGI application of a Web server to transmit the user's choice as a form result. If you are adept at JavaScript, your custom script can use the export value. To create a radio button, follow these steps:

1. Select the Radio Button tool from the Forms toolbar and define the size and position of the field in the document. After releasing the mouse button, the Radio Button Properties dialog box appears.
2. In the General tab Name field, enter a name for the field and modify additional parameters as discussed previously in the "Create Form Fields" section.

3. Click the Appearance tab and define the appearance parameters for the list box, as discussed previously in the "Specify Field Appearance" section.
4. Click the Options tab.
5. Click the triangle to the right of the Button Style field and from the drop-down menu choose one of the following: Check, Circle, Cross, Diamond, Square, or Star. This option determines what the radio button looks like when selected.
6. In the Export Value field, Yes is entered by default. This means that the value of "Yes" will be exported when users select the check box. Enter different text to export a different value when users select the check box.
7. Choose Button Is Checked By Default and when the document loads, Acrobat will fill the field with the radio button style you selected in Step 5. If you create a group of radio buttons with the same name, only one button can be set up with the Default Is Checked option.
8. Click the Buttons With The Same Name And Value Are Selected In Unison if you have more than one radio button with the same name and export value in the document. When you select this option, all buttons with the same name and export value will be selected when the button you are creating is selected.
9. Click the Actions tab and specify the actions you want to occur when users interact with the button.
10. Click Close to complete the creation of the radio button.

TIP

To create an exact copy of any field, select the field with the form tool with which it was created and then, while holding down CTRL (Windows) or COMMAND (Macintosh), drag the form field. After you begin dragging the form field, press SHIFT to constrain motion vertically or horizontally. Release the mouse button to complete copying the field. If the copied field is part of a group of radio buttons, choose Properties from the Context menu and change the export value of the field but not its name.

Create a Text Field

You can create text fields to accept user input or you can use them to display text strings, such as the current date. You can also use text fields to display multiple lines of text. You can limit the number of characters in the field and determine whether the field is visible or not. To create a text field, follow these steps:

1. Select the Text Field tool from the Forms toolbar and define the area for the field in the document. After releasing the mouse button, the Text Field Properties dialog box appears.
2. In the General tab Name field, enter a name for the field and then modify other parameters as outlined in the "Create Form Fields" section.
3. Click the Appearance tab and set the appearance options for the field, as outlined previously in the "Specify Field Appearance" section.

4. Click the Options tab to modify the following parameters:
   - Click the triangle to the right of the Alignment field and choose to align the field contents to the Left, Center, or Right.
   - In the Default Value field, enter the default value for the field. This value will be submitted unless the user enters different data. Alternatively, you can leave this field blank.
   - Enable the Multi-Line option to display the contents of the field on multiple lines. If this option is unchecked and the contents of the field exceed the width of the text box, the text will be truncated.
   - Enable the Scroll Long Text option, and users will be able to scroll through the contents of a multiline text box. This option is selected by default; users of the form can scroll through the field and edit the contents. Furthermore, if you use the text box to display Read Only Text and the Scroll Long Text option is deselected, users will not be able to scroll the contents of the field as no scroll bars will be present. If you create a Read Only text box with multiple lines of text with this option deselected, be sure to properly size the box so every line of text is visible.
   - Enable the Allow Rich Text Formatting option to allow users to apply styles such as Bold, Italic, or Underline to the text they enter in the field. Users with Adobe Reader 6.0, Acrobat Standard, or Acrobat Professional can format text by choosing View | Toolbars | Properties Bar, selecting the text and then selecting a style from the toolbar.
   - To limit the number of characters a user can enter in the field, enable the Limit Of [ ] Characters option and enter a value in the field.
   - Enable the Password option, and each character of text displays as an asterisk. The option is not available until you deselect the Check Spelling option.
   - Enable the Field Is Used For File Selection, and a path to a file can be entered as the value of the field. This option is dimmed out until you deselect the Check Spelling option. It is also unavailable if you have specified a default value for the field or enabled the Multi-Line, Limit Of Characters, or Password options. Likewise, it is unavailable if you have defined the field with formatting script.
   - Enable the Check Spelling option (selected by default), and users can perform a spell check for the field.
   - To spread a given number of characters evenly across the width in the field, enable the Comb Of [ ] Characters option and enter a value in the field. This option is available only if you deselect all other choices in the Options tab.
5. Click the Actions tab and specify which actions occur when a user's mouse interacts with the field.
6. Click the Format tab to specify the type of data that will be accepted in the field. For more information on formatting a field, refer to the upcoming "Format Form Fields" section.

7. Click the Validate tab if you want to restrict the range of data that can be entered in the field. For more information on this option, refer to the upcoming "Validate Form Fields" section.
8. Click the Calculate tab if the field will be used to perform a mathematical calculation. For more information on creating a calculating form field, refer to the "Calculate Form Fields" section in the latter part of this chapter.
9. Click Close to finish creating the text box.
10. Select the Hand tool and click the text box to test it.

Create a Digital Signature Field

You can create a digital signature field when you want the user to sign the form. When you create a digital signature field, you can specify what occurs after the field is signed. To create a signature field, follow these steps:

1. Select the Digital Signature tool from the Forms toolbar and define the area for the field. After releasing the mouse button, the Digital Signature Properties dialog box appears.
2. In the General tab Name field, enter a name for the field and set additional parameters, as outlined in the "Create Form Fields" section.
3. Click the Appearance tab and set the appearance options for the field, as outlined previously in the "Specify Field Appearance" section.
4. Click the Actions tab and select the actions that occur when a user's mouse interacts with the field. This step is optional.
5. Click the Signed tab and choose one of the following options:
   - **Nothing Happens When Signed** Choose this default option, and the signature transmits with the submitted form, but nothing else happens.
   - **Mark As Read Only** Choose this option, and you can limit certain fields on the form to read-only status after the document is signed. When you select this option, choose one of the following from the drop-down menu: All Fields, All Fields Except These, or Just These. When you choose either of the latter options, click the Pick button to select the fields to include or exclude.
   - **This Script Executes When The Signature Is Signed** Choose this option to create a JavaScript that executes when the field is signed. After you choose the option, click the Edit button and create the JavaScript in the JavaScript Edit dialog box.
6. Click Close to complete the creation of the Signature field. For more information on digital signatures, refer to Chapter 11.

Spell Check Form Fields

You can spell check form fields and comments you create in a PDF document. You can add words to the Acrobat Spell Check dictionary and edit the dictionary as needed. To spell check form fields and comments in a document, follow these steps:

1. Choose Edit | Check Spelling | Comments And Form Fields to open the Check Spelling dialog box.
2. Click Start to begin the spell check. When Acrobat finds a word that is not in its dictionary, the word is highlighted in the Word Not Found field, as shown in the following illustration. Acrobat supplies a list of suggested replacements in the Suggestions field. You can choose one of the following options:
   - Edit the suspect word and then click Change.
   - Double-click a word from the Suggestions list to replace the highlighted word.
   - Click Ignore to leave the highlighted word unchanged and continue with the spell check.
   - Click Ignore All to leave the highlighted word and all future instances of the highlighted word unchanged.
   - Click Add, and Acrobat adds the word to your personal dictionary.
   - Select one of the words from the Suggestions list and then click Change to replace the highlighted word.
   - Select one of the words from the Suggestions list and then click Change All to change all occurrences of the highlighted word to the selected correction.
   - Click Done to end the spell check.

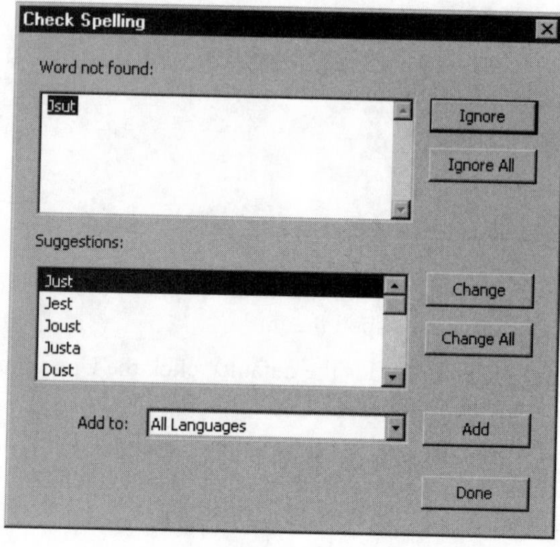

Specify Spell Check Preferences

Acrobat Spell Check is a powerful feature that you use to guard against typographical and spelling errors in your form fields and comments. You can configure the Spell Checker to suit your preferences by following these steps:

1. Choose Edit | Preferences to open the Preferences dialog box.
2. Choose Spelling from the list in the left-hand window to open the dialog box, as shown here:

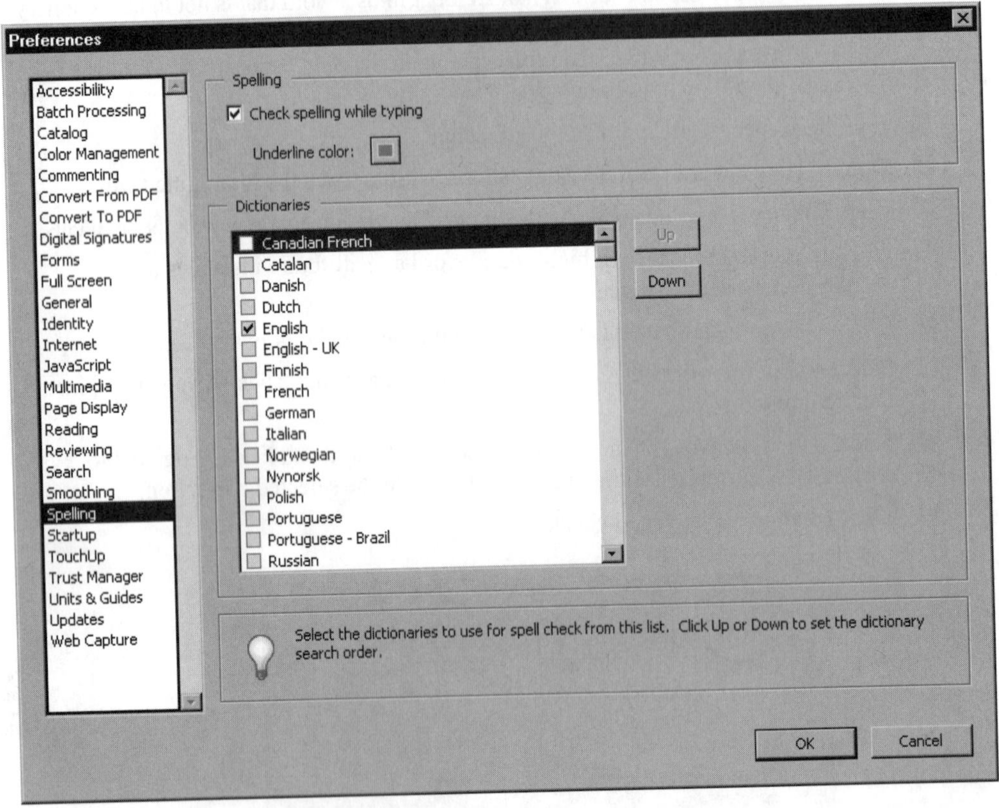

3. Choose Check Spelling While Typing (the default option) to have Acrobat underline any words immediately after you misspell them.
4. To change the underline color (red is the default), click the Underline Color button and choose a color from the pop-up palette.
5. To add a dictionary to the list, select one from the list on the left. The default dictionary is the one you selected when you installed Acrobat. When you have multiple dictionaries, Acrobat searches the dictionary at the top of the list first.

6. To change the order in which Acrobat searches the dictionaries, select a dictionary from the Dictionary Search list and then click the Up button to move the dictionary toward the top of the list; click Down to move the dictionary toward the bottom of the list.
7. To remove a dictionary from the Dictionary Search List, click its check box.
8. Click OK to apply the changes.

Edit the Dictionary

When you perform a spell check and Acrobat locates a word that is not present in any dictionary in the Dictionary Search List, you have the option to add the word to your personal dictionary. You can add or delete words from your personal dictionary when they are no longer needed by following these steps:

1. Choose Edit | Check Spelling | Edit Dictionary to open the Edit Custom Dictionary dialog box, shown here:

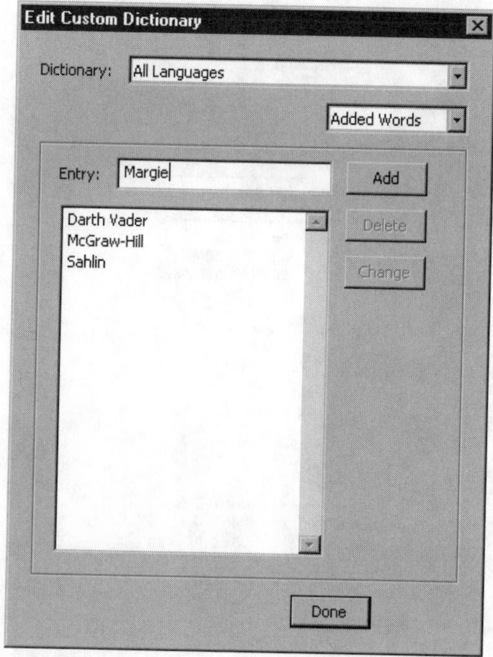

2. To add a word to the dictionary, type it in the Entry field and then click Add.
3. To remove a word from the dictionary, select it from the window on the left and then click Delete.
4. Click Done to finish editing the dictionary.

Format Form Fields

When you create a form field that accepts data input, you can format the field for a specific type of data. For example, if the form field requests the user's fax number, format the field using the Phone Number option. If the user fills out the form and enters **5555551212**, when the data is submitted, Acrobat reformats the entry to read (555) 555-1212. To format a form field, follow these steps:

1. Create a form field as outlined in "Create Form Fields."
2. Click the Format tab in the field Properties dialog box.
3. Choose one of the following categories: None, Number, Percentage, Date, Time, Special, or Custom. Each category has different formatting options. The following illustration shows the available options for the Number category:

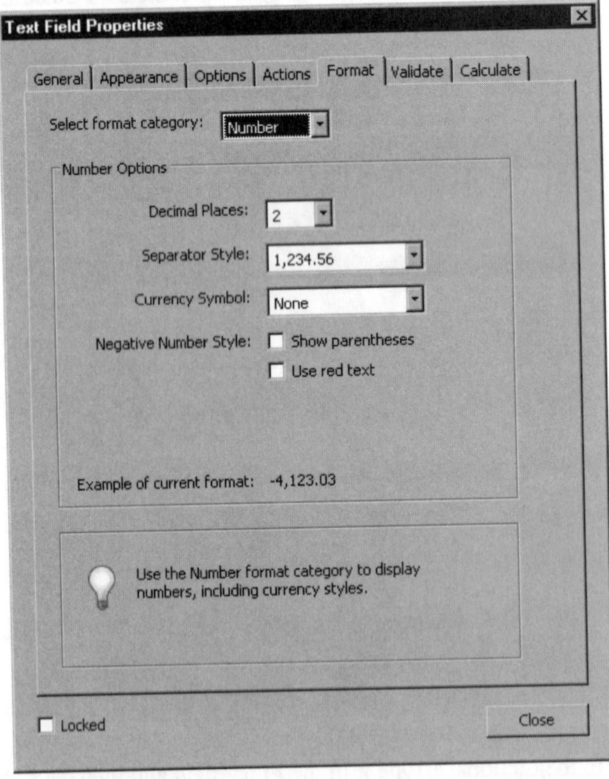

4. Choose the options that best suit the form you are creating.
5. If you choose the Custom category, click the Edit button beside Custom Format Script or click the Edit button beside Custom Keystroke Script to open the JavaScript Edit dialog box. Enter the script or paste an existing script into the dialog box and then click OK.

Validate Form Fields

When you create a form field that accepts data, you can limit the amount of data the user enters by validating the form field. Validating a form field is useful when you put a form on the Internet. By limiting the amount of data you let the user enter, you eliminate a potential server bottleneck when a malicious user submits a form with copious amounts of data. You can only validate text and combo box form fields. To validate a form field, follow these steps:

1. Create a form field, as discussed in previous sections of this chapter.
2. Click the Validate tab in the field Properties dialog box to open the dialog box, as shown in the following illustration. The options you have available will vary depending upon the format you specify. By default, Acrobat does not validate a field.

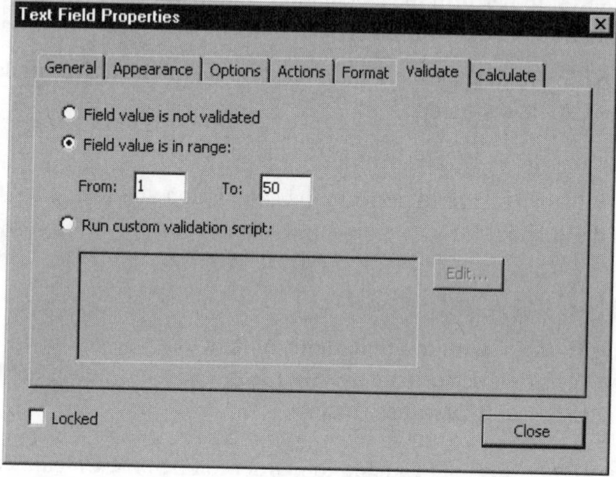

3. If you choose either the number or percentage format (refer to the "Format Form Fields" section presented previously in this chapter), you can limit the range of data the user can enter by clicking the Field Value Is In Range radio button. Enter values in the From field and To field to define the acceptable range of data.
4. To create a validation script using JavaScript, click the Run Custom Validation Script radio button and then click the Edit button to open the JavaScript Edit dialog box. Enter the script you want used to validate the form field and then click OK.

Calculate Form Fields

When you create form fields with numeric data, Acrobat can calculate the value of two or more fields. You can choose from common arithmetic functions or you can create a complex calculation using JavaScript. To calculate two or more form fields, follow these steps:

1. Create the form field that will display the result of the calculation, as outlined previously in this chapter.

2. Click the Format tab and choose Number from the Select Format Category drop-down menu.
3. Select the options that pertain to the calculation. For example, if you want to calculate a price, choose the appropriate style from the Currency Symbol drop-down menu.
4. Click the Calculate tab to open the Calculate section of the field's Properties dialog box.
5. To use one of the present mathematical operations, choose the second option listed, and from the drop-down menu choose the operation you want performed, as shown here. You can choose from Sum (+), Product (x), Average, Minimum, or Maximum. Alternatively, you can choose Simplified Field Notation to calculate the selected fields using simplified notation such as `Sum=Field1+Field 2`. Another option is to choose Custom Calculation Script, click the Edit button to open the JavaScript Edit dialog box, create the JavaScript to perform the calculation, and then click OK to close the dialog box and apply the custom calculation script.

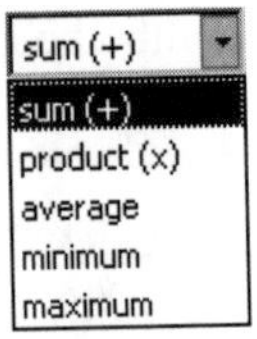

6. Click the Pick button to display the Field Selection dialog box. This dialog box lists all the fields present in the document.
7. Click a field check box to use the field in the calculation.
8. Add the other fields necessary to perform the calculation and then click Close to exit the Select A Field dialog box.

Set Field Calculation Order

When you create a complex form with multiple fields of data that you call upon for calculation, the order in which the calculation performs may differ from the tab order of the fields. To change the order of the calculated fields, follow these steps:

1. Choose Advanced | Forms | Set Calculation Order to open the Calculated Fields dialog box. This dialog box shows all the calculable fields in your form and the order in which the calculations are performed on them.
2. To change a field order in the list, select it and then click the Up button to move the field one position higher in the list. Click the Down button to move it one position lower in the list.
3. Click OK when you finish reordering the fields.

Create a Reset Form Button

If you create a form with multiple fields, you may want to consider creating a reset button. Adding a reset button gives the user the option of starting over again by clicking a button. When you create a reset button, you can specify which form fields are cleared when the button is used. To create a reset button, follow these steps:

1. Select the Button tool from the Forms toolbar and define the size and position of the field.
2. In the General tab Name field, enter a name for the field (Reset is a good choice).
3. Modify the button appearance and options to suit your form, as presented previously in the "Create a Button Field" section of this chapter.
4. Click the Actions tab and choose the Mouse Up as the trigger.
5. Click the triangle to the right of the Select Action field and from the drop-down menu, choose Reset A Form.
6. Click the Add button to open the Reset A Form dialog box, shown next:

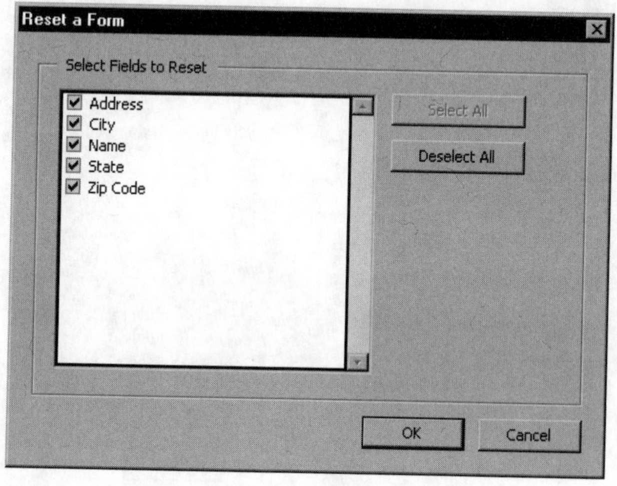

7. Select the fields you want to reset. Alternatively, you can click Select All to select all form fields in the document.
8. Click OK to exit the Reset A Form dialog box; then click Close to assign the action to the button.

14

Create a Submit Form Button

When you create a form for use on the Internet or a local intranet, you can add a submit form button to transmit the results to a Web server. You can specify the export format and specify which fields are submitted. To create a submit form button, follow these steps:

1. Select the Button tool from the Forms toolbar and define the size and position of the field.
2. In the General tab Name field, enter a name for the field. Remember to choose a unique name for the button; "Submit Form" is a good choice.

3. Modify the button appearance and options to suit your form, as discussed previously in the "Create a Button Field" section.
4. Click the Actions tab and choose the Mouse Up for the trigger.
5. Click the triangle to the right of the Select Action field and from the drop-down menu, choose Submit A Form.
6. Click the Add button to display the Submit Form Selections dialog box, as shown here:

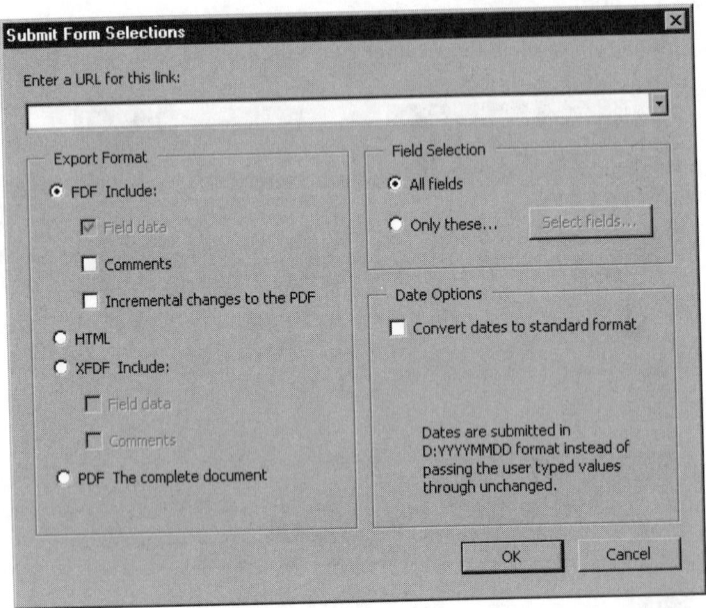

7. In the Enter A URL For This Link field, enter the destination URL for the form results.
8. In the Export Format section, choose one of the following options:
   - **FDF Include** Acrobat exports the data as an FDF (Forms Data Format) file. With this format you can choose to export field data, comments, incremental changes to the PDF, or all the preceding. When you choose the Incremental Changes To The PDF option, data from digital signature fields can be exported in a manner that is recognized by a Web server.
   - **HTML** Acrobat exports the form data in HTML format.
   - **XFDF Include** Acrobat exports the form data as an XFDF file.
   - **PDF The Complete Document** Acrobat exports the entire PDF file that contains the form data.

How to ... Create a Form Table

You can create a table of form fields by first creating a row or column of fields. Remember to give each field a unique name. Select the fields and then choose Advanced | Forms | Fields | Make Multiple Copies to open the Create Multiple Copies Of Fields dialog box. From within the dialog box, you can specify the number of copies to make and the direction to which the new fields will be copied. By default, Acrobat provides a preview so you can fine-tune the table before exiting the dialog box. When you click OK, Acrobat creates the multiple copies and appends the name of each copied field so that the field is unique.

9. In the Field Selection section, choose All Fields or Only These. If you select the Only These option, click the Select Fields button to open the Field Selection dialog box. Click a field check box to select it or click Select All to select all form fields in the document. After selecting the fields, click the Include Selected radio button (the default) to include the selected fields when the form is submitted or click the Exclude Selected radio button to exclude the selected fields when the form is submitted. If you choose the Empty Field option, fields with no data will be exported. Click OK to exit the Field Selection dialog box.
10. Choose Convert Dates To Standard Format, and Acrobat exports date information in a standard format, regardless of what the user entered.
11. Click OK to apply the options.
12. Click Close to assign the action to the button.

dit a Form

After you create a form, you may find that you need to edit the form in order to make it more aesthetically pleasing. You can resize, align, reposition, and duplicate form fields to achieve this result. You may also find it necessary to edit the properties of individual fields, if, for example, an action does not execute as planned or a calculation does not give the expected result.

Use the Form Context Menu

You find many of the commands needed to modify forms by choosing Tools | Advanced Editing | Forms and then selecting the desired command from the drop-down menu. You can also quickly access a command from the Context menu. To modify a form field with a command from the

Context menu, select a form field with the forms tool with which it was created or the Select Object tool, and then right-click (Windows) or CTRL-click (Macintosh) and choose a command from the Context menu, as shown in the following illustration. Note that some of these commands are exclusive to the Context menu.

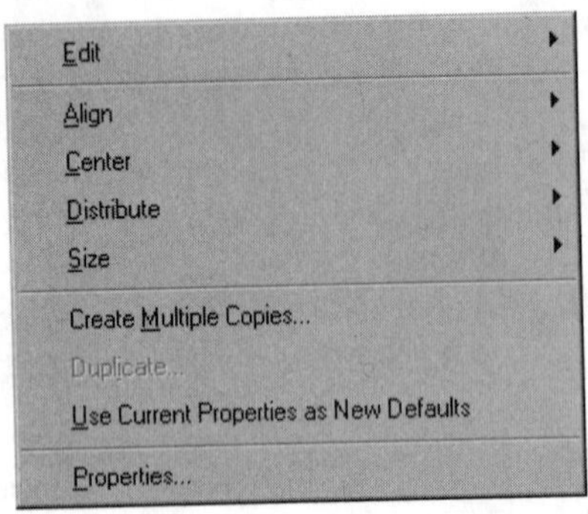

Use the Fields Tab

You can use the Fields tab to edit the form fields within your document. The Fields tab lists every field in your document. You can use the Fields tab to delete fields, navigate to fields, change field properties, and more. Open the Fields tab, as shown in the following illustration, by choosing View | Navigation Tabs | Fields.

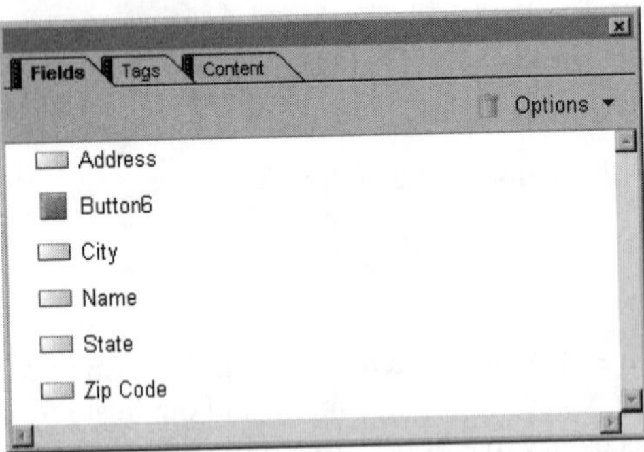

To edit any field from the list in the Fields tab, select the field, click the Options icon in the upper-right corner of the tab, and choose a command from the drop-down menu. Alternatively, you can select a field in the tab, right-click (Windows) or CTRL-click (Macintosh), and then choose a command from the Context menu. The Go To Field command at the top of the menu is unique to the Context menu.

To delete selected fields, click the icon that looks like a trash can near the top of the Fields tab.

Edit Form Field Properties

When a form works exactly as planned, it's time to move on to the next task—or take a quick break and bask in the glow of accomplishment. However, more often than not, you will need to tweak one or more properties of a form field. To edit form field properties, select the field with the tool with which it was created, right-click (Windows) or CTRL-click (Macintosh), and then choose Properties from the Context menu to open the tool's dialog box.

TIP *When you're editing a document with multiple fields of different types, you can edit them by choosing the Select Object tool from the Advanced Editing toolbar. After you select the tool, every object in the document including form fields are highlighted. You can select an object's properties by right-clicking (Windows) or CTRL-clicking (Macintosh) and then choosing Properties from the Context menu.*

Delete a Form Field

When you revise a form and no longer need a particular form field, you can easily delete that form field. First, select it with the form tool with which the field was created; then choose Edit | Delete. Alternatively, you can choose Delete from the Context menu or press DELETE.

Align, Reposition, and Resize Form Fields

If you use the Layout Grid to align and size the fields in your form, you generally end up with a form that is neatly laid out. However, you may still need to make some minor adjustments to the position or size of a field. You can resize individual fields or select multiple fields and then size and align them to each other.

To resize or reposition an individual form field, select the field with the forms tool with which it was created. After you select the field, eight handles appear around the field perimeter. You can then modify the field by doing any of the following:

- To reposition the form field, click the center of the field with the tool used to create the field and drag the field to the desired location. As you drag the field, a bounding box gives you a preview of the current position of the field. When the field is in the desired position, release the mouse button.
- To resize the field, click any corner handle and drag. To resize the field proportionately, press SHIFT while dragging. As you resize the field, a bounding box appears that gives you a preview of the current size of the field. Release the mouse button when the field is the desired size.
- To modify the field width, click the center handle on either side of the form field and drag left or right to change the width of the field.
- To modify the field height, click the middle handle at the top or bottom of the field and drag up or down to change the height of the field.

You can also modify the size and alignment of several fields—just select the forms tool that was used to create the fields or use the Select Objects tool to select different types of fields you want to modify and then click a form field. To add fields to the selection, hold down SHIFT and click the fields you want to add to the selection. The last form field you click highlights in red. All fields will be modified to the applicable parameter of the first field selected. After selecting two or more fields, you can do any of the following:

- To change the size of the selected fields, right-click (Windows) or CTRL-click (Macintosh) and from the Context menu choose Size; then choose Height, Width, or Both.
- To change the alignment of the selected fields, right-click (Windows) or CTRL-click (Macintosh) and from the Context menu choose Align; then choose Left, Right, Bottom, Top, Vertically, or Horizontally.
- To center the selected fields to the current document, right-click (Windows) or CTRL-click (Macintosh) and from the Context menu choose Center; then choose Vertically, Horizontally, or Both.
- To equally distribute the selected fields, right-click (Windows) or CTRL-click (Macintosh) and from the Context menu choose Distribute; then choose Vertically or Horizontally. Note that the fields will be distributed relative to their center points.

TIP

You can set the tab order of the form field by opening the Pages tab and clicking the thumbnail for the page on which the form is displayed. Right-click (Windows) or CTRL-click (Macintosh) and choose Page Properties from the Context menu. In the Tab section, choose Row Order to tab from left to right, Column Order to tab from top to bottom, or Document Structure to tab in the order in which the fields appear on the structure tree.

Duplicate a Form Field

If the information or data entered in a form field needs to be in multiple locations of the document, you can duplicate the form field. You can duplicate a form field on the same page or across a range of pages. When you duplicate a form field, the field retains all the attributes you assigned to the original field. When you change a parameter in a field that has been duplicated (in other words, a field with the same name that appears more than once in the document), the parameter changes in the duplicated fields as well. You can duplicate a single form field or a selection of form fields.

To duplicate form fields on a page, follow these steps:

1. Choose Tools | Advanced Editing | Select Object Tool and then select the field(s) you want to duplicate. Hold down the SHIFT key and click additional fields to add them to the selection.
2. Hold down CTRL (Windows) or OPTION (Macintosh) and drag the selected fields. To constrain the motion of the fields vertically or horizontally, hold down SHIFT (along with CTRL or OPTION) after you begin to drag the fields.

3. Release the mouse button, and Acrobat duplicates the selected fields where you released the mouse button.

To duplicate fields across a range of pages, follow these steps:

1. Choose Tools | Advanced Editing | Select Object Tool and then select the field(s) you want to duplicate.
2. Choose Advanced | Forms | Fields | Duplicate to open the Duplicate Field dialog box, as shown here:

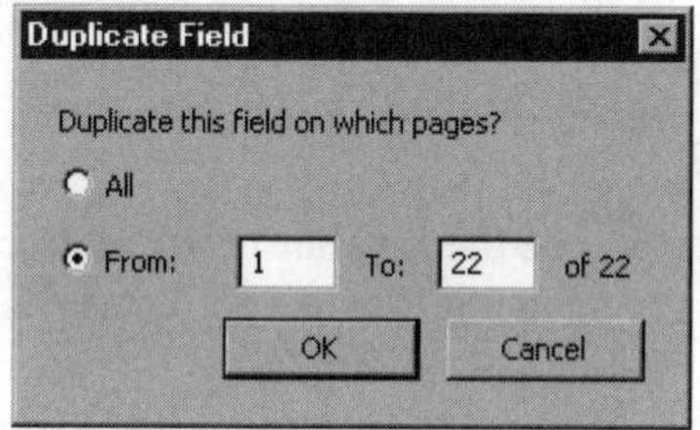

3. Accept the All option (the default) to duplicate the field on all document pages or choose the From option and enter the range of pages to duplicate the field on.
4. Click OK, and Acrobat creates the duplicates per your specification.

Export Form Data

You can export data from a form for use in other PDF forms that have the same field names. When you export data, you create a smaller file with data only. You can export the data as an FDF file or as an XFDF (an XML representation of the FDF data) file. To export form data, follow these steps:

1. Choose Advanced | Forms | Export Forms Data to open the Export Form Data As dialog box.
2. Enter a name for the file and the folder where you want the data file stored. If you do not assign a name for the file, Acrobat uses the current name of the file by default.
3. Click Save.

Import Form Data

You can import FDF files to automatically fill in form fields. When you import an FDF file, Acrobat automatically inserts the data in document form fields with the same names. To import data into a PDF document, follow these steps:

1. Choose Advanced | Forms | Import Forms Data to open the Select File Containing Form Data dialog box.

2. Navigate to the file containing the data you want to import and select the file.
3. Click Select to open the file.

You can also share form data with other users. For example, if you work in a corporate environment, you can post a form that contains fields pertaining to product information, such as current cost and list price. When the data needs to be updated, you can update the master version of the form and export the data. The version of the form that is posted on the corporate intranet can be programmed to automatically update using the Import Form Data action that you program to execute when the page opens or when the user clicks a button. For more information on actions, refer to Chapter 8.

Use JavaScript Actions

When you create a form field, you can use the JavaScript action to create a custom script for the field. You can create a JavaScript and assign it to a button for use as navigation. You can also use JavaScript to augment Acrobat mathematical functions.

Use JavaScript to Subtract and Divide

In the "Calculate Form Fields" section, you may have noticed Acrobat does not provide the ability to subtract or divide form fields. In order to perform either operation, you must create a JavaScript. To subtract a text field named *Field B* from a text field named *Field A*, follow these steps:

1. Select the Form tool.
2. Create a form field where you want the results of the calculation to appear.
3. Enter a name for the form field and choose Text from the Type drop-down menu.
4. Click the Appearance tab and set the parameters for the field text, background color, and border color.
5. Click the Format tab and choose a format option for the field. Choose the same format as Field A and Field B. For example, if Fields A and B work with currency value, choose Number and then choose the currency symbol that applies.
6. Click the Calculate tab, choose Custom Calculation Script, click the Edit button, and then enter the following in the JavaScript Edit dialog box:

```
var a = this.getField("Field A");
var b = this.getField("Field B");
event.value = a.value - b.value
```

7. Click OK to exit the JavaScript Edit dialog box.

You can modify the script to perform division by entering the following JavaScript in Step 6:

```
var a = this.getField("Field A");
var b = this.getField("Field B");
event.value = a.value / b.value
```

NOTE *Division by a value of zero is not possible. If the user enters a value of zero for the second field, an error message appears warning the value does not match the format of the field. To guard against this, click the Validate tab and specify that the number must be greater than or equal to one. Validating the field in this manner will also result in an error message if the user enters a value less than one; this includes dividing by negative numbers.*

You can use JavaScript to perform complex calculations involving multiple form fields in a document. Simply create a variable for each form field and use the `getField` method to get the value of the field. To calculate the result, set the value method of the event object equal to a mathematical calculation using the value of each variable and the applicable operands. For example:

```
var a = this.getField("Field A");
var b = this.getField("Field B");
var c = this.getField("Field C");
event.value = c.value * (a.value + b.value)
```

ld JavaScript Actions to Form Fields

You can use the Run A JavaScript Action with form fields (Professional only), bookmarks, and links, or you can create global JavaScript that can be used for an entire document. When you choose the Run A JavaScript action, you create the actual script in a text editor. As previously mentioned, there are myriad uses for JavaScript with PDF documents. The following steps show how to use JavaScript to display the current date when a page loads:

1. Select the Text Field Tool from the Forms toolbar.
2. Navigate to the document page where you want the date to appear.
3. Drag to define the shape of the field. When you release the mouse button, the Text Field Properties dialog box is displayed.
4. In the General tab Name field, enter ***todaysDate***. This is the name of the form field that will display the current date, which will be retrieved from the host computer using JavaScript you'll create in a future step.
5. Click the Read Only check box.
6. Define the appearance and other parameters of the text field, as outlined previously.
7. In the Pages tab, select the thumbnail for the page to which you just added the text field.

8. Right-click (Windows), or CTRL-click (Macintosh) and choose Properties from the Context menu. The Page Properties dialog box opens.
9. Click the Actions tab and choose Run A Javascript from the Select Action drop-down menu.
10. Click the Add button to open the JavaScript editor.
11. In the Create And Edit JavaScripts window of the JavaScript Editor (see the following illustration), enter the following JavaScript code:

```
var today = util.printd("mmmm d, yyyy", new Date());
this.getField('todaysDate').value = today ;
```

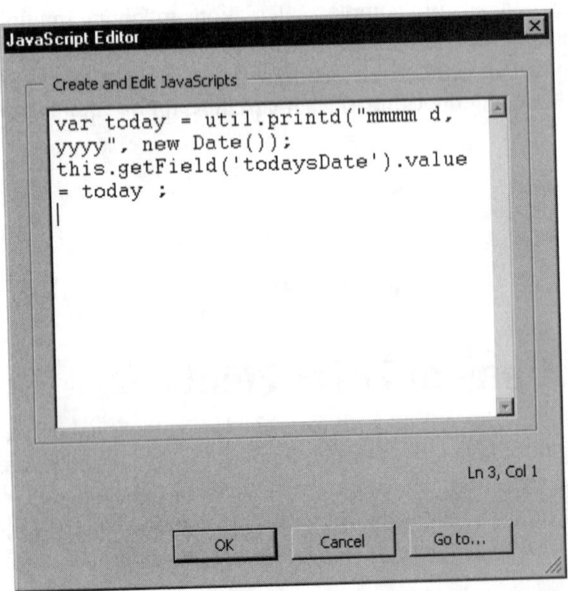

The first line of code creates a variable called `today` and sets its value to the current date (`new Date()`). The first part of the value `printd` method of the `util` object formats the date where mmmm is the long form of the month, *d* is the day in numeric form and *yyyy* is the four-digit representation of the year. The second line of code sets the value of the `todaysDate` field you created in Step 4, equal to the variable `today`. To display the day name before the date, modify the code to read as follows:

```
var today = util.printd("dddd, mmmm d, yyyy", new Date());
this.getField('todaysDate').value = today ;
```

NOTE

When you create JavaScript that uses variables, be aware that variables are case sensitive. For example, if you refer to the variable as today *in one line of code and* Today *in another, the JavaScript will not function as you desire because the second instance of the variable is not lower case.*

The addition of *dddd* adds the name of the day to the value of the variable *today*. The date is returned as text data, or as it is known in the programming world, *string* data. The code between the quotation marks is what returns the current date when the page opens. Notice the addition of commas and spaces. This tidies up the formatting. Without them, everything would run together and the result would be something like, MondayAugust22010 instead of Monday, August 2, 2010.

NOTE

JavaScript programming language has formatting rules, as does the language with which this book was written. In programmer speak, formatting protocol is known as syntax. *When your JavaScript has a syntax error, it is noted at the bottom of the Edit JavaScript dialog box.*

12. Click OK to close the Edit JavaScript dialog box.
13. Click Close to close the Page Properties dialog box and then save the document.

The next time you open the document, the date will be displayed where you created the form field. If the date does not appear or if the formatting is incorrect, you will have to edit the JavaScript.

TIP

If you prefer working in a text editor when creating JavaScript, choose Edit | Preferences and then choose JavaScript. In the JavaScript Editor section, choose external editor, and then enter the path the external editor executable (.exe) file. After changing the preference, whenever you edit JavaScript, Acrobat launches the external editor. After you enter the JavaScript, choose the external editor Save command before setting the JavaScript action in Acrobat. If you prefer working with the Acrobat JavaScript Editor, you can use this dialog box to change the font type and size as displayed in the JavaScript Editor.

Summary

In this chapter, you learned to use Acrobat tools to add form elements to your PDF documents. You learned how to create and edit form fields that collect data, allow viewers to make a choice from a list or combo box, and choose items using radio buttons or check boxes. You also learned to create form fields that calculate numeric data and validate data. In the next chapter, you'll learn to add multimedia elements to your PDF documents.

Chapter 15 Add Multimedia Elements to PDF Documents

How to...

- Work with images
- Extract images from documents
- Add sound to documents
- Add movies to documents

When most people think of creating multimedia presentations, they think of programs such as Macromedia Director. Indeed, Director is one of the most frequently used programs to create full-fledged multimedia presentations. However, with a bit of imagination, Acrobat Professional, and a smidgen of JavaScript, you can create impressive multimedia presentations.

When you create a multimedia presentation for CD-ROM, file size is generally not an issue. A CD-ROM can hold 700 MB of data, which means you can fill your PDF documents with stunning full-color images, sound files, and movie files. In this chapter, you'll learn how to integrate multimedia files into your PDF documents to create multimedia presentations that will impact your viewing audience.

Work with Images

When you create a multimedia PDF presentation, images are a must. Whether you create a corporate portfolio presentation, educational media, or product catalog, images add visual spice that pique user interest and make the presentation a success. When you prepare images for multimedia PDF presentations, you can crank up the resolution and use file formats that are not compressed, or if you do use an image file that is compressed, you can apply less compression to create a sharper image.

If you create documents with images and intend to use these as the basis for a Multimedia PDF, consider investing in a page-layout program such as Adobe InDesign, Adobe Pagemaker, or Microsoft Publisher. When you use a page-layout program, you have better control over image placement, especially when text wraps around the image. In lieu of a page-layout program, many popular word processing applications support embedding images in documents. If the authoring program supports PDF export, export the document with little or no image compression. If PDF export is not supported, choose Adobe PDF as the printing device to convert the document to PDF format and use the High Quality conversion setting.

TIP *When you're working with a PDF document with images that you want to use in another document, you can export the images by choosing Advanced | Export All Images. This opens a dialog box that you use to specify the export format for the images and the folder in which you want to store the images.*

How to ...

Optimize Images for Multimedia PDF Presentations

If you have image editing software such as Adobe Photoshop or Macromedia Fireworks, scan your images into the program at 200 *DPI (dots per inch)*. If you're capturing images with a digital camera, shoot them at the highest resolution possible. Resample the image to the desired size for your presentation. Ultimately, your presentation will be viewed on a 72 DPI monitor; however, you can leave the resolution at higher value and the images will look better if your viewers magnify the document. Export the finished image as a BMP file (Windows) or an uncompressed TIFF file (Macintosh and Windows) for the best results.

Add Sound to Documents

No multimedia experience is complete without sound. When you add sound to a presentation, you involve another one of the viewer's senses, which of course makes the experience more complete. You can use sounds in a variety of ways, including with buttons, when a page opens, or when a page closes. Acrobat now supports sounds for all popular formats including MP3. When you add a sound to an Acrobat document, you can choose to embed the sound or not. When you embed a sound in a document, it is saved with the document. When a sound is not embedded with a document, Acrobat records the path to the sound and the file is summoned when the trigger occurs. If you move a sound that is not embedded in a document to a different folder on your computer, it will not play. Adding a sound to a document you plan to display on the Internet would result in an extremely long download for users with a dial-up connection, unless the sound file is extremely small. However, when you create a PDF document with sound for a multimedia CD-ROM, Internet bandwidth is no longer a concern.

Add Sound to a PDF Document

You can use the Sound tool to add sound to a PDF document. When you use the Sound tool, you create an activation area that, when clicked, plays a sound. This is useful when you want to augment an image with a pre-recorded narration or perhaps a song. When you use the Sound tool, you enable viewers to play a sound on demand.

15

You can also play a sound when a page opens or closes using the Play Media (Acrobat 6 Compatible) action. This option gives you complete control over the sound file you want the user to hear when the page opens. Depending on the type of presentation you create, you can have a short musical piece play when a page opens or have a vocal introduction. You can also use a sound when the page closes. (For more information on actions, refer to Chapter 8.) When you use the Play Media (Acrobat 6 Compatible) action and choose Page Close as the trigger, you can choose to play a sound that's been added to the page using the Sound tool as outlined in the next section.

Sound can enhance your presentation, but the blatant use of sound will have your viewer turning down the speaker volume, or worse yet, exiting your presentation before it is concluded.

Another method you can use to add sound to your PDF presentation is the button. Create a button and then assign a sound to it. You can assign a sound to the Mouse Enter event to alert viewers that the button warrants their attention or you can assign the sound to the Mouse Down event, which alerts the viewers that the button has successfully been clicked. For more information on events refer to Chapter 14.

CAUTION

If you use sounds for both events and the sound assigned to the Mouse Enter event is longer than the sound you use for the Mouse Down event, the first sound will play until conclusion. This means that the button action may execute before the second sound ever plays.

If you create a CD-ROM product catalog or an educational tool, you can have a product description or tutorial play when an image is clicked. To have a sound play when an image is clicked, select the Link tool and create a hotspot around the image as outlined in Chapter 7. Choose Invisible Rectangle for the Link appearance type and from the Action Type drop-down menu, choose Play A Sound and then select the sound you want to play when the image is clicked. If you already have Acrobat 6.0–compatible media embedded in the document, you can choose the Play Media (Acrobat 6 Compatible) action and then select a sound file previously embedded in the document.

Use the Sound Tool

When you use the Sound tool, you define an active area of the document that viewers can click to play a sound file. You can embed the file with the document or not. When you do not embed the sound file with the document, Acrobat plays the sound from the folder where it resides on your computer. If you intend to send a PDF document with a non-embedded sound to someone, you have to send the sound file as well. The only time you should consider not embedding a sound file is when the document is for playback on your own computer or for a CD-ROM product where the sound file will be used by several documents. When you compile the assets for burning the CD-ROM and you have PDF documents with sounds that are not embedded, be sure to include the folder with the sound clips. You will also have to maintain the same relative path to the sound files. In other words, if the sound files were in a subfolder to the parent directory named Sounds, you'll have to create a subfolder named Sounds at the web site or on the CD-ROM from which the PDF presentation will be viewed.

To add a sound to a document using the Sound tool, follow these steps:

1. Navigate to the page to which you want to add the sound file.
2. Choose Tools | Advanced Editing | Sound Tool. Alternatively, click the triangle to the right of the currently selected media tool on the Advanced Editing toolbar and click the Sound Tool, whose icon looks like a speaker.

3. Drag a rectangle inside the document to define the active area that will play the sound when clicked. This opens the Add Sound dialog box shown here:

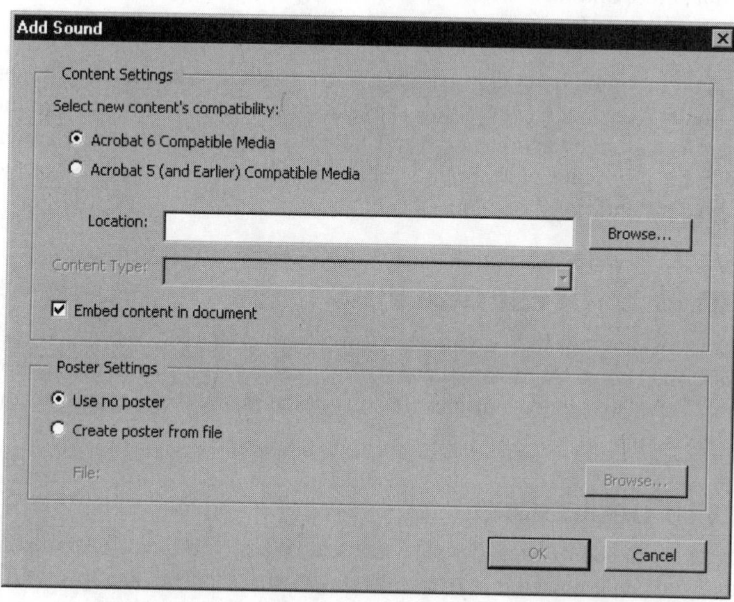

4. In the Content Settings section, click a radio button to choose Acrobat 6 Compatible Media or Acrobat 5 for earlier media. Note that if you choose Acrobat 5 and earlier, you will not be able to embed the sound with the document.
5. Click the Browse button to open the Select Sound File dialog box; then select the desired sound file and click Select to exit the Select Sound File dialog box.
6. If you choose Acrobat 6 Compatible Media, the Embed Content In Document check box is selected by default. Deselect the check box if you do not want the sound embedded with the document.
7. In the Poster Settings section, choose one of the following options:
   - **Use No Poster** Accept the default option, and the active area that plays the sound is designated by a border whose attributes you can modify.
   - **Create Poster From File** Select this option, and the Browse button becomes available. Click the button and select an image that will designate the active area for the sound file. Note that when you select an image, its dimensions are reconfigured to fit the area you defined with the sound tool.
8. Click OK to finish adding the sound to the document and close the Add Sound dialog box.

NOTE *If you use an image as a poster for a sound object, you may have to resize the area to conform to the dimensions of the image by clicking the poster with the Sound tool or Select Object tool and then dragging the handles around the perimeter of the object until the image is no longer distorted.*

Viewers can play the sound by clicking the active area with the Hand tool. Alternatively, you can use the Play Media (Acrobat 6 Compatible) page action to play the sound when the page opens. (For more information on actions, refer to Chapter 8.) When you use this action to play a sound, you can edit the properties of the sound to hide the playback location, as outlined in the upcoming "Edit Media Renditions" section.

Add Movies to PDF Presentations

You can also add movies to your PDF documents using the Movie tool. When you add a movie to a PDF document and choose Acrobat 6.0 compatible media, you can embed the movie with a document or not. You also specify multiple versions of the movie that are tailored for playing from a CD-ROM or from an Internet web site.

Add Movies to Documents

You use the Movie tool to add movies to your document. When you specify Acrobat 6.0–compatible media, you can embed the movie in the document. You can also specify different renditions of the file for users who view the document with different desktop sizes or access the document via the Internet at different connection speeds. Finally, you can specify a rendition using a different format; for example, you may want to include one rendition of the movie in the WMV (Windows Media Viewer) format for viewers with the Windows Media Player installed and another rendition in the MOV (**MOV**ie) format for viewers who have the QuickTime player installed on their systems. If you choose Acrobat 5.0–compatible media, you will not be able to embed the media with the document and are limited to your choice of media. Of course, your viewing audience largely determines the compatibility you choose. If the majority of your audience does not have the Adobe 6.0 Reader, you will have to include it with your CD-ROM

Create Audio Tracks for Your PDF Documents

Acrobat does not have the capability to edit soundtracks. If you intend to use sound extensively when creating multimedia PDF presentations, you may want to consider investing in sound-editing software. You can use sound-editing software to record your own sound clips and then edit them to fit your presentation. Most popular sound-editing software can be used to enhance a recording, remove noise from a recording, add special effects (such as echo or reverb) to a sound recording, and much more. Some sound-editing programs give you the capability of mixing soundtracks with other recordings. There is also software available to create musical soundtracks. Sonic Foundry sells both sound-editing and music-sampling software for Windows-based PCs. For more information, visit their web site at http://www.sonicfoundry.com.

presentation, or provide a link to the page at Adobe's site from which the software can be downloaded. Alternatively, you can use Acrobat 5.0–compatible media if your audience is not likely to have the latest reader.

By default, Acrobat Professional will snap the movie window to the size of the movie and use the first frame of the movie as a poster in the document. To add a movie to a PDF file, do the following:

1. Choose Tools | Advanced Editing | Movie Tool or select the Movie tool from the Advanced Editing toolbar, as shown here:

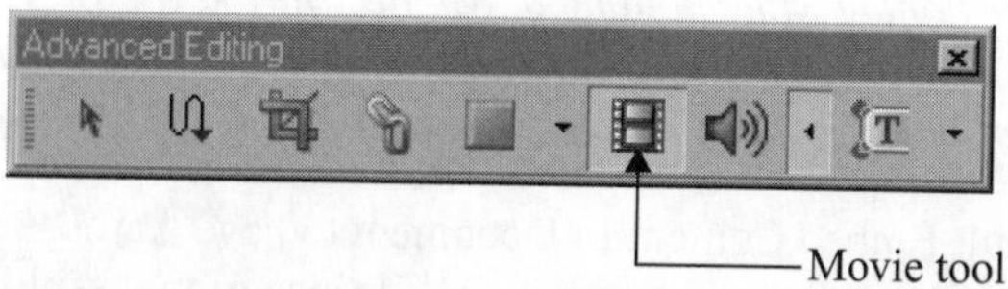

2. Click and drag inside the document to specify the position in which the poster frame of the movie will appear. You don't have to worry about sizing the area; by default Acrobat snaps the activation area to the dimensions of the movie. After releasing the mouse button, the Add Movie dialog box appears, as shown here:

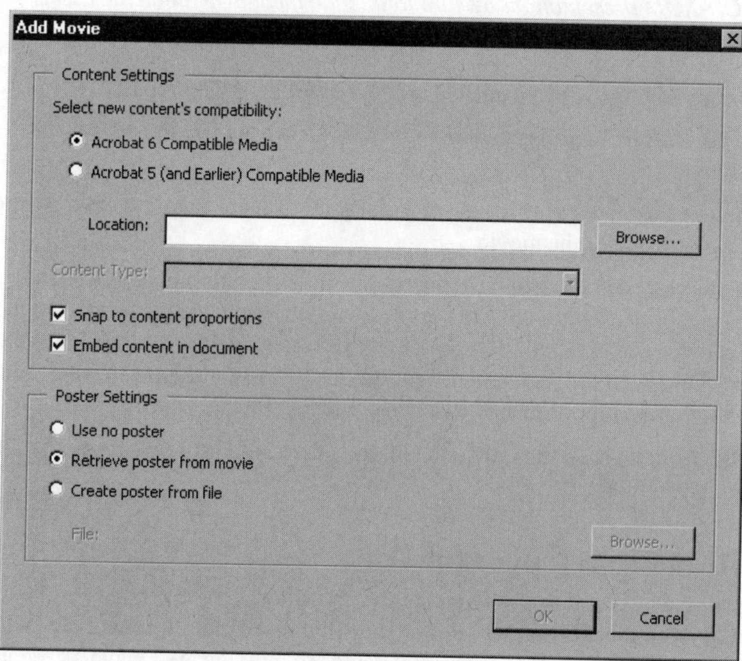

3. In the Content Settings section, choose Acrobat Compatible Media (the default) or Acrobat 5 (And Earlier) Compatible Media. If you choose the Acrobat 5.0 compatibility, the options to embed the movie in the document and create a poster from file are no longer available.

15

4. Click the Browse button to open the Select Movie File dialog box, then select the file and click Select.
5. Deselect the default Snap To Content Proportions option if you want to manually resize the movie.

CAUTION *If you resize the movie to smaller dimensions manually, you may distort the moving images if you do not resize the movie proportionately. You will also distort the images if you resize the movie to larger dimensions. You can proportionately resize the movie by dragging a corner handle while holding down the SHIFT key; however it is recommended that you size the movie to standard dimensions (320×240, 160×120, and so on) in a video editing application prior to adding the movie to a PDF document.*

6. Deselect the default Embed Content In Document to have Acrobat create a link to the movie's location. If you select this option, the file size of the resulting PDF document will be smaller, but if you move or delete the movie, the link is broken and the movie will no longer play when the activation area is clicked.

CAUTION *If you choose not to embed the movie and upload the document for a Web server for Internet viewing, be sure to upload the movie file, or if the document will be included with a CD-ROM presentation, be sure to include the movie file in the assets you burn to disk. Make sure the relative path is the same as well.*

7. In the Poster Settings section, choose one of the following options:
   - **Use No Poster** Displays a rectangular border to signify the activation area for the movie.
   - **Retrieve Poster From Movie** Displays the first frame of the movie to signify the activation area for the movie.
   - **Create Poster From File** Activates the Browse button that, when clicked, enables you to choose a supported file type that will be displayed as the activation area for the movie. The selected file snaps to the dimensions of the movie if you have not deselected the Snap To Content Proportions. If this option is selected and image is not the same proportion as the movie contents, the image is distorted.
8. Click OK. Acrobat adds the movie to the document and displays a poster according to the options you selected.

Add Renditions to a Document

After you add a movie or sound to a document, you can add different versions of the media and specify the system requirements that will determine which rendition Acrobat plays when the activation area is clicked. In Acrobat, different versions of a movie are known as *renditions.* To add a rendition to a document, follow these steps:

1. Choose Tools | Advanced Editing, and then select the Select Object tool. Alternatively, you can select the tool from the Advanced Editing toolbar.
2. Select the media clip, right-click (Windows) or CTRL-click (Macintosh), and choose Properties from the Context menu. Acrobat displays the Multimedia Properties dialog box shown here:

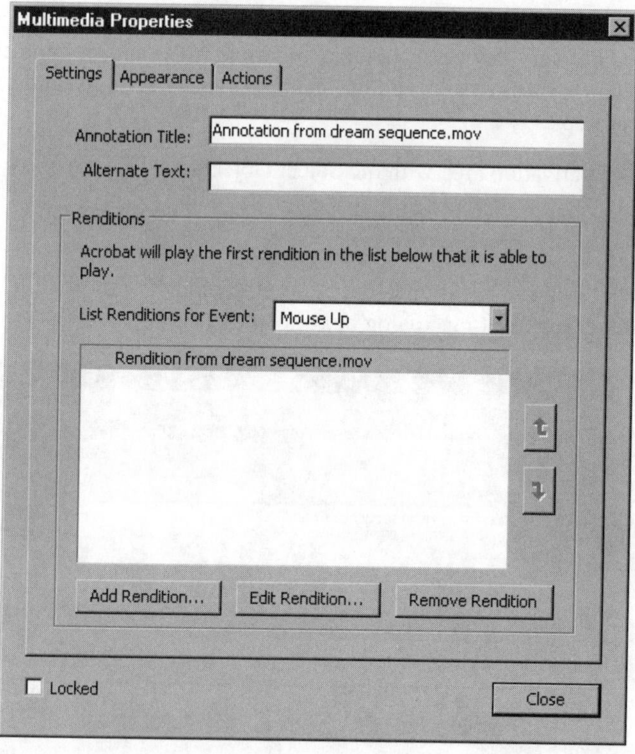

3. Click the Add Rendition button and from the drop-down list choose to add the rendition by specifying a URL, choosing a file, or copying an existing rendition. When you copy an existing rendition, you can choose different options, such as whether to display media player controls or not. After choosing an option, Acrobat displays the applicable dialog box. If you choose a rendition from file, Acrobat gives you the option of embedding the file with the document or not.
4. After choosing a rendition, click OK.

You can add as many renditions as needed to cover the different viewers, processors, media players, connection speeds, and so on, to compensate for the different scenarios that you anticipate users will encounter when viewing the document. If you embed several renditions, the document will have a rather large file size, especially if you are embedding lengthy movies, movies with large dimensions, or both. You may want to consider embedding the rendition the majority of your viewers will be using and then linking the other files. After adding several renditions to a document, you can edit each rendition to compensate for situations under which the rendition will be viewed.

Edit Media Renditions

If you add several renditions of a movie to a document, chances are you've optimized each movie for the intended delivery device or viewing situation. You can fine-tune each rendition by modifying parameters such as system requirements, playback settings, and so on. To edit a rendition, follow these steps.

1. Click the movie activation area with the Select Object tool.
2. Right-click (Windows) or CTRL-click (Macintosh) and choose Properties from the Context menu.
3. Select the Rendition whose parameters you want to modify and then click Edit Rendition to open the Renditions Settings dialog box shown here:

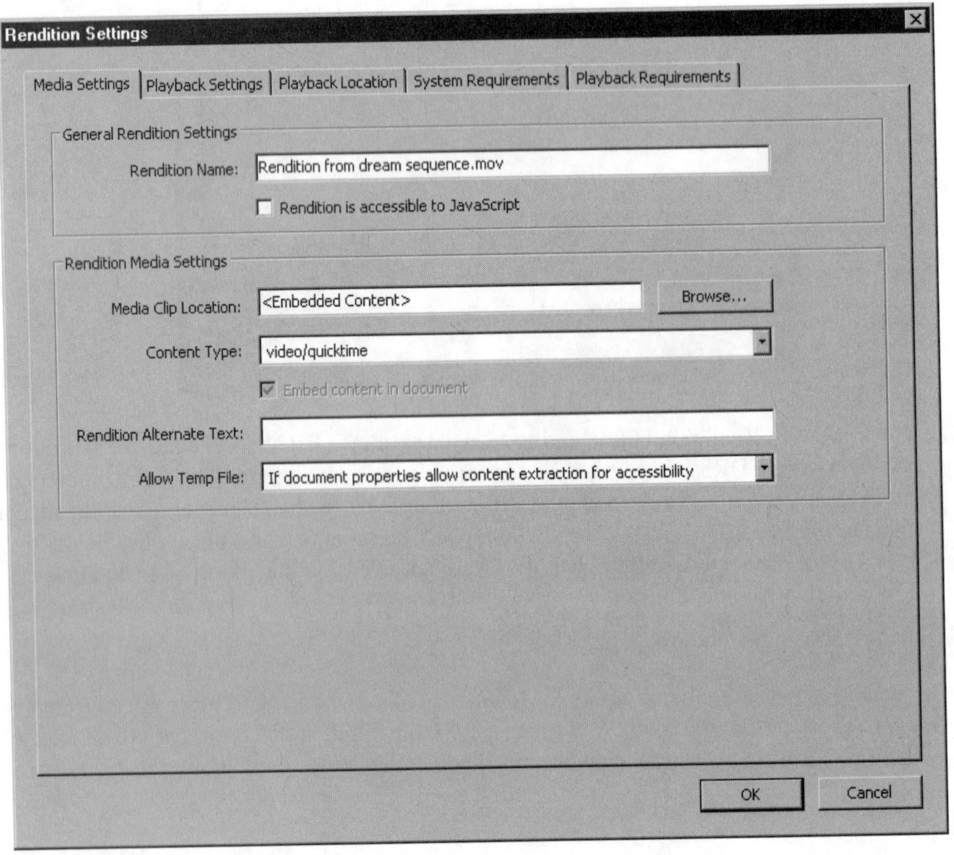

4. In the General Rendition Settings section of the Media Settings tab, you can specify the following settings:

   - **Rendition Name** Determines the name of the rendition as displayed on the Renditions list. The Rendition Name does not determine which file is played.
   - **Rendition Is Accessible To JavaScript** Enables you to control the movie with JavaScript code.

5. In the Rendition Media Settings section of the Media Settings tab, you can specify the following settings:

   - **Media Clip Location** Enables you to specify the location from which Acrobat plays the file. You can accept the default option (which varies depending on the rendition option you chose), or specify a different clip location.
   - **Content Type** Enables you to specify a different content type for the media clips. In most instances you'll want to stick with the default content type Acrobat chooses. If you choose the wrong content type, the clip may not play.
   - **Rendition Alternate Text** Enables you to enter Alternate Text for the movie clip, which is used by visually impaired viewers.
   - **Allow Temp File** Enables you to specify whether the user's system will be able to write a temporary file of the movie.

6. Click the Playback Settings tab to modify the following options:

   - Click the triangle to the right of the Keep Player Open field and choose one of the following options: For Normal Length Of Content; Forever Once Activated; or For A Number Of Seconds. If you choose the final options, the Seconds field becomes available. Enter the number of seconds for which you want the player to remain open after the movie ends, or click the spinner buttons to specify the duration.
   - In the Volume field, enter a value to specify the percentage at which you want the volume of the clip to play. Alternatively, you can click the spinner buttons to select a value. Note that you can play a clip at a higher percentage than its original volume; however, this may result in distortion or poor sound quality.
   - Click the Show Player Controls check box to display the controllers associated with the media type.
   - Click the Repeat check box if you want the movie to play more than once. After selecting this option, click the Continuous radio button (the default) or Times radio button. If you choose the Times option, a text field becomes available. Enter the number of times you want the movie to play or click the spinner buttons to select a value.

7. Click the Playback Location tab to specify the following options:

   - **Playback Location** Gives you the option of choosing a different playback location other than the default Document location. You can choose Hidden, Floating Window, or Full Screen. When you embed a sound in a document and use an action to play the sound when the page opens or closes, your best choice is Hidden. If you choose Floating Window, the media plays in a window that users can move to a different location.

If you choose this option in conjunction with Player Controls, viewers will be able to manipulate the volume, pause the media, and so on. The options vary depending on the default system player for the media type associated with the rendition you are editing.

- **Background Color** Click the color swatch and select a background color for the media player. This option has no visible effect on a movie player, but you will be able to see the background color if you choose to display player controls for an embedded sound.

8. If you choose Floating Window, the following options are available:
   - **Show Title Bar (selected by default)** Displays the title bar at the top of the floating window.
   - **Show Control For Closing Window (selected by default)** Displays a control viewers can use to close the window prior to the movie finishing.
   - **Title Text** Enables you to enter text you want displayed in the title bar. This field is not available if you deselect the Show Title Bar option.

   The remaining options in this tab allow you to specify resizing options for the window. It is recommended that you accept the default Acrobat options as resizing the window may cause image distortion.

NOTE *In order to view title text, users will have to change preferences for non-trusted documents by choosing Edit | Preferences | Trust Manager, then choosing Non-Trusted Documents from the Display Permissions For list and allowing the document to set the title when a movie is displayed in a floating window. Otherwise, Acrobat displays generic title text.*

9. Click the System Requirements tab to specify which conditions cause the rendition you are editing to appear. For example, if you have two renditions of a movie, one sized at 160 pixels × 120 pixels and another sized at 320 pixels × 240 pixels, you can use this tab to specify that the smaller clip plays if the user's desktop size is 800 pixels × 600 pixels and the other clip plays for 1024×68 screen resolution. You have other options in this tab to play a rendition based on a user's connection speed to the Internet and so on. Acrobat determines which system requirements are satisfied and serves up the rendition you specify.
10. Click the Playback Requirements tab to specify which requirements must be met by the user's hardware in order to play the clip. Note that users will have to change permissions for non-trusted documents to allow the document to control the playback of the media.
11. Click OK to exit the Renditions Settings dialog box and then click Close to exit the Multimedia Settings dialog box. Alternatively, select another rendition whose settings you want to modify.

Create a Multimedia Presentation

When you use Acrobat to create a PDF document multimedia presentation, you can include documents with images in other applications and then use Adobe PDF as a printing device to convert the documents into PDF format. You can augment the images with text documents you convert to PDF files. But the real power of Acrobat Professional comes when you add multimedia files such as Flash SWF movies, video clips, and sound files.

You can create a single multimedia document or create a series of documents that you link with interactive menus. When you create a multimedia presentation for CD-ROM distribution, you have considerable leeway. You can create a menu with multistate rollover buttons that play sounds, trigger movies, and much more. As long as you can fit the entire production on a CD-ROM, you are good to go. You can use the Button tool as the basis for your menu. For more information on using the Button tool, see Chapter 14.

You can spice up a CD-ROM presentation by adding interactivity to the Navigation menu buttons. When you create a multistate rollover button for a multimedia presentation, use the Push Highlight option and choose a different image for each button state. For example, you can use an icon for the Up state, use an icon with text for the Rollover state, and then use a variation of the icon for the Down state. You can add additional interactivity to the button by assigning multiple actions. For example, you can play a short movie file on Mouse Enter, stop the movie file on Mouse Exit, and play sound on Mouse Down. Note that if you use a large movie file with a mouse event, the movie may not load before the user clicks the button. For more information on events, refer to Chapter 14.

Create an Introduction

You can create an effective introduction to your multimedia presentation by creating a series of pages that play one after the other, similar to a movie's opening credits. After Acrobat displays the last page, you use an action to open the main page of the presentation. The number of introduction pages varies depending on your presentation. You could create an interesting introduction by gradually increasing the size and opacity of a corporate logo until it fills the entire page. Another visually stimulating introduction for a presentation is to have various images assemble into a splash screen, like the pieces of a jigsaw puzzle coming together. If you have image editing software such as Adobe PhotoShop, Corel Photo-Paint, or Macromedia Fireworks, you can create the individual images for the introduction. Create the images with the same dimensions as your PDF presentation and convert each image to PDF format using the Standard conversion setting. Name each file in the order it will appear in the introduction—for example, intro1.pdf, intro2.pdf, and so on. After you convert the images to PDF format, launch Acrobat and do the following:

1. Choose File | Create PDF | From Multiple Files to open the Create PDF From Multiple Documents dialog box and select the files created for your introduction.
2. In the File To Combine window, arrange the files in the order in which they will appear and then click OK to convert the files to a PDF document.

3. In the Pages tab, select the first thumbnail, right-click (Windows) or CTRL-click (Macintosh), and then choose Properties from the Context menu. When the Page Properties dialog box appears, click the Actions tab. Page Open is selected by default.
4. Click the triangle to the right of the Select Action field and choose Run A JavaScript.
5. Click the Add button to open the JavaScript Editor dialog box.
6. Enter the following code in the Create And Edit JavaScripts text window:

```
var interval = app.setInterval("this.pageNum = this.pageNum + 1;", 3000);
```

7. Click OK to close the JavaScript Editor dialog box, and then click Close to exit the Page Properties dialog box and assign the action to the page. Before you go on to the next step, take a look at the preceding JavaScript code. You created a variable named `interval` and set it equal to the `setInterval` method of the `app` object. The `setInterval` method is used to pause the application for a certain amount of time, in this case 3000 milliseconds, which is equal to 3 seconds. The code in quotation marks executes after the interval has passed. In this case, it increases the value of `pageNum` property of the document by 1, which advances the document to the next page. The code will continue to execute every three seconds until you stop the code by clearing the interval.
8. In the Pages tab, select the thumbnail for the last page in the document and then right-click (Windows) or CTRL-click (Macintosh) and choose Properties from the Context menu. When the Page Properties dialog box appears, click the Actions tab. Page Open is selected by default.
9. Click the triangle to the right of the Select Action field, choose Run A JavaScript from the drop-down menu, and then click the Add button to open the JavaScript Editor dialog box.
10. Enter the following code in the Create And Edit JavaScripts text window:

```
app.clearInterval(interval)
```

11. Click OK to close the JavaScript Editor dialog box. Now that you have created the JavaScript to stop the pages from turning, you need to specify which document will open after the introduction plays.
12. Click the triangle to the right of the Select Action field, choose Open File, and then click the Add button to open the Select File To Open dialog box.
13. Select the file that you want to open after the introduction plays, click Select to select the file and exit the Select File To Open dialog box, and then click Close to exit the Page Properties dialog box.

That is all you need to do to create an automated introduction. You could have created each page of the introduction as a separate PDF file and used the Open File action to advance to the next PDF document. However, on all but the slowest computer, the files would open too quickly for the viewer to get a good look at them. When you use JavaScript, you can control the amount of time each page of the introduction is displayed. To increase or decrease the interval time, enter a new value in Step 6. Remember that 1 second equals 1000 milliseconds and that you can precisely control the amount of time each page is displayed.

Did you know?

You Can Create an Automated Slide Show

You can use the `setInterval` JavaScript object to create a slide slow. Assemble the images you want to present, choose File | Create PDF | From Multiples Files to combine them as separate pages of a PDF document, and follow the steps in the preceding section to set the interval between each image. At the end of the document, create two buttons: one to replay the show and one to exit. For the Replay button, use the Execute Menu Item action and choose View | Go To | First Page; for the Exit button, use the Execute Menu Item action and choose File | Close.

Create a Pop-Up Menu Using Named Destinations

You can create an effective pop-up menu for your multipage PDF documents using Named Destinations and a bit of JavaScript. Pop-up menus are useful as they do not take up much space and you can cram several destinations into a single menu. To create a pop-up menu, do the following:

1. Choose View | Navigation Tabs | Destinations to open the Destinations tab.
2. Click the Scan Document button, and Acrobat displays a list of destinations in the document. If the document contains no destinations, create the desired destinations. For information on creating named destinations, refer to Chapter 8.
3. Decide which destinations you want included as menu items.
4. Change the name of each menu item destination to the name you want to appear on the menu. For example, if the menu item will be called Chapter 1, change the name of the destination to Chapter 1. Note that this technique is intended for desktop viewing. Note that if you create a document for viewing in a Web browser, spaces may cause inconsistent results.
5. Using the Button tool, create a field where you want the pop-up menu to appear. Acrobat opens the Button Properties dialog box.
6. In the General tab, enter a name for the button.
7. Define the appearance and options for the button as outlined in Chapter 14.
8. Click the Actions tab, click the triangle to the right of the Select Action field, and then choose Run A JavaScript from the drop-down menu to open the JavaScript Editor dialog box.
9. In the Create And Edit JavaScripts text window, enter the following code replacing the `Dest` designations with the names of your destinations exactly as they appear in the Destinations window—named destinations are case sensitive. If you have the Destinations tab open when

you create the JavaScript, refer to the tab when adding each destination to your code as shown here:

```
var c = app.popUpMenu ("Dest1","Dest2","Dest3","Dest4");
this.gotoNamedDest(c);
```

10. Click OK to close the JavaScript Editor dialog box; then click Close to close the Button Properties dialog box. When users click the button with the Hand tool, the JavaScript pop-up menu appears, listing each named destination. When the named destination is clicked, Acrobat displays the page view associated with the named destination.

NOTE *After you modify document destinations but before you save the document, choose Advanced | PDF Optimizer. Click the Clean Up tab and deselect the Remove Unused Destinations option section to prevent inadvertently removing a named destination you plan to use later.*

Summary

In this chapter, you learned to add multimedia elements to your PDF documents. You learned to embed multimedia elements with the Sound and Movie tools. You also learned to add different renditions of multimedia objects to a document for users who view the document with different systems configurations and Internet users who view the document at different connection speeds. You learned to use JavaScript to create an automated introduction and pop-up menus. In the next chapter, you'll learn to use the Acrobat Professional Catalog command to create PDF indexes. You'll also learn to automate your work using batch processing.

Chapter 16

Create a PDF Index

How to...

- Use batch processing
- Create an index
- Prepare the documents
- Build an index
- Purge and rebuild an index

Whether you use Acrobat personally to maintain a collection of information or use it to create and maintain documents in a large corporation, you can make the information in your PDF documents more accessible by creating a PDF index. Whether you use a few or several hundred PDF documents to create your PDF index, the result is a searchable database. After you create an index, or several indexes, you can quickly find the information you need using the Search command.

In this chapter, you'll learn how to prepare PDF documents for the creation of a PDF index. You'll also learn how to use the Catalog command to create a searchable database of PDF documents. (Catalog is available in Acrobat Professional only.) In addition, you'll learn to use the Batch command to automate your work.

Edit with Batch Processing

When you prepare a large number of PDF documents for a specific audience or destination, you often end up performing the same task on every document, for example, optimizing several documents for Internet viewing. Instead of opening up every document you need to modify and then repeating the same task, you can perform the same command on several documents at once using batch processing. You can choose from preset batch sequences or create your own batch sequence. When you create a custom batch sequence, you can specify the order in which the commands execute. You can also use batch processing to perform a specific sequence of commands on a single document or multiple documents.

Use Preset Batch Sequences

When you choose a preset batch sequence, Acrobat prompts you for the files to process. If a command in the batch sequence requires user input, the applicable dialog box appears. To perform a batch sequence, follow these steps:

1. Choose Advanced | Batch Processing to open the Batch Sequences dialog box and then choose a preset batch sequence from the menu. If, for example, you want to print the first page of several documents, choose Print 1st Page Of All.
2. Click Run Sequence after you select a batch sequence and the Run Sequence Confirmation dialog box appears, as shown in the following illustration. Note that this illustration is of the Print 1st Page Of All batch sequence, which actually uses JavaScript to accomplish

the task. The triangle to the left of the actual batch sequence command has been clicked to illustrate the JavaScript used to run the batch sequence.

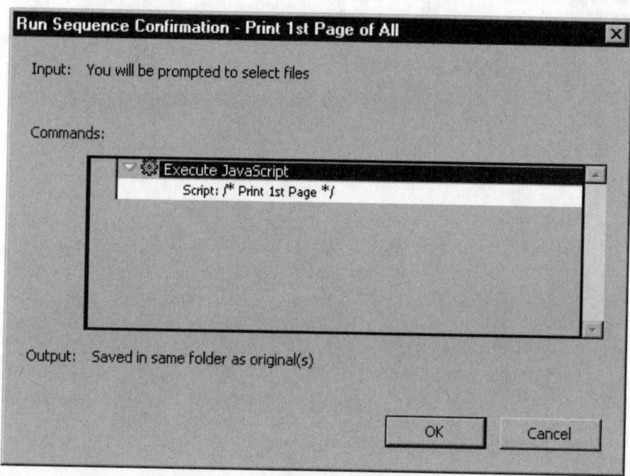

3. Verify that the commands in the Run Sequence Confirmation are the tasks you want to perform. If the batch sequence command has a triangle before it, you can click the triangle to see the exact command Acrobat will perform. If the batch sequence is the one you want, Click OK to open the Select Files To Process dialog box.
4. Select the files you want to process.
5. Click Select to have Acrobat perform the batch sequence commands and save the modified files in the original folder.

When you choose a preset batch sequence, Acrobat saves the files in the same folder by default. It is advisable to store processed documents in a separate folder. If the batch sequence does not perform as you expected, you can modify the batch sequence and perform it again on the original. You can specify in which folder processed files are stored as well as other options by editing the batch sequence.

Edit a Batch Sequence

When you edit a batch sequence, you can modify an existing batch sequence, create a new batch sequence, rename a batch sequence, or delete a batch sequence. When you modify an existing batch sequence, you can add or remove commands from the sequence, change the order in which the commands execute, change the files the commands run on, change the folder the files are saved in, and modify the output options. To edit an existing batch sequence, follow these steps:

1. Choose Advanced | Batch Processing and from the Batch Sequences dialog box, select the sequence you want to edit.

2. Click Edit Sequence to open the Batch Edit Sequence dialog box, as shown here:

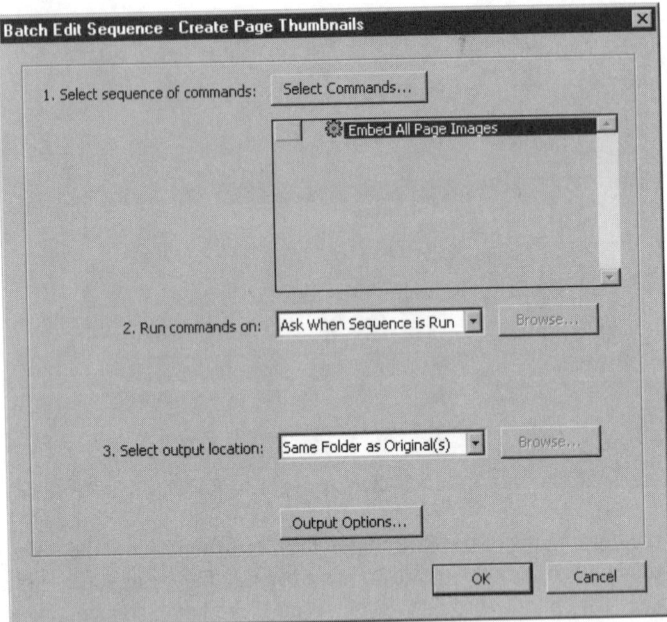

3. To add additional commands to the sequence, click the Select Commands button to open the Edit Sequence dialog box, as shown here:

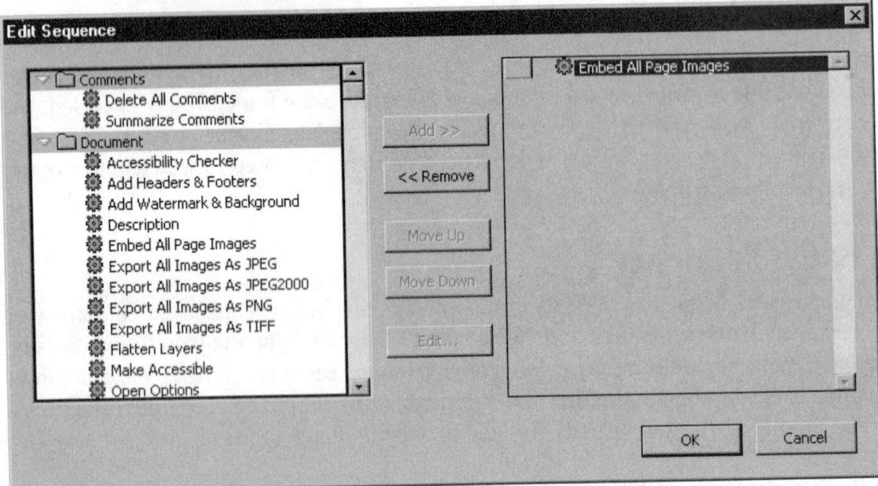

4. In the Edit Sequence dialog box, you can modify the sequence as follows:

- To add a command to the sequence, in the left window, select the command and then click the Add button.
- To remove a command from the sequence, in the right window, select the command and then click the Remove button.
- To modify the order in which Acrobat executes multiple commands in the batch sequence, select a command in the right-hand window and click the Move Up button or Move Down button to change the order of the command list. Commands are executed in the order they appear in the list.
- To edit a command, click the Edit button to open the applicable dialog box for the command. For example, if you add the Execute JavaScript command to a batch sequence, clicking the Edit button opens the JavaScript Editor dialog box, enabling you to edit the script that will be executed when the batch sequence runs.

5. Click OK to close the Edit Sequence dialog box and go back to the Batch Edit Sequence dialog box.
6. Click the triangle to the right of the Run Commands On field and from the drop-down menu, choose one of the following:
   - **Selected Files** Choose this option, and Acrobat runs the sequence on selected files. When you choose this option, the Browse button becomes active. Click the button and choose the files you want the sequence to run on.
   - **Selected Folder** Choose this option, and Acrobat executes the batch sequence on all PDF files and other applicable files in the selected folder. After you choose this option, the Browse button and Source File Options button become available. Click the Browse button and choose the folder you want the batch sequence commands executed on or click the Source File Options button. By default, all supported source file types are selected and will be processed in the batch unless you deselect file types you don't want processed.
   - **Ask When Sequence Is Run** Choose this option (the default), and a dialog box appears when the sequence runs, prompting you to select the files to execute the commands on.
   - **Files Open In Acrobat** Choose this option, and when you choose this batch sequence, it runs on files currently open in Acrobat.
7. Click the triangle to the right of the Select Output Location field and from the drop-down menu, choose one of the following options:
   - **Specific Folder** Choose this option to specify the folder in which the modified documents are stored. After you choose this option, the Browse button becomes active. Click it and choose the folder in which to save the output files.
   - **Ask When Sequence Is Run** Choose this option, and Acrobat prompts you for a folder to save the files in when the sequence executes.

- **Same Folder As Original(s)** Choose this option (the default), and Acrobat saves the processed files with the same name(s) as the original(s). Note that if you choose this option and choose the same output folder as the originals, Acrobat will prompt you for a new filename as each file is processed, so as not to overwrite the original file(s).
- **Do Not Save Changes** Choose this option, and Acrobat will not save the changes or output the processed files. This option enables you to test the batch process. After you have ascertained that the batch sequence is working correctly, you can remove this option to process files with this sequence.

8. Click the Output Options button to open the Output Options dialog box. In the Output Options dialog box, you can modify the filename and output options as shown in the following steps.
9. In the File Naming Section, choose one of the following options:
   - **Same As Original** Saves the batch processed files with the same name as the original document.
   - **Add To Original Base Name(s)** Changes the original base filename. When you select this option, the Insert Before and Insert After fields become available. You can add text to either or both to create a new name for the processed files.
   - **Do Not Overwrite Existing Files** Prevents Acrobat from overwriting any files with the same name as those being processed.
10. In the Output Format section, click the triangle to the right of the Save File(s) As field; from the drop-down menu, choose to save the processed files in one of the following formats: Adobe PDF Files, Encapsulated PostScript, HTML 3.2, HTML 4.01 with CSS 1.0, JPEG, JPEG2000, Microsoft Word Document, PNG, PostScript, Rich Text Format, Text (Accessible), Text (Plain), TIFF, XML 1.0, or XML Data Package Files.
11. If you save the files in PDF format, choose Fast Web View (PDF Only) to optimize the files for Internet viewing.
12. Choose the PDF Optimizer option, and all files processed with this batch sequence will run through the PDF Optimizer. If you choose the PDF Optimizer option, the Settings button becomes available. Click the button to configure the PDF Optimizer for the Batch Sequence you are editing.
13. Click OK to close the Output Options dialog box, click OK to close the Edit Sequence dialog box, click OK to close the Batch Edit Sequence dialog box, and then click Close to exit the Batch Sequences dialog box and apply the changes.

Note that you can also use the Batch Sequences dialog box to delete a sequence, rename a sequence, run a sequence, or create a new sequence—the topic of discussion in the next section.

Create a New Sequence

You can create a new sequence and tailor it for operations you perform frequently on your PDF documents. When you create a new sequence, you specify the commands that are run when the sequence executes, the order they run in, and how the processed files are saved. To create a new batch sequence, follow these steps:

1. Choose Advanced | Batch Processing and from the Batch Sequences dialog box, click the New Sequence button. Acrobat opens the Name Sequence dialog box.
2. Enter a name for the sequence and click OK to open the Batch Edit Sequence dialog box.
3. Click the Select Commands button to open the Edit Sequence dialog box.
4. Select the commands you want to execute when the sequence is run. If the command has options, such as the Crop Pages command, you can set the options by clicking the Edit button or by double-clicking the command name in the right-hand window. Remember, when you create a sequence with multiple commands, you can use the Move Up and Move Down buttons to change the order in which the commands are executed.
5. Click OK to close the Edit Sequence dialog box and then follow Steps 6 through 11 in the preceding section to specify how and where the files are saved.

After you create a new batch sequence, it is displayed on the Batch Sequence menu list. To run the new batch sequence, choose Advanced | Batch Processing, and then select the name of the custom batch sequence from the list.

Create an Index

To create an index of PDF documents, use the Catalog command. You can create an index of files stored in one folder or several folders. When you create an index from a folder, Acrobat includes all PDF files located in the specified main folder plus all PDF files located within the main folder subdirectories. You can specify which directories to add or remove from the catalog, as well as specify certain words you want to exclude from the index. Create as many indexes as you need to organize specific documents. For example, you can keep corporate documents in one index, personal documents in another, and research information downloaded from the Internet in yet another index. The long and the short of it is that you can use this powerful tool to create custom PDF indexes to suit your specific needs.

16

Prepare the Documents

Before you can actually create the PDF index, you need to prepare the documents you want to include in the index. When you create an index, Acrobat creates a PDX (index definition) file and support folders in the same folder as the documents. To prepare your documents for inclusion in a PDF index, follow these steps:

1. Create a folder in which to store the PDF documents you want to index. If you create an index that will be shared cross-platform, choose a folder name with no more than eight characters and no spaces. Also, refrain from including any nonstandard characters such as *$,%,^,&,*,£,$,"*, or *!*.
2. Locate the PDF documents you want to index and move them into the index folder. If desired, break the index folder into subfolders to keep sub-genres of the index separated. Be advised, however, that deeply nested folders may adversely affect the performance of the index. If you have deeply nested folders path names longer than 256 characters, you will also get unexpected results. Moving the PDF files to their own index folder is optional, but it is an excellent way to keep track of related PDF files. You can create an index using any folder as the root and Acrobat will index all PDF files in the subfolders you specify.
3. After you add the PDF documents to the index folder, you can begin the preparation process. Examine the documents in the folder and pay special attention to the following:
   - If you have an exceptionally long document in the index, consider breaking it down into several documents. For example, if you have a manual in the index, break the manual down into individual chapters or sections. This will speed up the search process after you index the documents.
   - Rename any documents that have long filenames. Long filenames may adversely affect the performance of the index when truncated. This is especially true if you share the index cross-platform. Stick with the old tried-and-true DOS naming convention of eight letters followed by the three-letter .pdf extension.
   - Rename any documents with spaces using DOS naming conventions. For example, empbnfts.pdf would be an acceptable alternative for Employee Benefits.pdf, while emp bnfts.pdf would not.
   - Rename any documents that use ASCII characters 133 through 159 (as shown in the following table), as Acrobat Catalog does not support these characters.

133	à	134	å	135	ç	136	ê	137	ë
138	è	139	ï	140	î	141	ì	142	Ä
143	Å	144	É	145	æ	146	Æ	147	ô
148	ö	149	ò	150	û	151	ù	152	ÿ
153	Ö	154	Ü	155	¢	156	£	157	¥
158	_	159	ƒ						

- If any of the documents need structure editing, perform the edits before renaming and adding the files to the index. If you change the document filename after creating cross-document links and other document structure, the links may not be functional. If a file needs extensive editing and you do not have the time, move the file to another folder. You can always perform the necessary edits, add it to the folder, and then rebuild the index.

4. After you create the index folder and modify filenames, you can modify the documents for optimal search performance by following the steps in the upcoming section.

Optimize PDFs for the Index

When you create a PDF index, the resulting index will be more efficient if you pay a little attention to detail when preparing the documents that will be included in the index. Acrobat uses the contents of the Document Properties Description section when conducting a user query. For example, a user can search a document by author or keywords—information that can be added to the Document Properties Description. Recipients of your PDF documents will be able to search more efficiently if you consider the following when preparing your files:

1. Optimize each document for space. This may seem like an arduous task if you have a large document collection to index; however, if you run a batch process on the documents and choose Fast Web View and PDF Optimizer as outlined in the previous "Edit A Batch Sequence" section, you can quickly optimize a large number of documents.
2. Audit the content of the Document Properties Description section of each document to be included in the index. This may prove to be a lengthy task with a large document collection. If Acrobat users have their search preferences configured to search by document information, they can search an index by Title, Subject, Author, or Keywords, the same information included in the Document Properties Description section. If you create documents with the intention of including them with an index, you can include the necessary document information when you publish the document. If you index a collection of documents prepared by other authors or modify your own documents, open each document and then choose File | Document Properties and add the desired information to the Description section. Review each document description and pay attention to the following:
   - **Title** Make sure the document title accurately reflects the contents of the document.
   - **Author** Include the author's name for each document. Remember that users of the document collection can specify a search by author. If you index a document for a large corporation, remember that personnel frequently change. For this reason, use the department information in this field rather than the author's actual name.
   - **Subject** When you create an index with a variety of documents that contain different subject matter, be consistent with your naming conventions. For example, when indexing documents pertaining to employee benefits, do not use Employee Benefits for the subject of some documents and Benefit Package for others.

- **Keywords** Acrobat can also use keywords to select documents for a user's search query. Enter the keywords that pertain to the document you include in the collection. Again, be consistent with your naming conventions. If your organization uses a numbering system for memos and correspondence, you can include it in this field.

After you modify a document description for a PDF index, it should contain information similar to what is shown here:

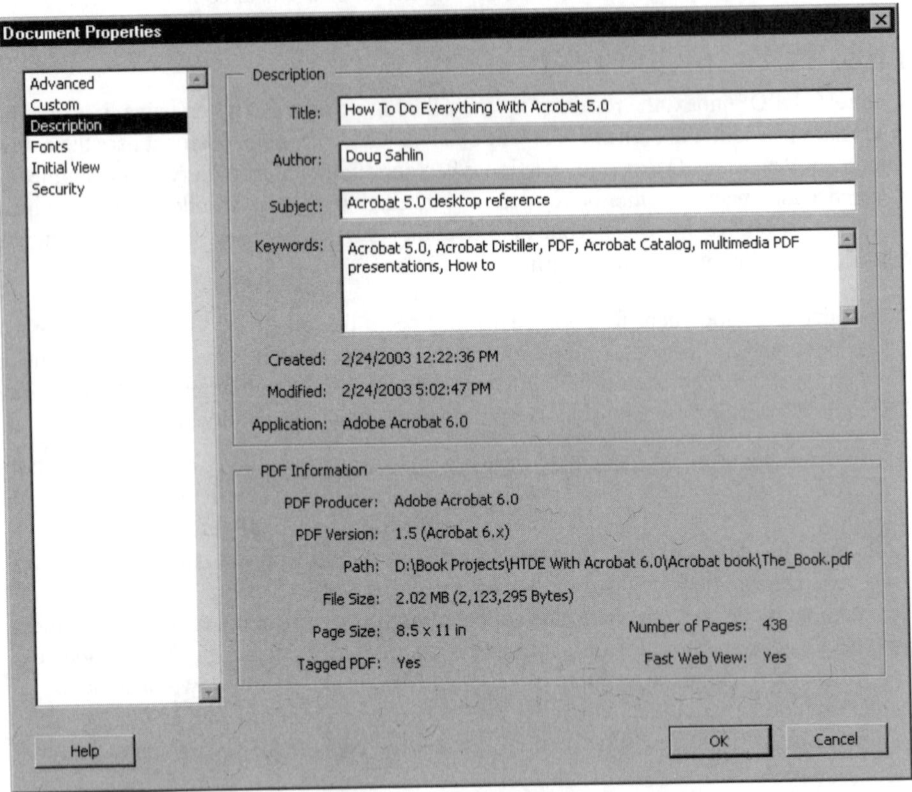

Build an Index

After preparing the documents, you are ready to build the document index using the Catalog command. When you build the index, you specify a name for the index and the document folders to include in the index. You can also add a description of the index, as well as modify the index options to exclude certain words from a search. To create a PDF index, do the following:

1. Choose Advanced | Catalog to open the Catalog dialog box, as shown next.

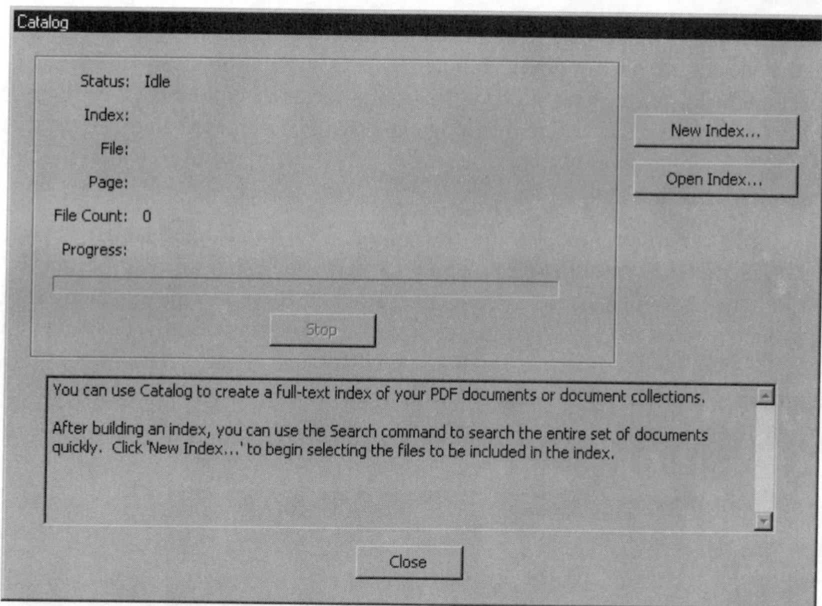

2. Click the New Index button to open the New Index Definition dialog box, as shown here:

3. Enter a name in the Index Title field. People within your organization use the index name when they decide whether or not to include the index in a search. Enter a descriptive name that accurately reflects the type of documents in the document collection (such as Employee Benefits Documents). Remember that long names will be truncated on the list of available indexes. Stick with a short two- or three-word index title that will fit within the bounds of the Index Selection dialog box.
4. In the Index Description field, enter a description. This step is optional. However, adding a brief description that describes the type of documents in the index makes it easier for users to decide whether or not the index contains the information they are searching for before adding the index to the currently selected indexes. The information you enter in this field is available in the Index Information dialog box that appears after a user clicks the Info button from within the Index Selection dialog box.
5. Click the Options button to open the Options dialog box, as shown here:

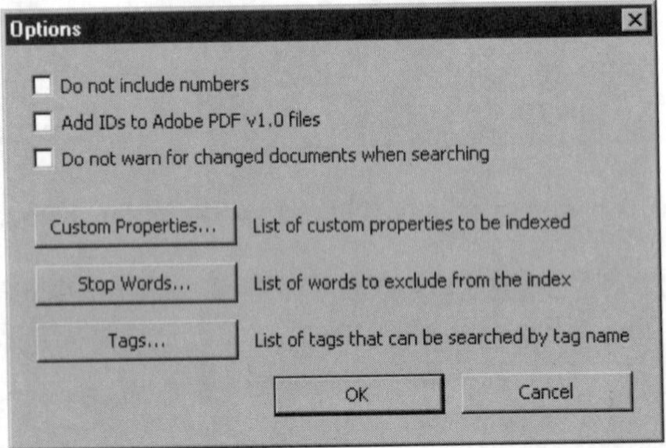

You can fine-tune your index by modifying the following parameters:

- To exclude numbers from the search, enable the Do Not Include Numbers option.
- Click the Custom Properties button to include custom properties that are relevant to the documents you are indexing. Custom Properties are added to PDF documents by choosing File | Document Properties and then adding the Custom Properties to the Custom section of the Document Properties dialog box. Custom Properties are added to the Search These Additional Criteria list after the index is built. For example, if you wanted users to be able to search by document name, you would add the custom property Document_Name and choose String as the property type.
- To exclude any words from a search, click the Stop Words button and enter your stop words one at a time in the Word field and then click the Add button. To speed up a search, eliminate words such as *a, an, the,* and so on.

- To include tag names as searchable objects in an index, click the Tags button and add the tag names one at a time in the Tag field and then click the Add button. Remember, tags are elements used to define document structure.
- If you have Acrobat PDF 1.0 documents in the collection, you can add cross-platform identifiers to the document by choosing the Add IDs To Adobe PDF v1.0 Files option. If you have a large quantity of 1.0 files to add to a collection, convert them to 6.0 by opening the documents in Acrobat 6.0 and then saving them. While you have the 1.0 file open, you can also modify the Document Properties Description information to include pertinent data for the search index.
- Choose the Do Not Warn For Changed Documents When Searching to prevent Acrobat from displaying a warning dialog when a document has been changed since being indexed.
- After you modify the search index options, click OK to exit the Options dialog box and return to the New Index Definition dialog box.

6. In the Include These Directories section, click the Add button to open the Browse For Folder dialog box, select the folder that contains the documents you want to index, and then click OK to close the dialog box. Remember, you can add more than one folder of documents to an index as long as the additional folders are nested in the main index folder. Acrobat automatically indexes documents in each subfolder of the directory unless you exclude certain subdirectories, as outlined in the Step 7.
7. In the Exclude These Subdirectories section, click the Add button to open the Browse For Folder dialog box, select the subdirectory you want to exclude from the index, and click OK to close the dialog box. Repeat as needed to exclude additional subdirectories.
8. Click the Build button, and Acrobat displays the Save Index File dialog box. Accept the default name for the index that you entered in the Index Title field or enter a different filename. If the index will be accessed from an intranet server or shared cross-platform, remember to choose an eight-letter filename with no spaces.
9. Click Save As to have Acrobat Professional begin building the index. If you have not entered a name in the Index Title field, the Save Index File dialog box appears, prompting you for a filename. After you do this, click Save; Acrobat begins building the index. As Acrobat builds the index, the build progress and applicable comments are displayed in the Catalog dialog box, as shown in Figure 16-1. You can stop a build by clicking the Stop button. If you stop a build, you can still search the partial index and then finish building it—just choose Advanced | Catalog and then choose Open Index. When the partially built index is open, click the Build button and Acrobat scans the index to determine how many files were indexed and then completes building the index.
10. Click Close to exit the Adobe Catalog dialog box. Your index is now ready for use.

After you create an index, you can add it to the list of indexes to search by following the steps outlined in Chapter 3.

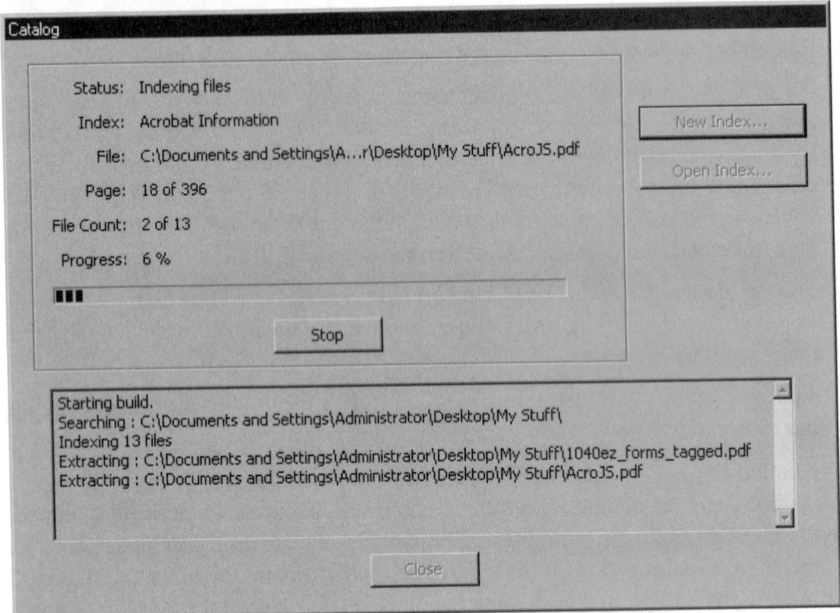

FIGURE 16-1 When you create a PDF index, Acrobat displays the build progress in this dialog box.

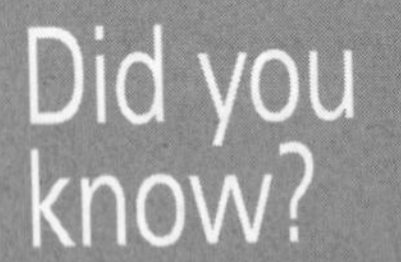

Searching a PDF Index with Adobe Reader

Indexes you create can be searched by anyone with a copy of Adobe Reader 6.0, as installed or distributed from the Acrobat application CD-ROM. If users download Adobe Reader 6.0 from the Adobe web site, they must specify the version with the Search plug-in. If you have sensitive documents that you only want available to certain parties, then apply Acrobat Security to the documents. When Acrobat or Adobe Reader users search an index and their search returns a document with security, users can only view the document if they have the proper password, or in the case of a document that has been encrypted for certain users, users not listed on the document author's trusted certificate list will not be able to view the document.

Purge and Rebuild an Index

After you create an index, it becomes obsolete as you add and delete documents from the index folder. When you open an index with deleted documents, the original versions of modified documents and deleted documents remain in the index. When you try to select a document whose title still appears in the index but the document has been moved or deleted, Acrobat displays a warning dialog box to that effect. You should periodically purge an index of obsolete documents and rebuild it to reflect the current content. To purge a PDF index, follow these steps:

1. Choose Advanced | Catalog to open the Adobe Catalog dialog box, as shown previously in Figure 16-1.
2. Click the Open Index button and open the index you want to purge. Remember that the index will be in the index root folder with a .pdx extension.
3. Click the Purge button. Note that if you purge an index in a network situation, it is advisable to notify co-workers in advance in case they are searching the index when you intend to purge it.
4. After Acrobat completes the purge, repeat Steps 1 and 2 to reload the index.
5. Click the Build button.

TIP *You can specify the default Options for each Catalog you create by choosing Edit | Preferences to open the Preferences dialog box and then choosing Catalog from the window on the left. The options allow you to modify the defaults for every index you create.*

Move an Index

You can use your operating system utilities to move an index to another folder, another hard drive, or another network server. When you relocate a PDF index, you need to move the index root folder and all associated subfolders. This maintains the necessary links for the index to function properly. After moving an index, you will need to load it again, as outlined in the previous section.

Summary

In this chapter, you learned to automate your work using batch processing. You learned to use the preset Acrobat batch sequences, how to edit them to suit your working situation, and how to create new batch sequences. You also learned to create a searchable index of PDF documents using the Acrobat Professional Catalog command. You also learned to maintain indexes by purging and rebuilding them.

Part VI

Appendixes

Appendix A

Acrobat 6.0 Keyboard Shortcuts

If you use Acrobat frequently, and find yourself doing the same tasks repeatedly, you can streamline your workflow by memorizing the keyboard shortcuts for the commands you use most frequently. You don't have to memorize every keybord shortcut in one sitting; begin memorizing the shortcuts for the commands you use most often. Soon the shortcuts will become second nature and you can memorize additional shortcuts to become more proficient with Acrobat.

Tool selection keyboard shortcuts are disabled by default when you install Acrobat. To enable keyboard shortcuts for tools, choose Edit | Preferences to open the Preferences dialog box. Click General to open the General section of the dialog box and then enable the Use Single Key Accelerators To Access Tools option. After closing the dialog box, you'll be able to use any of the keyboard shortcuts in this appendix. Where you see an asterisk (*) following a tool description, you can toggle to the next tool in the group by pressing SHIFT and the keyboard shortcut. For example, press N to select the last used commenting tool; press SHIFT-N to select the next commenting tool in the group.

Tool	Windows Keystroke	Macintosh Keystroke
Article	A	A
Crop	C	C
Drawing Tool Last Selected *	D	D
Form Tool Last Selected (Professional only) *	F	F
Snapshot	G	G
Hand	H	H
Stamp	K	K
Attach File *	J	J
Link	L	L
Movie (Professional only)*	M	M
Pencil *	N	N
Select Object	R	R
Note	S	S
TouchUp Text	T	T
Highlight Text *	U	U
Select Text *	V	V
Text Box	X	X
Zoom In	Z	Z
Zoom Out	SHIFT-Z	SHIFT-Z

TABLE A-1 Tool Selection Shortcuts

Desired Navigation	Windows Keystroke	Macintosh Keystroke
Previous Screen View	PAGE UP	PAGE UP
Next Screen View	PAGE DOWN	PAGE DOWN
First Document Page	HOME	HOME
Last Document Page	END	END
Previous Page	LEFT ARROW	LEFT ARROW
Next Page	RIGHT ARROW	RIGHT ARROW
Scroll up one line	UP ARROW	UP ARROW
Scroll down one line	DOWN ARROW	DOWN ARROW
Show/Hide Full Screen View	CTRL-L	CMD-L
Go to Page command	CTRL-SHIFT-N	CMD-SHIFT-N
Go to previous view	ALT-LEFT ARROW	CMD-LEFT ARROW
Go to next view	ALT-RIGHT ARROW	CMD-RIGHT ARROW
Go to Previous document	ALT-SHIFT-LEFT ARROW	OPTION-SHIFT-LEFT ARROW
Go to Next document	ALT-SHIFT-RIGHT ARROW	OPTION-SHIFT-RIGHT ARROW

TABLE A-2 Navigation Shortcuts

Desired Action	Windows Function Key	Macintosh Function Key
Complete Acrobat Help	F1	F1
Show/Hide How To..? pane	F4	F$
Show/Hide Navigation pane	F6	F6
Spell check comments or form fields	F7	F7
Show/Hide Toolbars	F8	F8
Show/Hide Menu Bar	F9	F9
Open Context Menu	SHIFT-F10	CONTROL-CLICK
Navigate to Next Window (in cascade or tile mode)	CTRL-F6	-
Rename Selected Bookmark	F2	-

TABLE A-3 Function Key Shortcuts

Desired Action	Windows Shortcut	Macintosh Shortcut
Select All	CTRL-A	CMD-A
Copy	CTRL-C	CMD-C
Zoom To Command	CTRL-M	CMD-M
Open Document	CTRL-O	CMD-O
Print Command	CTRL-P	CMD-P
Exit Acrobat	CTRL-Q	CMD-Q
Show/Hide Rulers	CTRL-R	CMD-R
Save Document	CTRL-S	CMD-S
Paste	CTRL-V	CMD-V
Close Document	CTRL-W	CMD-W
Cut	CTRL-X	CMD-X
Undo	CTRL-Z	CMD-Z
Fit Page	CTRL-0	CMD-0
Actual Size	CTRL-1	CMD-1
Fit Width	CTRL-2	CMD-2
Fit Visible	CTRL-3	CMD-3
Zoom In	CTRL-+	CMD-+
Zoom Out	CTRL--	CMD--
Deselect All	SHIFT-CTRL-A	SHIFT-CMD-A
Delete Pages command	SHIFT-CTRL-D	SHIFT-CMD-D
Insert Pages command	SHIFT-CTRL-I	SHIFT-CMD-I
Page Setup (for printing)	SHIFT-CTRL-P	SHIFT-CMD-P
Save As	CTRL-SHIFT-S	CMD-SHIFT-S
Use Local Fonts	SHIFT-CTRL-Y	SHIFT-CMD-Y
Show/Hide Grid	CTRL-U	CMD-U
Snap to Grid	SHIFT-CTRL-U	SHIFT-CMD-U
Rotate Clockwise	SHIFT-CTRL++	SHIFT-CMD++
Rotate Counterclockwise	SHIFT-CTRL--	SHIFT-CMD--
Add New Bookmark	CTRL-B	CMD-B

TABLE A-4 Document Editing Keyboard Shortcuts

Desired Result	Windows Shortcut	Macintosh Shortcut
Open Document Properties dialog box	CTRL-D	CMD-D
Open Preferences dialog box	CTRL-K	CMD-K

TABLE A-5 Document Information and General Preferences Shortcuts

Desired Result	Windows Shortcut	Macintosh Shortcut
Cascade documents	SHIFT-CTRL-J	SHIFT-CMD-J
Tile documents horizontally	SHIFT-CTRL-K	SHIFT-CMD-K
Tile documents vertically	SHIFT-CTRL-L	SHIFT-CMD-L

TABLE A-6 Display Multiple Documents Shortcuts

Desired Result	Windows Shortcut	Macintosh Shortcut
Create PDF From Web Page	SHIFT-CTRL-O	SHIFT-CMD-O
Automatically Scroll Document	SHIFT-CTRL-H	SHIFT-CMD-H
Read Out Loud Current Page	SHIFT-CTRL-V	SHIFT-CMD-V
Read Out Loud to End Of Document	SHIFT-CTRL-B	SHIFT-CMD-B
Pause Out Loud Reading	SHIFT-CTRL-C	SHIFT -_ CMD-C
Stop Out Loud Reading	SHIFT-CTRL-E	SHIFT-CMD-E

TABLE A-7 Miscellaneous Shortcuts

Appendix B Acrobat Resources

The Internet is a treasure trove of information. All you need to do is navigate to your favorite search engine and let your fingers do the walking. With the right keywords, you can find out almost anything about almost everything. Acrobat is no exception. In this section, you'll find some Acrobat web resources. As of this writing, Acrobat 6.0 is in the final development stages and hasn't been released. However, you can rest assured that all of the sites in this section are working with the latest development version of Acrobat and are updating their resources for Acrobat 6.0. Currently, the web sites in this appendix feature only Acrobat 5.0 resources. By the time this book is in your hands, all of Adobe's resources will be updated for Acrobat 6.0, and most of the other sites should be as well. As of this writing, the information is accurate, the URLs have been verified, and the web sites are online. However, the Internet is in a constant state of flux and some of the URLs may have changed, or the resource may have gone by the wayside by the time you read this.

Adobe Resources

The Adobe web site features a wealth of information about Adobe Acrobat and the other products that Adobe distributes. The following sections list individual pages in the Adobe web site that may be of interest to Acrobat users.

The Adobe Web Site (http://www.adobe.com)

This is the gateway to the Adobe web site. Here you will find links to all Adobe products, including Acrobat. You can use the Adobe search engine to find specific information about Acrobat and other products. The Adobe web site features technical support sections for all their products.

Acrobat Reader Download Web Site (http://www.adobe.com/products/acrobat/readstep2.html)

If you distribute PDF documents from a web site, you can include a link to this web page where web site visitors can download a free copy of Adobe Reader 6.0.

Distribute Adobe Reader 6.0 (http://www.adobe.com/products/acrobat/distribute.html)

At this section of the Adobe web site, you can download the Get Reader and Adobe PDF logos. To download the logos, Adobe requires that you fill out the Adobe Trademark License Agreement.

eBook Reader Download Web Site (http://www.adobe.com/products/ebookreader/)

At this section of the Adobe web site, you can download the free Acrobat eBook Reader. If you distribute eBooks formatted for the Acrobat eBook Reader from a web site, include a direct link to this page, and your visitors will be able to download a free copy of the software.

Third-Party Resources

The PDF format is tremendously popular; so popular, in fact, that there are a number of web sites devoted to Acrobat tutorials, tips, and plug-ins. The web sites listed in the following sections are home to products you can use when creating your PDF documents and information about Acrobat PDF.

Sonic Foundry (http://www.sonicfoundry.com)

If sound is a staple element in your PDF documents and other multimedia projects, you can find some sophisticated sound-editing software at this web site. Sonic Foundry's Sound Forge application enables you to manipulate a sound and apply effects to it. You can use the software to record sounds directly into your PC and then edit and mix them with other sounds. Sonic Foundry Acid Music and Acid Pro is software you can use to create sound loops for your PDF documents. You can also use the Sonic Foundry software to create soundtracks for Flash movies and videos you composite with the Apple QuickTime Pro and other video-editing software. If you embed movies in your PDF documents, you'll find sophisticated tools you can use to edit videos at Sonic Foundry's web site as well. Unfortunately, the software is only for the Windows platform.

Planet PDF (http://www.planetpdf.com/)

At this web site you'll find all manner of resources for Acrobat. Peruse their many tutorials, check out the latest PDF news, and browse through their store, which is chock-full of useful third-party PDF plug-ins. Check out their forums at forum.planetpdf.com where you can exchange information and ideas with other Acrobat users.

Active PDF (http://www.activepdf.com/)

At this web site you'll find a collection of server-based PDF products. The web site purveyors promise no licensing hassle, no per user costs, and no per document costs, as you find with many other plug-in products. You pay one price for each server you use their products on. Active PDF also features developer tools.

Planet eBook (http://www.planetebook.com/)

If you use Acrobat to create eBooks, you'll find useful information here related to the publishing of eBooks. The web site features news and articles related to eBooks, as well as a tools section where you can locate eBook software and hardware.

Dionis (http://www.dionis.com/)

This web site features plug-ins that you can use to check document links, split large documents for the web site of CD-ROM catalogs, copy links, and more.

Enfocus (http://www.enfocus.com)

This web site features third-party plug-ins for PDF creation and editing. Enfocus' PitStop software makes it possible to edit large volumes of PDF documents. This web site also features software that enables you to perform enhanced editing of a PDF document without having to modify the original document in its native application.

PDF Zone (http://www.pdfzone.com/)

Here's another web site that features a plethora of PDF information. Browse through their Resources section for useful PDF tips and tricks. Check out their Toolbox section that features a sophisticated search engine you can use to locate PDF plug-ins.

Mark Anderson's Web Site (http://www.yeardley.demon.co.uk/)

The PDF devotee's web site features Acrobat tutorials and tips. There is also a section with links to other useful PDF information.

010.com.au (http://www.010.com.au)

This PDF guru's web site features free PDF tools developed for Acrobat. Each PDF tool is provided with the VB (Visual Basic) code used to create it. The webmaster, Dave Wraight, is a very talented fellow. In addition to doing a thorough job as the technical editor of this book, Dave has contributed to the Planet PDF AcroTips section. Stay tuned to this web site for future programs, tips, and other Acrobat- and PDF-related material.

Index

References to figures and illustrations are in italics.

A

B

C

D

E

F

G

H

I

J

K

L

M

N

O

P

Q

R

S

V

W

X

Z

INTERNATIONAL CONTACT INFORMATION

AUSTRALIA
McGraw-Hill Book Company Australia Pty. Ltd.
TEL +61-2-9900-1800
FAX +61-2-9878-8881
http://www.mcgraw-hill.com.au
books-it_sydney@mcgraw-hill.com

CANADA
McGraw-Hill Ryerson Ltd.
TEL +905-430-5000
FAX +905-430-5020
http://www.mcgraw-hill.ca

GREECE, MIDDLE EAST, & AFRICA (Excluding South Africa)
McGraw-Hill Hellas
TEL +30-210-6560-990
TEL +30-210-6560-993
TEL +30-210-6560-994
FAX +30-210-6545-525

MEXICO (Also serving Latin America)
McGraw-Hill Interamericana Editores S.A. de C.V.
TEL +525-117-1583
FAX +525-117-1589
http://www.mcgraw-hill.com.mx
fernando_castellanos@mcgraw-hill.com

SINGAPORE (Serving Asia)
McGraw-Hill Book Company
TEL +65-6863-1580
FAX +65-6862-3354
http://www.mcgraw-hill.com.sg
mghasia@mcgraw-hill.com

SOUTH AFRICA
McGraw-Hill South Africa
TEL +27-11-622-7512
FAX +27-11-622-9045
robyn_swanepoel@mcgraw-hill.com

SPAIN
McGraw-Hill/Interamericana de España, S.A.U.
TEL +34-91-180-3000
FAX +34-91-372-8513
http://www.mcgraw-hill.es
professional@mcgraw-hill.es

UNITED KINGDOM, NORTHERN, EASTERN, & CENTRAL EUROPE
McGraw-Hill Education Europe
TEL +44-1-628-502500
FAX +44-1-628-770224
http://www.mcgraw-hill.co.uk
computing_europe@mcgraw-hill.com

ALL OTHER INQUIRIES Contact:
McGraw-Hill/Osborne
TEL +1-510-420-7700
FAX +1-510-420-7703
http://www.osborne.com
omg_international@mcgraw-hill.com

Know How

How to Do Everything with Your Digital Camera
Second Edition
ISBN: 0-07-222555-6

How to Do Everything with Photoshop Elements 2
ISBN: 0-07-222638-2

How to Do Everything with Photoshop 7
ISBN: 0-07-219554-1

How to Do Everything with Your Sony CLIÉ
ISBN: 0-07-222659-5

How to Do Ever with Macromedi Contribute
0-07-222892-X

How to Do Everything with Your eBay Business
0-07-222948-9

How to Do Everything with Your Tablet PC
ISBN: 0-07-222771-0

How to Do Everything with Your iPod
ISBN: 0-07-222700-1

How to Do Everything with Your iMac,
Third Edition
ISBN: 0-07-213172-1

How to Do Ever with Your iPAQ P
Second Edition
ISBN: 0-07-222950-0